EurographicSeminars

Tutorials and Perspectives in Computer Graphics

Edited by G. Enderle and D. Duce

Eurographics Tutorials '83

Edited by Paul J. W. ten Hagen

With 164 Figures

Springer-Verlag
Berlin Heidelberg New York Tokyo 1984

EurographicSeminars
Edited by G. Enderle and D. Duce
for EUROGRAPHICS –
The European Association for Computer Graphics
P. O. Box 16
CH-1288 Aire-la-Ville

Editor:
Drs. Paul J. W. ten Hagen
Stichting Mathematisch Centrum
Kruislaan 413
NL-1098 SJ Amsterdam

ISBN-13:978-3-642-69908-5   e-ISBN-13:978-3-642-69906-1
DOI: 10.1007/978-3-642-69906-1

Library of Congress Cataloging in Publication Data.
Main entry under title: Eurographics Tutorials '83. (EurographicSeminars) Bibliography:
p. 1. Computer graphics–Congresses. I. Hagen, P. J. W. ten. II. Series. T385.E975
1984 001.64'43 84-13905 ISBN-13:978-3-642-69908-5 (U.S.)

© 1984 EUROGRAPHICS The European Association for Computer Graphics,
P. O. Box 16, CH-1288 Aire-la-Ville
Softcover reprint of the hardcover 1st edition 1984

2145/3140-543210

Editors Introduction

This book is the first issue of a EUROGRAPHICS publication series in the field of computer graphics, an important field of research and a versatile tool for various application areas. The availability of powerful hardware at an affordable price and the evolution of high standard software have led to a rapidly increasing expansion of computer graphics and the penetration of computer graphics techniques and systems into a wide range of application areas.

This book series will cover state-of-the-art surveys as well as scientific contributions on specific areas of research and development.

The first book in the series contains the Tutorial Notes of the EUROGRAPHICS '83 conference, held in Zagreb, Yugoslavia, in September 1983. It covers four major aspects of computer graphics today:

- The first part contains a detailed **introduction into computer graphics,** its concepts, its methods, its tools, and its devices. It gives an easy access for the newcomer to the field and it offers an overview of the state of the art in computer graphics.
- The second part is devoted to **interactive techniques.** This is currently one of the most important fields of research in computer graphics. Important aspects of this research and its current state are reported. From the developments described here, in the near future powerful generally applicable user interface management systems are likely to evolve.
- The third part gives broad information on the most important software development in computer graphics in the past years: The first computer graphics standard, the **Graphical Kernel System,** GKS. Concepts, functions, and interfaces of GKS are described, a case study reports on implementation experiences.
- The fourth part covers important aspects of a major application area of computer graphics – namely the field of **three-dimensional models.** Contributions in this book describe both the fundamental concepts of surface design and of solid modelling.

The description of implemented solutions offers a bridge from the theoretical fundamentals to the reality of applications.
We are sure this book will serve as a thorough, detailed, yet easily comprehensible introduction to four important computer graphics areas. It will offer easy access to the fields of computer graphics fundamentals, interactive techniques, computer graphics standards, and three-dimensional modelling techniques.

	David Duce
Paul ten Hagen	Günter Enderle
EUROGRAPHICS '83	EurographicSeminars
Tutorial Chairman	Series Editors

Table of Contents

VI. The Graphical Kernel System
J. Schönhut

VII. Case Study of GKS Development
C. D. Osland

VIII. Surface Design Foundations
W. Böhm, G. Farin

IX. Geometric Modelling – Fundamentals
M. A. Sabin

X. Solid Modeling: Theory and Applications
M. Mäntylä

I. Introduction to Computer Graphics (Part I)

R. J. Hubbold

1.0 ACKNOWLEDGEMENT

I should like to thank my colleagues Tony Arnold and Terry Hewitt for their help in producing these notes. The notes on graphics hardware are based partially on those written by Tony for Eurographics 82.

2.0 GENERAL INTRODUCTION

The main parts of a system for interactive computer graphics are:

o A computer. Used to store information from which pictures are constructed, to execute calculations, to generate the information needed to drive the graphical output device (e.g. display), and to monitor input tools controlled by the operator. This might be a large time-shared host. However, the popularity of this is diminishing because of poor response times - the trend is towards powerful personal computers.

o An interactive display. Used to show pictures.

o Input tools. Used to control the information which is displayed and how it is calculated. Examples include keyboard, joystick, graphic tablet, function buttons. (These will be described later.)

o Hard-copy devices. Plotters, printers etc., used to obtain a permanent record of pictures and other data.

Graphics equipment falls into two broad categories:

o Calligraphic. Pictures are drawn with lines. Suitable for many types of graphics and until recently the commonest type of equipment.

o Raster (or raster-scan). Pictures are made up from rows of dots which are drawn row by row in a similar manner to a domestic T.V.

There are three main aspects of computer graphics:

o Entering data into the computer, known as digitising. This can be performed manually, semi-automatically, or with a fully automatic scanner or T.V. camera.

o Viewing data graphically and updating it with some kind of display device and input tools.

o Obtaining hard-copy on paper with some kind of plotter or printer, or on film or video tape.

We will examine what equipment is available in each of these areas.

3.0 DIGITISING

There are three main ways in which information can be recorded from existing diagrams and other sources:

o Using a manual digitiser.
o With a semi-automatic line-following digitiser.
o With a scanner or T.V. camera.

3.1 MANUAL DIGITISERS

The manual digitiser consists of a flat drawing surface, rather like a draughtsman's drawing board, with many wires embedded in X and Y directions. Each wire carries a unique signal which is detected by a puck which is capacitively coupled to the tablet. These signals are decoded to produce the X and Y coordinates of the puck's position.

Usually there are several buttons on the puck which the operator may use to signal different types of data being recorded. Information can be picked off diagrams, charts, drawings, maps, X-ray films etc. by positioning the puck's cross-hairs over a point and pressing a button. Some systems also permit stream-mode recording, where points are sampled at either fixed time or distance intervals.

These digitisers produce coordinates of points and line segments.

3.2 SEMI-AUTOMATIC DIGITISERS

Manual digitising is tedious and error prone. One solution is to use a scanner which will follow lines. One such is the Laser-Scan Fastrack digitiser. This scans back and forth on either side of a line, recording the line's centre coordinates as it traces from one end of the line to the other. The system is interactive, so that ambiguities about which direction to take at nodes between different line segments can be resolved by the operator.

As with manual digitisers, the output is a set of coordinates of points and line segments.

3.3 SCANNERS AND T.V CAMERAS

These record pictures in the form of a raster image, with intensity information recorded for each point (pixel) in the picture. The various features within the picture must be derived using image analysis techniques. Such methods are increasingly popular with the growth of raster display systems, but need sophisticated software if they are to be used to input line diagrams.

4.0 GRAPHICAL DISPLAYS

Graphical displays vary enormously in cost, complexity and capabilities. At one end of the spectrum is the simple display terminal, and at the other are systems with considerable local intelligence, typified by the Evans & Sutherland PS300, which contains a Motorola 68000 together with highly specialised graphics processors.

We will examine three different types of display technology:

- o Direct view storage tube.
- o Refresh display.
- o Raster-scan display.

then look at various display processor architectures.

4.1 DIRECT VIEW STORAGE TUBE DISPLAY (DVST)

Marketed by Tektronix since early 1970s, this display has been very popular because of its relatively low cost and ease of programming and interfacing. It has become a de-facto standard and many newer displays employing other technologies (e.g. raster-scan) are "Tektronix compatible".

It is usually configured as a terminal operating via an RS232 interface. Drawing instructions received from a host computer are decoded by the display logic and used to trace the picture on a special type of CRT shown in Figure 1. The storage tube is a calligraphic display.

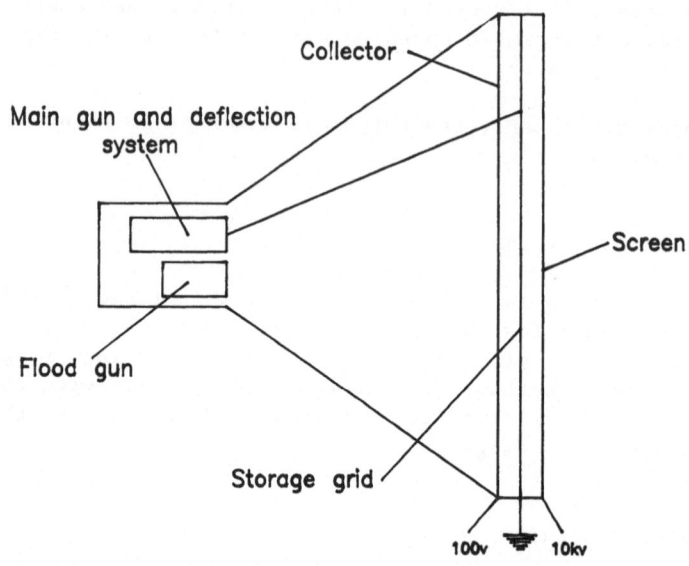

FIGURE 1 : DIRECT VIEW STORAGE TUBE (TEKTRONIX)

The picture is drawn on a storage grid by the main electron gun. This leaves a charge on the storage grid. Low-velocity electrons are emitted by the flood gun. The collector smooths the flow of electrons from the flood gun. In areas of the storage grid charged by the main gun, flood gun electrons can pass through and are attracted to the positively charged screen. These electrons strike the phosphor coating of the screen and produce a visible image.

The DVST is very popular mainly because:

- o It's easy to program – uses ASCII codes.
- o It's easy to interface – typically RS232.
- o Can be used as an ordinary VDU.
- o Picture is flicker free.
- o It's relatively cheap (cheaper alternatives now available, however).

Problems are:

- o Cannot remove charge selectively from grid - no selective erase. Screen must be cleared by applying high voltage to storage grid for up to half a second resulting in bright green flash. Limits its potential for interactive graphics.

- o Charge leaks from storage grid eventually rendering picture invisible.

- o Overall charge builds up on storage grid due to electron supply from flood gun resulting in overall background glow.

With an RS232 interface picture drawing times can be quite long. Because there is no selective erasure the whole picture must be re-drawn when deletions are made. Later models have local intelligence and only changes to the picture need to be re-transmitted from the host. This cuts re-draw times to about half a second.

4.2 REFRESH DISPLAYS

The refresh display is also a calligraphic device. Figure 2 shows a simple refresh display system. The picture is drawn on a CRT screen by controlling the deflection voltages so that the lines, text and other picture parts are traced by the CRT beam. The phosphor is excited by the electron beam and glows for a short period. To maintain a steady image, the picture must be re-drawn before the phosphor glow fades completely; usually 30 or 50 times a second.

The picture is refreshed from a stored description called the display file. If the display file contains more much data than can be processed in 1/50th of a second (i.e. a very complex picture is defined), the result is a flickering picture caused by fading of the image between frames.

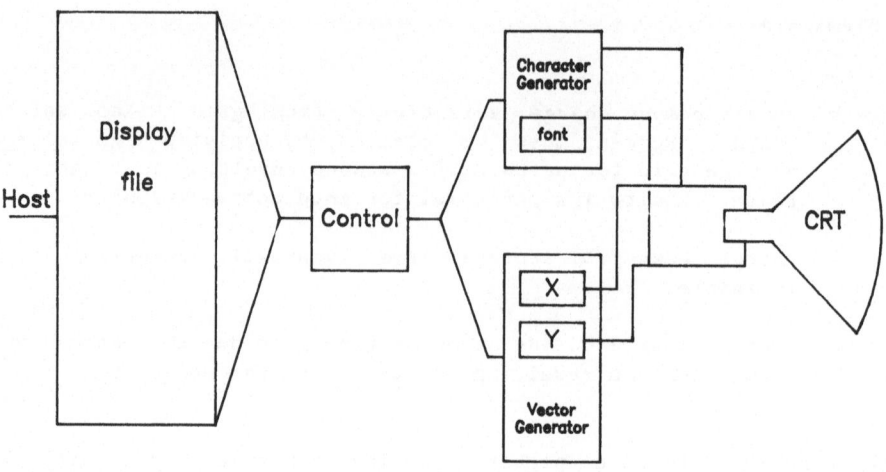

FIGURE 2: SIMPLE REFRESH DISPLAY

The display file may be modified dynamically by the host CPU, allowing
selective erasure and animation. Display file may be in in host CPU
store (cheap but requires high-speed DMA interface and puts considerable
load on host I/O bus), or in display's own refresh buffer.

The display file contains two main classes of instruction:

- o Drawing instructions.
- o Control instructions.

Drawing instructions.

Figure 3 shows hypothetical instruction format. Some drawing
instructions are:

- o MOVE - draw invisible line.
- o LINE - draw visible line.
- o TEXT - display character string.
- o ARC - draw part of a circle.

Lines and text are usually drawn by special vector and character
generation hardware. More expensive systems can also draw arcs, curves
etc. using special generators.

By modifying code within the display file, dynamically changing pictures
can be drawn. Each time the code is altered the new picture appears
instantaneously, because the display processor is continually refreshing

the picture using the current display file contents. This makes the refresh display a powerful interactive device.

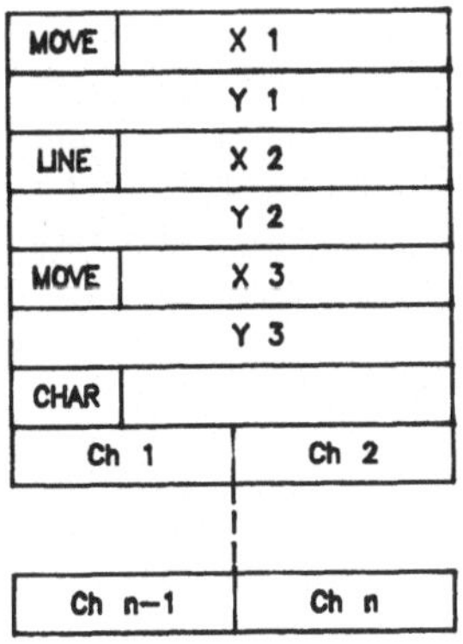

FIGURE 3: SIMPLE REFRESH DISPLAY INSTRUCTION FORMATS

Control instructions.

These control drawing parameters (e.g. line style, character size, intensity) and flow through display file. Typical instructions might be:

1. SET_LINE_STYLE - select solid or dashed line style.
2. SET_CHAR_SIZE - select character size.
3. SET_INTENSITY - select intensity of displayed information.
4. JUMP - specify address from which next display file instruction is to be fetched.
5. JUMP_TO_SUBROUTINE - as JUMP but remembers current address in display file.
6. RETURN - JUMP to address saved by JUMP_TO_SUBROUTINE + 1.

The JUMP instruction provides a way to add structure to the display file. Instead of a simple sequential list of instructions, a linked list of blocks of instructions can be constructed, making it easy to add new pictures and delete old ones by linking new blocks to the list and un-linking those no longer required.

The subroutine instructions permit more complex structuring. If a picture contains many copies of a sub-picture, JUMP_TO_SUBROUTINE allows its description to be stored once but invoked many times thus saving display file space. Coordinates specified inside subroutine need to be relative to current point.

Colour refresh displays

Refresh displays are usually monochrome, but typically have several intensity levels. Colour can be obtained by use of a special CRT with several phosphor layers. The required layer is selected by altering the potential on the anode of gun. This involves fast switching of high potentials (25kv) and is expensive.

A better approach is to use a shadow mask tube (similar to those used in T.V. and raster displays), but to drive it in a calligraphic fashion. Evans & Sutherland and Vector General both make displays of this type.

Advantages of refresh displays

The advantages of the refresh display are:

- o Can selectively erase parts of the picture.
- o Display file permits structure of picture to be represented. This can be very beneficial for interaction.
- o Can modify contents of display file to animate pictures.

Disadvantages of refresh displays

The main disadvantages are:

- o If a picture is too complex then the display may flicker. The capacity usually increases with cost and may be anywhere between 2,000 and 60,000 or more vectors.
- o Requires local processing capability which increases the cost. Can also be complex to program.

4.3 RASTER DISPLAYS

On a raster display the picture is drawn by scanning from the top of the screen to the bottom, like a domestic television. In order to draw a picture we must compute intensities of each point on the screen. The screen is divided into small areas called PIXELS. The number of dots along each axis determines the resolution of the display. Typical resolutions are 512*512, 640*512, 768*512, 1024*1024, 1280*1024 and 1536*1024.

The intensity value for each pixel is stored in a pixel memory. This is scanned in the correct order and the outputs are used to drive a T.V. monitor via digital to analogue converters (DACs).

Scan can be either interlaced (alternate scan-lines drawn on alternate frames), as in domestic T.V., or non-interlaced. One-pixel wide horizontal lines tend to flicker on interlaced displays. Long-persistence phosphors used to alleviate this.

Simple bi-level or grey-scale raster display

A simple system would have 1 bit per pixel giving two intensity levels, 0 and 1 (see Figure 4). Because of their relatively low cost these displays are commonly used as Tektronix look-alikes.

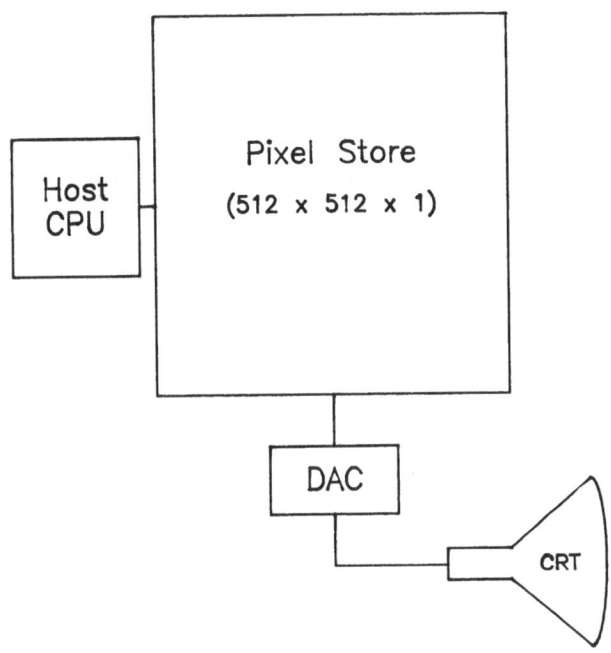

FIGURE 4: BI-LEVEL RASTER DISPLAY

By adding more bits per pixel and a slightly more expensive DAC we can have several intensity levels. E.g. 4 bits per pixel gives 16 intensity levels.

Colour raster displays

Colour is achieved by driving the red, green and blue guns of the T.V.
monitor separately. One bit per pixel per gun (i.e. 3 bits per pixel)
gives 8 colours (see Figure 5).

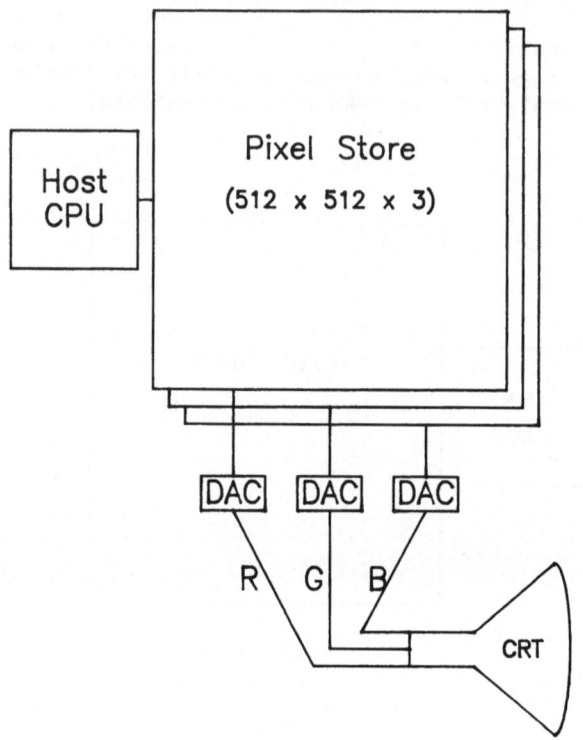

FIGURE 5: 8-COLOUR RASTER DISPLAY

Nine bits per pixel allow 512 colours (see Figure 6).

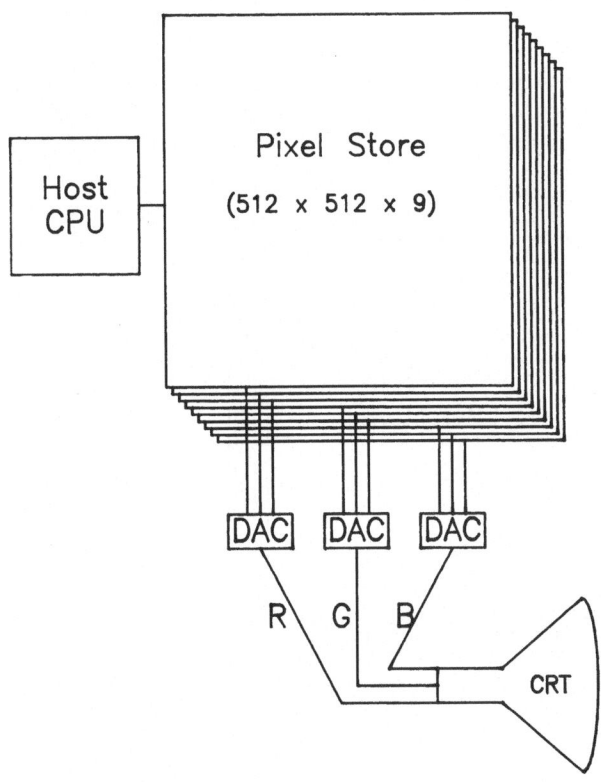

FIGURE 6: 512-COLOUR RASTER DISPLAY

Selective update and display of pixel memory planes

Most displays offer a facility whereby individual planes can be written without affecting other planes. Simplest mechanism is temporal priority: last thing drawn overwrites things drawn previously. By selecting planes to be written we can achieve other effects, including storing different pictures in different memory planes.

When different pictures are stored in different planes, a mechanism is needed for selecting which planes are to be displayed. Can be useful for applications like printed circuit board layout, where each layer is drawn in a separate memory plane. By alternating the choice of which planes are to be written and which are to be displayed a double-buffering technique can be employed: useful for interaction and small-scale animation.

Some displays permit other ways of writing data to memory, such as ANDing, ORing, inverting.

Colour maps

In order to avoid having very large amounts of memory in order to provide more colours/intensities many displays use a colour map (colour translation table, video look-up table), as shown in Figure 7.

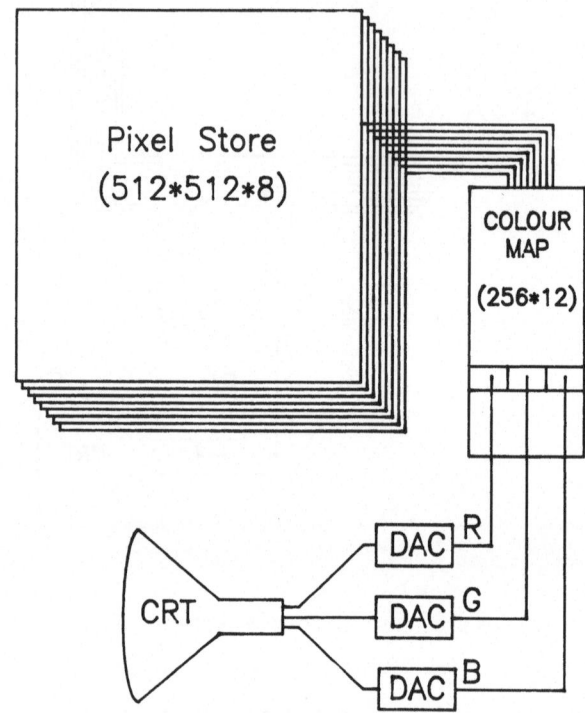

FIGURE 7: 256-COLOUR RASTER DISPLAY WITH 4096 COLOUR REPERTOIRE

This type of display shows so-called "false colour", because the value stored in the pixel memory is not the value of the colour, but an indirect reference to it. It has some other advantages too:

    o Can alter colours retrospectively.
    o Can control colour mixing.
    o Simulate overlay.
    o Can switch planes on and off.
    o Use for limited animation.
    o Can perform gamma correction.

For applications where shaded pictures are needed the colour map should ideally have 8 bits per colour. Such displays can be used for simple shading, but full shading calls for eight bits of colour information for each of red, green and blue to be stored in the pixel memory, i.e. 24 bits per pixel. An expensive, but flexible, configuration for this is shown in Figure 8.

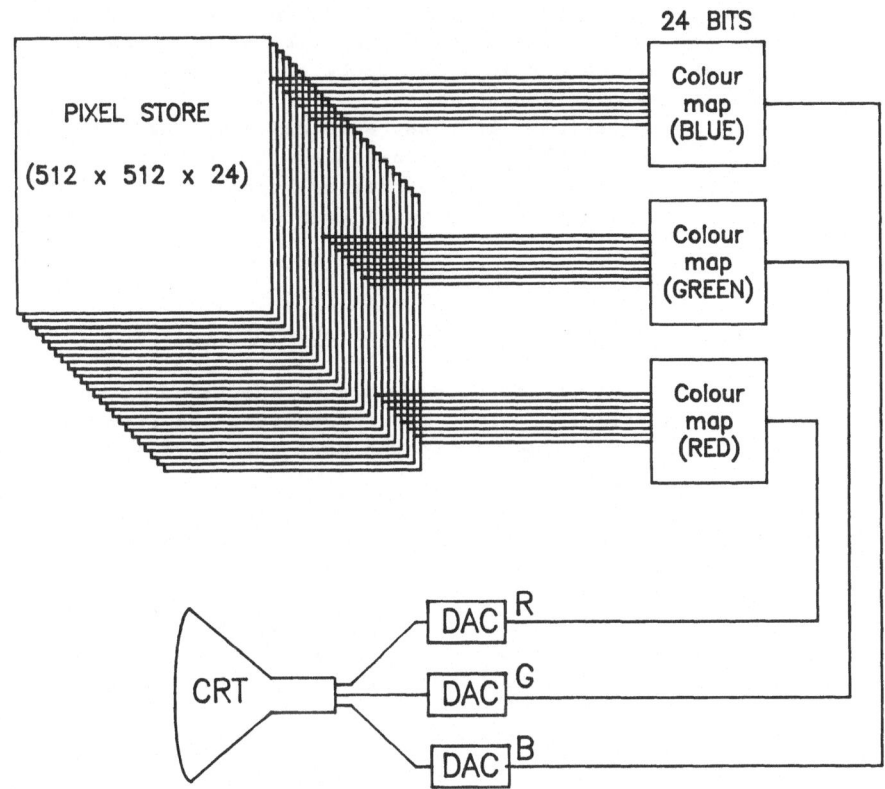

FIGURE 8: FULL COLOUR (EXPENSIVE) RASTER DISPLAY WITH COLOUR MAP

Advantages of raster displays

- o Flicker-free image, therefore can display very complex pictures.
- o Filled areas possible.
- o Full colour allows realistic shaded images.
- o Makes use of T.V. technology. On suitable systems can video record output, and use with video discs.
- o Cheap and getting cheaper as price of memories come down. Prices range from 2000 to 20,000 pounds plus.

Problems with raster displays

- o Jagged lines. Straight lines approximated to nearest pixel resulting in staircasing. Known as aliasing.
- o Limited resolution. Highest resolution is typically 1500*1000. Resolution limited by memory cost, speed and monitor quality.
- o Selective erase. Possible if done with care. Erasing a line is done by re-drawing in background colour, this may erase parts of any overlapping lines.
- o Real-time animation. It takes a relatively long time to load pixel memory with complex picture. To animate need to load, erase and re-load. Double buffering can help. Advances in display system architecture will eventually overcome this.

4.4 DISPLAY SYSTEM ARCHITECTURES AND MORE ADVANCED FEATURES

Even at the low-cost end of the display market the trend is towards more intelligence in displays, using microprocessors and firmware. It is therefore worth examining some of today's more expensive systems to see what facilities they contain.

The use of display files for non-refresh displays is one trend which can be expected to grow. The benefits of a display file include:

- o Ease of updating without re-computing the whole picture.
- o Reduced frequency of picture regeneration.
- o Software compatibility between refresh and non-refresh displays.
- o Support for picture structure for interaction.
- o Local picture processing, e.g. hard-copy.
- o Display can implement 3-D viewing transformations.
- o Reduced load on host computer.

Refresh displays with hardware transformation

With cheaper refresh displays the coordinates stored in the display file are in device units and are two dimensional. Therefore, to represent 3-D objects we must transform the coordinates from 3-D to 2-D according to a viewing transformation (described later) and put the 2-D coordinates in the display file. If we then wish to alter our viewpoint, we must re-calculate the 3-D to 2-D transformation and re-compute the coordinates. This amounts to re-calculating all the picture coordinates each time the viewpoint is changed. For small pictures this is O.K. but will be slow for complex displays.

To solve this problem, more expensive refresh displays allow 3-D coordinates to be stored in a structured display file (SDF) and converted to 2-D by the display processor. In order to permit large numbers of vectors to be displayed flicker-free the transformed output is put in a linear display file (LDF). This is done by special transformation hardware using matrix multiplication techniques. Figure 9 shows a functional model of this, taken from Foley and van Dam, page 407 (originally from I. Carlbom, System Architecture for High-Performance Vector Graphics, Ph. D. Thesis, Brown University, 1980).

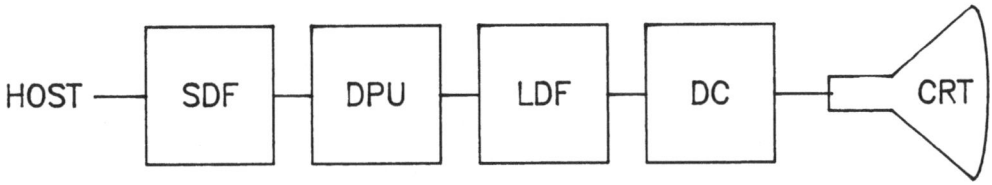

FIGURE 9: FUNCTIONAL MODEL OF HIGH-PERFORMANCE DISPLAY

Examples of systems like this are the Evans & Sutherland (E & S) Multipicture System 2 and the Vector General 3400.

The more recent E & S PS300 uses a highly pipelined design which obviates the need for the intermediate LDF. The system is fast enough to transform and display between 20,000 (full 3-D with complex hierarchical structure) and 95,000 (2-D with relatively little structure) vectors, flicker-free at 30 frames per second.

High-performance raster displays

In order to gain some of the advantages of refresh displays (3-D transformations, structured pictures) some raster displays use a display file. Instead of generating vector output, the display controller performs vector to raster conversion and stores its output in a pixel memory, as shown in Figure 10. The pixel memory is double-buffered to achieve smooth transition between successive frames. Dynamically changing pictures with shaded, filled areas can be drawn by this system. Suffers from aliasing effects when pictures are animated. (Megatek 7200.)

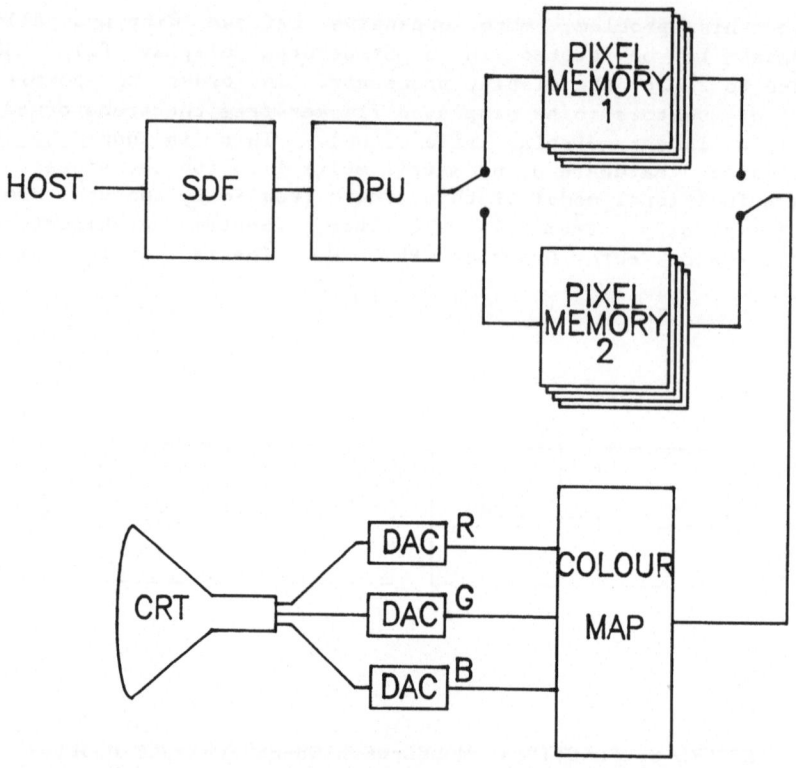

FIGURE 10: HIGH-PERFORMANCE RASTER DISPLAY

4.5   BIT-MAPPED RASTER DISPLAYS

The last three or four years have seen the emergence of this new type of
display   and variations of it.   Best-known example is Three Rivers PERQ.
Present systems are essentially one-bit per pixel raster   displays   with
part of the main CPU memory used as a pixel store (see Figure 11).

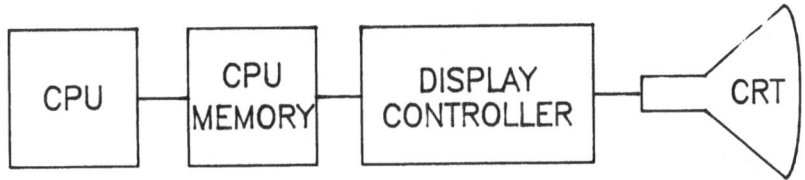

FIGURE 11: BIT-MAPPED DISPLAY

The major advantage of this system is its high speed. There is no interface to act as a bottle-neck between the computer and display. Programs can directly manipulate the pixel store using CPU instructions. Usually, special (microcoded) instructions are available for drawing lines and writing and operating on rectangular areas of the screen memory (RASTER-OP).

The raster-op instruction has three components:

    o A source raster.
    o A destination raster.
    o An op-code (or, in some cases, a modifier raster).

The source raster contains the new data which are to be combined in some way with the screen image. The destination raster specifies where on the screen the new data are to be plotted. The op-code or modifier raster specifies how the new and old data are to be combined:

    o Copy source to destination.
    o Copy inverse of source to destination.
    o Destination becomes source ANDed with destination.
    o Destination becomes source ORed with destination.
    o Destination becomes source XORed with destination.
    o Destination becomes inverse of source ANDed with destination.
    o Destination becomes inverse of source ORed with destination.
    o Destination becomes inverse of source XORed with destination.

These give considerable flexibility. E.g. XOR permits non-destructive alterations to the bit map for plotting a cursor. The raster-op function can also be used to copy pictures between visible (on-screen) and invisible areas of the memory.

Advantages of the bit-mapped display

o Very fast. No interface to act as a bottle neck.
o Flexible. Can be used to display images (black/white) and graphics.
o Good resolution (typically 100 dots per inch).
o Well suited to multiple page mixed text/graphics, i.e. future office systems.

Problems with bit-mapped displays

o Appears difficult to extend to colour without using separate graphics store because of memory bandwidth required. E.g. Apollo Domain has separate store and fast block transfer between CPU memory and graphics store. This makes the graphics slower and loses some of the flexibility.

5.0 INPUT TOOLS

Input tools are needed by a program operator to interact with graphics programs. Most commonly used input tool is a keyboard, but this is inadequate for many graphical operations. Two common requirements are:

o **Positioning**. Supply X,Y coordinates for drawing or positioning objects on screen. Typing coordinates on a keyboard very tedious and inconvenient.
o **Pointing**. Used to identify object on screen for manipulation or used to pick item from menu. Could use naming convention and let user type names on keyboard but this is messy and inconvenient.

The GKS international standard defines the following logical classes of input tool:

o Locator. Generates coordinates.
o Stroke. Generates strings of coordinates which form a connected sequence of points.
o Choice. Allows alternatives to be specified.
o Pick. Used to identify parts of a picture by picking them or pointing at them.
o Valuator. Generates real values in a prescribed range.
o String. Generates a text string. E.g. alphanumeric keyboard.

Tools commonly available can be programmed to match these different logical categories. Many tools can serve as more than one logical tool. For example, a graphic tablet, which generates pairs of coordinates, can be used as a pick device. Some displays have special hardware which permits a pair of coordinates to be correlated with a display file, allowing a locator tool like the tablet to be used as a pick tool.

Joystick (locator/valuator). Consists of a stick that manipulates two potentiometers arranged at right-angles to each other. Each potentiometer gives X and Y coordinates respectively. Some joysticks allow the stick to be rotated thus giving Z coordinate. Often used to control position of cursor on screen thus giving essential visual feed-back of operation. Joystick may be used to control absolute position of cursor or may be used to control the rate at which cursor moves.

Trackerball (locator/valuator). Similar to joystick except rotating ball in socket used to control two digital counters.

Mouse (locator/choice). Consists of a box supported by two wheels at right angles to each other. Axles of wheels drive digital counters giving X and Y coordinates. The box is placed on any flat surface and moved to alter cursor position. The box may be lifted and moved without affecting cursor position. Mouse also has buttons on the box which can be read under program control. Thus with one hand, the user can control position and select functions making the mouse very ergonomic. The mouse is becoming popular on personal computers.

Tablet (locator/choice). The tablet is a small digitiser and is identical in operation to that already described. It is mainly used for positioning but can also be used for pointing with the aid of software. If a puck with several buttons is available it can be used to signal different choices to the program.

Lightpen (pick/locator). This device is used mainly on refresh displays. Some raster displays also offer this device. Consists of tube with a photocell that is pointed at the screen. When a line is detected by the photocell, the display processor is stopped and the CPU informed. The CPU interrogates the display processor to find the address at which it stopped and from this determines what was being drawn. Software must organise display file to make this operation easy. Lightpen may be used for positioning with the aid of software. A cursor is displayed and the lightpen is pointed at it. As the lightpen moves it sees a different part of the cursor. The software determines which part of the cursor was seen and repositions the centre of the cursor. If the lightpen is moved too quickly and no longer sees any part of the cursor, a scan of dots is displayed in the region of the last cursor hit to try to find the lightpen. Lightpens used on raster displays return X and Y coordinates directly and therefore operate as a positioning tool.

Programmable function keys (choice). A box of keys (switches) which can be used to indicate an operator's choices to a program. Often, the switches have programmable lights which can be used to indicate the switch states.

Control dials (valuators). Potentiometers which returns values in a prescribed range. Useful for controlling parameters such as picture scale factors.

6.0 HARD COPY DEVICES

Hard copy devices fall into two main categories, like other graphics devices: vector (line drawing, calligraphic), and raster. With suitable vector to raster conversion software, raster devices can be used to draw line diagrams, although the quality of output will depend on the device's resolution.

The following devices will be discussed:

- o Flat-bed plotter.
- o Drum plotter.
- o Electrostatic plotter.
- o Matrix printer (with multi-coloured ribbon).
- o Ink-jet plotter.
- o Camera.
- o Camera system.
- o Computer output on microfilm (COM).

6.1 FLAT-BED PLOTTER

This operates with pens that can be wet ink, liquid ink ball, ballpoint or fibre-tip. The pens are supported on a gantry. Pens (and lifting mechanism) can move along gantry (Y movement). Gantry can move (X movement). Movement achieved with stepping motors or DC servo motors. Stepping motors give 'jagged' line effect. Servo motors require negative feed-back mechanism giving possible stability and accuracy problems. Movement of heavy gantry limits acceleration and speed. Typical speed is 25cm per second. Different coloured lines can be drawn by using different pens. Filled areas can be drawn using cross-hatching methods, but often not of very good quality.

6.2 DRUM PLOTTER

Pens are supported above a drum. Pens may move along axis of drum (Y movement). Paper is wrapped around drum which is rotated under the pen (X movement). Drive mechanisms may again be stepping motors or DC servo motors. Drum and pen both very much lighter than gantry system and so higher speeds and accelerations possible. Typical speed is from 5cm/sec up to 80cm/sec and up to 6G acceleration. Flat-beds used to be favoured for accuracy (but not speed) but modern day fast drum plotters are accurate. Flat-bed is required if plotting onto pre-printed stationary or card is required. Drum plotter can be loaded with continuous rolls of paper, requiring minimal operator intervention.

6.3 ELECTROSTATIC PLOTTER

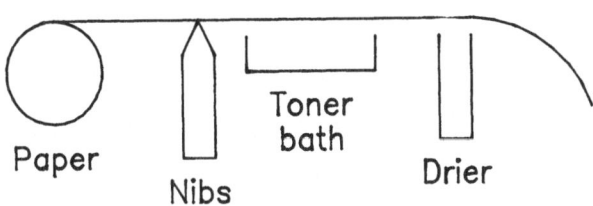

FIGURE 12 ELECTROSTATIC PLOTTER

Picture is drawn as successive rows of dots across paper (see Figure 12). Each row produced by depositing a charge from a row of writing nibs on to the paper. The paper is passed through a toner bath and graphite particles adhere where there is a charge. Paper is dried leaving a black and white image on the paper. Capable of filled areas and grey scale images with software half-toning/dithering technique. Typical resolution is 200 dots/inch.

Recently, Versatec have announced a colour version of this device, which makes multiple passes over the plotting area (by rewinding the paper) to print each primary colour.

6.4 MATRIX PRINTER

Consists of a modified dot matrix printer with a multi-coloured ribbon. Each colour (secondary colours yellow, magenta and cyan because it uses dyes not light) is plotted in turn, with the paper being wound back to the start of the plot each time. Basically 8 colours although more can be obtained with half-toning technique. Usually low resolution and there can be problems aligning the different colours. Relatively cheap.

6.5 INK-JET PLOTTER

A raster device which plots dots by squirting very small drops of ink at a sheet of paper held on a rotating drum. Recent models use a drop-on-demand technique. Eight basic colours can be printed but dithering techniques permit larger range of colours to be simulated. Typical resolutions are 120 to 160 dots per inch.

6.6 CAMERA

A simple way to get copies of pictures on a display screen is to photograph them with an ordinary camera. Commercial systems that include a hood that fits screen are available. Polaroid film gives quick results but is not particularly cheap, nor is it of high quality.

6.7 CAMERA SYSTEMS

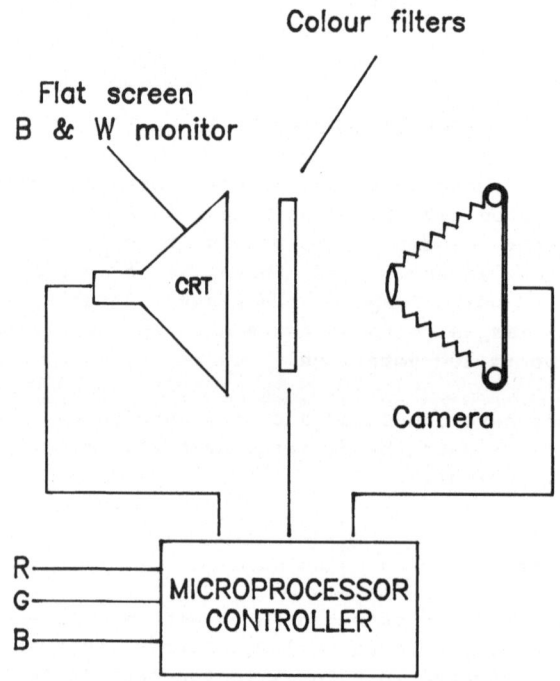

FIGURE 13 CAMERA SYSTEM

Various camera systems are available for direct connection to a raster display. Under microprocessor control, R, G and B video signals are each fed in turn to a high-quality black and white monitor with a screen phosphor as near to white as possible (see Figure 13). The film is exposed through colour filters. This is repeated for each primary colour resulting in composite full colour picture. Systems offer alternative cameras e.g. 35mm, 4" by 5" colour negative, polaroid. No extra software is required to drive such a system as it is connected at the monitor through the video signals. Some systems take several minutes to produce one picture.

6.8 COMPUTER OUTPUT ON MICROFILM (COM)

These systems are essentially expensive and high-quality versions of the camera system just described. Input is usually from magnetic tape, because very large amounts of data are necessary to define high-quality pictures. Devices can usually be driven in vector (calligraphic) or raster mode. There are also more coloured filters than in the camera system. Resolutions are up to 64K by 64K and cameras include 16 and 35 mm, and microfiche.

6.9 RECOMMENDED READING

[1]   J.D. Foley and A. van Dam: Fundamentals of Interactive Computer Graphics, Addison-Wesley, 1982.

[2]   W.M. Newman and R.F. Sproull: Principles of Interactive Computer Graphics, McGraw-Hill, second edition, 1979

II. Introduction to Computer Graphics (Part II)

R. J. Hubbold

1.0 PROJECTIONS AND VIEWING

1.1 PLANAR GEOMETRIC TRANSFORMATIONS

NOTE: This section is based on the excellent paper by I. Carlbom and J. Paciorek: Planar Geometric Projections and Viewing Transformations, Computing Surveys, Vol 10, No 4, December 1978.

Use of perspective is an example of a projection technique with which we are all familiar. Engineers and others commonly use other types of projection for their drawings, such as multi-view orthographic projections and axonometric projection.

The many different types of projection are summarised in Figure 1.

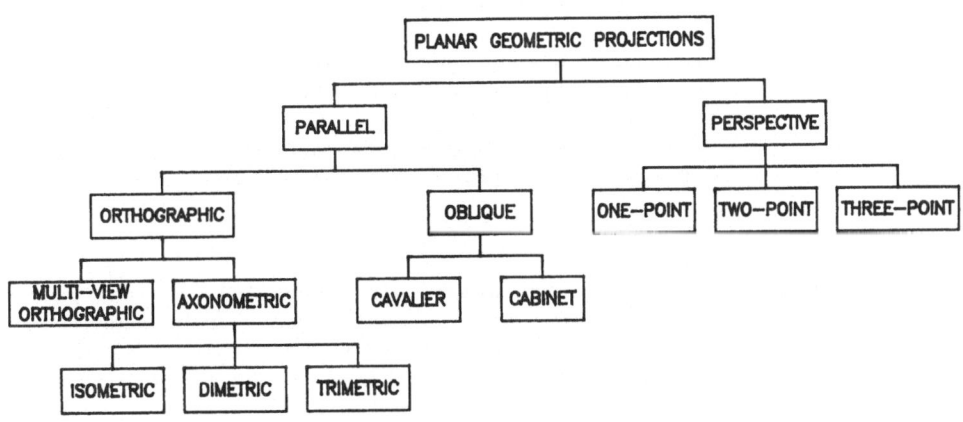

FIGURE 1: CLASSIFICATION OF PLANAR GEOMETRIC PROJECTIONS

Each type can be obtained by choosing a suitable projection plane (which in computer graphics is the display surface) and centre of projection. Broadly, the various types of projection are:

o Parallel. The projection centre is at infinity, so the projectors (projection lines) are parallel. This category sub-divides into:

   o Orthographic. The projectors are perpendicular to the projection plane. Further sub-divides into:

      o Multi-view orthographic, such as are used in engineering drawings (e.g. top, side and front elevations).

      o Axonometric, where parallel lines are equally foreshortened. An axonometric projection is further qualified by the angles between the principal coordinate axes and the projection plane: if all three angles are equal the projection is isometric; if two are equal it is dimetric; if all three are different it is trimetric.

   o Oblique. Here, the projectors are not perpendicular to the projection plane. Usually, the aim of this is to show at least one face of the projected object so that measurements may be made directly from the drawing; often, the face with most detail is chosen. Two (not particularly common) examples:

      o Cavalier, where the angle between the projectors and projection plane is 45 degrees. This produces perpendiculars projected at full scale without foreshortening, so measurements can be made directly.

      o Cabinet, where the angle is arccot(0.5) (approx. 64 degrees). This produces a foreshortening of 1/2.

o Perspective. Objects drawn with parallel projections are useful because they permit measurements to be made from the picture, but they produce unreal looking pictures (a kind of inverse perspective effect which makes the front look smaller than the back). Perspective projection results in apparently normal view of an object, as one would expect it to appear to the eye in real life, but measurements cannot usually be taken from the picture.

Figure 2 illustrates a perspective projection and plan view.

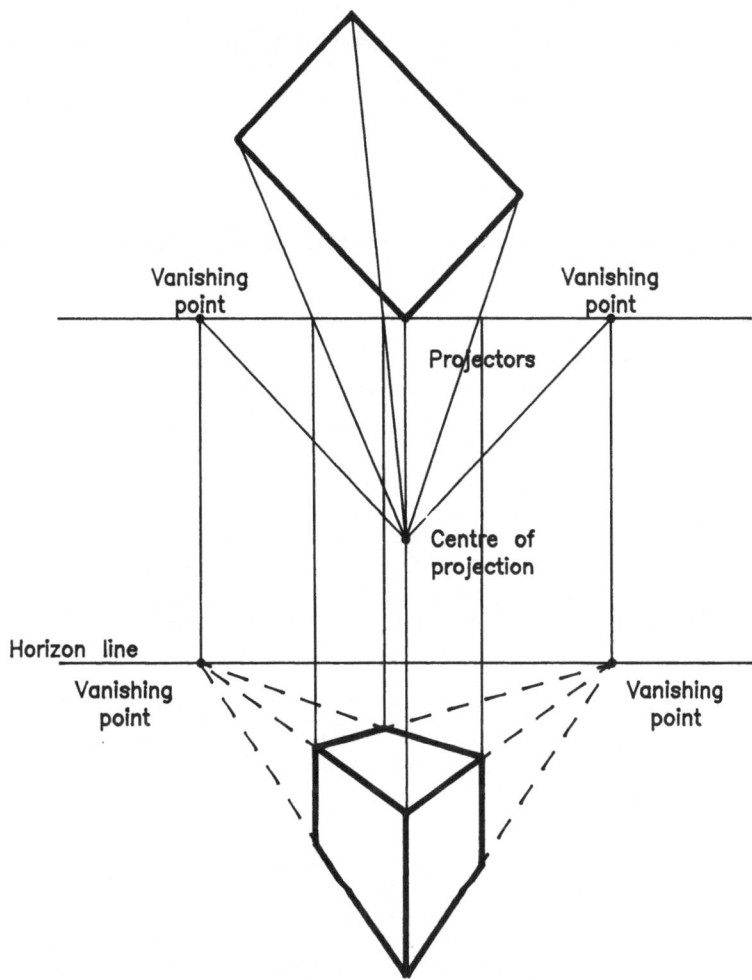

FIGURE 2: PERSPECTIVE PROJECTION

Perspective projections can be further qualified as one-, two-
or three-point.

Stereoscopic views

An interesting 3-D effect can be obtained by choosing two slightly
different view points and creating two views of an object. The two
views correspond to the view of the object seen by the left eye and the
right eye. A special viewer is required to combine the two images.
This technique is popular for viewing molecular structure diagrams.

1.2   SPECIFYING PROJECTIONS IN A GRAPHICS SYSTEM

Parameters which define the projections described can be specified via
procedure or subroutine calls or by language statements.   The parameters
are:

   o The direction of view (usually a vector in world coordinate
      space). This defines the direction of the projectors.

   o For perspective projection, the position of the eye.   This
      defines the centre of projection.

   o The position and orientation of the projection plane. This can
      be given as a point (a centre of interest) and a view-up
      vector, which defines which direction will be "up" (parallel to
      the vertical axis of the display surface) in the projected
      picture.

   o Details of how to position the projected picture on the display
      surface.   This can be given in various ways, such as the
      position in normalised device coordinates (NDC) of the centre
      of interest.

All of the projections described so far can be represented conveniently
by a 4 by 4 transformation matrix, using homogeneous coordinates. This
matrix formulation is a standard method in computer graphics and is
particularly convenient for viewing transformations for two reasons:

   o It allows viewing transformations to be concatenated with
      modelling transformations by simple matrix multiplication.
   o It can be handled by displays with special transformation
      hardware.

1.3 CLIPPING IN 3-D

For parallel projections the clipping process is similar to that used for 2-D, but a rectangular clipping volume is used which has front (hither) and back (yon) faces.

For perspective, the clipping volume is a right regular pyramid (see Foley and van Dam for details). Care is needed to ensure that objects behind the viewing position are not visible.

1.4 REPRESENTING SOLID OBJECTS

Drawing realistic pictures of 3-D objects has long been a major area of research in computer graphics. This is because the computer provides us with a convenient way to view theoretical models and designs which do not in reality exist, but which we may wish to build. Line drawings of 3-D objects are notoriously difficult to interpret; it can be difficult to tell which is the front and which is the back of an object, even though perspective is employed.

Early work centred on removal of hidden lines, because early systems were calligraphic devices. In practice the task is to remove hidden surfaces. In order to illustrate this we will examine some simple techniques for raster displays.

Because of its ability to show filled areas the raster display is ideal for producing pictures of solid objects. The pictures can be shaded to indicate the shapes of objects for various lighting conditions and recent work in this field has resulted in quite realistic pictures. For good results the display (or other output device, such as a film recorder) needs to have 64 intensity levels for grey pictures and up to 256 levels for each of red, green and blue, for full colour.

Most work in this field has concentrated on representing surfaces of objects by polygonal facets, although spheres are also very useful for some applications (e.g. molecular modelling [3]). Recent work has also been done on developing methods for drawing surface patches [4]. To illustrate the subject we will limit discussion here to planar polygons.

Many surfaces can be approximately represented by planar polygonal facets. In general, for curved surfaces the larger the number of polygons the better the approximation. Flat surfaces, of course, can be modelled precisely by planar polygons. Figures 3 and 4 show surfaces modelled in this way.

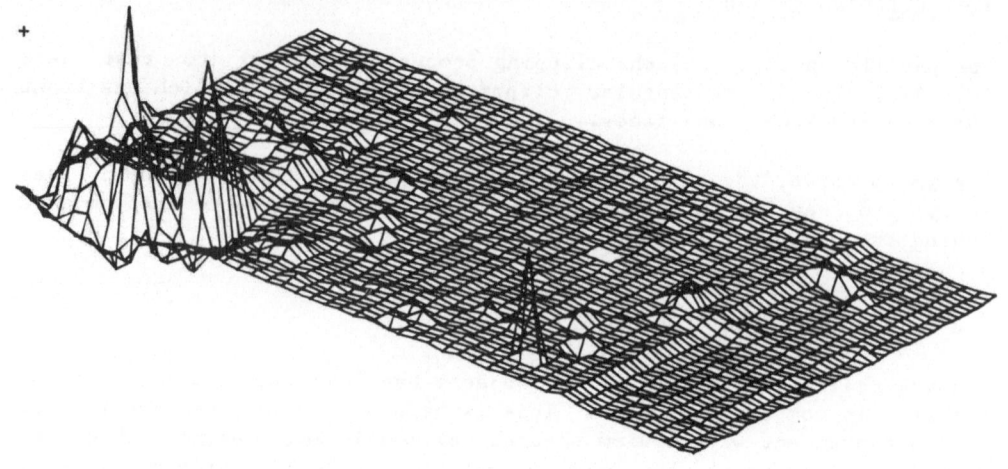

FIGURE 3: SURFACE DRAWN WITH LINES

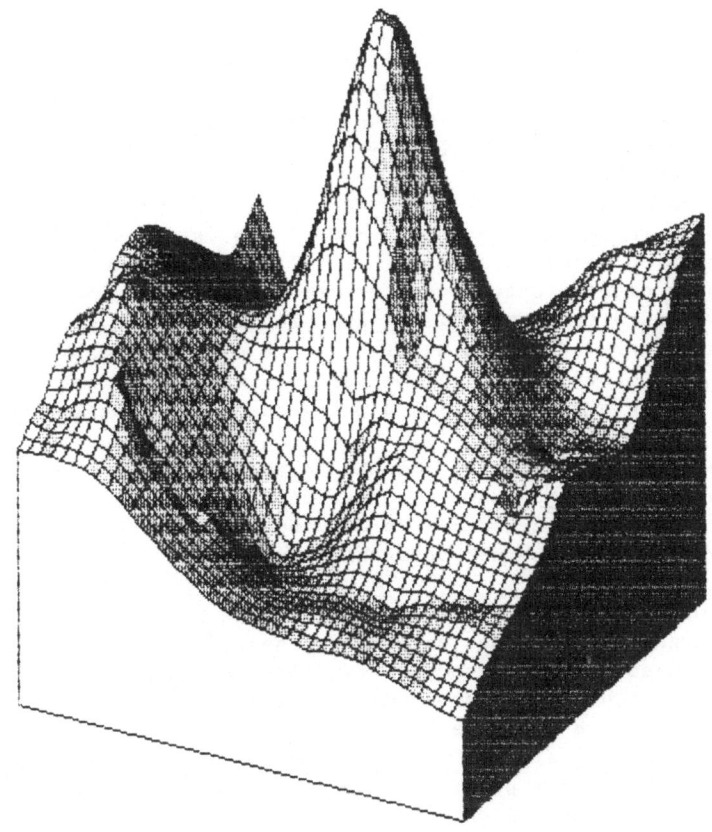

FIGURE 4: SURFACE DRAWN WITH SHADING (ORDERED DITHER, SEE LATER)

Three steps are involved in generating such shaded pictures:

1. A viewing transformation is applied to map the polygons in to the display coordinate system.

2. Hidden surfaces are removed.

3. Intensity (shading) calculations are made.

The viewing transformation

Viewing transformations have already been described. Most raster displays do not support hardware transformations, so the transformations are performed in software; only the X and Y coordinates are needed to draw the polygon boundaries, after transformation. However, in order to perform depth calculations during hidden surface removal the Z coordinates must also be preserved.

Hidden surface removal

Many hidden line and surface algorithms have been developed. Several of these are classified as "image space" algorithms which operate in the coordinate space of the output device and capitalize on its limited resolution, and these are popular for raster devices. We will very briefly examine three:

o **The painter's algorithm** is one of the simplest which can be used on raster displays. It relies on the picture being drawn in an ordered sequence, starting with those parts which are furthest from the viewer and progressing towards the front of the scene. New data written to the display overwrites anything drawn previously, in the same way that an artist working with oil paints can overpaint a background with foreground detail.

o **The Newell, Newell, Sancha algorithm** A problem with the painter's algorithm is that the polygons must be sorted into the correct order prior to drawing. The Newell, Newell and Sancha algorithm performs this sorting [5].

A preliminary sort is made with the Z coordinates of each polygon, with that polygon furthest from the viewer placed at the head of the sorted polygon list, and the closest at its tail. The sort produces a roughly correct ordering. The polygons are then drawn in the order of the list. Because some overlapping polygons may have been placed at the wrong place in the list by the preliminary sort further processing takes place as the list is traversed. Specifically, where an ambiguity exists polygons are compared using their plane equations to determine the correct priorities.

With this and some other algorithms care is required to detect self-overlapping polygons (circuits). In such cases polygons must be sub-divided. Many objects can be constructed so they do not include these situations to begin with.

o **Z-buffer algorithms**. The simplest Z-buffer algorithm is one which keeps a large array of Z coordinate values, one for each pixel. The array is intialised with large negative values (assuming a right-handed coordinate system). Objects are then drawn in any order. Each time a pixel is generated its Z coordinate is compared with the corresponding value in the Z-buffer. If the new pixel is closer to the viewer than anything plotted previously at that point the new pixel value is plotted and its Z coordinate is saved in the Z-buffer. This is a very simple algorithm, but can be used to generate quite good results. Some display manufacturers have incorporated a Z-buffer into their hardware, thanks to reducing memory costs.

The algorithm can be adapted to work on a single scan-line at a time. This dramatically reduces the memory requirements at the expense of a more complicated program, particularly if primitives other than planar polygons are allowed.

In all of these algorithms (except if transparent surfaces are employed) it is usual to cull away-facing surfaces. These can be found by taking the vector dot product of the surface normal and line-of-sight vector. If the result is positive, the face is pointing away from the viewer. If negative, it is pointing towards the viewer. (This doesn't mean it is visible, however. It might be obscured by another surface closer to the viewer.)

For a review of hidden surface algorithms see [6].

Shading calculations

These are performed using lighting models. In general there are three main contributions to the intensity of light reflected from a point on the surface of an object:

o General background illumination.
o Diffusely reflected light from specific light sources.
o Specularly reflected light which "bounces" off the surface.

For transparent or translucent objects there will also be light which passes through the visible surfaces from behind.

For greyscale pictures a single intensity value must be computed for each pixel from the sum of the above components. For colour pictures intensities must be calculated for each primary component (usually R, G, B).

o **Background illumination.** This is usually assumed to be constant:

$$Ib = constant * R$$

where R is the reflectance coefficient for the surface.

o **Diffuse reflections.** The intensity of light falling at a point on a surface, which will be diffusely reflected, is computed from Lambert's Cosine Law:

$$Id = Ip * R * cos(i)$$

where R is the refectance coefficient, Ip is the intensity of the light source, and i is the angle between the incident light and a vector normal to the surface (see Figure 5). The value

of cos(i) can be found by taking the vector dot product of a
unit vector along the direction of the light rays and a unit -
surface normal vector.

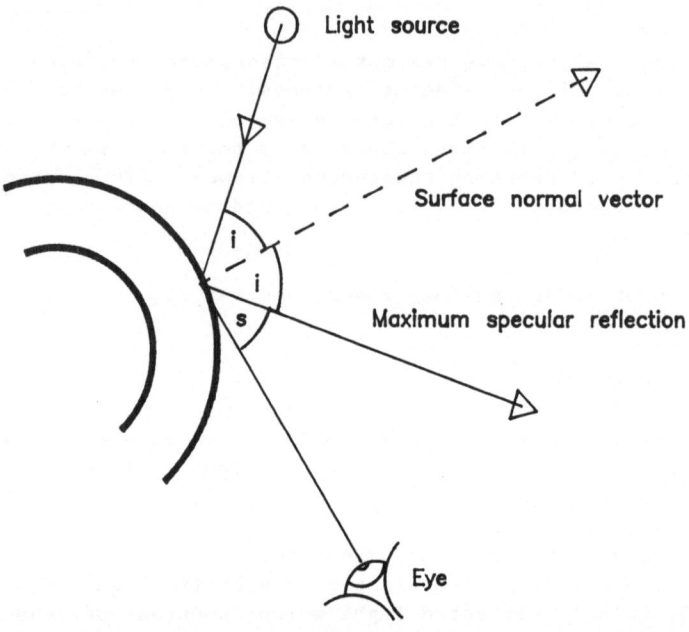

FIGURE 5: DIFFUSELY AND SPECULARLY REFLECTED LIGHT

o Specular reflections. These cause a surface to look shiny.
  Several methods have been developed, one of the best known by
  Phong (derived empirically), (see Figure 5):

$$Is = Ip * W(i) * (\cos(s))**n$$

where $W(i)$ is a specular refection coefficient which varies
with the angle of incidence i and the material, and n is an
exponent which determines how shiny the surface looks. (W is
in the range 0 to 1 and n varies, typically between 1 and 10.)
It should be noted that the "colour" of the specular component
is the same as the light source and does not depend on the
surface colour (which determines R).

An assumption which simplifies the calculations is that point light
sources are located at infinity. This makes all light rays parallel, so
a single vector can be used in the calculations.

Recently, work has been done to develop much more elaborate models,
including that by Whitted which uses a light ray tracing approach [7].
These methods produce some beautiful results but are very expensive

computationally.

If a single intensity is plotted inside each polygon, disconcerting discontinuities occur at the boundaries (known as Mach banding). Several techniques have been devised to remove these by varying the intensities across the polygons to produce a smooth shading effect. Two of the best known are:

o   Gouraud shading [8], in which intensities are computed at each polygon vertex and linearly interpolated across the polygon.

o   Phong shading [9], in which surface normals are computed at each vertex and interpolated across the polygon.

Although these produce reasonable results they do give some problems, particularly when animation is used since inaccuracies in the shading model can cause the surfaces to appear to change in shape. Other methods have been developed, see [10] for example.

1.5   HALF-TONING TECHNIQUES

Half-toning is the name of a collection of ways of simulating different grey levels on devices with a limited range of output values (often only 0 or 1, as with bi-level displays, matrix printers and electrostatic plotters).

Patterns

Patterns of dots can be used to represent different intensities. For example, with a 2 by 2 dot pattern we can get 5 intensity values corresponding to 0, 1, 2, 3, or 4 dots.

Effectively, this technique produces grey levels by using several dots to plot one pixel, i.e. it trades resolution against grey levels.

Dithering

This is a technique which keeps resolution unaltered, but gives the effect of extra grey levels by an appropriate spatial distribution of dots (rather like newspaper pictures). Dithering works by comparing the desired intensity at a point with a threshhold value to see whether that point should be plotted or left blank. If the desired intensity level is greater than the threshhold the point is plotted. For ordered dithering, the threshhold values are stored in a two-dimensional array accessed by the point coordinates. Random dither uses a random number generator to compute the threshhold for each point.

The surface plot in Figure 4 was made with a 4 by 4 array of threshhold
values capable of simulating 16 grey levels. [11] gives details of the
method.

2.0 COLOUR

Colour is now recognised as a major development in computer graphics and
is becoming increasingly common. It is a complex subject, so only a few
simple aspects are presented here. [1] contains an excellent discussion
of the subject. See also [12] and [13].

Uses for colour include:

  o Coding information.
  o Highlighting important detail.
  o Natural images.
  o Contouring.

There are two major colour systems:

  o Additive, in which the primary colours are red, green and blue
    (RGB).   This is the usual colour system for display monitors.
    Zero values for RGB give black, equal mixtures of RGB give a
    grey level, and maximum values of RGB give white.

  o Subtractive, in which the primaries are yellow, cyan, magenta
    (YCM).   These are used for plotting on paper, as with ink-jet
    plotters. Zero values for YCM give white, maximum values give
    black.   (In theory!   In practice black is often printed
    separately.)

Colour models

Several different models have been devised for specifying colour. Among these are:

o The RGB colour cube. RGB is useful for computation (e.g. shading). The RGB colour space can be visualised as a cube, see Figure 6.

Each of R, G, B is in the range [0..1]. (0,0,0) is black and (1,1,1) is white. All combinations lie inside or on the surface of the cube.

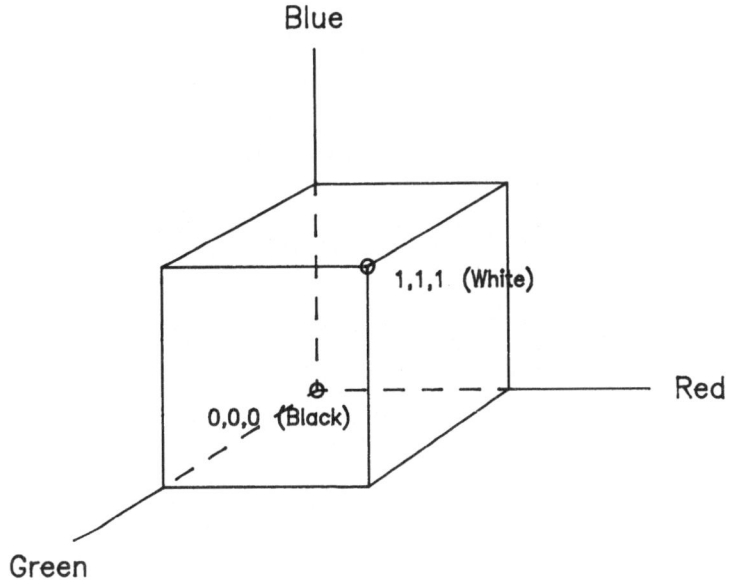

FIGURE 6: THE RGB COLOUR CUBE

o   The hue/saturation/value hexcone (HSV). Hue is how a colour is
    classified as red, yellow, green etc., i.e. a way of naming a
    colour. Saturation determines the degree to which a colour
    differs from a grey or white of the same intensity. Value
    determines how light or dark a colour is along a linear scale
    from black to full brightness.

    Figure 7 shows the HSV hexcone. Hue is measured as an angle
    (R=0, G=120 degrees, B=240 degrees), saturation as distance
    from the centre axis, and value as position along the centre
    axis. The base point of the hexcone is black, and the top
    contains the maximum intensity colours for different levels of
    saturation.

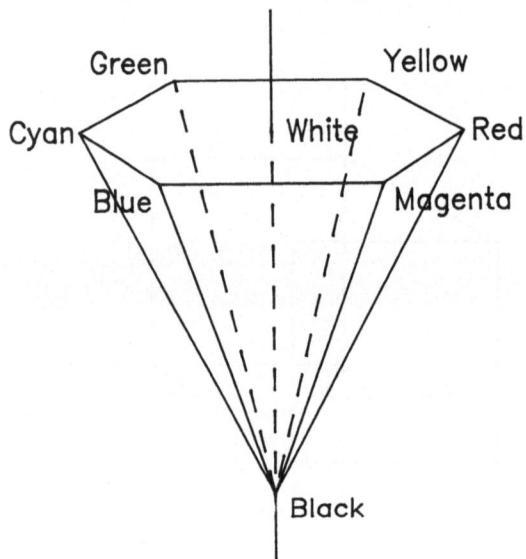

FIGURE 7: THE HSV HEXCONE

o The hue/lightness/saturation double-ended cone (HLS). This is
   similar to the HSV hexcone but has maximally saturated colours
   at 50% value (lightness), as in Figure 8. The top point of the
   cone is white, the bottom point is black.

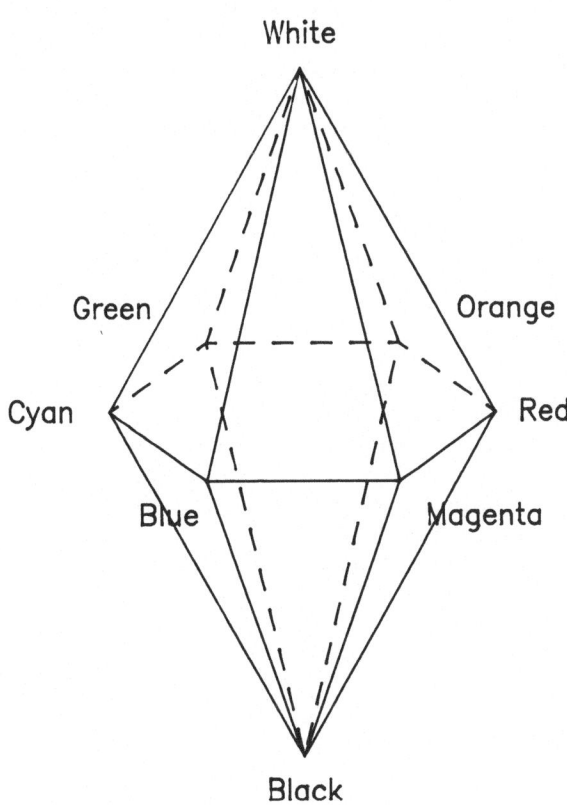

FIGURE 8:THE HSL DOUBLE-ENDED CONE

o The YIQ model. This is commonly used in TV broadcasting. Its importance is that it provides downward compatibility with black and white TV. YIQ is a simple transformation of RGB:

$$|Y| = |0.30 \quad 0.59 \quad 0.11| \quad |R|$$
$$|I| \quad |0.60 \ -0.28 \ -0.32| \quad |G|$$
$$|Q| \quad |0.21 \ -0.52 \quad 0.31| \quad |B|$$

By ensuring that different colours have different values for Y they can be guaranteed to have different intensities on a black and white TV.

Some basic colour usage rules

In practice certain colour combinations go well and others do not. Some general guidelines are:

o No blue lines on black background.
o No yellow lines on white background.
o Use "natural" background for full colour images.
o Use complementary background to accentuate dominant hue.
o Colour edging enhances polygons.
o Complements mix to give grey.
o Colours near in hue make pleasing combinations.
o Complements give warm/cool contrast.
o Use of dominant tint gives mellow picture.

Recommended reading and references

[1]   J.D. Foley and A. van Dam: Fundamentals of Interactive Computer Graphics, Addison-Wesley, 1982.

[2]   W.M. Newman and R.F. Sproull: Principles of Interactive Computer Graphics, McGraw-Hill, second edition, 1979

[3]   T.K. Porter: "Spherical shading", ACM Computer Graphics, 12(3), 1978.

[4]   J.M. Lane, L.C. Carpenter, T.Whitted, J.F Blinn: "Scan line methods for displaying parametrically defined surfaces", CACM, 23(1), January 1980.

[5]   M.E. Newell, R.G. Newell and T.L. Sancha: "A new approach to the shaded picture problem", Proc. ACM National Conf., 1972.

[6]   I.E. Sutherland, R.F. Sproull and R.A. Schumaker: "A characterisation of ten hidden surface algorithms", Computing Surveys, 6(1), 1974.

[7]   Turner Whitted: "An improved illumination model for shaded display", CACM, 23(6), 1980.

[8]   H.   Gouraud: "Computer   display   of   curved   surfaces", Department   of   Computer   Science,   University   of   Utah, UTEC-CSc-71-113, June 1971.

[9]   Bui Tuong-Phong: "Illumination   for   computer   generated pictures", CACM, 18(6), 1975.

[10]   J.   Blinn: "Models of light   reflection   for   computer synthesised pictures", ACM Computer Graphics, 11(2), 1977.

[11]   C.N. Judice: "display of two-dimensional functions using grey scale simulated on a bi-level display", ACM Computer Graphics, 9(1), 1975.

[12]   Alvy Ray Smith: "Color gamut transform pairs", ACM Computer Graphics, 12(3), August 1978.

[13]   G.H Joblove and D. Greenberg: "Color spaces for computer graphics", ACM Computer Graphics, 12(3), August 1978.

III. Introduction to Computer Graphics (Part III)

R. D. Bergeron

1. Graphics Concepts

1.1. Graphics Software Overview

As shown in Figure 1, there are two major functional components to every graphics application:

-construct objects by extracting information from the data base.

-convert the object specifications into image specifications.

An important step in the development of graphics software was the categorization of these two major components [Guedj76]:

MODELLING - the process of creating an object specification

GRAPHICS - the process of transforming an object specification into an image specification

Modelling is inherently application-dependent, which makes it very difficult to establish general purpose programming support for it. Graphics is substantially application-independent and can be reasonably well supported by general purpose, application independent software.

This separation into modelling and graphics functions provides the basis for both the recent major advances in general purpose graphics software support, the Core System [GSPC79] and GKS [GKS82].

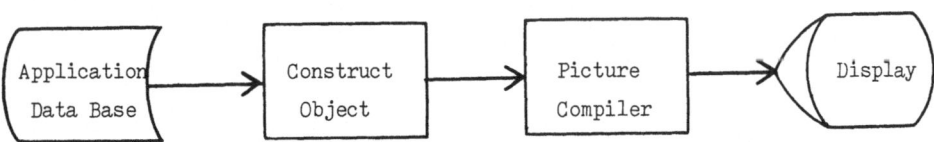

Figure 1. Major steps in a graphics application.

Based on this approach, the overall structure of a prototypical graphics application is shown in Figure 2.

The "Graphics System" in Figure 2 has the responsibility for converting object specifications defined by the application program into images. Furthermore, Figure 2 is based on the assumption that the "Graphics System" aims at providing a device-independent interface to the application program. This goal is crucial in the organization and design of the graphics system. Following the GKS [GKS82] terminology, it is convenient to separate the "graphics system" of Figure 1 into two parts -- the device independent part and the workstation or device dependent part. This is shown in Figure 3.

The device independent part accepts a standard object specification from the application program and uses the currently defined viewing parameters to convert that specification into a standardized image specification which is passed to the workstation. It is the responsibility of the workstation to interface to the peculiarities of the specific display by converting the standardized image definition into appropriate commands that cause the image to be displayed.

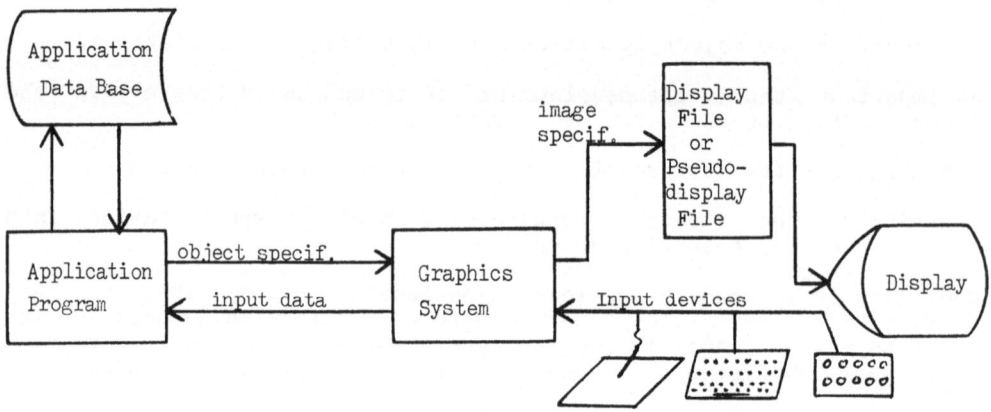

Figure 2. Structure of a graphics application

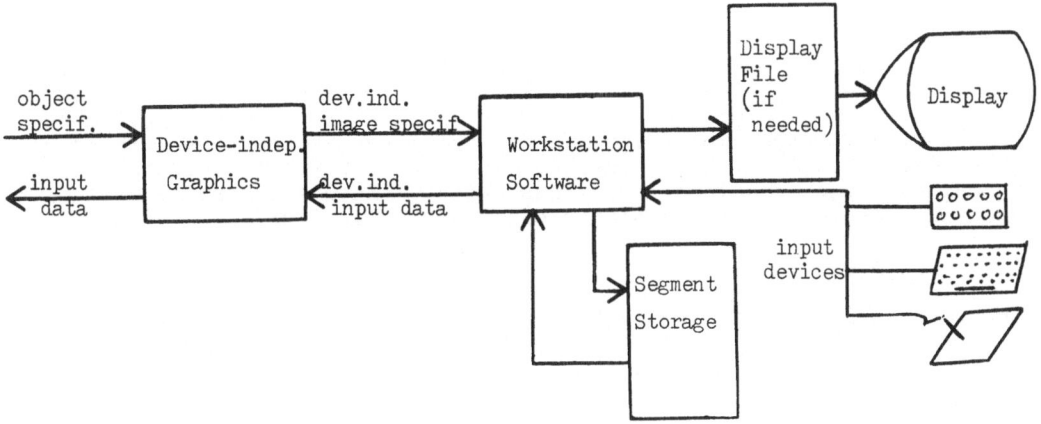

Figure 3. A device-independent graphics system.

Below are a few more or less rigorous definitions of terms that are often used ambiguously or interchangeably:

object – a conceptual entity which can be presented to the viewer, such as a "house" or a "circuit", etc.

scene – a collection of objects and a specification of a view of those objects.

image – the visual display resulting from a particular view of an object. I.e., lines, etc. drawn on a view surface. Note: it is possible for an object to have an "empty" image for some views.

picture – the set of images representing a scene.

workstation – the display device plus interaction tools utilized by the end user of the application program.

1.2. Device Independent Graphics Standards

Since 1976, there have been major efforts invested in attempting to develop standards for computer graphics software. The task was (and still is) a formidable one. In the beginning, a considerable amount of energy had to be invested in trying to understand and formalize the basic concepts behind graphics programming. Many of these issues are well presented in [Gued76, GSPC77, Newm78]. The earliest significant proposal for a graphics standard was generated by the ACM SIGGRAPH Graphics Standards Planning Committee [GSPC77, GSPC79]. The system proposed has come to be called the Core System. At about the same time the early versions of GKS were being developed, first in Germany and later as an ISO effort. GKS is now an ISO Draft Standard [GKS82]. Although there are significant differences between the two systems, there has been much cross-fertilization and the fundamental approaches are similar. The most significant difference is that the Core is a three-dimensional system, whereas GKS is only two-dimensional. Throughout the remainder of these notes, these two systems will be used as examples for explaining "how" graphics is done.

1.3. Graphical Output

In order to produce an image, the graphics system must be given:

   object – "what" is to be viewed

   viewing specification – "how" the object is to be viewed

Object definition

Object definition requires the specification of:

primitives – geometric information defining the primitive components
      that make up the object (such as lines, polygons, text, etc.)

attributes – visual information specifying how each primitive is to be
      displayed (such as color, line style, etc.)

We need to have a coordinate system for defining the geometric proper-ties of the primitives. For the convenience of the application pro-gram, this coordinate system should be natural and convenient for the application. Because of the enormous range of potential applications, the only feasible coordinate system for specifying primitives is one which spans the representable real numbers in a machine. This is called the world coordinate system and is used for primitive specifi-cation.

Viewing specification

The application program must also define the portion of the world coordinate system that is to be viewed. The viewing specification in a two-dimensional system is straightforward. The program specifies a window which is a rectangular region of the world coordinate system which is to be displayed. Since it is often desirable to use only a portion of the view surface for a given display, the application pro-gram also specifies a viewport which is the portion of the view sur-face in which the contents of the window will be displayed. In order to specify a viewport, it is necessary to have a coordinate system to represent the view surface. Since this representation should be device-independent, we define the normalized device coordinate space (NDC) as a 2-dimensional system in which the range 0 to 1 in x and y represent the visible area of the view surface. (Note that for non-

square view surfaces, additional conventions are needed for determining the mapping to the actual display.)

Finally, the workstation software must map the NDC coordinates to the
display coordinate space for a particular device.

The sequence of coordinate transformations is shown in Figure 4.

Given the window-to-viewport mapping defined above, what happens to
primitives or portions of primitives that are defined outside the window? In most graphics systems, primitives outside the window are
clipped to remove those pieces that are outside the window. Figure 5
shows an example of how primitives might be clipped to the window.

The actual clipping process can take place at different points in the

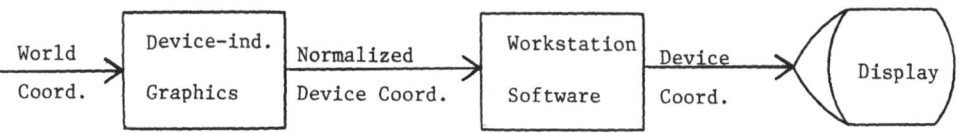

Figure 4. The viewing pipeline.

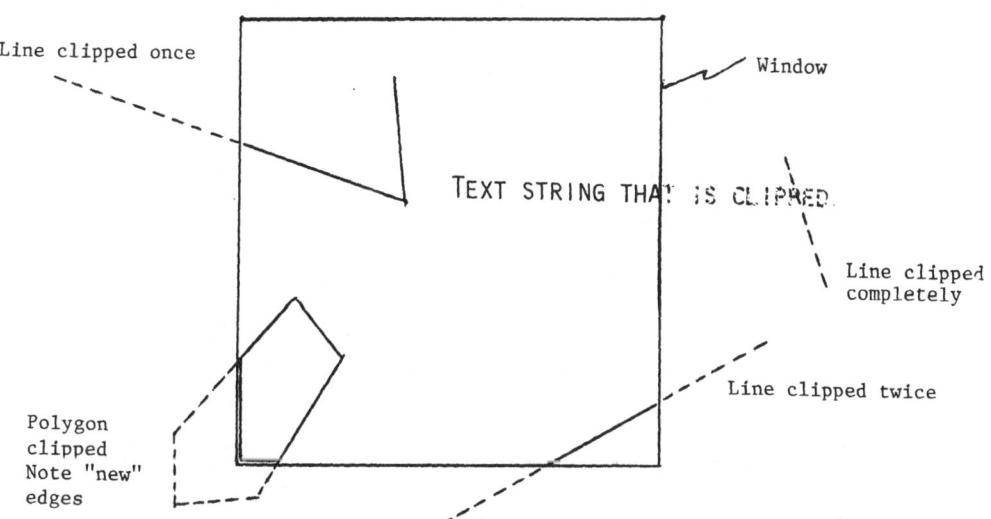

Figure 5. Clipping of primitives.

viewing pipeline. The Core System is defined such that clipping is done to the window in world coordinates, prior to the mapping of world to NDC coordinates. GKS, on the other hand, defines clipping to take place to the viewport in NDC coordinates, prior to mapping to device coordinates. The former approach has the advantage that primitives that are completely clipped never need be transformed; this is especially advantageous if a large percentage of the primitives is typically clipped away, thus reducing the information that must be sent to and maintained by the workstation. The second approach has advantages that are apparent when segment transformations can be applied (see next section).

Segmentation

In order to deal with large pictures interactively, it is desirable to have a mechanism for defining the picture as a collection of segments that can be manipulated independently. Each segment can be created, deleted, made visible or invisible, without affecting the remainder of the picture. Since many physical devices support a selective erase feature, segmentation is extremely important in terms of providing fast user-friendly picture update. Even with a device without selective erase, segmentation improves response time by minimizing the effort necessary to recreate the picture.

Every segment is created with an unique "name" (usually an integer value), which is used to identify that segment in future references.

Each segment has a number of segment attributes associated with it. Typically, the value of these attributes can be changed dynamically as long as the segment exists. Typical segment attributes (supported by both the Core System and GKS) include

    visibility - indicates whether segment is visible

    highlighting - a generalized "blink" feature

    detectability - whether segment can be selected by the PICK device

    segment transformation - translation, scaling and rotation factors
                    to be applied to the NDC coordinates of the primitives
                    in the segment

The segment transformation capability interacts with the viewing features differently in the Core and GKS. In the Core clipping occurs prior to mapping coordinates to NDC space, so that segment transformations (called "image transformations" in Core terminology) are applied to the clipped coordinates as shown in figure 6b. Consequently, a primitive that has been clipped, then translated away from the edge of the viewport, remains clipped, even though its new position would not appear to warrant it.

In GKS, clipping does not occur until segments are converted by the workstation to device coordinates. This occurs **after** segment transformations have been applied. Consequently, as shown in figure 6c, GKS segment transformations do not produce the "surprises" that can occur in the Core System although it does produce the situation that objects defined **outside** the window can appear inside the viewport. The GKS strategy also entails additional overhead:

-a substantial amount of primitive data may have to be stored and processed by the workstation, even though it is always clipped.

-it is less likely that hardware features can be used to implement the segment transformations. (This is a major goal for the Core System).

Picture storage and retrieval

In order to improve picture portability, some modern graphics systems provide a well-defined format for storing pictures in a device independent manner on secondary storage. Such files are called **metafiles** and are an important feature in the drive towards device

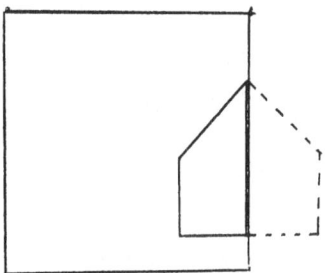

a. Before segment transformation.

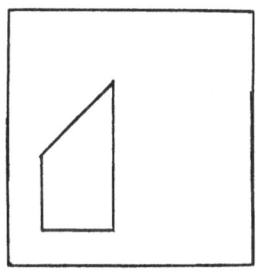

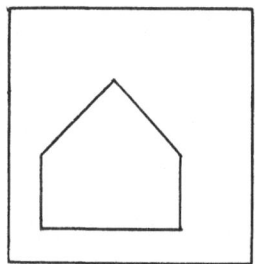

b. After segment transform - Core   c. After segment transform - GKS.

Figure 6. Clipping and segment transformation.

independence and portability. For more information see [GSPC79, GKS82, Reed82].

Sample program

Below is the skeleton of a graphics program that could be used to produce and manipulate a simple picture. To avoid the details of a particular package, the algorithm is presented in pseudo code with graphics calls that are semantically equivalent to both the Core System and GKS. The program creates three segments with only the first one visible. It then cycles through the segments alternately making the previous invisible and the next visible.

```
    initialization;

    define window and viewport;

    create_segment (1);
      define attributes for primitives;
      define primitives;
      define new attributes;
      define primitives;
    close_segment;

    create_segment (2);
      set_visibility (2, off);    { segment invisible while created }
      define attributes and primitives;
    close_segment;

    define window and viewport; { another view can be specified }

    create_segment (3);
      set_visibility (3, off);    { also invisible }
      define attributes and primitives;
    close_segment;

    { Cycle through the 3 segments making them visible in turn.}

    vis := 1;
    while still cycling do
      set_visibility (vis, off);
      vis := vis + 1;  { make next segment the visible one }
      if vis = 4 then  { but wraparound at 3 }
         vis := 1;
      set_visibility (vis, on);
      wait a bit;
      endwhile;
```

1.4. Graphics-Based Input

Logical input devices

Just as with graphics output, it is important to provide device independent support for accessing the input facilities of a graphics workstation. To achieve this goal the Core System and GKS both define a set of logical input devices which attempt to incorporate the basic functionality of common physical devices. The basic function of a logical devices is to return (from the operator of the program) a particular kind of value. The GKS logical devices and common corresponding physical devices are listed in Figure 7. If a particular workstation does not have a convenient physical device for a particular logical device, some form of simulation must be implemented in order to support the logical device.

Logical Device	Returns	Typical Physical Devices
LOCATOR	an x,y position	tablet, mouse, trackball
STROKE	series of x,y positions	tablet, mouse, trackball (plus extra software)
VALUATOR	a real number	control dial
CHOICE	integer indicating selection from a number of choices	function buttons
STRING	a character string	alphanumeric keyboard
PICK	identification of picture primitive selected by operator	lightpen

Figure 7. GKS Logical Devices.

Events and sampling

Physical devices produce information in two quite distinct methods. Devices such as control dials, joysticks, etc., can continuously provide a value to the program -- at any time, the program can choose to sample the current value of such a device. A device such as a keyboard, on the other hand, produces meaningful values at discrete points in time (when a key is pressed by the operator). For such devices, it is important that the application program be able to determine when an appropriate event has occurred that signifies that the value of the device is meaningful and can be used.

Both the Core System and GKS define their logical input devices in such a way that they incorporate the concepts of sampling and event-handling.

The logical input devices of the Core System are defined to be either sampled devices, or event devices, but not both. PICK, KEYBOARD (like the GKS STRING), BUTTON (similar to the GKS CHOICE) and STROKE are event devices, while LOCATOR and VALUATOR are sampled devices. This approach reflects a fairly close association between the logical devices and the corresponding physical devices upon which the logical devices are based.

GKS, on the other hand, provides a more unified approach to its definition of logical devices -- all devices can be used as either sampled devices or event devices (and may also be used in "request" mode).

sample mode

> In sample mode, the program can issue a SAMPLE command which returns the current value of the logical device, without waiting for operator action.

request mode

> In request mode, the program can issue a REQUEST command which requests input from the operator as follows: a prompt is issued indicating that input is requested for the particular logical input device; the program waits until the operator has specified a new value for the device; this value is returned as the result of the REQUEST command.

event mode

> In event mode, the operator may use the device at any time. When the value of the device is "correct", the operator invokes a "trigger" for the device which causes an event. (Usually the trigger is a natural part of the device such as the "return" key of a keyboard). When the trigger is fired, the current value of the device is saved by the graphics system on an event queue that is ordered on a first-come first-serve basis. The application program issues an AWAIT EVENT command in order to remove information from the queue. If the queue is empty, this command waits until the next event occurs.

For further details on the input facilities of GKS see [GKS82] or [Rose82].

1.5. Human factors in interactive programming

Writing a good interactive program requires considerably more effort than writing a similar batch program. The programmer must address the needs of the operator in terms of providing a human-oriented interface that is convenient and easy to use and that responds efficiently to requests.

Below are some guidelines for writing interactive programs (taken from [Berg78] and [Fole82]):

simplicity

> Provide simple, consistent interactions sequences; do not over-load the user with too many different methods for interacting with the program.

prompting

> Provide some kind of prompt to the user at each stage of the interaction. A novice user should be provided with reasonably complete and self-defining prompts, while an expert user should be able to bypass these in favor of a very terse or unobtrusive prompt.

feedback

> The program should provide feedback to the user after every user request. In fact, there are actually two kinds of responses that should occur. As a direct result of using an input device, the user should receive some immediate echo to indicate that the graphics system is responding to the use of that input device and has acquired values from it. This form of feedback corresponds to the echoing of characters as keys are struck on an alphanumeric keyboard. The echo of the use of an input device is normally the responsibility of the graphics system (although there is some control that can be exercised by the application program. A user utilizes input devices to prepare information and requests for processing by the application program. Once the application program has satisfied such a request, it must produce some visual feedback to the user to show that the requested pro-cessing has been performed. Furthermore, it is highly desirable that intermediate feedback also be generated in cases in which the satisfaction of the request requires considerable processing time or a number of distinct steps. Such intermediate feedback is very reassuring to the user because the continuing progress of the computation is clearly demonstrated.

graceful recovery from user mistakes

It is highly desirable to provide as much "backup" protection as possible to allow a user to recover from mistakes. In some circumstances the cost of allowing a particular action to be "undone" may be sufficiently high, that the user should be forced to explicitly confirm that the action should indeed be taken. However, a more desirable form of recovery is the implied confirmation. As each request is made by the user, the program performs the request (or enough of the request so that the visual display corresponds to how it should be at the conclusion of the action), but saves sufficient information to "undo" the request. If the user's next action is UNDO, the previous request is cancelled and the system returned to the state it was prior to that request. If the user's next action is anything except UNDO, the previous action is completed and can no longer be undone.

1.6. Interaction techniques

Below is a brief compendium of typical programming techniques for interactive programs. These techniques are described algorithmically in terms of pseudocode using a graphics system such as the Core or GKS. However, an important requirement for some of these techniques to be effective is that the implementation must be very efficient. With some implementations of any general purpose graphics package and/or with some devices, it may be impossible to achieve satisfactory performance for many of these techniques. (The information below has been derived from [Berg78, Fole82, and Newm79].)

Basic event-driven processing

Events are the critical facility that allows synchronization between the program and its user. The following is the standard schema for a typical interactive program:

```
initialize
enable interaction devices to be used
generate a picture

repeat
  wait for user-generated event
  if the event is legal then
    case event of
      .
      .      [perform an action based on event -
      .       typically involves updating display
      .       and/or the data structure ]
      .
    endcase
  else
    generate error indication
until exit specified
```

Command hierarchy

A common approach to implementing a graphics application is to provide the user with a hierarchy of commands. At the highest level, the choices available to the user each lead to a set of possible selections at a lower level. In such a situation the graphics program is composed of a hierarchy of procedures that have the above format. Corresponding to each procedure is a menu defining the actions a user can take at that stage of the interaction.

A standard issue often associated with the design of an interactive command language of this sort is whether a given "command" should specify one action, or should put the user into a mode allowing many action of the same type to be specified. For example, should the user have to pick "ADD" for every symbol to be added, or does "ADD" enter a mode in which any number of symbols can be added, followed by an explicit "return" to the higher level. If the user typically adds many symbols at once, the second option is clearly preferable.

Menus and prompts

At most stages in an interaction sequence, the user must select one of a number of actions to be performed. In keeping with the goals of good prompting, it is very effective to present the user with a textual or visual prompt briefly stating what kind of action is required and a menu of the legal selections. In most cases it is preferable to reserve a portion of the display area for prompts and another for a menu area, rather than using a full-screen menu. Figure 8 shows a typical screen layout with prompt and menu areas. Menus can be composed of entries that are simple text strings, or icons (symbolic

representations). With color raster devices it is effective to place
text strings in a colored box to draw attention to the choices.
Iconic representations are usually preferable to text, especially if
the symbols are "natural" and obvious. Figure 8a shows a text menu
and figure 8b shows a symbolic menu.

The user's selection of an item from the menu can be required in
several different ways:

- entering commands with a keyboard (STRING)
- pressing buttons (CHOICE)
- picking with a PICK
- positioning with a LOCATOR

The last two alternatives generally provide the best combination of
device independence and user convenience. Using a PICK device is the
simplest approach from the programmer's point of view, but some implementations of the PICK device may be somewhat inefficient and may
result in excessive delays in the responses to the user. Using a
LOCATOR requires a little more effort from the programmer since the
physical location of the entries in the menu must be saved and compared with the position of the LOCATOR, but this approach is less
likely to be affected by the efficiency of the graphics system.

The program segment below shows how a text menu such as shown in Figure 8a might be created if it were to be used with a PICK device.

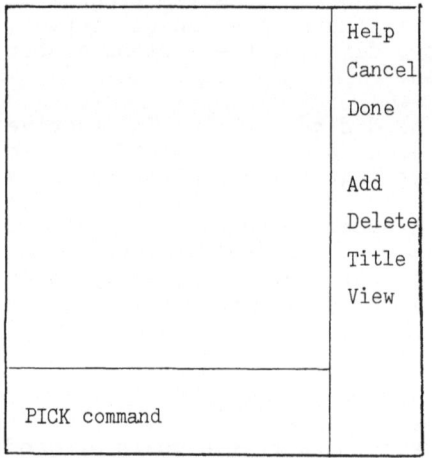

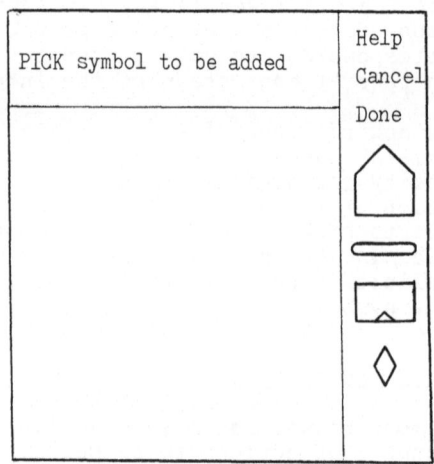

(a) Text menu   (b) Icon menu

Figure 8. Typical screen layouts with menu and prompt areas.

Each entry in the menu is assigned a distinct value for the PICK_ID
attribute. When the entry is picked, the PICK device returns both the
segment name and the PICK_ID of the entry picked.

```
                      { creating a text menu }

     establish appropriate view;
     initialize x,y to location of first item of menu;

     create_segment (menu);
       set_visibility (menu, off);
       for i:= 1 to num_entries do
         set_pick_id (i);
         generate string[i] at x,y;
         update y;
       endfor;
     close_segment;
```

The following program segment could then be used to allow the user to
pick an element from the menu. We assume that this menu is a command
menu in the middle of the hierarchy of commands. In other words, each
selection from this menu invokes a procedure that presents a lower
level menu to the user. Consequently, this menu is made invisible as
soon as a selection is made and made visible again after the lower
level procedure returns.

```
                      { selecting from a menu }

     initialization;

     repeat
       set_visibility (menu, on);      { make menu visible }
       set_visibility (menuprompt,on) {    and an appropriate prompt }
       wait for user event;
       set_visibility (menu, off);     { make menu invisible }
       set_visibility (menuprompt,off) {    and prompt }
       if event is PICK and segment picked is menu then
         case pick_id of
           1:  new_title;
           2:  add_symbol;
           3:  delete_symbol;
           4:  change_view;
           5:  exit := true;
         endcase
       else
         perform other action or give error message;
       until exit;
```

A minor variation of the above code can be used to perform the

selection based on a LOCATOR. Using GKS, the LOCATOR should be in
event or request mode. Using the Core, it would also be necessary to
define a BUTTON whose event would be used to indicate that the current
value of the LOCATOR is the one to use.

Double buffering

During the interaction process, it is often necessary to update a particular segment. The brute-force technique for doing this would be:

```
delete_segment (i);
create_segment (i);
  generate primitives for new version of i;
close_segment;
```

If the segment is at all complicated, this approach has the unpleasant
effect of having nothing visible for some period of time. To minimize
this effect, it is good practice to utilize "double buffering" for the
segment. That is, create the new version of the segment before deleting the old version. This would be done with code such as the following:

```
create_segment (temp);
  set_visibility (temp, off);    { new segment is invisible }
  generate primitives for new version of i;
close_segment;
set_visibility (i, off);         { now switch the visibilities }
set_visibility (temp, on);
delete_segment (i);              { delete old one }
rename_segment (temp, i);        { and rename new one to be i }
```

With this code, there is no segment visible only between the pair of
set_visibility calls.

Soft delete

Deletion of components is one of the most important areas for graceful
recovery of user errors. The most effective method for supporting this
is to implement what is called a soft delete. That is, when the user
requests deletion of segments, the application program initially only
makes them invisible. Once confirmation of the deletion is made
(preferably an implied confirmation), the segments and corresponding
elements in the application data structure are actually deleted. This
technique provides the user with the visual feedback concerning the
effect of the command, while minimizing the cost of recovery if the
command was not the desired one.

Dragging

When a user needs to place or move an object on the screen, it can be easily done by first specifying the object and then a location for it. This technique, however, requires that the user know what part of the object corresponds to the location and to visually estimate whether that location is the desired one. A more user-friendly approach is to allow the user to drag the object from its old position to its new position. In this way, the user has constant visual feedback and can more easily place the object in the desired place. In fact, this only works well if the re-positioning of the object can be done very rapidly. The segment transformation facilities of the Core and GKS provide some expectation that this can happen. The Core definition of segment transformations are more likely to provide real-time translation of segments than is possible with GKS. The code segment below uses the LOCATOR in sampled mode to derive a position which is then used as the segment translation factor for a segment called, seg. Obviously it is necessary to be able to stop the dragging somehow. This is done be waiting for a user event inside the dragging loop. With both the Core and GKS, the functions which wait for a user event ("await_event") also accept a parameter which is a maximum number of seconds to wait. If no event occurs during that time, the await returns with an indication of "time-out". In the code below, we wait for just 1/30 of a second and normally expect the time-out to occur.

```
repeat
   sample_locator (x,y);    { get locator position }
   translate_segment (seg, x,y); {transformation NOT cumulative}
   await_event (0.033, event);
until event is not time-out;
```

Panning/zooming

When viewing a large complicated picture, it is useful to be able to change the view easily and rapidly. If the user is presented an overall view showing the entire picture, it should be possible to zoom in to some portion of that picture in order to get a more detailed view. Similarly, it ought to be possible to zoom back out to a more comprehensive view. Once viewing a portion only, it is often desirable to shift the view in some direction to bring in neighboring areas (and losing areas to the opposite side). This is called panning. Although panning and zooming are most effective if they can be performed in real-time, this can only be done with very expensive hardware or with moderately priced hardware and very limited functionality.

Even if expensive hardware is not available, however, it is very convenient to implement a non-dynamic mechanism for re-specifying the view. Zooming in is actually quite straightforward and reasonably effective. It is only necessary to allow the user to define the "new" window as a rectangular area within the current viewport. The coordinates in the viewport can be easily be converted to corresponding locations in world coordinates. These then become the new window and the picture is re-created. Panning and zooming out are more difficult. If these are often required in a particular application, they can be most effectively supported by always providing a small auxiliary view representing an overview of the entire picture. The "current" window (shown in the main view) is represented in the auxiliary view as a rectangle. The user can move this rectangle around and change its size in the auxiliary view until it seems to be at the desired place, then request an update of the main view. The auxiliary view may or may not contain an actual picture of the entire view. In order to minimize computation time and display space, it may even be acceptable to have nothing displayed in the auxiliary view except the window. Alternatively, in some applications it is possible to display objects at several levels of detail, such that the auxiliary view might be able to contain only the largest objects and only in a very simple form. Figure 9 shows an example of an auxiliary view which contains only the window. In this case the current window is shown as a solid line and the new window which the user is in the process of specifying is a dashed line.

Line drawing

endpoint positioning

The simples method for drawing lines is to require the user to enter the locations of the two endpoints. This technique is easy to program

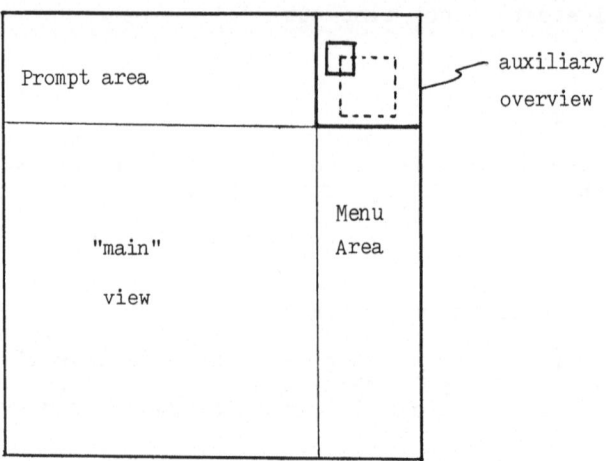

Figure 9. Screen layout with an auxiliary overview.

and works on all devices. Normally, a LOCATOR is used to specify each endpoint. In GKS, the LOCATOR would be used in either request or event mode; in the Core, a BUTTON device would be used to cause the event indicating that the current LOCATOR position is the one to use.

A minor, but important improvement is to allow the user to specify a series of connected lines. This then requires the user to specify only N+1 positions for N line segments. In this case, another event has to be defined to indicate that the series of lines is completed. In GKS, this prevents the use of request mode for the LOCATOR.

rubberbanding

A more effective method of line drawing uses rubberbanding to define the second endpoint. In this mode, a line is drawn from the first endpoint to the LOCATOR position (with the GKS LOCATOR in sample mode) until an event occurs. 20-30 times a second, the LOCATOR position must be sampled and the line redrawn to the new position. Obviously, in drawing a series of connected lines, the last of the series can be rubberbanded.

Rubberbanding is not always possible if programmed at the application program level. There is no capability in either GKS or the Core to dynamically update the coordinates of primitives in a segment; the segment must be deleted and recreated with new values for the line endpoints. Although a segment with only one line in it is very simple, the basic overhead of creating and deleting a segment is substantial and may not allow for truly dynamic rubberbanding. On the other hand, GKS and the Core define an "echo type" for the LOCATOR that allows a workstation to do the rubberbanding. Rubberbanding can also be used very effectively in defining rectangles with one fixed corner and the opposite corner following the LOCATOR position.

inking

The final technique for line drawing has been called "sketching" or "inking". With this technique the position of the LOCATOR is constantly sampled and a series of short lines is drawn following the path of the LOCATOR. Usually there is a minimum distance allowed for a line -- as soon as the LOCATOR gets that far from the previous endpoint, a new line is drawn. If the distance is reasonably large, the last line segment can be rubberbanded. Except for rubberbanding the last line, "inking" can be implemented using GKS or the Core, but the feature is also provided by both as an echo type for the logical device STROKE.

Constrained drawing

horizontal/vertical lines

In many circumstances it is necessary or desirable to constrain the user's drawing capability in some way. The simplest form of constrained drawing requires that all lines be either horizontal or vertical. Typically the first endpoint specified by the user is considered an actual line endpoint, while the second (LOCATOR position) is adjusted to insure that the line is horizontal or vertical. A particularly convenient technique for implementing this is to force all lines to either horizontal or vertical depending their slope. (This is a simple test: abs(x2-x1) > abs (y2-y1) implies horizontal.)

drawing grids

Often it is desirable to force endpoints of lines to lie on specific grid points rather than allowing them to be placed arbitrarily. This can be accomplished implicitly, by simply adjusting all endpoints to the nearest grid point, although it is also often desirable to allow the user to see and utilize the grid. Typically the display of the grid should be optional and should be done at a lower intensity than the remainder of the picture. Otherwise, the grid will clutter and obscure the display. Another alternative is to display a limited size grid in the area of the LOCATOR. This provides the advantage of having the grid visible in the area of the user's interest, but not cluttering up the entire screen. Figure 10a shows a full screen grid displayed at low intensity, while figure 10b shows a limited size grid.

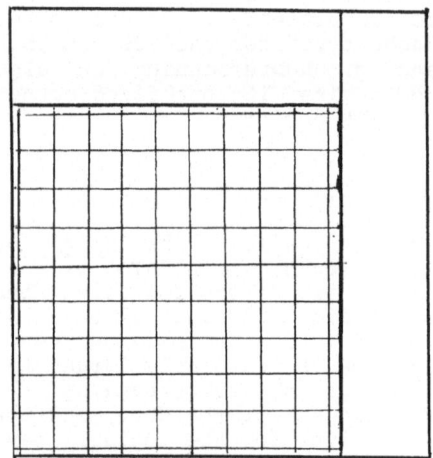
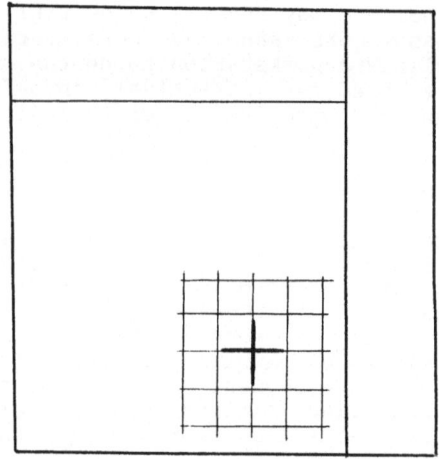

a. Full screen grid   b. Partial screen grid

Figure 10.   Use of a visible grid for constrained positioning.

gravity fields

In many applications it is desirable to connect new primitives to old
ones. In such situations it is helpful if the system, forces position
specifications that are "near" a line to be "on" the line. In effect,
the existing line acts as a gravity field for a LOCATOR position. In
the sausage form of gravity field all points on the existing line have
equal mass. A simple method for implementing the sausage gravity
field is to utilize the same code used for clipping. A small "window"
is defined around the LOCATOR position as shown in figure 11a. The
size of the window determines the size of the sausage. All visible
lines are "clipped" to this window. Since the window is so small, most
lines are trivially rejected. If any part of a line remains after the
clip, it is a relatively simple task to find the point on the line
that is nearest to the position.

Often the endpoints of lines are more important than the interior and
should have greater mass. This results in a gravity field shaped like
a dumbbell. Implementing a dumbbell gravity field requires a preliminary comparison of the LOCATOR position with each of the endpoints of
the line, which can also be done using the clipping code. Prior to
the sausage test, a larger "window" such as shown in figure 11b is
defined around each endpoint to determine if the LOCATOR position is
near.

Logical device simulations

An important problem for the implementer of workstation code for a
system like GKS or the Core is the need to provide facilities for the
logical devices. If a rich set of physical devices is available at the
workstation, there may be a relatively straightforward mapping of physical to logical devices. If this is not the case, the programmer
must simulate the features of one or more logical devices with physical devices that are available. Some common simulations are listed in

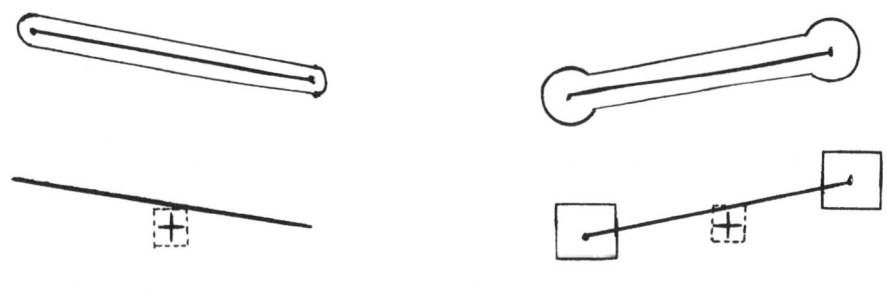

a. Sausage   b. Dumbbell

Figure 11. Gravity fields.

Figure 12 and described in more detail in [Fole82].

Logical Device	Physical Device	Technique
LOCATOR	lightpen	-tracking cross -cross with prediction
PICK	position device	-segment extent test -line extent test -use clipper with "window" around position
VALUATOR	position device (and display)	-x or y coordinate -graphical dial or scale
	keyboard	-value type in
KEYBOARD	position or pick (and display)	-character recognition -character menu
BUTTON	position or pick position voice recognizer	-light button menu -character recognition -voice recognition

Figure 12. Possible logical device simulations.

2. Modelling Concepts

As discussed earlier, the Core System and GKS are based on the separation of "modelling" and "graphics" first developed in [Guedj76].
Since the term "modelling" incorporates whatever facilities any application might need in order to produce an object specification for the
graphics system, it is impossible to summarize all such modelling
facilities. On the other hand, there are some basic concepts and
facilities that are useful for a wide range of applications.

2.1. Object Definition

For the application to utilize the facilities of a typical graphics
system "easily", that application must be able to describe its objects
in a manner compatible with that of the graphics system -- i.e., as
lines, polygons and text. This does not necessarily mean that the
data base for the application must contain these primitives explicitly, but that from the application data base, the application program is able to create line, polygon and text specifications for the
graphics system. In the remainder of this section, however, we assume
that objects are explicitly stored in the data base in some graphical
form.

Coordinate system

Objects must be specified to the graphics system using world coordinates. Consequently, it can be convenient to actually store the
objects in the data base in world coordinates. On the other hand, it
is often convenient to define the object's primitives in a local coordinate system and, then, specify the location and orientation of that
local coordinate system in the world coordinate system. This is
equivalent to defining the object at the origin of the world along
with a transformation to move it somewhere else.

Masters -- instances and copies

In many applications, pictures are composed of a few graphical symbols
that are replicated at different places and or sizes. In such an
application, the geometric information defining the component is
stored in a local coordinate system in the application data base. This
definition is called a master.

The application program can use the master definition to create an
object either by defining an instance or a copy. An instance of the
master includes a reference to the master along with a transformation
specification. To produce an image of an object that is an instance,
the primitives in the master definition are extracted, transformed and
passed to the graphics system. If the master definition is changed,
the image of the instance of the master also changes. A copy of the
master, on the other hand, results in copying the current primitives
from the master, transforming them by a specified amount and storing

them back in the data base as an independent object. Since producing an image of the copy does not require access to the master definition, a change to the master definition is not reflected in the copy.

Both copying and instancing can be nested: the object containing the instance or copy can itself be used as a master for a higher level copy or instance. In such cases, the transformation maps one local coordinate system to another, rather than to the world.

2.2. Two-dimensional transformations

The "standard" two-dimensional transformations normally used in the definition of objects include:

> -scaling
> -rotation
> -translation

These transformations can be most conveniently defined by using a vector and matrix notation. There are several alternative conventions that can be used in such a notation -- we will follow those used in [Fole82]. Coordinates in 2D are represented as row vectors of the form:

> $v = [x, y]$

A 2x2 matrix, M, that post-multiplies v, can be used to define scaling and rotation and transforms v to v':

> $v' = vM$ or
> $[x', y'] = [x, y]M$

Scaling

In order to scale an object by some amount, s, all coordinates in the object must be scaled by s. Scaling the coordinates uniformly by s can be achieved with:

> $x' = sx$
> $y' = sy$

This is represented as the matrix, S:

$$S = \begin{vmatrix} s & 0 \\ 0 & s \end{vmatrix}$$

Non-uniform scaling (by sx in x and sy in y) can also be easily represented:

$$S = \begin{vmatrix} sx & 0 \\ 0 & sy \end{vmatrix}$$

Rotation

A rotation of the coordinates [x, y] through an angle of Q degrees about the origin (where positive angle of rotation is counter-clockwise from x toward y) is given by:

$$x' = x \cos Q - y \sin Q$$
$$y' = x \sin Q + y \cos Q$$

or, in matrix form:

$$[x', y'] = [x, y] \ R$$

where

$$R = \begin{vmatrix} \cos Q & -\sin Q \\ \sin Q & \cos Q \end{vmatrix}$$

Because of the uniform representation, it is possible to compose scaling and rotation transformations into a single matrix. Thus, the composite transformation representing a scale by 2 followed by a rotation of 30 degrees is:

$$M = \begin{vmatrix} 2 & 0 \\ 0 & 2 \end{vmatrix} * \begin{vmatrix} \cos 30 & -\sin 30 \\ \sin 30 & \cos 30 \end{vmatrix}$$

Rather than applying two separate transformations to all the coordinates that define an object, it is much more efficient to perform the matrix multiplication once and apply the one composite transformation to each of the coordinates.

Translation

Perhaps the simplest transformation is translation. A translation of dx in x and dy in y is given by:

$$x' = x + dx$$
$$y' = y + dy$$

or

$$[x', y'] = [x, y] + [dx, dy]$$

Homogeneous coordinates

Unfortunately, translation does not fit into a 2x2 matrix. This makes
the implementation of a generalized transformation scheme a bit awkward since the composite transformation must be maintained as two
parts -- a 2x2 matrix containing the scale and rotation parts plus a
2x1 vector containing the translation part. Furthermore, since
transformations are not normally commutative it is sometimes necessary
to apply scale and rotation factors to the translation component in
order to properly represent the final composite transformation. This
is not difficult, it is just another complicating factor.

These problems can be overcome by using homogeneous coordinates. By
imbedding the two-dimensional world as a plane at z=1 in a three
dimensional world, translations in that plane can be implemented as a
"shear" in the three-dimensional space. Since a shear is an affine
transformation (leaves the origin fixed), it can be incorporated into
the same 3x3 matrix as scaling and rotation transformations. Consequently, a two-dimensional position [x,y] is represented in the homogeneous world as the three-dimensional point:

$$v = [x, y, 1]$$

A translation of [dx, dy] is defined by the matrix:

$$
T = \begin{vmatrix} 1 & 0 & 0 \\ 0 & 1 & 0 \\ dx & dy & 1 \end{vmatrix}
$$

A scale by s is defined by the matrix:

$$
S = \begin{vmatrix} s & 0 & 0 \\ 0 & s & 0 \\ 0 & 0 & 1 \end{vmatrix}
$$

A rotation of Q degrees about the origin is defined by:

$$
R = \begin{vmatrix} \cos Q & -\sin Q & 0 \\ \sin Q & \cos Q & 0 \\ 0 & 0 & 1 \end{vmatrix}
$$

Homogenous coordinates provide one consistent uniform representation
for scaling, rotation and translation which allows composition of
transformations to occur correctly.

A simple example of composition occurs when we wish to perform a rotation about a point that is NOT the origin. This is done by first translating the point [cx, cy] to the origin, performing the rotation, then translating the origin back to [cx, cy]. The composite matrix below will perform this entire operation:

$$
M = \begin{vmatrix} 1 & 0 & 0 \\ 0 & 1 & 0 \\ -cx & -cy & 1 \end{vmatrix} * \begin{vmatrix} cosQ & -sinQ & 0 \\ sinQ & cosQ & 0 \\ 0 & 0 & 1 \end{vmatrix} * \begin{vmatrix} 1 & 0 & 0 \\ 0 & 1 & 0 \\ cx & cy & 1 \end{vmatrix}
$$

Figure 13 shows an example of this series of transformations. In practice, the matrix multiplications would be performed to compute a single matrix M. The matrix M would then be multiplied by all the coordinates defining the object in order to perform the transformation.

Simple scaling also occurs about the origin, so a similar set of matrices would be used to perform scaling about an arbitrary point. In addition, the definition of hierarchical pictures using masters and instances or copies, requires matrix compositions to place the objects.

2.3. Three-dimensional transformations

The move from 2D to 3D is relatively straightforward, complicated mainly only be the distinction between **left-handed** and **right-handed** coordinate systems. Figure 14 shows the difference between a left-handed and a right-handed coordinate system. Traditionally, right-handed systems have been used more commonly, but a left-handed system is convenient in graphics -- it seems very natural to represent a display space as lying in the xy plane, with the positive z-axis going

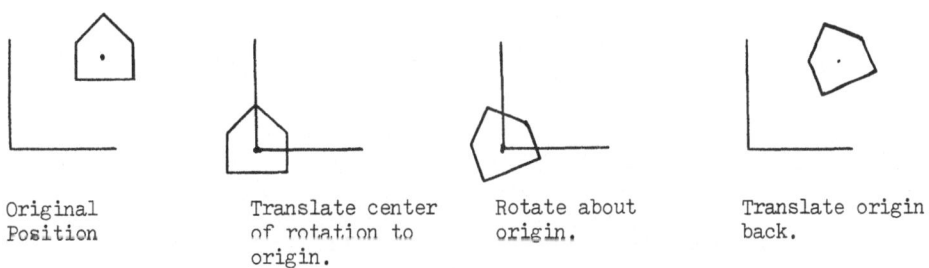

| Original Position | Translate center of rotation to origin. | Rotate about origin. | Translate origin back. |

Figure 13. Rotation about an arbitrary point.

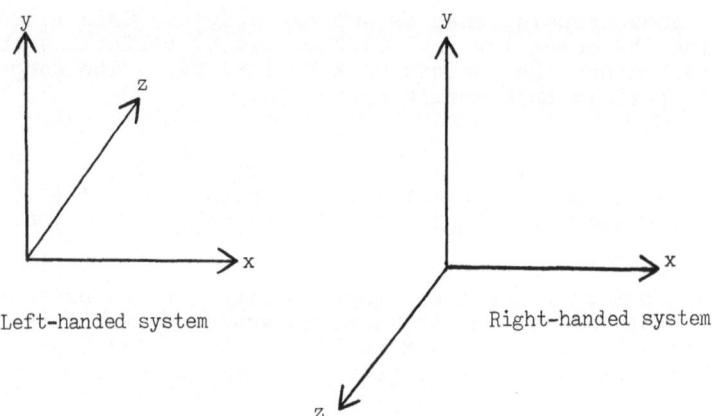

Figure 14. Left-handed and right-handed coordinate systems.

away from the viewer.

Homogeneous coordinates in three dimensions require the use of 4x4 matrices and a 4x1 coordinate vector of the form:

[x, y, z, 1]

Scaling

The general homogeneous matrix for non-uniform scaling (sx in x, sy in y and sz in z) is:

$$
S = \begin{vmatrix} sx & 0 & 0 & 0 \\ 0 & sy & 0 & 0 \\ 0 & 0 & sz & 0 \\ 0 & 0 & 0 & 1 \end{vmatrix}
$$

Rotation

In keeping with [Fole82], positive angles of rotation are considered to be counterclockwise when looking from a positive axis towards the origin. (Note: Be careful! There are different conventions used in different texts that can lead to confusion with regards to the location of the minus sign in rotation matrices.)

In 3D, rotation occurs about an axis. The basic rotations are defined about the 3 principal axes. Rotation about an arbitrary axis has to be done by composing the basic rotations along with possible translations. The basic rotations are defined by:

About the x-axis:

$$
Rx = \begin{vmatrix} 1 & 0 & 0 & 0 \\ 0 & \cos Q & \sin Q & 0 \\ 0 & -\sin Q & \cos Q & 0 \\ 0 & 0 & 0 & 1 \end{vmatrix}
$$

About the y-axis:

$$
Ry = \begin{vmatrix} \cos Q & 0 & -\sin Q & 0 \\ 0 & 1 & 0 & 0 \\ \sin Q & 0 & \cos Q & 0 \\ 0 & 0 & 0 & 1 \end{vmatrix}
$$

About the z-axis

$$
Rz = \begin{vmatrix} \cos Q & \sin Q & 0 & 0 \\ -\sin Q & \cos Q & 0 & 0 \\ 0 & 0 & 1 & 0 \\ 0 & 0 & 0 & 1 \end{vmatrix}
$$

Translation

Translation by [dx, dy, dz] is defined by:

$$
T = \begin{vmatrix} 1 & 0 & 0 & 0 \\ 0 & 1 & 0 & 0 \\ 0 & 0 & 1 & 0 \\ dx & dy & dz & 1 \end{vmatrix}
$$

References

[Berg78] Bergeron, R.D., P. Bono and J.D. Foley, "Graphics Programming Using the Core System", Computing Surveys 10(4), December 1978, 389-443.

[Fole82] Foley, J.D. and A. van Dam, Fundamentals of Interactive Computer Graphics, Addision-Wesley, 1982.

[GKS82] "Draft International Standard ISO/DIS 7942: Graphical Kernel System Functional Description", November 1982.

[GSPC79] "Status Report of the Graphics Standards Planning Committee," Computer Graphics, 13(3), August 1979.

[Gued76] Guedj, R.A. (ed), Report on the IFIP W.G. 5.2 Workshop on "Methodology in Computer Graphics" (July 1976). Also published as Methodology in Computer Graphics, North-Holland, Amsterdam, 1978. ???

[Newm78] Newman, W.M. and A. van Dam, "A Brief History of Efforts towards Graphics Standardization", Computing Surveys, 10(4), 1978, 365-380.

[Newm79] Newman, W.M. and R.F. Sproull, Principles of Interactive Computer Graphics, 2nd. ed., McGraw-Hill, New York, 1979.

[Reed82] Reed, T.N., "A Metafile for Efficient Sequential and Random Display of Graphics", Proceedings of SIGGRAPH '82, Computer Graphics 16(3), July 1982, 39-43.

[Rose82] Rosenthal, D.S., J.C. Michener, G. Pfaff, R. Kessener, and M. Sabin, "The Detailed Semantics of Graphics Input Devices", Proceedings of Siggraph '82, Computer Graphics, 16(3), July 1982, 33-38.

IV. Interactive Techniques

P. J. W. ten Hagen

1. Introduction.

The programmer of an interactive program has a complex task to perform. In addition to the specification of correct, efficient algorithms he must pay continuous attention to the way the program will manifest itself to the observing user when run and by what means the user can influence the problem solving process. The success of the program depends as much on how easily the user can interact with it as on the efficiency and correctness of the algorithms.

In these lecture notes we will concentrate on techniques for programming the interactive part of a program. We will not attempt to define what constitutes high quality interaction. This is a multidisciplinary subject. Psychologists (perception, cognition), journalists, artists, application specialists, etc., all have something to say about this. Very likely no two of them will agree about which are the more important rules and issues.

The techniques that will be presented, and the fundamentals for such techniques, ideally will be such that they can be used or misused for implementing any type of interaction. At best the programmer may discover that the techniques he is using follow some rules of thumb like:
- give the user value for his efforts. (e.g. keep the amount of work he has to do to obtain some information sufficiently small).
- present only relevant information; remove rubbish.
- don't be ambiguous without reason.

However, no systematic is present. Sometimes one rule prevales, sometimes another. Also, many of the principles can be traded off against each other.

2. User Interface.

The user interface to a program is the collection of visualisation and manipulation facilities and their interpretation (right or wrong) given to them by the user. Each of these facilities as perceived by the user is made up of three entities: the physical part of a facility, the way it can be used and the way it is controlled by the program, and, its contribution to the interactive process.

The fact that each facility depends on a physical realisation is reason for questioning by many people whether generally good interfaces can be specified in a device independent manner.

Also many people believe that good interfaces cannot be described unless taking into account the general model of the whole program and the role of each interaction facility in such a model. The problem here is that different users may perceive different models and that such models are not a bases for specifying (designing) interaction, because they are difficult to perceive or formulate.

The optimists however, consider the capability of human beings to adapt and to use abstractions sufficient for interactive systems that can be realised on a wide variety of devices and would work with a great variety of user models.

The attention of researchers and system designers has, with respect to user interfaces, shifted from the conceptual model to the realm of devices and interaction techniques. The recognition that the techniques used are substantial in determining what you can say, or, that communication and expression are as important as understanding has emerged with the use of rich interaction devices.
The computer graphics experts are for the time being also the experts who can build user interfaces. It is through graphics that communicating with computers has become fun. That is to say, it has become a fun for non-experts in programming. Before the breakthrough of graphics every one enjoying the use of computers was considered to be a bit freaky.

3.   **Interaction and Graphics.**

One may wonder what is so special about a computer interface involving graphics.

The first important property of communicating through pictures is the directness. That is to say using pictures removes at least one level of encoding-decoding. If one accepts that pictures are much closer to the concepts one wants to convey, either as input or as output, then one may consider both the method of constructing a view from a picture description, or constructing a picture description from input activities, as local activities, which have only to do with the syntax of an interaction language. This is a very important justification for situating graphics viewing facilities both for input and output in a local terminal, to be used by arbitrary applications. The fact that the CORE -once proposed- standard and to a lesser extend the GKS standard failed to support picture input at the same level as picture output, had more to do with the state of the art, than with the principles underlying the standard.

A second important property is the non-sequential nature of a picture. Two or three dimensional objects cannot be linearly ordered. Therefore a user cannot be expected to react only to the last item presented. In principle he must be able to act upon every aspect of the information presented.
The program must be prepared to receive input referring to picture elements from the past. It is up to the program to reconstruct the association with the semantic context.

A third property is the opportunity to convey a meaning by changing something rather than adding something new. Hence manipulation and "gesture" become part of the dialogue.

Last but not least the syntax of a dialogue allows many degrees of freedom and variable feedback. So that adaptation to user skills becomes feasible.

By no means can one say that today a general solution and method exists for exploiting these possibilities in interactive systems.
A great number of programming tools and basic support programs have to be developed to make this possible. We will now turn our attention to the problem a programmer encounters when he wants to specify an interactive program. We will then identify the key issues and describe possible tools by introducing language constructs that are adequate for solving the specification problems, and the implementation of which can provide the tools. The advantage of doing that through a special purpose language is that it becomes possible within the same framework to explain how the tools will have to work together.

4.   Dialogues.

In these notes a human-computer dialogue, or dialogue for short, is the exchange of information (commands, results, explanation) between a human operator and an interactive computer program in execution.
As part of writing an interactive program it is specified which information can be exchanged. Besides defining algorithms, a programmer also defines a dialogue language, i.e. he specifies which exchanges can take place at any time and what their effect (=meaning) will be. We can therefore consider a program to consist of two parts: the algorithmic part and the dialogue part. Whether both parts can be mutually separated depends on the program structure.

The state of the art very much is that the algorithmic part of a program is designed before it is implemented whereas the dialogue part is merely designed while implemented.

For a proper method of designing a dialogue language prior to implementation three conditions have to be met:
1.   The dialogue part must indeed be a separate program section (not interwoven with the algorithms).
2.   The programming method for the dialogues must allow for easily readable dialogue specifications, so that a programmer can conclude what happens at the user interface when reading the program text. This is a "structured programming" requirement for dialogues.
3.   The constructs for dialogue programming must provide complete control over the physical part of the user interface, with or without device independence.

Generally speaking the program structure required for algorithms differs from dialogue structure. For instance, the algorithm may ask for parameters in a format and order quite different from the way most users would naturally provide them.

4.1 The separation of algorithm and dialogue.

A separate dialogue module would provide a number of advantages:

- The algorithmic part is relieved from all details concerning in- an output such as: test whether input is correct, check whether output is possible right now.
- One can alter the dialogue part (e.g. adapt to new hardware), without having to change the algorithms.
- Dialogue specialists can write a dialogue most suitable for a given environment and/or application.
- Interactive techniques may become available as (sub)dialogue libraries.
- A dialogue run time support system may provide facilities for user help, error recovery and audit-trails.

The most simple and may be adequate method for separating algorithms from dialogues is by introducing dialogue procedures. They would, when called, look quite similar to, say, subroutines.
However, the dialogue procedure itself may be specified by a method or language quite different from the general purpose programming language used for the algorithms.

Dialogue procedures provide a structure different from input- or menu-driven systems. Here the program block- and subroutine structure can be seen as a directed graph (the arrows are the procedure calls or block nestings), the top levels of which are the input handlers.

One can imagine that dialogue procedures in turn can call algorithmic routines, for instance, to do conversions of input data. At run time dialogue and algorithm can be conceptually two cooperating processes which exchange messages (=procedure calls). The language construct that will be presented here for specifying a dialogue can become very complex, when both processes can cause side effects in the other.
Current practice does not allow for such complicated structures. Especially situations requiring backtracking over algorithms or dialogues cannot be dealt with satisfactory. A better strategy seeks to avoid the necessity of such mechanisms.
As we will see this can be achieved without becoming too restrictive.

4.2 **Dialogue Cells**

The language construct that will be presented here for specifying a dialogue procedure is called **dialogue cell**.
A dialogue cell is a unit which can completely specify one step in a dialogue. Each step comprises the following parts:

- an action from the user,
- the corresponding external reaction from the system,
- the effect on the internal state of the system
- the environment and conditions in which the action takes place.

Dialogue cells can be organised in hierarchies. This means that a big unit can be built from a combination of smaller units. In a hierarchy the way smaller units are combined can be precisely controlled. The overall action of two combined units is determined by the individual actions and the combining operator. This hierarchy therefore allows at the same time the specification of dialogue syntax (how words combine to sentences), the internal semantics (how a structured state vector is changed component by component), how the effect of changing the visible interface is built from little changes and last but not least how sub-dialogues get activated and deactivated.
The four groups of dialogue cell activities as given here are specified in four separate cell components that make up a dialogue cell.
These components are:

Prompt:The section which initialises the sub-dialogue and activates all sub-cells required. In addition it informs the user that it is ready to accept the input.

The appearance of the prompt can vary from a simple "continue" sign to a whole new screen set up plus initial message (question) for the user. This means that it can express where the initiative lies, or, who asks the question and who provides the answers.

Symbol:The section which specifies an input sentence. It will tell how the input monitor will try to read the input words and when the cell input is completed.

First of all specifying how the system will read symbols is different from specifying how (and in what order) a user must produce the inputs. Only in strictly synchronous, sequential systems can these two be the same.
Sub-symbols (i.e. "words" of the sentence) are produced either by the user directly (basic symbols) or are obtained from sub-cells.

Echo: The acceptance of a symbol by a dialogue cell causes a message sent back to the user.

These messages (echoes) may remain visible when the dialogue cell is completed (global echo) or may have to be removed (local echo) when the cell is deactivated. Thus the echo mechanism is the basis for dynamic control of the screen.

Value: Each symbol accepted has a value associated with it. This value may with or without conversion contribute to the complex value to be produced by the cell.

Also here a local-and-global value scheme is used which is controlled through the cell hierarchy. The value section contains an extensive mapping mechanism including input validity checks. The result of mapping and checking may be fed back to the symbol section by means of synchronisation tokens which can be used to select among alternatives or end repetitions. In this way attributed grammars can be handled.

In appendix A a complete syntax for dialogue cells is given, whereas appendix B contains some examples.
The somewhat simplified version we will use through these notes will allow us to discuss some fundamental problems of interaction specification and control. This is by no means an attempt to show that dialogue cells constitute the ultimate solution for interaction specification. This can only be concluded when a full and working implementation (which is underway) is available.

4.3 The Basic cycle of a Dialogue Cell

What happens when a dialogue cell becomes active?
The answer is: its four components become (simultaneously) active. However, implicit in the dialogue cell semantics are synchronisation rules and some form of abstract data typing. We will give an informal description here because the understanding is more important than the precise form.

In each of the sections names of sub-cells may be used. It is understood however, that when a prompt part names a dialogue cell it only refers to the prompt section of that sub-cell. A similar rule holds for all other sections.

The next rule is that only symbols appearing in the symbol part of a cell may appear in the other parts. This guarantees that only cells are activated which inputs can be read and also that values and echoes of cells that are to be produced stem from active cells.

An additional very important rule states that symbols can only be read when a cell is active (i.e. the prompt section must be executed before symbol parsing) and the value and echo actions specified for a symbol must be triggered by the parser. This guarantees that value expressions cannot be evaluated further unless all values required become available and all output echoes (e.g. pictures) produced are either prompts or echoes.

A refinement of this rule allows for mutual synchronisation between value and echo, so that the change to the internal state can be visualised. An active cell proceeds for each symbol in the symbol expression through the sequence, P ->S ->V ->E. When the last symbol is encountered the cell will deliver a symbol, value and echo to the external environment.
After delivery of the external results the cell is ready for a new complete basic cycle. Whether this will happen or not is controlled by the surrounding cell.

The activation of dialogue cells.

A dialogue cell, as we have seen, is either activated by the algorithmic part as dialogue procedure (root-cell), or it is activated as sub-cell of a dialogue cell closer to the root-cell. This activation can generally be either synchronous or asynchronous. In the synchronous case a cell is activated just prior to the action by the symbol part to accept this symbol. The activating dialogue cell is forced to wait until the symbol asked for has been produced. The cell is deactivated immediately after its symbol has been accepted. This activation mode is a generalisation of the REQUEST mode defined for GKS input. Similarly the asynchronous activation is a generalisation of the GKS concept SAMPLE and EVENT.

All asynchronously used sub-cells of a dialogue cell are activated in the prompt section as part of the initialisation. So all these subcells are active simultaneously. This has two important consequences:

1. The user is allowed to produce input long before it is being used and he **can** produce input in an order quite different from the order in which the symbol part will accept them.

2. Symbols may be produced in parallel, the symbol expression of many cells may simultaneously attempt to accept the symbol produced for it. Therefore the symbol parsing process goes on in many rules at the same time although ultimately one start symbol will be produced. This requires a so-called dynamic multi-stream parser.

In order for both user and programmer to limit the complexity of this parallel parser a number of restrictions must be imposed on the dialogue cell semantics. These will be discussed in the next section.

Simultaneously active dialogue cells model the actual situation of many graphics workstations, having for instance, a keyboard, menu on the screen and a locator all simultaneously enabled. They then leave it up to the user which one to select.

A dialogue cell activated in SAMPLE mode puts the initiative with the computer program. It can decide at any time to "sample" the value produced, even before the user has provided one, or, after the user has provided several, in which case all but the last get lost.

A dialogue cell activated in EVENT mode gives the initiative to the user. Firstly the program is forced to wait if no symbol is yet produced. Secondly, the program is forced to read all symbols produced one after the other from a queue. Unlike GKS, the various event queues of the individual dialogue cells are not merged into one.

4.4 Input Parsing

The symbol part of a dialogue cell consist of a grammar rule. This rule directly controls the input parser. (See the syntax rules for symbol in Appendix A). Two kinds of problems with respect to input parsing must be dealt with.

The first one has to do with ambiguous grammars. An ambiguous situation occurs when a symbol is produced which might fit in more than one place. Then the parser cannot decide where to continue. In addition, a parallel parse over a non-ambiguous grammar may introduce ambiguities, because more than one active rule (= symbol part of the active cell) may require such a symbol. Ambiguous situations are generally speaking, not wanted in interactive dialogues because they leave the user confused. They either force the system into multiple reaction (try all possibilities for some time) or they postpone one reaction or they choose one arbitrarily. Each of those has its own contribution to confusion to make. A user who makes an error in an ambiguous situation forces the system to reject, without having the possibility to direct the user where to go.

A dialogue cell system can be, an in fact is, provided with a strong mechanism to remove ambiguities. First observe that in order to be able to obtain a symbol, a sub-cell or basic cell must be activated first. The run time system can easily detect through some kind of lock-out mechanism that the subcell is already activated. Disambiguating means that it will in this case activate a different instance of the same cell, which will be guaranteed to manifest itself to the user in a different way (e.g. on a different place on the screen, or with a different cursor and prompt or eventually at a different time (local synchronisation by priority)).
This mechanism is closely coupled to the resource manager which assigns and deassigns hardware and firmware interaction resources.

This strategy is based upon a principle which is very fundamental. That is the strict separation of type and value. In a dialogue cell type is the realm of the symbol part whereas value is in the realm of the value part. For instance, a syntax rule which has two alternatives:

A: all letters and digits
B: all punctuation marks and zero.

is ambiguous when a zero is encountered.
In a dialogue cell either A and B would use different keyboards or the same keyboard at different times, or there is only one syntax rule (say C), and the value mechanism associates a value with C in all cases. So, the ambiguity is either removed before the activation or it is not a syntactic but a semantic ambiguity.
An additional benefit is that the system is at first instance always prepared to accept all user inputs. The inputs it cannot accept are not enabled.

4.5 The input pool.

When the parallel production of symbols for input is served by only one processor one needs a scheduler to determine which symbol will next be processed by the parser. We will now show how this arbitration mechanism can influence the behaviour of the system as perceived by the user. The situation we are confronted with is as follows:
Each time an active cell produces a symbol this symbol is either immediately consumed by the requesting cell (synchronous mode) or it is placed in the cell's corresponding sample or event register.
The input pool is the collection of all sample and event registers.
Only a subset of the symbols in the pool is candidate for reading by the parser. All others are, one could say, produced too early.
Each time an elementary parse action has been completed, (i.e. the parser moves to the next symbol of the symbol expression), the arbitration unit can be activated to decide which symbol for which cell to parse next.
The decision procedure chosen, favours high level cells over low level

cells, and also favours cells in left branches over cells in right branches. This achieved by considering the syntax graph which is implied by the dialogue cell hierarchy and appending a preorder code to each dialogue cell, being the preorder code from the node in the corresponding graph. The root will get the highest code. Then the scheduler will search the pool for the symbol with the highest preorder code.

The effect of all this at the user interface is that the highest level result implied by any input is always produced first and also that cells trying to empty an event queue have priority over cells adding a new symbol to the queue.

5. **The interface to the graphics system.**

For discussing the interface problems to graphics systems we will refer to GKS. GKS can be expected to be widely used. It is one of the few systems which are sufficiently well-structured to make this discussion not too complicated.

The graphics system must provide the basic input cells. We will assume that they are the logical input devices or behave in a similar way. We have already seen that this fits the activation modes and the symbol/value separation. What concerns us more here is the effects on a graphics screen and how we can control those effects through dialogue cells.

Basic cells produce prompts and echoes on the screen as specified in the input type which is chosen when the device is initialised.
Higher level cells can either inherit or refuse the effects caused by lower cells. In case of refusal, the effect together with the local effects are removed. There must therefore be an extra function not provided by GKS which can retain or delete the effects on the screen caused by input devices. Higher level cells can add to these effects by means of output functions such as creating primitives, segments, changing segment attributes or attribute bundle values. All these functions control picture aspects which can be manipulated dynamically.

The problem is however, that GKS requires (for good reasons!) that these functions are called in the right state. And also that if the pictures generated must be manipulated, then this must be prepared for by putting them in a segment. Segments in GKS cannot be nested, therefore, a dialogue cell which opens a segment cannot call a subcell which also opens a segment, without closing it first. Even more serious, if two arbitrary dialogue cells can be active in parallel in a non-deterministic way only one of them may have a segment open. In this case having a segment open must be a critical section excluding other cells to be active. Because a reopen segment is not allowed only new segments can be created after closing the most recent one. This makes it unattractive to have a dialogue cell deliver its echo in one segment unless new functionality is added on top of GKS first. If not than the only way of delivering one segment is to copy the ones to retain via new segment and then delete the original ones.

5.1 A symmetric I/O layer on top of GKS

The analysis of the interface to the graphics system has revealed two problems:
One is the mixing of input and output primitives into new pictures and another is the control of the screen in terms of the same coordinate system. The latter is necessary to be able to position input and ouput primitives relative to one another (e.g., how can one position an echo area next to an ouput window on the screen).

A symmetric I/O layer would firest of all allow for controlling the input devices in the same world coordinates as the output functions. Next the input primitives will on the level of the basic cells be converted to the same type of graphical primitives as the output primitives. E. g., one will have a REQUEST POLYLINE for input.

Next this will make clear that in very many interactive applications, datastructures such as segments are for controllling high level input rathe than output, for instance draughting.

The dialogue cell will provide the following support as part of the echo function. Local to a dialogue cell one can have so-called primitive radicals. They are not in a segment and would disappear on, say, a redraw.

Radicals can be considered to be (cheap) segments containing only one primitive. They can be produced by basic cells or by output functions. Radicals will disappear when their dialogue cell is deactivated. At most one can be handed over.

In addition a function DELIVER SEGMENT is introduced which in one indivisible action can create a segment from radicals and other inserted segments.

Radicals can also be subjected to editing operations if supported by the corresponding input device.

All of these functions can be realised efficiently on top of GKS.

Appendix A: Complete Syntax for Dialogue Cells

```
%{
# include <stdio.h>
# include <ctype.h>

        /* declaration section */
%}

%term LETTER
%term DIGIT
%term IDENT
%term ENUMIDENT
%term STRUCTIDENT
%term NUMBER
%term EXPRESSION

%term BINOP
%term LCURLY
%term RCURLY
%term LPAREN
%term RPAREN
%term SEMICOLON
%term COMMA
%term EQS
%term MULT
%term DOLLAR
%term RELOP
%term COLON

%term STRUCT
%term TYPEDEF
%term POINTER
%term ENUM
%term CHAR
%term INT
%term REAL
%term EMPTY

%term DICE
%term PROMPT
%term  PRS
%term  PRV
%term  PRE
%term SYMBOL
%term VALUE
%term  RULES
%term  FAIL
%term  RESULT
%term ECHO
%term  PRINT

%term REQUEST
%term SAMPLE
%term EVENT

%term IPRIM
%term OPRIM
```

```
%term SEGM
%term SEGM_ATTR
%term BUNDLE
%term BUNDLE_ATTR
%term SELECT
%term PRIM

%term ACCEPT
%term OFF
%term TRANSF

%term TRIGGER
%term IF
%term CASE
%term IN
%term MAP
%term TO
%term REJECT
%term EMPTY
%term RETURN
%term CONT
%term STOP

%left  BINOP

%start dialogue_program

%%      /* rules section */

/***** dialogue program *****/

dialogue_program      :    declaration_list
                      ;

declaration_list      :    declaration |
                           declaration_list declaration
                      ;

declaration           :    type_definition |
                           cell_definition
                      ;

/***** dialogue cell definitions *****/

cell_definition       :    cell_header cell_body
                      ;

cell_header           :    DICE IDENT cell_type
                           LPAREN cell_params RPAREN
/*
                           cell_attributes
*/
                      ;

cell_body             :    prompt_component
```

```
                              symbol_component
                              value_component
                              echo_component
                    ;

/*
cell_attributes     :    cell_resources | cell_environment ;
cell_resources      :    viewport | cursor ;
cell_environment    :    empty ;
viewport            :    empty ;
cursor              :    empty ;
*/

cell_params         :    empty |
                         prompt_params SEMICOLON
                         symbol_params SEMICOLON
                         value_params SEMICOLON
                         echo_params

                    ;

prompt_params       :    param_list
                    ;

symbol_params       :    param_list
                    ;

value_params        :    param_list
                    ;

echo_params         :    param_list
                    ;

param_list          :    IDENT |
                         param_list COMMA IDENT

                    ;

/***** type definitions *****/

type_definition     :    struct_definition |
                         enum_definition

                    ;

struct_definition   :    TYPEDEF STRUCT IDENT
                         LCURLY struct_field_list RCURLY SEMICOLON

                    ;

struct_field_list   :    struct_field |
                         struct_field_list struct_field

                    ;

struct_field        :    type_specifier IDENT SEMICOLON
                    ;

enum_definition     :    TYPEDEF ENUM IDENT
                         LCURLY enum_list RCURLY SEMICOLON

                    ;
```

```
enum_list              :    IDENT |
                            enum_list COMMA IDENT
                       ;


/*
 * identifiers :
 * yylex must recognize them and return IDENT
 */

/***** types *****/

cell_type              :    type_specifier
                            picture_part
                       ;

picture_part           :    empty |
                            COMMA picture_type
                       ;

type_specifier         :    basic_type |
                            struct_type
                       ;

basic_type             :    standard_type |
                            empty_type |
                            enumaration_type
                       ;

standard_type          :    CHAR |
                            INT |
                            REAL
                       ;

empty                  :    /* EMPTY */
                       ;

empty_type             :    EMPTY
                       ;

enumaration_type       :    ENUMIDENT
                       ;

struct_type            :    structure |
                            pointer
                       ;

structure              :    STRUCTIDENT
                       ;

pointer                :    POINTER type_specifier
                       ;

picture_type           :    empty |
                            primitive |
                            segment |
```

```
                                segment_attribute |
                                bundle |
                                bundle_attribute |
                                select
                        ;

primitive               :       PRIM empty ;
segment                 :       SEGM empty ;
segment_attribute       :       SEGM_ATTR empty ;
bundle                  :       BUNDLE empty ;
bundle_attribute        :       BUNDLE_ATTR empty ;
select                  :       SELECT empty ;

/***** values *****/

cell_value              :       value_expression
                        ;

/* for the moment */
value_expression        :       EXPRESSION
                        ;

/***** prompt component, globals *****/

prompt_component        :       PROMPT
                                inform
                                init_symbol
                                init_value
                                init_echo
                        ;

inform                  :       empty |
                                message COMMA
                                output
                        ;

message                 :       prim_list
                        ;

output                  :       prim_list
                        ;

prim_list               :       empty |
                                prim_list
/*
                                global_state
                                segment
*/
                                inprim outprim
                        ;

/* what to do with global states and segments */
/*
global_state            :       empty ;
segment                 :       empty ;
*/
```

```
inprim                 :    IPRIM IDENT
                       ;

outprim                :    OPRIM IDENT
                       ;

/***** prompt component, inits *****/

init_symbol            :    empty |
                            PRS activ_list
                       ;

activ_list             :    activ_list_element |
                            activ_list activ_list_element
                       ;

activ_list_element     :    activ_mode activ_cell_list SEMICOLON
                       ;

activ_mode             :    REQUEST |
                            SAMPLE |
                            EVENT
                       ;

activ_cell_list        :    activ_cell_element |
                            activ_cell_list COMMA activ_cell_element
                       ;

activ_cell_element     :    IDENT
/*                          LPAREN cell_params RPAREN

                            cell_attributes
*/
                       ;

init_echo              :    empty |
                            PRE echo_list
                       ;

echo_list              :    echo_list_element |
                            echo_list echo_list_element
                       ;

echo_list_element      :    IDENT
                            echo_mode
                            echo_function
                       ;

echo_mode              :    ACCEPT |
                            OFF |
                            TRANSF
                       ;

echo_function          :    empty
                       ;
```

```
init_value            :    empty |
                           PRV
                           local_inits
                           cell_inits
                      ;

local_inits           :    empty |
                           local_inits local_init
                      ;

local_init            :    type_specifier variable_decl_list SEMICOLON
                      ;

variable_decl_list    :    variable_decl |
                           variable_decl_list COMMA variable_decl
                      ;

variable_decl         :    variable_ident variable_assignment
                      ;

variable_assignment   :    empty |
                           variable_value
                      ;

variable_ident        :    IDENT
                      ;

variable_value        :    EXPRESSION
                      ;

cell_inits            :    empty |
                           cell_inits cell_init
                      ;

cell_init             :    IDENT EQS cell_value
                      ;

/***** symbol component *****/

symbol_component      :    SYMBOL symbol_expression
                      ;

symbol_expression     :    symbol_expression MULT |
                           symbol_expression MULT trigger |
                           symbol_expression BINOP symbol_expression |
                           symbol_case_statement |
                           primary
                      ;

trigger               :    TRIGGER
                      ;

primary               :    LPAREN symbol_expression RPAREN |
                           IDENT |
                           constant |
```

```
                            stop
                    ;

symbol_case_statement : CASE cell_case_key IN
                            LCURLY symbol_case_list RCURLY
                    ;

cell_case_key       :   IDENT
                    ;

symbol_case_list    :   symbol_case_element |
                        symbol_case_list symbol_case_element
                    ;

symbol_case_element :   left_element COLON right_element
                    ;

left_element        :   cell_value |
                        REJECT
                    ;

right_element       :   symbol_expression |
                        EMPTY
                    ;

constant            :   cell_value
                    ;

stop                :   DOLLAR
                    ;

/* binary operators can be terminals */
/* binop            :   SEMICOLON  |     /*  ;  */
/*                      LOGOR |         /* \\/ */
/*                      LOGAND |        /* /\\ */
/*                      MULT            /*  *  */
/*                  ;
 */

/***** value component *****/

value_component     :   value_assignment
                        DOLLAR
                        rules
                        fail
                        result
                    ;

rules               :   empty |
                        RULES rules_expression
                    ;

rules_expression    :   value_expression RELOP basic_type
                    ;

fail                :   empty |
```

```
                            FAIL fail_expression
                    ;

fail_expression     :       RETURN value_expression
                    ;

result              :       empty |
                            RESULT result_expression
                    ;

result_expression   :       cell_value
                    ;

/*
 * relop can be a terminal symbol
 */
/*
relop               :       '<'  |
                            '<''='  |
                            '>'  |
                            '>''='  |
                            '=''='  |
                            '!''='
                    ;
*/

value_assignment    :       empty |
                            value_case_statement |
                            value_map_statement
                    ;

value_case_statement :      CASE cell_case_key IN
                            LCURLY value_case_list RCURLY
                    ;

value_case_list     :       value_case_element |
                            value_case_list value_case_element
                    ;

value_case_element  :       cell_value COLON value_assignment
                    ;

value_map_statement :       MAP map_source TO map_destination
                            LCURLY value_map_list RCURLY
                    ;

map_source          :       IDENT
                    ;

map_destination     :       IDENT |
                            IDENT IDENT
                    ;

value_map_list      :       value_map_element |
                            value_map_list map_separator
                            value_map_element
```

```
                         ;

map_separator       :    COMMA
                         ;

value_map_element   :    cell_value COLON map_value trigger_value
                         ;

map_value           :    cell_value |
                         FAIL
                         ;

trigger_value       :    empty |
                         CONT |
                         STOP
                         ;

/***** echo component *****/

echo_component      :    ECHO
                         print_list
                         DOLLAR
                         print_list
                         ;

print_list          :    empty |
                         print_list print_stat
                         ;

print_stat          :    PRINT IDENT |
/*
                         PRINT picture_type |
*/
                         IF value_expression print_stat

%%      /* start of program section */

yylex()
{
        c = getchar();
        if ( isdigit(c) ) {
                yylval = c + '0';
                return( DIGIT );
        }
        if ( islower(c) ) {
                yylval = c;
                return( LETTER );
        }
        if ( isupper(c) ) {
                yylval = c;
                return( LETTER );
        }
        return( c );
}
```

Appendix B: Examples for Dialogue Cells

```
DICE number real
{
        /* number reads symbols from the keyboard  and interprets
         * them as a real number;  all reactions  on checking the
         * input are given immediately;  the effect on the screen
         * is completely specified.
         */
PROMPT:
        REQUEST sign, unsint, fraction, exponent, separator.
        /* these symbols and  their  static resources  are  made
         * available;  they  will  manifest  themselves  when the
         * parser asks for (requests) a symbol from them.
         */
        PRINT "number?"
SYMBOL:
        [sign]; [unsint]; [fraction]; [exponent]; separator.
        /*
         * the components are REQUESTED one after the other(;)
         */
VALUE:
        /* error checking: */
        $
        /* at the end i.e., when begin symbol is produced */
        RULES
        {
        (unsint.d + fraction.d + exponent.d <= 0)->
                ER( "skipped" )
        (unsint.d + fraction.d > 12)->
                ER( "too many digits in mantissa" )
        (exponent.d > 4)          ->
                ER( "too many digits in exponent" )
        }
        FAIL
                return(0.0)
        RESULT
                (unsint.r + fraction.r) * sign * exponent
ECHO:
        $
        IF (separator != CR) PRINT "\n";
        /* ensure beginning of new line */

}
```

```
DICE fraction real(r,d)
{
PROMPT:
SYMBOL:
        CASE KB IN
        {
                '.'      : unsint,
                REJECT  : EMPTY
        }
VALUE:
        MAP unsint TO fraction
        {       (r,0) -> FAIL,
                (r,d) -> (10^(-d)*r,d).
        }
        FAIL    ER( "fraction not completed" )
        $
ECHO:
        KB, unsint
}


DICE exponent real(r,d)
{
PROMPT:
SYMBOL:
        CASE KB IN
        {
                'E'      : unsint,
                REJECT  : EMPTY
                /* reject means: the symbol (KB) is not used,
                 * it is pushed back on the input stream
                 */
        }
VALUE:
        MAP unsint TO exponent
        {
                (r,0) -> FAIL,
                (r,d) -> (10^r , d)
        }
        FAIL    ER( "exponent not completed" )
        $
ECHO:
        KB, unsint
}


DICE separator char
{
PROMPT:
SYMBOL:
        KB.
VALUE:
        MAP KB TO separator
```

```
                    TAB -> CR,
                    SPACE -> CR,
                    CR -> EMPTY,
                    REJECT -> FAIL

ECHO:
        separator
}


DICE sign real(r,d)
{
PROMPT:
        /* empty means: all subcells in REQUEST mode, echo ON */
SYMBOL:
        KB*t.
VALUE:
        MAP KB TO sign,t
            {
                    '+' -> (1,1), STOP;/* plus sign */
                    '-' -> (-1,1), STOP;/* minus sign */
                    ' ' -> (0,0), CONT;/* skip leading spaces */
                    EMPTY -> FAIL, STOP;/* error from KB,
                                    sign fails */
                    REJECT -> (1,0), STOP;
            }
            $
ECHO:
        KB
        /·· export KB echo */
}


DICE unsint real(r,d)
{
        d = r = 0;
        int     v = 0;
PROMPT:
SYMBOL:
        KB*t
VALUE:
        MAP KB TO v,t
            {
                    '0'-'9' -> 0-9, CONT;
                    REJECT -> -1, STOP;
                    v >= 0 : r*10+v -> r;
                    (d += 1) >= 10: t = STOP;
            )
            }
            $
ECHO:
        KB
}
```

V. Specification Tools and Implementation Techniques

H. G. Borufka, H. Hanusa, H. R. Weber

1. Introduction

1.1 Overview

Within the last few years, more and more research work
has been invested in the area of man-machine communication. This is a natural consequence of the ongoing
demand for improved man-machine-interfaces of a growing user
community. Reviewing the history of computing starting with
batch processing steps of improvement have been the fixed
dialogue, offering the user on-line editing, testing and
computing, and the programmable dialogue, allowing the
system's programmer or expert user to adjust the dialogue to
applications' and users' requirements. Today's efforts aim
at systems capable to adjust the dialogue structure themselves to user characteristics. It is assumed that a
successful solution to this problem would increase acceptance and efficiency of computer usage.

An important prerequisite for the successful design of user
adaptive systems is the development of appropriate tools
that allow to consider user aspects in a predictable and
measurable way. Therefore, one of the primer goals of the
SEILLAC II - workshop, France 1979 /GUE80/, was to work on a
model for interaction in order to be able to develop
guidelines for a design methodology of interactive systems.
Several propositions were discussed and one of the results
of SEILLAC II was the development of a basic interaction
model with the levels of abstraction shown in fig. 1.1.

Our approach is heavily influenced by the experience with
graphics systems. The important progress in designing
graphics systems (i.e. graphic kernel system) has been
possible by the separation of modelling from I/O-functions.
We think that an analogue approach, namely the separation of
the dialogue from the application is the key to the
successful design of user adaptive systems.

We will present a strategy for the design and construction
of interactive graphics systems, as well as a tool to

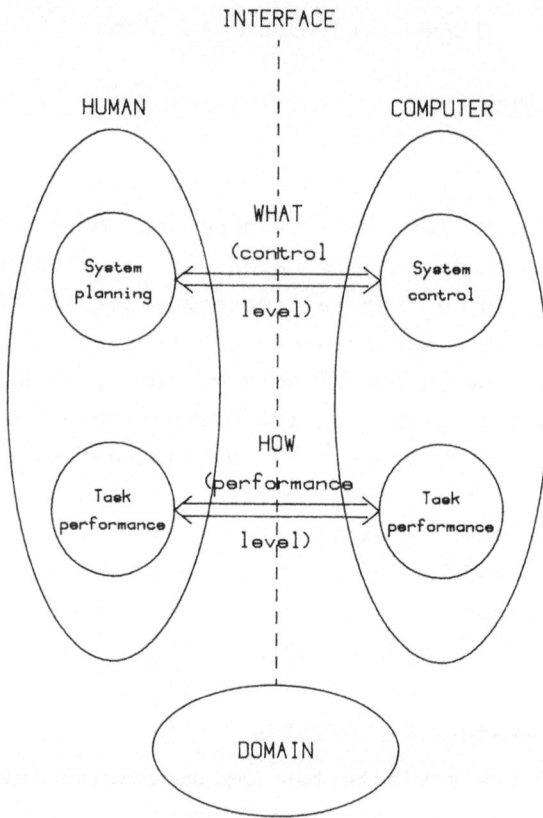

Fig. 1.1   Interaction Model

support the construction phase and the evaluation of the
man-machine behaviour at run-time. We will also deal with
aspects and guidelines for the design of man-machine interfaces, especially from the user's point of view. Lastly,
tools and techniques for the design and implementation of
interactive man-machine dialogues will be introduced.

1.2 Notions

With the following, we want to clarify some of the notions
used within these tutorial-notes; this seems to be necessary, for some of them may be used in other publications
with different understandings.

USER

The man/woman using an interactive system to accomplish a given task. He/she knows, what kinds of problems can be solved, but need not necessarily know how this is realized.

USERMODEL

A model within the interactive system representing the system's knowledge about how a user will behave on a certain problem.

USER'S MODEL

This is the idea of the user, how to solve a given problem and how an interactive system will react.

DIALOGUE

The flow of interaction between user and machine.

IMPLEMENTATION

This is the coding of algorithms and the mapping of the logical data-structures and logical operations on them to programming language types and constructs.

DIALOGUE MODULE

This is a module within an interactive system, which is responsible for the communication with the user, the dialogue support for the user, and supplying the application functions with the necessary parameters.

INSTALLATION

Putting the implementation modules on to a specific machine and specific peripheral environment, resulting in an executable program system.

MACHINE

Hardware, firmware, and basic software needed.

DESIGN

This is the process of mapping out a given problem to

realizable solution for a machine.

MAN-MACHINE INTERFACE

The consideration and/or realization of the way man and machine cooperate.

BEHAVIOUR

The perceptable and recognizable out-look of man and/or machine in a dialogue.

METHOD

How to combine given tools and techniques and to make use of them.

EVALUATION

The measuring and analysation of data, giving information about man and machine behaviour in an interactive dialogue.

INTERACTION

The nucleus of a dialogue; this is a prompt, echo, acknow-ledgement sequence.

Following, an overall scheme for generating graphical user interface management systems is given. To do so, various components have to be developed and the coherence and the interfaces between these system components have to be defined. It is also desired that results of the study of human factors can be used to influence the design and implementation.

2. Models and Design Strategy

Most studies of human factors of interactive systems are behavioural experiments, for the real use of a system is a direct way to find out whether the system is easy to use or not (/BLA83/). Another advantage is that the test can be done with those groups of users, which are to be the end-users of the system.

A disadvantage of such behavioural experiments is that they are costly and rather time consuming. Furthermore, the results of the analysation of the experiments may come so late in the phase of designing and developing an interactive system that they do not have any impact. Thus, these kind of tests are applicable to evaluate existing systems, but the results can only effect the design of a next system.

To overcome these problems, research work has been done to develop analytic tools to determine the quality of the man-machine interface. Hopefully, this will help to speed up the study of interfaces, giving the chance to influence the system-design at an early stage.

2.1 Models

The analytical tools of models are a way of determining the user-interface of interactive systems. They more or less represent design and development methodology, than giving rules for particular systems. An analytic tool, a model, serves for some abstract representation of relevant aspects of man-machine interfaces, and helps to predict what would happen if actual users use the system. Some examples of models are described below.

Keystroke Level Model

This model predicts the time it will take a user to perform a task in an interactive system. It is based on counting the number of keystrokes necessary to perform the task. A disadvantage of this model is that it is difficult to describe performances containing errors. It helps to predict the task time for an expert user, knowing the precise sequence of commands.

Action Language Model

The action language model describes the man-machine interface by defining the actions a user has to perform at the interface using a formal grammar (BNF). All terminal symbols of the grammar or user actions. This model was used to compare interfaces and validated by results of a behavioural experiment. The grammar for the interface-description gets rather extensive, even for not too complex interfaces.

Command Language Grammar

Using this model, a system can be described in a conceptional, communication, and physical level. The description starts at the conceptional level and gets down to the physical level by refinement, from the definition of the task to be performed, to the physical input devices used.

The next models presented, will be discussed more detailed. They are based on mathematical descriptions of operator's behaviour in process control environments. The ones described are currently under discussion, to what extend the can support an automated evaluation of man-machine interfaces (/HAN83/) using a "Monitor". The monitor (/HAN83/) is a means of selecting, registering, measuring, and analysing data with the goals of justifying the system behaviour as well as the user behaviour, in order to provide decission criteria for configuring an interactive system.

Classical Power Form Model

- total time for n-tasks

$$T_n = K\ n^{1-s}$$

where n = 1, 2, ... is the number of tasks

K > 0 is the initial cycle time

0 < s < 1 is the learning factor

- cumulative mean time for one task

$$A_n = T_n/n = K n^{-s}$$

where $n = 1, 2, \ldots$

- individual cycle time for the n-th cycle

$$X_n = K(1-s) n^{-s}$$

$X_n = T_n - T_{n-1}$ because for large n there is

$$\frac{dT_n}{dn} = K(1-s) n^{1-s-1} = K(1-s) n^{-s}$$

- percentage of learning rate

$$r = \frac{A_{2n}}{A_n}$$ where $n = 1, 2, \ldots$

that is $\log r = -s \log 2$

The problem when using this model is, that n has to be very large to end up with useful results, and that the function is 0-asymtotic.

Exponential Model

The Exponential Model corrects the 0-asymtotic effect of the former one, but still keeps the problem of the large amount of sample-data.
- individual cycle time at a given time t is

$$Y(t) = Y_c - Y_f(1-e^{-t/\tau})$$

where Y_c is the time needed for the first execution of a task

$Y_c - Y_f$ is the final cycle time

t   is the execution time

τ is the learning time constant.

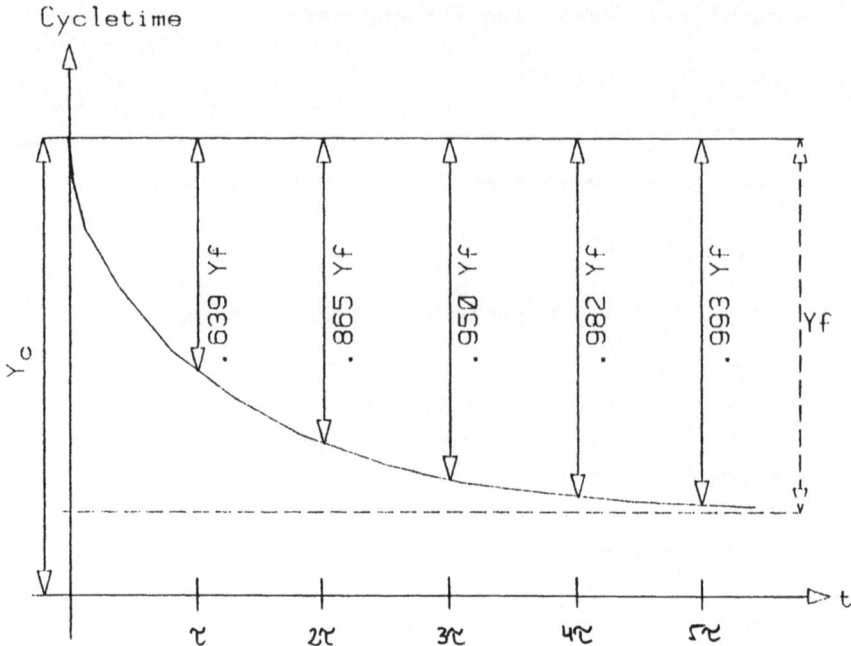

Fig. 2.1   Exponential Model

De Yong

- individual cycle time for th n-th cycle

$$X_n = X_1 M + \frac{1-M}{n^m}$$

where n = 1, 2, ... is the number of tasks

X_1 is the time used for the first execution of the task

m is a factor to represent the frequency of performing the task

M is a non-reduction factor in percentage, representing a timevalue which can not be less than a certain level.

All of these models have in common, that the criterion to simulate the user's behaviour is the individual cycle time for performing a given task.

The requirements for such a model being used as a reference model by a monitor, are:

- the models have to be simple; that means, simple to realise within the monitor, as part of the analyser, with respect to time restrictions in case of parallel monitoring.

- they should make do with a small number of parameters.

- they should help to find meaningful interpretations of the data measured.

- they should be as correct as possible, even for small sampling rates, and a small number of sessions.

A minimum set of parameters derived from the existing models, which have to be in a revised version of one of the models - used as the reference model - is:

- Frequency factor.
  A value representing the time of session duration, combined with the time gap between two sessions.

- Non-reduction factor.
  A value (given in percentage), representing a time which can never be reduced in using a system (initial cycle time, time for program execution) on the one hand, and the user's ability to handle the system on the other.

- Learning factor.
  A value $(0 < s < 1)$ representing the learning ability of a user.

A model for man-machine interfaces can be regarded as a conceptional "what" has to be considered during the design and implementation phase. Now, this has to lead to a precise "how" design strategy.

2.2 Design Strategy

We now present a design strategy, which is based on the concept explained in /ENC83/, how to construct an inter-

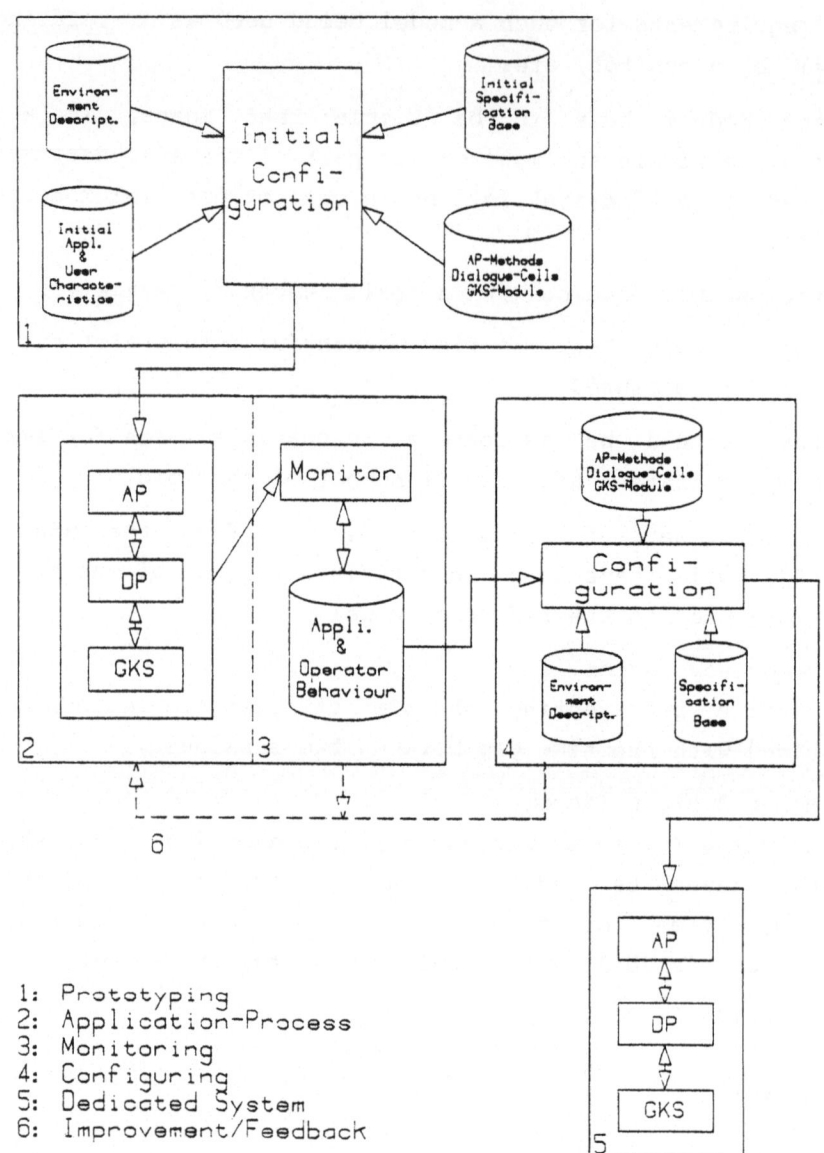

Fig. 2.2 Design Strategy

active system, promising to result in a solution which will
be regarded to be a good one. We will also point out some
items still under discussion (/BOR83/):

Monitoring

Monitoring /HAN83/ as said above is a means of selecting, registering, measuring and analysing data with the goals of:

a) justifying the system behaviour

b) justifying the operator behaviour

in order to provide decision criteria for configuring a system (by static or dynamic configuration).

There are two aspects concerning monitoring:

a) two-phase execution (selecting, registering and measuring happenings in the first place; analysing the data in the second.)

b) simultaneous execution of selecting, registering, measuring and analysing in a parallel running process.

From the analysation of the data, configuration parameters are derived either by a human expert or automatically.

Configuring

Configuring /PFA82a/ is a means of adapting a system according to given parameters with the goals of:

a) minimising the system's overhead

b) tailoring the system to operator requirements

c) tailoring the system to the application needs

There are two possible realisations (both of which are used in the following):

a) static system generation (by compilation/preprocessing)

b) dynamic configuration (selection of an execution path and routing out of a given number of realisations)

Having tools to generate a system from a set of programs, the basic elements for system construction have to be defined as well as corresponding descriptions for selecting the appropriate modules for given parameter data. These elements are called methods.

Methods

A method is a system component that

- can be executed independently
- is a solution for a (partial) problem

For every method, there exists a method description, containing at least the descriptions of the interface and the effect of the method.

NOTE:- Methods may range from very simple procedures or subroutines, to complete system packages.
  - Methods may be hierarchically structured thus providing a means for building complex methods.
  - Methods may only have one entry, i.e., they may be used via one welldefined name. They may have one or more "uses interfaces" to other methods, i.e., may call several other program modules.

Next, a tool is needed to define program skeletons to determine how the methods interact with each other in possible configurations. This should be some kind of simple description language suitable for occasional users (perhaps providing a graphical interface).

Method Interaction Language (MIL)

MIL /GOE83/ is a means to describe the interaction of methods, where

a) methods are used with their interface description

b) there are language constructs to define independent execution instances of methods and the communication between them.

With the above given definitions of monitoring, configuring, method definition, and method interaction language, we are able to generate graphical user interface manager systems in a prototyping process, i.e, by stepwise improvements. The prototyping approach is explained in this section. Before that, we give the definition of a user interface manager.

User Interface Manager (UIM)

A UIM is a means to mediate the interaction between a user and an application; satisfying user requests for application actions and application requests for data from the user.

In our approach, a UIM consists of the following components:

a) a set of output, input, and dialogue functions,
b) a monitor for protocolling certain interaction flow,
c) a system controller for configuring resources,
d) a graphics system.

Prototyping

A) Building a prototype.

A prototype is a system constructed from a set of available system components (e.g. program modules) according to a given specification.

The goals, when setting up a prototype, are:

a) to implement the functional behaviour of the given specification

b) to fix the final internal program structure as far as possible

c) to find a fast and inexpensive solution for an intermediate system.

NOTE: (a) and (b) are necessary requirements to find realistic system execution data when running the prototype.

B) The prototyping process

Prototyping is a sequence of stepwise improvements and refinements of a prototype, consisting of the following phases:

a) configuration of a first prototype according to a given initial specification

b) monitoring of the prototype and modifying the specification (see Note 2)

c) configuration of a new prototype according to the modified specification

The iteration loop over steps (b) and (c) are repeated, until the data measured and analysed by the monitor fulfills the specification requirements.

Note 1: Results of monitoring and adapting should be two-fold:

  (i) possible operator classes are found for the given system application

 (ii) the system (especially the dialogue part) fits exactly to these operator classes

Note 2: The specification from which a system is configured, may be realised in several ways:

  (i) a specification language defining the execution paths between methods

 (ii) a set of tables, the entries of which control pre-processors or compilers, when generating object cards

(iii) a set of tables, the entries of which determine the actual execution path, in a system that integrates several possibilities

Generating the Program Specification

The next open question is how to set up the specification of
the dialogue and the application components of UIM systems.
From this specification the actual implementation of the
final program system should be generated after prototyping
either various versions of realisations of the same specifications (then several dialogue possibilities have to be
foreseen) or various versions of specifications. In the
latter case, for new prototyps new specifications have to be
generated. We are looking for ways to ease the generation of
the specification. One way could be the application of an
expert system by which specifications could be generated
automatically according to requirement parameters given by
an expert.

Requirement:

A system user describes an application problem in a suitable
way (e.g. using a system with guided graphical dialogue). We
assume a target function, for the classes of problems and a
description of the methods' effects for this function. A
system component selects methods and puts them together,
such that a programmed realisation of the problem exists.
The methods and the interaction between the methods are
selected according to the problem description, the target
function, and the method descriptions. The generated realisation of the problem may be in terms of the method
interaction language.

In order to achieve an application system, two processes
have to be considered. We are calling them "Dialogue-
Generating-Process" and "Application-Generating-Process".

The "Dialogue-Generating-Process" is as follows:

The given methods for dialogue leading and graphical interaction (realised perhaps by Dialogue Cells and GKS) form the
basis for that dialogue system. A dialogue author sets up a
solution for dialogue leading for the given goals of the
required application. A resource for doing this, is the
Method Interaction Language (MIL) or the Dialogue Cell
Language (DZS). In the case of a MIL specification, a

first prototype is configured (otherwise it was programmed).
An improvement on this prototype is made with monitoring and
configuring a new prototype, until the best fitting require-
ments are found. The resulting system, called "Dialogue
System", consists of a User Interface Manager and the
Graphical Kernel for Interaction, and is the result of the
"Dialogue-Generating-Process".

The "Application-Generating-Process" is as follows:

The methods, given in a method base, which in their
community form a solutionfor the application requirements,
are transformed by a "Method Manager" into the MIL. Together
with the given Dialogue System, an application system is
configured out of this MIL, without the prototyping process
which was involved in the "Dialogue-Generating-Process".

If no "good" system has been achieved, the Application-
Generating-Process is done once again, with changes in the
constellation of methods.

Dialogue Cells and their Relation to MIL

Dialogue cells (/BOR80/, /BOR82a/) represent the basic
building blocks for programming a dialogue component. They
are constructed using the program skeleton scheme known as
Prompt - Symbol - Echo - Value, and provide syntactical
elements (statements) for its definition. Control flow constructs allow the combination and conditional execution of
these statements. The symbol elements may be represented by
other dialogue cells thus allowing for hierarchical program
structures. Prompts may be of type picture, text or menu;
echo items of type picture or text. A dialogue author may
define pictures using graphics output and attribute functions (e.g., GKS function calls). At runtime prompt and echo
objects are associated with the hierarchy level of the
generating cell; relative to this level the object lifetime
is defined (usually it ends at the cell end). Menus and
pictures may be passed to other cells by parameters.

The dialogue cell language (DZS) is an FORTRAN extension and compiled to FORTRAN by a preprocessor (GEP) for portability reasons. Its concepts are based on sequentiell processing and therefore, the dialogue type is restricted to the well-known REQUEST input model.

We aim at meaningful extensions of tools for dialogue programming. The most important criteria of a language suitable for setting up a general dialogue component are:

a) the concept of parallel processes should be included, i.e., an dialogue function may be realised by several independently active processes using each other (inquiring values from and sending event messages to other processes).

b) The concept of methods should be included. A dialogue component should be constructable from a set of interaction technique methods in flexible ways, i.e., the single methods should be basic enough to be used in several environments; references to other methods should be in such a way that a single method may be replaced by another one providing the same interface. This may be achieved by defining classes of methods. All methods of a class must have the same functional interface. Each method has to have a method description by which it can be selected as the actual instance of the class.

c) The language should allow for describing functional coherences between methods, i.e., the data and control flow between methods being executed as processes. From this description and the method modules executable programs should be generated consisting of a number of processes which execute instances of methods.

d) Defining a dialogue method existing ones should be usable decreasing the design effort and enabling well structured systems.

The requirements of parallel processes together with the concept of methods resulted in the definition of the method interaction language (MIL). It concentrates on defining the control and data flow between parallel processes. It is in an early stage of development ("dream phase" as being described by Hatvany /HAT83/).

In this context each dialogue cell can be seen as a method which is constructed from a set of already defined dialogue methods. By this other methods are used and hierarchies can be built. Data passing is performed via parameters. Each referenced method inside a cell can be replaced by another-one with the same interface (in a configuration process).

Further development should result in a unique language providing the facilities both of the method interaction language and the dialogue cell language.

Description Language and Relation to Expert Systems

Assuming a method base containing method entries each of which consists of an independent program function and a description of the function's interfaces and effects, user interface management systems can be created. To that purpose, UI programs are defined by means of the MIL, which consist of the program modules of the methods and of control statements between these modules, i.e., the interaction between the methods. As can already be deduced from this, methods are items which are independent from all other methods. Nevertheless, they can only be performed in a certain program environment using other and being used by other program modules.

There were two major objectives in our mind when defining the method interaction language: first, there should be some kind of process or independently performing program which provides an externally visible state that may be inquired by other programs. Secondly, the overall system consisting of a number of these independent programs should be distributable to a structure of several processors. It should be possible to derive this structure from the software structure, i.e., from the communication links between the independent programs.

We have to deal with the two aspects of a method, namely the method as a static declaration and an "action unit" as a runtime instance of the method being embedded in a programming environment. Then there is the problem, whether instances of the methods should be generated at system runtime (because only then the number of parallel performing instances of a method may be known) or at the time of generating the software (because then the distribution of parallel tasks to several processors can be better decided upon).

To describe the communication between methods resp. between their runtime instances, data and control structures are needed. The range of possibilities starts with strictly sequential executions and ends with the well-known control constructs of programming languages like PASCAL, MODULA, or ADA.

The MIL specification elements have to be mapped onto languages providing multiprogramming and distribution facilities for program modules, but it may also be possible to emulate some MIL features by simpler language constructs.

The way we look upon the generation of UIM systems leads us to the areas of expert systems. For a given problem (generate a UIM program for special application demands, specific user characteristics, and a given graphics device support) a solution (a UIM system) should be automatically constructed where the expert (an expert in user interface engeneering) sets up the configuration parameters.

The method interaction language MIL may serve as a tool for describing the function and control flows between independently running processes. It also serves as a description for a MIL preprocessor which generates instances from methods and the appropriate interaction control flow statements in order to set up a program consisting of method processes. These elements are called action units. To that purpose a set of language constructs is selected that gives a person setting up the dialogue component enough possibilty to describe this in terms of dialogue, input, output, prompt, echo, etc. methods and of dependencies between these

methods, i.e., the "uses" of other methods. The MIL interpreter generates an executable program in a language allowing for multiple processes.

Finally, a possibility was considered to create the dialogue
component in a completely automated way. An expert system
generates the MIL specification of the dialogue component or
it selects one of the possible dialogue realisations within
an existing MIL specification according to actually given
target system parameters. In both cases, the resulting
system will no longer contain the configuring possibilities
but rather provide a dialogue component being adapted to the
end users.

The rest of this chapter deals with some of the problems we
have to consider, when trying to embed facilities to measure
and analyse user-system behaviour.

User Classification

Problem:
Classification of users depend on their individual behaviour
and reaction to the system, their ability to learn how to
use the system and the handling of the interaction tools.

Classification is necessary to combine the variety of those
values which describe the user's behaviour within the
description model, to a single value. The determined user
class is considered when prototyping the system.

There are two ways to classify users:
(a) to distinguish between the criteria evaluated by the
    user model, in a classified set including
    - learning factor, error rate ...

(b) to combine the values mentioned above to a user
profile. E.g., if the dialogue is set up by logic I/O
elements (Measure, Echo, Trigger = MET), the user
profile is based on valid MET combinations and describes
which realization is preferred by the user.

The individual profile is compared with a "standard
user profile", which is:
- predefined (for the first step)
- the average of all evaluated user profiles (for the
  i^{th} step, i > 1) in the analysation phase of the monitoring process for achieving monitor decisions.

Levels to Gather Data

Each system consists of a set of subsystems, e.g. a dialogue
system using graphics I/O system, data bases, etc. Data
collection is performed only at the defined interfaces to
each subsystem, at least at the application interface
and/or the operator-interface.

It is assumed that monitoring takes place at the highest
level (i.e. the application interface) data is gathered and
integrated, decisions are elaborated upon.

Non-determinisms at that level require the monitor to
collect data from the lowest level. Given a choice, the
monitor returns to the higher level, or else it steps down
to a lower level.

The hierarchical monitor concept has to be well defined,
otherwise situations can arise where monitoring is switching
between two levels without evaluating any results.

Different solutions for data collection:
(a) collecting and interpreting at only one level (the
highest); if a choice is available, use the next lower
level.
- no consideration of lower level data which concerns
  the decision to step downwards
+ fast monitoring

(b) always monitoring protocols at <u>all</u> levels and inter-
    preting the highest level (use lower level in undefined
    situations)
    - enormous amount of data
    + consideration of the past concrete values
    + possibility to determine the correct state of the
      system, exactly (looking back)
    + detection and consideration of errors made by the user

(c) Monitoring senses the lowest level (the Operator Inter-
    face) to draw conclusions about the user's activity in
    any situation. The data collection and interpretation
    level is chosen by the monitor, (i.e. alternative, a
    positive lowest level registration).
    + no undefined system state for the monitor
    + decision whether user is active or inactive
    + looking bach facility
    + acceptable amount of collected data

Analysation

By analysation, we mean the interpretation of the data
gathered by the ED module of the monitor.

It should be no problem to measure time differences at the
application program, the dialogue control, and the I/O
system, not concerned with the part where the user has
control. The interpretation of such time values may lead to
a problem such as the following:

   If there are large time intervals between user reactions,
   this may result in the assumption that the user is unable
   to handle this special part of the dialogue in a proper
   way. In reality, the user is not using the system at all
   this point in time, for one reason or another.

This leads to the requirements that the lowest level of monitoring has to answer the question: "is the user still working or not?" The problem of how to interpret whether the user is not using the system or whether he is thinking how to proceed, is not yet resolved.

Other points of interpretation, like errors, levels of errors, and effects of fatigue, have to be discussed in detail.

Connection of the Monitor

Parallel   - The data measurement and analysis is done in parallel with the dialogue (Type B monitoring, see below). The pros are that the system has not to be modified by inserting monitor-activation points as the connection is done via synchronised buffers whose supervision is part of the monitor itself. This also allows the dynamic configuring process, i.e. decision on what part of the dialogue alternatives is to be used at a certain time for the actual user. The parallel connection also has as few effects as posible on the system behaviour, with respect to response time.

Sequential - The measuring is done via monitor activation points, within those parts of the system to be monitored (automatically generated). Thus some parts of the FD module have to be executed before the dialogue goes on. This may have the result that the system performance could be affected in a negative way, leading to wrong conclusions during analysation. This will be so more especially, when dynamic modification is used. The sequential connection is, therefore, recommended for the prototyping phase, where time dependencies are of lower interest. Sequential connection may also be used when system modification is required, before every interactive session, but with question/answer help by the user himself.

Monitor Data

Problem when monitoring with analysation in parallel with dialogue session (Type B - parallel): the monitor should verify that the ration of time spent in the monitor versus "productive time" max result in "time-monitoring" for the monitor.

Monitoring Type A   (installation monitoring)
Time to evaluate the relative effort compared with the total time
Dataflow between processes
 - amount of data
 - direction of data

Control Flow which part/parts of the system are active at a time
 - evaluation of frequency of usage
            of parallel active parts

Monitoring Type B
Physical level   sense whether there is activity at this level or not
Signal#   #protocol the activities at the lowest level for having the possibility to simulate the userbehaviour when going back to Type A for reconfiguration.
Actual Objects   these are the objects regarded as relevant for monitoring each time.
Actual Time
 - direction of data
 - content of data

Control Flow

Two different versions of Type B monitoring:

B1: The control of what is being monitored is part of the monitor supervisor. It determines the parts of the system being monitored; either they are active or not. OBJECT-MONITORING

B2: The control is implicitly within the system, for al parts of the system which are active at a certain time, have to be monitored. ACTION-MONITORING

As the monitor supervisor does not have the control, it does not know when to start analysation (if needed in parallel). One solution may be to start all possible analysation functions and these have to be "intelligent" to decide when to begin their analysation.

Errors

lexical: illegal value   detectable if description
              impossible value   is available

syntactical: correct
              incorrect

semantical: correct   if description of applica-
              incorrect   tion is available

              context ???

conceptional: _____

(1) If a description for the different error-levels is available (perhaps generated during Type A monitoring) a comparison with the actual dataflow is possible - error detection without knowledge of the objects.

(2) Errors are reported to the monitor by the objects which detect the error.

Special Error: Deadlock

The monitor has to detect deadlocks. The problem is to find the criteria for the analysation to decide on deadlock situations.

The problems presented may give an impression, what difficulties occur to provide a "universal" monitor for interactive man-machine behaviour. The difficulties become more,
the more analysation with respect to human factors is
desired. The monitor is still under development and improvement, especially the analysation part of it. Some aspects of
what has to be dealt with in evaluating user-interfaces are
pointed out in the next chapter.

3. Guidelines and Observations

3.1. Theoretical Aspects

The question "What is a good user interface?" cannot be answered here. We do not want to add another failure to the answering of this question.

To illustrate the content of this part we want to cite a prologue of Harold Thimbleby, given at a conference of software ergonomics in Nurenberg /THI83/. He writes:

"There are several major obstacles to designing good user interfaces:

(a) The standard ergonomics issue: designers tend to design for themselves unless they are intentionally humble and consciously aware of actual user needs.

In computing, the problem is possibly worse than in other technologies because there is no intermediary (e.g. a craftsman) between formalism and user interface. There is consequently considerable confusion between user and designer interfaces.

(b) User interface design appears to be simple.

Indeed, it is if the interface design takes advantage of users' almost limitless capacity for adaptability (and acceptance).

(c) People who construct interfaces have considerably more control and understanding of them than any other class of user.

In particular, a computer scientist's training (and delight?) is specifically to handle complexity. This results in system designs with an excess of technical options. Users are not necessarily computer experts nor want to become so, by using a system which apparently expects them to be. Users may react emotionally to computer interfaces which require abstract computing skills and experience.

(d) What knowledge there is, is multi-disciplinary and not systematized and thereby may be ignored in preference for necessary but more obvious design constraints (e.g. formal properties of correctness).

Crucially, ergonomics cannot be used inductively - it is notoriously hard to reason about a design except by hindsight. Consequently, there is a temptation to define human requirements in terms of abstract metrics. Yet computers are very small (in mind and etiquette) and it is nonsense to define 'rational' behaviour vis-a-vis the interface purely in their terms.

(e) Ergonomics is essentially experimental and case-study driven; and the technology continues to outstrip any experimental basis.

Computer scientists are neither trained in experimental procedures nor have the motivation. Thus, computer scientists tend to over-generalize from specific experimental results. Furthermore, the innovative areas where ergonomists might have widest influence, are generally too specialized.

(f) Social, psychological and other issues which are outside the immediate man-machine domain are readily ignored.

As an illustration, Carroll /CAR82/ presents the 'Adventure' metaphor: why does a person get addicted to a game interface (where the user takes risks and faces unknown and under-specified tasks) but is unmotivated and feels lost with a structurally similar interface in a 'work' context (e.g. the straight computer interface)?

(g) There is considerable confusion between legitimate design principles and mere slogans.

Particular principles may become no more than slogans without the backing of applied reasoning from other ergonomic knowledge - and designer motivation. A particularly distracting activitiy consists of promoting prejudice as principle.

(h) Finally, the 'human factor' has become a euphemism for poor design.

The human user is perceived as a source of trouble, and many of his troubles (if noted) are classified as irrelevant to the functional specification and are dismissed as his own responsibility."

The reader may have noticed that no problem of hardware, algorithms, or other computer science proper problems were described. The reason is that most of the problems on achieving good performance and good acceptance of the increasing man-machine interface, concentrate on man - an "object" uncalculable with technical resources. The theme of the tutorial, "Specification Tools and Implementation Techniques", was, therefore, wrongly concentrated on machine aspects. We believe that:

To achieve a good man-machine interface, the activity of development has to concentrate on both the machine and man, with equal energy.

The problem in presentation is that models and algorithms in part of a machine are easily described and their functional proof can be verified by pilot implementations.

On the part of man, the situation is really different. No acceptable models exist; the "functional proof" of any effort is uncertain, since no evaluation methods exist, etc. So it would be a simple task to concentrate on the machine side, present examples here and leave the confusing world of user variables to the reader.

In this part of the tutorial, therefore, we will briefly (and naturally incompletely) concentrate on human factors and software ergonomics, in order only to deliver some guidelines and observations; guidelines /FOL81a/:

to apply at multiple levels of design,
to ignore when deadlines approach,
neither complete nor orthogonal,
which are obvious to users of poorly-designed interfaces

It should be mentioned here that there is great confusion on notions and interpretations on them, e.g. what doess "user-friendliness" or "ease of learning" mean? (See /STE83/.) This cannot be solved here. Similar to other areas of non computer science, the personal impact of the reader cannot be eliminated by simple definition.

We would invite you, while reading this part, to change your roles from designers and developers to some kinds of users, everyone looking upon his one part as a user of interactive systems.

3.1.1. Models of Usage and Learning

As described in Chapter 1.3, only a consistent flexible strategy in system design will lead to success. Before concentrating on the topics of this chapter, we would once again like to clarify what we regard as the main design failure of interactive systems: the concentration mainly on the machine. Our opinion is confirmed by HOLLNAGEL:

"Not only is the preferred approach in the study of MMSs to start from the description of one of the parts, but also to start from the machine rather than from man. This has the consequence that the description of the machine is extended to cover man as well, i.e. the description of the machine is assumed to be an appropriate basis for describing the MMS as a whole. ... Rather, each part should be described from its own point of view and with due regard to its inherent characteristics before an integration is attempted." /HLN83,136 f/

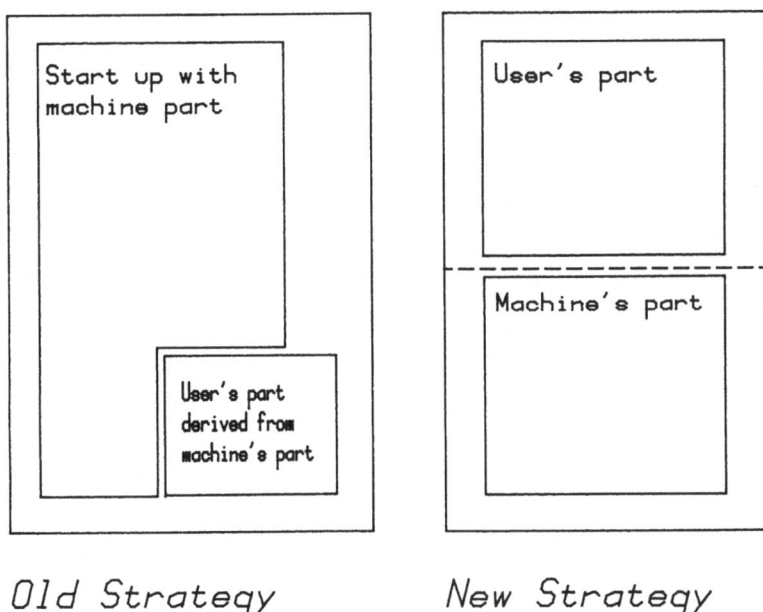

Old Strategy   New Strategy

Figure 3.1: Description of Machine-User Interfaces

We believe in the principle of discussing both parts separately and that investing similar effort in both will lead to better results. Arousing the awareness of the general public and designers will eventually lead to a point where errors like "SYNTAX ERROR" or system shut down, will cause systems designers to run for their lives. (Or something equally as drastic!)

As a result of Chapter 1.2 it becomes clear that there is a distinction between a usermodel and a user's model. Some models are based on "operators" and analyse or simulate their behaviour, others call for the use of consistent commands, etc. We want to clarify this:

A. A <u>usermodel</u> sets out how a user or class of user should behave, what kind of characteristics they have and how the intended system should react to the user's behaviour.

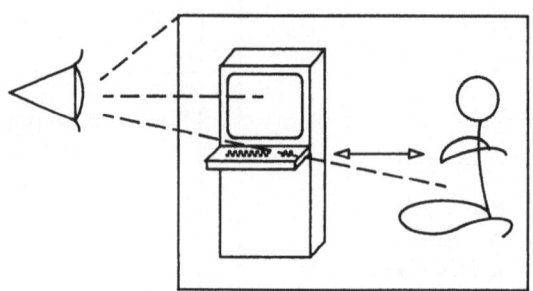

Figure 3.2: Usermodel

B. The <u>user's model</u> is the model that the user or class of user employs when operating the system. This model need not be comparable to any structure in the field of computer science.

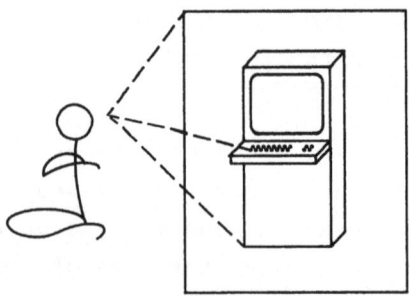

Figure 3.3: User's Model

When designing systems not explicitly concerned with human factors, a <u>usermodel</u> has always been present. Of course, few people have actually specified it, but some factors postulate a usermodel, e.g:

- The kind of errors the prospective user would be likely to make and how to deal with them

- Which part - man or machine - should have the control in interaction?

- Can all parts of the required application be dealt with by machine; which parts should be left to the user and how?

- Is it possible to split tasks among different users and machines?

- etc.

With a special task or application in mind, the designer's "usermodel" was checked against some of the above requirements and a solving strategy was developed. In actual use, the disadvantage of this strategy soon became apparent.

- The users made other errors than expected.

- When leaving control to the user, he became overburdened; leaving control to the machine, the user became angry through a lesser degree of freedom.

- The user did not understand what kind of solution was required to a given part on an application. ("I never did that before ...", "I never learnt to ...").

- Some users like to work on a general problem, while others prefer to find an expert solution to more specific problems.

- etc.

Now, we can argue about what may have caused reasons for failure. The appearance of errors when an actual user operated the system, was defined in terms of invalid operations during application, incorrect usage of input tools and disallowed sequences of operations. But the user's performance does not fall short on these aspects. The user himself analyses an error he may have made with carelessness, inefficient handling of devices, misunderstood prompting and nontransparent tasks.

Surrender .of control, in designers terms, requires programming a command parser or a menu-driven input device. Even
assuming an unrestricted design survey, control is defined
as a set of useable commands or selectable choices. From the
user's point of view, the interpretation is quite different.
When using the interface from a set of commands, a user
becomes angry about inconsistencies in the parameter sets,
and/or having to re-type a long command when a typing error
has been made. He is also frustrated with the appearance of
an unexpected effect of a command (e.g.

RENAME file1,file2

is a command to rename file1,"file2"). If we do not know how
to sequence commands in order to achieve the desired goal,
we are no longer able and should refuse to use the system.
(This is unfortunately not the case with all people!) Given
a menu or choice-driven interactive technique, we would
probably know the name of a required branch after inter-
acting with the system for some time, but would be still
forced to go through the tedium of stepping down to that
branch through five or nine other menus.

Dedicating parts of the application solution to the user is
dangerous. How can the designer be sure that the user can
solve the problem? How does he know what kind of tools the
user needs at that time and are they available then on the
system? What about access to them and return to the main
applications?

We think that should be enough to explain why we need a
user's model. If a system is running with respect to the
user's model, it will automatically lead to a situation
where the machine adapts to man and not vice versa.

Before going on to deal with learning, we shall mention some
aspects of user's models. We do not claim to have found the
only fitting one; this would be impossible. (See Chapter
3.1.3.) However, we want to give an incomplete list of terms
from which a user's model should be built or adopted
(/HLN83/, /BOS82/, /SHN83/):

- actual performance
- decision-making
- errors
- flexibility
- learning
- motivation
- problem solving
- satisfaction
- selection
- skills
- social climate
- training
- ....

Learning - something considered as a normal process that we are performing every day, hour and minute - becomes very complex on reflexion. The first thing to be observed is the time-consuming factor of learning: a process, therefore, which is not time-fixable. The second thing is that everyone has a different way of learning. One way may be the systematic repetition of sequences (e.g. learning a poem by heart), or another may be associative memorising (e.g. learning to speak our own language). (A good and amusing overview of psychological theories of learning is: /LF⁻72/.) With respect to users of interactive systems, we can derive the following styles of learning:

- manuals: similar to learning in school; a
                              good portion of self-motivation is
                              necessary to recognise the content
                              of the manual. Most of the existing
                              manuals only present information
                              and give no guidance for learning.
                              A controlled instruction manual has
                              to differ from a reference manual.

- trial and error: using a system often leads to erroneous situations. One of the best
ways of learning is to be provided
with information on how to deal
with these errors, since experience
can be widened through practise.
Problems arise through lack of support of information on how to deal
with errors and eliminate their
side effects. Computer support up
to now, has only been possible for
closed systems. (I.e. all reactions
pre-determined.)

- avoiding errors: Often, systems are constructed dis-
allowing users from making real
errors. Here, no learning is possible, as the system requires only
sequential leadership for some
applications, among few alternatives. The user has only to learn
to use some keys or something simi-
lary basic. Are you wondering about
less motivation in the background
applications? _Using_ the user
leads to objects performing like
machines stupid, unconcerned,
passive, not intellectually supporting the application.

- personal instruction: This can be the most relevant methods for teaching if two requirements are fulfilled. First, a good social atmosphere among teacher and student should exist, to enable the latter to learn without patriarchal, oppressive feelings. Second, the student must be allowed to decide on his rate of learning (self-motivation). In addition, the teaching methods must be geared up to the student. This method is seldom practicable, however, due to the high costs.

- computer-guided instruction during usage: The user is instructed whenever it becomes necessary. He himself can request instruction support and the system can offer help when necessary (error occurred, unsuitable usage, etc.) This can be an effective method when adapted to the user. (See Chapter 3.1.3.)

- mix: Possibly, the best results will arise when combining several methods. For example, starting with personal instruction supported by manuals based on didactic methods; making available a system which allows "trial and error" strategy, supported by computer guidance and instruction whenever requested or required.

Once again, you may notice that design of user interfaces requires special knowledge and sympathetic understanding of human factors. No model, theory or system, however it may be constructed, can relieve you of the responsibility of user and application-correlated tuning of machine-user interfaces.

3.1.2. Work Environment and Social Impact

Although the topic of this chapter is far beyond our research area, there are two main arguments here. The first states that besides users/operators, the programmers and designers of interactive systems are part of the same working environment and social world, as they communicate with the computer. Why divorce the product from the world of product development? Let us explain this giving an example of everyday life.

Suppose that you are a restaurant owner and you have to decide on the meals to be cooked. Not taking into account the fact that you tend to choose your own favourite dishes, it is a hard job, if you only have statistical information about cost of food, number of nearby residents and so on. Your decision would be much easier and, what is more important, much more effective, when analysing the wishes of your intended guests, the social and political situation around you, etc. If in addition, you yourself are the chef, knowing the cost, the effect of dishes, then it is more probable that you would establish a good restaurant in terms of pleasing the guests, than you would without that know-ledge.

Coming back to the design of interactive systems, as in the example above, the inclusion of work environment and other factors should be established in interactive system design. A second argument for discussing this topic is that research efforts of an interdisciplinary nature have shown the positive influence of other disciplines, such as psychology, ergonomics or social science (with regard, for example, to the description of work environment). For a good overview, see /DAV83/; for description on work satisfaction and work/personal factors, see /HOL83/. The incorporation of these results can be forced by trade unions, legislation /KNA83/, or, even better, by understanding the necessity of supporting the end user /KER83/. Be conscious of the growing community of computer users, the increasing broadening of personal computers, etc. Systems of former years, being controlled by experts, change into widely spread and used systems; similar to cars or televison.

But what we require, is not so new as is explained in an example by Shneiderman /SHN83/. Life critical systems like air traffic control, medical intensive care, or manned spacecraft, tried in former years to analyse and include human factors as a necessary improvement of system reaction to human operation. We think normal people in work and situations which are not life critical, would also be likely cases. In actual research areas, it has been accepted that the inclusion of more than "computer science interfaces" will lead to more suitable products, although these new interfaces and objects of concern do not always coincide with the topic of this chapter. /FNC82/

It is important to be conscious of these facts, working environment and social embedding, in order to make better decisions in interface design. We cannot give exact rules or requirements other than this one.

3.1.3. Different Users and Evaluation

Quite early on in the development of user interfaces, the phase of different users or user classes was introduced. The growing variety of machines on the one hand and the extension of access to those machines to non-expert users, on the other hand, influenced the need for differentiation between human users. But this was no urgent strategy. Why not teach the users the same model of usage that the experts and developers gained for themselves? Similar to other technological developments and their usage, there was no need to have all the details on the product for operation. Dissimilar to other areas of development, the product was not the computer itself, but an application using the computer as a tool for manipulation and generation

(mainly of information and data). This was a new situation,
as the tool becomes more complex to handle than the task
itself.

In Chapter 3.1.1, we agreed on the need of a model for the
user. Now we have to differ, just to integrate the different
users. What about classification of users? For example,
DZIDA /DZI78/ investigated the user-perceived quality of
interactive systems and they found three dimensions in user
classification: regular versus casual, experienced versus
inexperienced and interactive versus batch users. On this
classification, first systems were installed, acting in different ways to different categories of users.

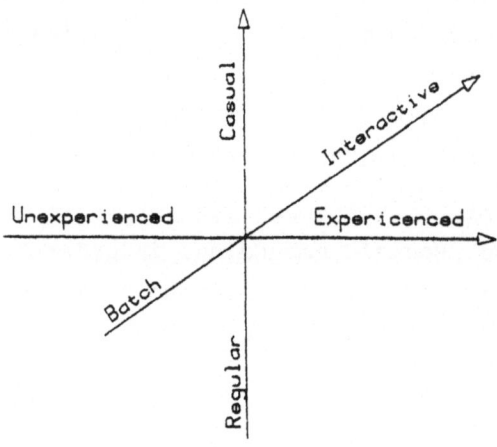

Figure 3.4: 3 Categories to Classify Users

For example, only a restricted set of commands for a text
editor was offered to the inexperienced and casual users,
while the experienced users were allowed to use the complete
set of functional possibilities.

But these categories soon showed to be insufficient in many
cases. There are some major reasons for this:

- the classification was postulated without regard to the
  influence of the actual application.

- the model of classification arose out of the mentality of
  computer designers, being restricted to their world of
  recognising interation.

- the assignment of an actual user to one of these categories was static and hard to reverse.

- the inclusion of temporary factors, such as physiological
and psychological health, grade of motivation, work environment, etc., on the actual behaviour of a user was not
regarded, although these factors seem to have a deep
influence on interaction with the computer /HOL83/.

Similar to /DZI78/ other categories have the same limitations. Another example given by Jim Foley /FOL81a/:

Intrinsic Personality Factors:

- secure/insecure
- bold/timid
- adaptable/rigid

Knowledge:

- Skill level
  - novice
  - intermediate
  - skilled

- Training
  - on the job
  - formally

- Intelligence
  - low
  - average
  - high

Work Environment
- stress level
  - low
  - high

- motivation level
  - low
  - high

Their existence is worth mentioning as they are one of the
first practicable elements in this area. For a system
designer, it is practicable to design systems for two or
four different classes of user, just as if there were two or
four different systems. This, of course, is a wrong way to
deal with different users.

We recommend the following guidelines:

1. There is nothing like "the" user or "the" classification of users of interactive computer systems. Computers must behave in a way which adapts to different users, requiring a special class of applications.

2. The assignment of one user to a special class of users must be variable, at best during normal interaction phases. This takes into account the learning ability and the situation-dependent productivity of the user. (Note: nevertheless, a uniform model of usage must be provided!)

3. Classification of users should not be done only by academic methods, but with consultation and incorporation of what the prospective user is hoping to achieve.

Trying to realise the above guidelines will cause much trouble. The main difficulty will be that at runtime, (the user operating on the system) a permanent assignment of the user to a fitting user class is necessary /HAN83a/. This leads us to the problem of evaluating user behaviour. Even in the simple user class model above, it is necessary to see if the chosen methods and techniques are legitimate, in order to achieve the required performance and acceptance. Up until now, there has been no proof that any activity in this area resulted in an expansion of performance or acceptability.

/HAN83a/ developed a monitor to evaluate user behaviour. Although the appropriate methods on evaluation are still missing, it was shown that the developed tool works on the basis of functional cooperation with the interactive application. This was the first time ever a specification language for describing user behaviour problems was developed, which involves computer experts, together with experts for behaviour and work environment. The complexity of this result showed that much effort must be put into investigating these problems, until suitable results will justify the enormous expense of user evaluation.

3.1.4. User Participation in System Design

As there is no "best way" to design a technical product, many circumstances may influence it to be less than "best". One of those circumstances is the fact that system designers tend to remain in their world of work. Each of them has its own experience and training in system design and it is the fate of man to use well known models and techniques quite more frequently than to explore new ideas and possibilities.

An example of these limitation has been discussed in Chapter 3.1.1. where the differences of "user" models have been explained. The system designer, developing and using his own product, is overcharged when thinking about a new user who knows nothing about the system with which he should operate /THI83, p.79/. Initial steps to integrate models of the user into system design models have failed, since they soon grew up to be very complex and difficult-to-handle models. Nevertheless there is a simple and successful way of improving the system design process, in order to relieve the usage of the system and to obtain better results in production:

ASK THE USER !

Not later than now, some people will cry and announce the impossibility of such participation. They are right and wrong at the same time. Let us focus on this problem.

At first we have to distinguish between several levels in the design process and several methods for users to partici-pate in the design process. Looking at the application design level it is, in most cases, not desirable and practicable to have user participation here. The goals of an application are not established by users (operator and not applicator), but by management, vendors, and applicators. For instance, what kind of modelling parts in a CAD-appli-cation in automobile design should be used? Of course, an engine, wheels, seats, and so on, but no swimming pool, TV, or garden fence. Although this would beautify work environment and job satisfaction (as some authors suppose), it would not be desirable and practicable in the near future. If we agree that in most cases the "what" in the design process should not be discussed with the users/operators (although some exceptions are presumable), what about the "how" in design process? This is also too weak a requirement, because only meaningful sequences (e.g. constructing an engine out of metal blocks or editing a letter) should be allowed in use. Operating on requirements and guidelines without involving an application is therefore very dangerous. Asking a user to decide on colour representation for a polyline in wireframe viewing of an aeroplane is harmless, whereas the same participation in editing a map, where a blue line represents a river, will change the context of application and must therefore be forbidden.

In any application there are some degrees of freedom, allowing the participation of users. To recognize these degrees of freedom is one of the main features of a good system design and we should try to make them fixable for the user, not for the designer.

Examples:

1. In every system, where parameters have to be varied, a default setting is used to avoid meaningless start and confusion. Some of these default parameters are set to initial values which the programmer or designer regards to be the best, if he himself had to use the system. As stated before, his use of the system may be quite different from that of a normal end-user of the system. Therefore the default setting of the intended user should be implemented or set and more than one person will be pleased with that initial behaviour of the system.

2. Think about left-handed persons. There are quite a lot! Leave the decision to them where, for example, the menu to pick should be placed on the screen - on the left-hand side, to use the lightpen with the left hand, or as normal right-hand side.

3. One of the commonly accepted requirements of display ergonomics is that the intensity of the display should be controllable by the user. But this is restricted to all objects on the display. Many modern displaying systems have the facilitiy to differ between several levels of intensity for different objects. So this gives the possibility of allowing a user to highlight those parts of a workstation surface which fit best to his individual kind of using an application.

On the other hand, there are different methods of participation. One is, to ask the user about special decisions, such as colour of lines, details of messages, etc. In most cases this procedure will not work, as it demands a local and temporal gathering. Only for special applications or a small distribution of systems is this possible. There are two other ways. The first method is to prepare a questionnaire, distribute it among intended users, and develop the system on the evaluation of that questionnaire. This would provide a better interface, especially if it were possible to switch between different user classes (see 3.1.3.). But this procedure has the disadvantage that users cannot control the result of their wishes, since only a one-time participation is realised. So we would investigate a questionnaire and feedback process, where users can investigate effort at time of design and at time of final refinement, regarding the change and limitation of degrees of freedom in that process. Examples 2 and 3 from above are of that kind.

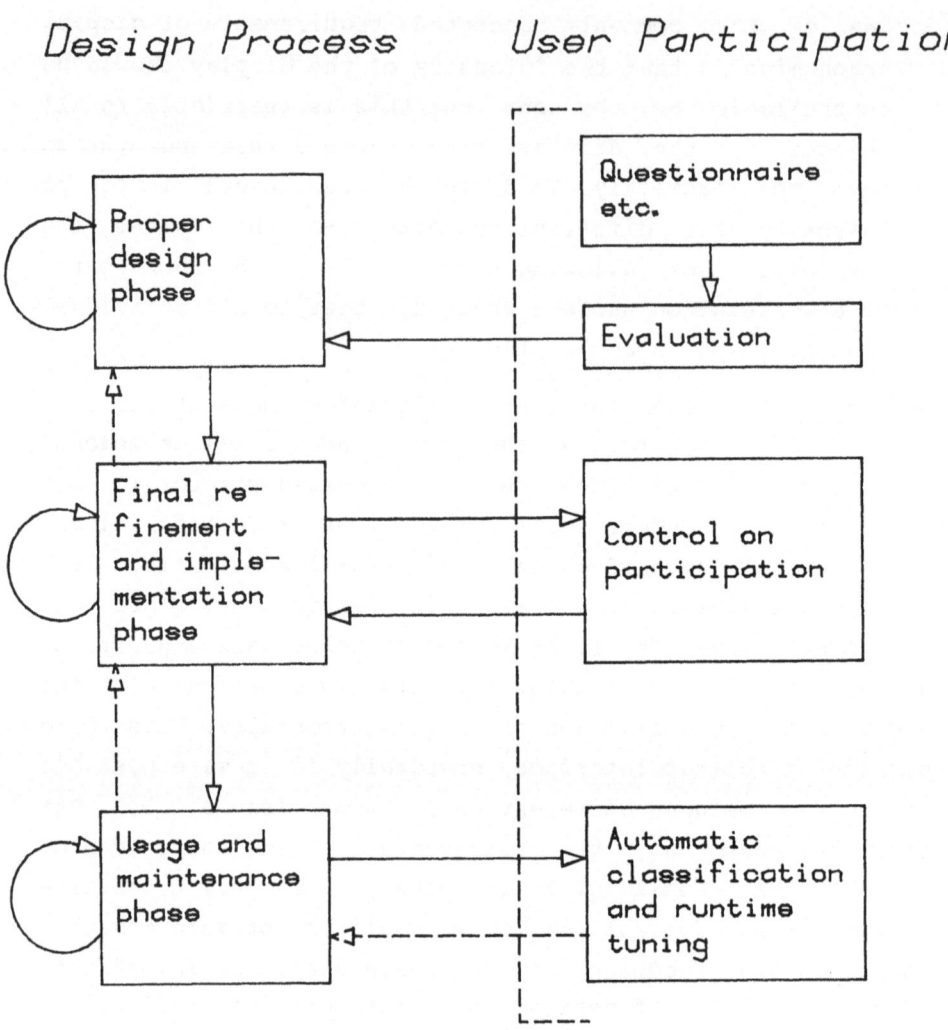

Figure 3.5: Design Process and User Participation

Nevertheless there are some chances and risks taken in participation. Involving users causes higher expense in the introductory and finishing phase, especially through the requirement of more workplaces and specialists in this area (e.g. /KNA83/, /SHN83/, /STE83/). Furtheron the "tuning" of the system causes more organisational and definitive decision. Of course, nobody is able to verify the positive influence on performance or acceptability. Even with complex evaluation procedures this will hardly be done. So primarily we have to believe in the following advantages:

- A deeper understanding, acceptance, and involvement of the persons concerned will arise.

- Resistance against new technology will decrease since more information and sufficient participation will cause users to judge on a more rational basis about installation and usage of the new system.

- Fault rates will decrease as the machine adapts to man and not vice versa.

- Every involved person will feel more a master of the machine with the machine serving his master. (Psychological and social problems in working environment should not be neglected as several research reports have shown /MAR83/. A new orientation in regarding the roles of man and machines in the social world will lead to more participation).

3.2. Practical Aspects

In Chapter 3.1, we discussed theoretical aspects of man-machine/user interfaces. It was necessary to go into detail, because many designers have not recognised the pressure of requirements resulting from the involvement of the human being. We know that no way of acting immediately came to light. The following chapters will fill in collected requirements.

As stated before, we do not enter into a theory or method, but just set out guidelines and observations which give the designer the freedom to develop his own method of dealing with different users and applications. Only the appearance to the user decides on the quality of the involved methods and efforts.

Chapter 3.2.1. introduces some development principles with comments and illustrated examples. The following chapter introduces results of several projects which consider human factors. Most of them are concerned with "hard" ergonomics like brightness, resolution, etc. But there are also many interesting facts about "soft" ergonomics (like information density, contour lines, colour-coding, etc.) which will be presented. We avail ourselves of a study, previously published in /DAV83/. Chapter 3.2.3 explains the usage of menus in different ways. Here, a special technical resource is examined, due to the user requirements.

3.2.1. Some Development Principles

Within this chapter, we want to follow a study gained by DZIDA et. al. /DZI78/. From a questionnaire of about six hundred users of computer systems in West Germany, factors of user-perceived quality were filtered by statistical analysis. Those notions are the basis for the German Institute of Standardisation (DIN) to work on a proposal for the modelling of dialogues (DIN 66234 part/Teil8) /DIN83/. This proposal is expected to be published in 1984/85. We will illustrate the principles with some examples given there.

The following are the principles:

- problem adequate usability
- self-descriptiveness
- user control
- ease of learning
- correspondence with user expectations
- fault tolerance

Before investigating each single principle, here are some guidelines. During this chapter, we will not alter the principles for different users. The content of Chapter 3.1.3 has, therefore, to be added. Additionally, all principles of Chapter 3.1 must be considered. Furthermore, the above principles are not contrary and may not be balanced against others.

Example: A dialogue, not allowing user control or being self-descriptive, can, nevertheless, be depended upon.

Problem Adequate Usability

A dialogue can be called problem adequate in usage, when the primary task of the user is supported by the system, without burdening it with additional work for the settlement of the task.

Preparing tasks resulting from the technical nature of the tool, should be performed by the system independently, unless they belong to the primary task of the user.

Example: The cursor on a display surface should be suitably positioned with regard to the progress of the task.

Dialogue should be mapped to application or usage area. Complexity of task content, as well as style and scale of information, have to be considered.

Example: Regard the filling in of forms. A form is divided
into several subforms, each of them occupying a
complete display surface. Parts of the task which
belong together are arranged on a subform. The user
can concentrate on those parts. He is also able to
request an overview of the complete subforms, in
order to be able to switch flexibly among them.

The way of input should correlate the information the
user has to perform.

Example: The input of data has not to be generated by menu,
but through input of an input area by alphanumeric
keystroke.

Existing default values in an application should be used to
disentangle the user from input, if exception is required,
the default values should be changeable.

Example: When modelling a crankshaft, initially the sizes
should be standardised. If correlation is obtain-
able, the standard sizes should fit to the previously modelled parts (e.g. a motor bearing).

Dialogue resources should be adaptable to periodical tasks
of the user.

Example: Input of data into a mask should be ordered
according to probability of appearance and normal
sequence of task settlement (e.g. investing a
complete address).

At the end of each description of a principle, we will cite
the requirements loaded in /DZI78/, ordered from most
relevant to less relevant items:

Factor 1: Problem Adequate Usability

  - have a data mangement system that obviates, as far as
    possible, the need for the user to perform clerical and
    housekeeping activities
  - manage formatting, addressing, and memory organisation
    without bothering the user
  - determine system decisions without consulting the user
  - accept free formatted command input

- have a command language easy to understand and easy to apply
- be tolerant towards erroneous user input
- have syntactically homogeneous command language
- have a command language easy to remember
- make repetitive or routine input unnecessary

Self-Descriptiveness

A dialogue is called self-descriptive when purpose and method of usage can be explained during dialogue at the request of the user. This is necessary if the information displayed is not immediately understandable.

On request, the capacity of the tool and the assumption of usage is explained to the user.

Example: Before starting an edit, the user is provided with information on how to create a file and how to access it. The necessary preparatory actions of user and machine are explained.

Situation and context-correlated descriptions should be available.

Example: The prompting of an input confuses the user. On typing a question mark, the format and interpretation of that input is explained.

The type and size of the explanation should be geared to the user, defined by the actual application and userclass.

Example: For casual users in a certain application (e.g. automatic timetable inquiry for arrivals and departures of aeroplanes) every input is explained with a line of comment.

Example: The technical terms, used for dialogue, belong to the application-defined working area. Explanations for each term can be requested by typing the keyword.

Explanations can be offered in different ways. Sometimes, a graphical representation of a tree structure for menu driven dialogue is sufficient; sometimes reference to a manual is necessary. In any case, the selected style of explanation must fit the situation and task, as well as userclass and application aspects. Think for a moment, of your experience on various systems. What kind of explanation and description do you know? What about self-descriptiveness? If, in any situation a system was not self-descriptive, was help available on the system? Was it easy to advance to that information?

Factor 2: Self-Descriptiveness

- explain system requests to the user if and when necessary
- supply explanations in different detail and different format upon user request
- supply help features pertinent to any dialogue situation
- enable transparency of dialogue organisation and dialogue sequence at any time
- explain each command and subcommand upon user request
- give clearly arranged presentation of system functions
- supply interactive programming aids which provide guidance for structured programming
- give decision aids if tasks cannot be executed as desired
- provide global information about the funtional range of the system
- make user thoroughly acquainted with system usage without human assistance
- by prompting, provide user guidance for the dialogue
- supply information about the current system status if desired

User Control

A dialogue is called user controllable if the user is able to control dialogue.

The user should be allowed to manipulate the process of dialogue. A task should be suspendable. After consulting provisional results, the user should be able to decide on termination or continuation. Until a task has been started, the revocation should be possible.

Example: The user can suspend the actual task, initiate a background task (e.g. print of a file) and then continue with the primary task.

Speed of dialogue should be able to be adapted to and by the user himself; no working cycle, no clearing of surface during thinking, no additional delay time for paging in files.

Example: The user should be allowed to continue typing his input, neglecting echoes of previous input.

Choosing a special, user-defineable way through dialogue should be possible, being restricted only by means of the application. A casual and inexperienced user should be able to advance in simple dialogue steps, while more experienced and/or regular users will be guided to combine simple steps to more complex ones.

Looking back to former steps in dialogue should also be possible. On finding himself at a dead end, the user should be allowed to return to an at best self-defineable, initial position. A re-entry point should be defineable in case of task suspension, to avoid initial task preparations. After system breakdown, a re-entry point should automatically be provided before the last dialogue step.

The last input or dialogue step should be reversable. If this is not possible, displayed input which cannot be changed, must be characterised by special features (colour, type of font, highlighting, etc.) It is desirable to be able to reverse sequences of dialogue steps. For special decisions, a user release is necessary (of course, there are other possibilities than: "Do you really want to ...?")

Primary data should be accessible in the case of comparison with previous actions.

Example: A detail on constructing the shape of a ship is changed. The difference between the old position and the actual new one is colour-coded.

Factor 3: User Control

- admit interuptions of a task to start or resume another task
- admit process cancelling without detrimental side effects
- allow abortion of particular dialogue steps or processes
- have a syntactically homogeneous command language
- be permanently available
- immediately detect syntax errors
- permit clustering of commands with a new name
- by prompting, provide user guidance for the dialgue
- allow user to make background processes visible
- supply information about the current system status if desired
- have a easily understandable command language which is easy to apply
- give decision aids if tasks cannot be executed as desired

Ease of Learning

A dialogue is easy to learn if the user is supported so he can gain knowledge about purpose and manner of application.

Inexperienced or casual users should gain knowledge about use of the tool being used during dialogue performance, to allow stepwise learning.

Technical terms used during dialogue should be adaptable to the usual knowledge of the user.

Example: During the instruction phase, the character "@" is defined as "end of input"; this is much better than "carriage return", saving the user from learning technical terms of computer science.

Small examples are helpful for beginners and casual users. Sometimes, a pointer to an instruction manual or online manual is necessary. Experienced or regular users need only be supported by help in recognising the pattern.

Of course, delivered information, explanations and learning facilities must agree with the dialogue behaviour of the system. (Remember the problem of updating documentation!). Explanations should be given to support users using their own knowledge to settle the task by obtaining useful ideas of system relations.

These explanations should also be so designed that as time passes by, the amount of self-description in the system should decrease.

Factor 4: Ease of Learning

- make user manuals superfluous
- facilitate the learning of system use without consulting manuals
- be usable without special data-processing knowledge
- largely offer on-line forms for user input
- be able to present user manuals in whole or in parts via display station

- provide global information about the functionality of the system
- make the least assumptions about user's prior knowledge on system structures and functions
- support user input by menu technique
- give error messages with correction hints
- explain each command and subcommand upon user request
- enable the learning of system use without referring to stored comprehensive texts

Reliability

A dialogue is called reliable if its behaviour corresponds to user expectations, based on his knowledge of former task settlement and actual use of the system.

Example: For all tasks on a system, the user can use the same language for communication because of homogenous syntax in all areas.

Shifting dialogue behaviour causes the user to adapt a changing performance in his work, leading to unnecessary mental effort.

Progress in the length of dialogue steps and their representation of information should appear similar in similar situations, taking into account user expectations.

Example: From time to time, system state messages are displayed. They always appear in the same area on the display surface.

Feedback of the system should lead to expectations focussing on tasks to be done in the future. The effect of each single dialogue step should be recognizable, but should not be a burden.

Example: The user dealt with a booking. Acceptance of the complete task by the system depends on the correct booking date. A cursor is positioned on the proper input line, which is called the "booking date". The default is the actual date of the day. Not changing the actual date will cause the acceptance of the task. The possibility of changing the booking date is given to the user by a message.

The relevant changes in the system state, necessary for changing the dialogue, have to be given to the user.

Example: In the interactive design of a house, the user changes the shape of a wall. By onscreen visual means, he can control changes to other walls and/or parts.

The input of characters should be echoed at once in order to relieve perception from deferred feedback. Execution time will lead to a performance model for the user. If, for some reason, execution time should increase, (e.g. due to increasing system load) the user should be informed; (e.g. "Because of growing system load, your task will last a little while longer.")

Feedback of the system announcing the state of processing is desirable, because the user is allowed to concentrate on other tasks apart from the display surface, e.g. sorting his documents or concept papers. Interrupting dialogue should force a state where a new dialogue step can be initiated and, in the case of system breakdown, information about kind, size and duration of breakdown can be delivered to the user.

Factor 5: Correspondence with User Expectations

- behave similarly in similar situations
- request analogous user actions to similar tasks to be performed
- offer minimum astonishment behaviour towards the user
- let user recognize effects of his input
- be tolerant towards erroneous user input
- enable transparency of a dialogue organisation and dialogue course at any time
- provide same response times to equal activities

Fault Tolerance

Fault tolerance is a quality of a system to process user's input in such a way that although wrong input may have gone into the system, the required result of the task can still be achieved and/or the user is provided with comprehensible information about the origin of the mistake, in order to initiate correction.

No input or use of devices may lead to an undefined system state or a breakdown. It may be advisable to correct unambiguous errors at once. The user should, in this case, be provided with acceptable information about correction. (See Learning, Chapter 3.1.1.) If an error can be corrected in many ways, the alternatives should be prompted to the user.

Example: A user chooses the name of a producer of small cars; he requires a car with an engine-size of about 120kW. The system announces the inconsistency of the input and asks the user to check both inputs. No system guided correction mode can be found here.

All system detectable errors should be announced (e.g. by marking the origin of the error).

Example: An input to a data area has caused an error, because the data was outside the application required boundaries. A message is displayed to the user and the cursor is positioned at the beginning of that area to prompt for correction.

Often, additional information ought to be displayed, (e.g. "This input is not interpretable; please choose the following format: ..." instead of the single format). All error messages output should be related to temporary requirements of the application. The attention of the user to his task may not be disturbed, but afterwards, the error information should be easily recognizable. The amount of attention provocation and the chosen coding, should be adequate for the application. (See Chapter 3.2.2.)

Error messages have to be comprehensible, relevant and constructive. They should have a uniform structure and uniform positioning. No value judgement may be present. (E.g. fatal error, senseless input, etc.) Long and short forms should be selectable. In the case of long forms, a pointer to a manual can be provided instead.

Factor 6: Fault Tolerance

- insist only on partical retyping if previous input was erroneous
- tolerate typical typing errors
- give error messages with correction hints
- enable user to submit concatenated commands as input
- accept reduced input when actions are to be repeated
- give error messages in full text
- give decision aids if tasks cannot be executed as desired
- support user to find his way

3.2.2. Studies on Human Factors

We want to move on to a different type of consideration when dealing with user interfaces. Although the human factor research is far behind the present advances being made in computer graphics technology and applications, some activities have been carried out.

For hardware designers especially, a well-established research area is noticeable /CAK80/. On dialogue types and display formatting, some results can also be observed. Guidelines become sparse (and in some cases, non-existent) in the cognitive areas of man-computer interfaces /DAV83/.

Consider a workstation with a colour raster display, a keyboard, a black-and-white alphanumeric display and a graphics tablet. This is a normal workstation for CAD applications. However, discussion about it can be easily applied to other configurations.

/DAV83/ gives a long list of guidelines and observations, collected from literature on human factors. With this list of special results, we want to give some examples of how to transfer them to design of user interfaces. We should also like to stimulate the reader into categorising for himself, the topics to be mentioned (hardware resources, cognitive factors, interface design). We shall omit citing the proper literature; for details see DAVIS's report /DAV83/.

Graphics Display

1. Resolution:

The minimum resolution of raster displays should be 70 dots/in or 28 dots/cm. As a result, a 1024 x 1024 raster display should have a maximum surface area of 36.6 cm x 36.6 cm.

Regardless of whether the display is raster-scanned or directly addressed, an illusion of a continuous image should be maintained. The resolution of individual scan lines seen by the observer is bothersome and can lead to small-area flicker which, in turn, results in disturbing and fatiguing effort with prolonged viewing. If, in addition, interlacing is carried out, a single line should have a width of two or more dots to avoid flickering.

2. Brightness:

The optimum brightness level depends on ambient light levels. For the more complex displays, this level falls into the range of 70-240 cd/m^2, assuming sufficient contrast is obtained. Optimal luminance is about 50 mL. However, screen luminance above 25 mL is probably adequate, again assuming adequate contrast. As surrounding light may change (influence of daylight), brightness should be controlled by the users; e.g. by the adjustable control knob on the lower right-hand front panel of a CRT.

3. Contrast:

Optimal contrast is 94%, minimum recommended contrast is 88%. At lower contrast levels, the segments begin to blur, necessitating continuous action of the human eye lens as it attempts to focus the retina on the image. This, of course, leads to eyestrain, headache and fatigue. Where contrast is lower than the minimum recommended level, the discrepancy can be reconciled either by increasing the symbol luminance on the CRT, or by decreasing the ambient luminence.

As a matter of fact, for normal users, it is impossible to decide on correct brightness/contrast levels. Additionally, dependency on the colours used and the amount of information on display, hinders correct adaptation. A standard testing picture at the beginning of a session would probably lead to correct adjustment.

As with brightness, contrast should also be adjustable by a control knob. Automatic contrast control using a dimmer switch control and/or station lighting and shading is required. If no adjustment is available to the user, the dialogue leading application has to be especially sensitive to the contrast and brightness of its displayed pictures; i.e. no great differences should occur.

4. Flicker Rate:

Wherever possible, flicker rate should be kept to an imperceptible level, as flickering is the principle cause of eyestrain and headaches to CRT operators. Using an inter-laced raster display, for example, avoid lines being displayed by one scan line. (See 1. Resolution.)

5. Colour:

Colour allows the inclusion of much more data in a single image, without confusion. High-quality raster displays offer superior quality images with full colour rendering capability. With low-priced systems, sometimes only 16, 24 or 256 colours are available. When setting colour tables, consideration has to be given to correlations and the side effects of colouring. (E.g. when 16 colours are available, they should not be used to realize only pastel colours. For special problems with colour coding, see /STR82/.)

6. Information Density:

As the number of displayed items increases, so does the time required by the user to detect and extract information that has changed. Therefore:

- only information which is essential to the user's needs should be displayed
- interim data should be removed from the screen once it is no longer needed
- users should have the option of eliminating irrelevant items from the displays and be able to reverse these decisions.

Techniques supporting these requirements are multi-viewport layout, where the user chooses for himself the viewport with the relevant information. Interim data should not disappear at one time, because a large amount of vanishing information can cause confusion for users. Instead, perception of the information should be reduced before deletion.

The amounts of visual and auditory stimuli presented to the user should be kept within his processing/storage threshold. Visual image storage capacity is approximately 17 letters; auditory capacity is about 5 letters. Visual image decay time (the time after which the probability of retrieval is less than 50%) begins at approximately 200 ms from perception; auditory image decay begins at approximately 1500 ms.

For example, when announcing an error, it is much more relevant to increase perceptibility of the event than to provide a lot of information which is less perceptible.

7. Orientation to User:

CRT displays should be placed between 35 and 88 cm above the seating surface. The optimal viewing distance is 46 cm. If this is not possible, distances less than 41 cm or greater than 71 cm should be avoided. The optimal horizontal angle of viewing is 90 degrees straight. In no instance should the user have to view the display from an angle smaller than 30 degrees. The greatest detail will be seen in the small area straight ahead of the eyes. The preferred visual area of the display panel centres around the normal line of vision of the user, which is approximately 15 degrees below the horizontal. All primary, secondary and auxiliary displays should be placed within the parameters illustrated in Fig. 3.6 so as to minimize potentially fatiguing eyes and head movements.

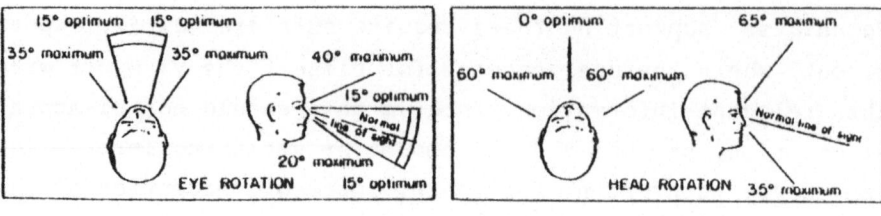

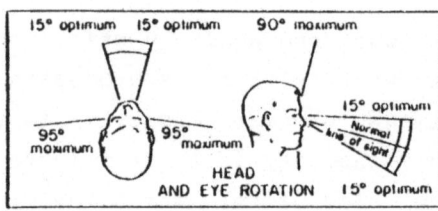

FIG. 1. Vertical and horizontal visual field (from MIL STD 1472B, 1974).

Figure 3.6: Vertical and Horizontal Visual Field

Once again, the multi viewport technique with user choose-
able priority of information, will provide best results on
placing information on displays. All other guidelines for
placing the user on workstations have to be considered in
addition. (/CAK80/)

8. Symbology:

Meaningful codes, which are consistent across all display
configurations, should be used to discriminate between
different classes of items presented simultaneously on the
screen. Users must be able to decode and interpret symbols
quickly without referring to comparison standards. Symbols
should conform to well-established habits or population
stereotypes. (A great help is to use graphical representation of symbols, e.g. special symbols for a chess game. In
future computer graphics will provide suitable methods for
doing this). See table for more information:

Comparison of coding types *(from Mallory et al., 1980)*

Code	Number of steps in code	Evaluation	
Alphanumerics	Unlimited	Excellent	High information-handling rate. Unlimited number of coding steps
Geometrics	20+	Excellent	Certain shapes easily recognized. Many coding steps
Color	4	Excellent	Difficulty in techniques of reproducing for CRT. Objects easily and quickly identified
Blink	2	Poor	Distracting and fatiguing. Interacts poorly with other codes. Best for attention getting. Few steps in code
Brightness	2	Poor	Limited number of steps. Fatiguing, detrimental to decoding performance
Line lengths	4	Fair	Limited number of steps. Clutters displays
Angular orientation	12	Fair	Ninety-five per cent of estimates correct within 15%
Inclination	24+	Fair	Many coding steps, especially with combinations
Visual number (dots)	6	Fair	Few steps
Combinations	Unlimited	Good	Avoid overloading symbols with too much information. Complex combination can degrade decoding speed and accuracy

Figure 3.7: Comparison of Coding Types

Appropriate coding of map symbols should be used, (i.e. blue colour for rivers and special symbols for landshapes would be unsuitable for ship designers).

Shape Coding should be used for search and identification tasks. A maximum of fifteen different shape codes should be used. Shapes should be used which are compatible to and associated with the coded objects. Where this is not possible, or where such shapes are easily confused with one another, symbols should be designed which are highly discrminatable. Symmetrical figures are more easily recognizable than asymmetrical ones. Symbols should be large enough to be clearly legible, but small enough to avoid clutter. In general, the size should be at least 20' of arc at the normal viewing distance. (E.g. with a viewing distance of 46 cm, the minimum size has to be 0.27 cm).

Colour should be used conservatively to avoid a cluttered appearance. The maximum number of colours that should be used is 11. When characters are formed by a combination of primary colours, colour registration problems occur, particularly near the corners and edges of the display. Also, characters which are formed by a combination of primary colours may appear as separate characters in each of the component primary colours. These registration problems do not apply to characters which are formed by a single primary colour. The meanings of the colours should be considered, as the colour itself may convey information. E.g. red means danger, yellow caution and green no danger. Colour coding is not valuable in a target search task. There seems to be a search speed superiority for various colours. The search speed order, from best to worst, is: red, blue, yellow, green, black and white. This persists across all background colours.

Colour identification decreases with the decrement of illu-minations. However, some colours appear to be more resistant to performance decrement than others. Red is superior for distance viewing, but will shift markedly in brightness with low illumination. Yellow, on the other hand, has been shown to be the most accurately identified. Furthermore, while users generally seem to prefer blue-green colours, these have produced the greatest identification variability. While they are useful for search and locate tasks, colour codes do not appear to be suited to situtations that demand rapid and precise identification. Approximately eight percent of males are colour blind, or have a colour weakness. Red is the colour the most likely to cause problems in this respect. Users should, therefore, be tested for colour blindness. Background features should have different colours from objects placed on top of them (e.g. no use of blue colour to display the name of a blue river which is to actually appear on the river).

Alphanumeric Coding should be used when absolute identifi-cation is essential. However, problems with alphanumeric coding include confusion with similar symbols, space con-straints and the time which is required to learn the meanings of the symbols. Numerical coding seems to invoke the fastest and most accurate performance in reaction time tasks. Alphanumeric coding should be avoided if it reduces legibility, is not distinct, increases transmission time, or calls attention to the display in a high-risk combat situation.

Studies of the accuracy of estimating <u>direction of movement</u> by line orientation indicate that 50 per cent of the direction estimates will have an error margin of less than 6 per cent and 95 per cent of the estimates by less than 15 per cent. These values are valid for lines as short as 0.25 cm. If the shape of a symbol suggests a direction of movement (e.g. an arrow), it should be oriented according to its real direction of movement.

The following methods of <u>highlighting</u> seem acceptable:

- contrast enhancement (dual level illumination)
- blinking (rate between two and three Hz with a minimum flash duration of 50 ms)
- graphics (boxes, asterisks, underlining)

Dynamic intensification is an effective form of highlighting, which involves the lighting of an individual item as it is being selected by the user. This provides timely, accurate feedback to the user at selection time. When it becomes necessary to draw the user's attention to a specific point on a filled screen, a moving or flashing point or cursor seems to be the most appropriate means, since the perception of movement is not specific to the central retina area. Highlighting should be limited to only one or two items in a display unit at a given point in time, as a field of flickering lights is quite irritating to the eye. Rather than blinking a displayed message to attract a user's attention, it seems preferable to present the message in a steady form and to indicate its importance by juxtaposing a separate blinking symbol. The user should be able to turn off any blinking.

Menu Selection Dialogues

Criteria for good design found in this area shall be discussed in more detail in Chapter 3.2.3.

Graphics Tablet

Direct graphical input devices enhance productivity by reducing the number of translations the user must perform. Keyboards usually prove less optimal for pick and locate operations from the human point of view. Graphics tablets may involve a performance decrement due to low stimulus response compatibility when the drawing surface is separated from the display surface. The major disadvantage of the graphics tablet is its remoteness from the display and the potential coordination problem due to displacement of visual feedback of motor activity.

Response time of the system to user input is quite critical to performance. The larger the deviation between input and response, the worse the uncertain effect on the user, who will begin to feel that the system has failed, or that his input was incorrect. In such cases, some kind of feedback, implying that the request is being processed, would improve the acceptability of the system. This may, for instance, be the lighting of the request button.

The maximum acceptable response time from input of point to display of point/line, or from selection of a visual field to visual verification, is 0.2 sec. From a command to a more complicated response (e.g. graphic display, message), the maximum response time is between 2 and 5 seconds. The more complicated the response which is perceived by the user, the longer he is likely to be willing to wait for feedback. When a displayed message or data is selected as an option, or input to the system, the subject item should be highlighted to confirm acceptance by the system. When the user must stand by, periodic feedback should be provided to indicate normal operation. Completion of an operation should be announced to the user. If input data is rejected, feedback as to the nature of the problem and the required corrective action should be provided.

In order to minimise the eye-hand co-ordination demands of
tracing with the pen on the tablet, the tablet could be
slanted at an angle (similar to a drafting table), so that
the user can see his hand at the lower portion of his visual
field. This aids in eye-hand co-ordination for the inexperienced user and can thereby relieve frustration and error.
Ideally, the slanting mechanism should be adjustable to
accommodate the user's particular anthropomorphic requirements.

Illumination of "activated" functions on the menu display is
a clear, easily understandable feedback mechanism when the
user returns to that display. If at all possible, the same
type of highlighting should appear on the tablet menu as
well.

Whenever possible, feedback should come from the tablet
where the user's attention is focused in the form of a
"click" or button backlighting.

In instances where the user either (1) inputs incorrect
data, or (2) requests an operation exceeding the machine's
capability, an error message should be generated and displayed, indicating the nature of the error.

The problem with graphics tablets is that only a little help
to improve performance and acceptability can be given by
software support. Primarily, a good hardware selection has
to be made, considering good feedback mechanisms (e.g.
"click" facility, highlighting buttons).

As the same problems arise with alphanumeric keyboards, we
will leave them out of our consideration. For some "hardware" ergonomics, see /DAV83/.

Alphanumeric Support Display

The same general characteristics as for graphics displays
have to be given here. Additionally, some "hardware" guidelines have to be considered when buying hardware equipment.

1. Symbol Characteristics

Text should be displayed in upper and lower case, rather than all in upper case.

The height-to-width ratio should be between 7:5 and 3:2. Stroke width should be in the range of 1:6 and 1:10 character height. Character separation should be between 25% and 63% of symbol height. Of the available methods of symbol generation, the 7 x 9 font is superior in legibility to both the 5 x 7 and stroke fonts. Legibility is further enhanced by the use of clear circular (vs elongated) dots and upright (vs slanted) strokes.

Spectral sensitivity is greatest in the yellow-green portion of the spectrum, since overall contrast is of greater importance than colour contrast; yellow characters on a green background are usually recommended. At the very least, the display should have bright (yellow, white) characters on a dark (green, grey) background.

2. Statistical Information Presentation

When five or more digits and/or alphanumerics are displayed and no familiar (i.e. population stereotyped) organisation exists, characters should be grouped in blocks of three or four characters each. Each group should be separated by at least one blank character. Lists containing decimals should use decimal alignment.

Example:	*Improved Example:*
165376,58 DM	165.376,58 DM
BLZ 50060060	BLZ 500 600 60
512.60	512.60
1.80	1.80
3,578.57	3,578.57
.78	0.78

Figure 3.8: Grouping of Data

Identical data should be displayed in a consistent, standardised manner, irrespective of their module of origin.
Data should be arranged in logical groups: sequentially,
functionally, or by importance. Contractions, hyphenations
and abbreviations should be avoided as they demand an
additional interpretation process.

Information contained in a message should be factual,
necessary, complete and readily usable. Reference to external documentation should be avoided. Critical information
should be presented at the beginning of a message.

The output speed of the terminal should be approximately the
average reading speed of the expected operator population.
Capability for adjusting output speed should be provided.
A re-run, scroll-back or halt capability should be incorporated to enable the operator to review missed information.
Blinking, contrast reverse, brightness level variation, or
the like should be used to highlight important messages or
statistics.

3. Tabular Information Presentation

When presented in tabular form, data should be aligned
vertically and left-justified; indentation should be used
for subclassification. When columns are not separated by
vertical lines, they should be separated by at least 0.166
inch (0.04 cm). When tables are long, numbers should be
separated into groups by providing a space between groups of
five.

When tables require more space than can reasonably fit on
the display screen, the operator should be able to scroll
the table upward, with the column headings remaining at the
top of the display screen. A capability should exist, in
this case, for both forward and backward scrolling.

4. Graphic Information Presentation

If the __shape__ of the function is important in making decisions, a graph should be used rather than a table.

Graphic displays that depict trends are read better if they are formed with lines rather than bars.

5. Split Screen Presentation

Screen presentation should be made apparent to the operator through the use of lines or some other form of visible demarcation. The physical location of specific data groups on the screen should be consistent throughout the operation of the system, irrespective of module in use. Important or infrequent messages should be placed in the central field of vision.

Critical messages requiring operator response should be highlighted and, when practicable, placed in the centre of the screen. Instructions should stand out. For example, they could be preceded by a row of asterisks. Commands should appear in the same area of the screen at all times. Alert messages should appear in the centre of the screen. In order to distinguish among types of information being presented, the screen could be split into sectors of different contrasts (e.g. the top third, black on white; middle third, white on black; lower third, black on white). It would be most beneficial to use the "different" contrast for the segment containing the most important data.

3.2.3. Menus - Limitation in Decision

Discussing the usage of menus is necessary because of great differences in their understanding. We would like to explain some features and details on the construction and use of menus.

Menus are tools for helping, sometimes being the main applications (e.g. information inquiry systems). With menus, the alternatives are given to the user with which he can operate. Menus explain the functionality of a system. The possibilities of the system are prompted at every moment. Menus are used to sequence programs and to select data. They are also one kind of communication between user and machine.

From a user's point of view, menus have several advantages. They help to memorize possible actions in processing. Not all names of commands have to be remembered at one time and the correct spelling is displayed when alphanumeric input is required. In addition, their position on screen and the constant sequence of alternatives, provide help when learning to use them. With menus, the assignment of names to functions is possible so that input (selection) can be associated with one alphanumeric character or function key ("soft keys"). Sometimes, menus can be pointed to. In this case, direct functional and local association is possible. Disadvantages arise when displayed menu information has to be typed in, resulting in possible typing errors.

Although the user is restricted in his decision when using menus, some support of input is nearly always guaranteed.

"Menu selection provides a very material dialogue if response-time criteria are satisfied and a "point-in" selection device is used. The principle advantage of a menu selection dialogue is that it requires little training, hence it is quite appropriate for use with inexperienced users. A well-defined menu of opportunities minimizes user confusion." /DAV83/

Besides support when inputting, the moment that the menu appears is a main factor in menu design. We have to differenciate: menus as echoes on a help request, menus as reactions either to user or system errors (correlation to help support is given in most cases), menus as reaction on user request (e.g. hierarchical design of menus), or menus whose appearance is system directed (e.g. WORDSTAR, SMALL-TALK). In the first example, the menu is the main application and the object of main interest, while in the last example, the menu is always present and is only helpful for memorizing and locating information to be selected. Location and appearance of menus must, therefore, be adapted to their special usage. Here are some observations:

"The main menu should be readily available at all times. The displayed menu should include only the appropriate options for that particular step. Whenever possible, the number of alternatives should be limited to 5-9 items." /DAV83/

When menus are required, several alternatives are possible for implementation. A teletype-oriented input and output of menus and selection on them is possible. However, this provides bad performance because no support can be maintained for location and the possibility of overwriting incorrect input. Sometimes, the menu itself is an alternative content on the screen to the application usage of the screen. But here, a sufficiently fast switch between the uses of both screens is required. Menus are offered through function keys, with static or dynamic assignment. The problem with dynamic load of function keys is to provide helps for learning and memorizing. Menus may be part of the screen ("splitscreen-technique"), giving content to the application, but reducing availability of the display surface. The best way of displaying menus is through the use of a multi-viewport system, where special menu areas can appear and disappear in different locations on the screen.

Guidelines and observations due to the offering and representation of menus:

"Formats should be so organised as to minimize the positioning movements of the cursor. Wherever possible, buttons should be arranged in order of frequently occurring sequences. The list of options should be organised according to the probability of selection for each item, with high probability items being presented first. Lists of equally-probable options should be listed in alphabetical or numerical order. Related options should be grouped from general to specific. If selection items are grouped, each group should be labelled.

When the number of selections can fit on one page in no more than two columns, a simple menu should be used. If the selection options exceed two columns, hierarchical menus should be used. Menu items should not be worded to imply a yes-no answer. Items should be phrased so that either alternative requires a possible choice." /DAV83/

3.3. Problems Arising

3.3.1. Adaptation to Accessible Resources

Provided with all the above information, nobody would be able to implement a real system. Too many details would be stored in the user's brain; there would be too many complicated decisions to make. At the beginning of this section, we mentioned that discussion on human factors would lead to confusion through lack of a uniform, implementable theory or model. We also tried to explain that arousing the awareness of all the people involved in these problems would lead to better results. How can we advance in practice?

We would like to suggest a strategy for human factor-guided design. Of course, our proposal is only one of many other possible strategies, since any strategy must be user and application dependent.

Consider on the one hand, the content of chapter 3.2.2. Within that chapter, boundaries, minimum or/and maximum values, etc. were given. They all refer to optimal tuning on each factor, not taking into account correlative relationship among other factors. Given firm hardware, software support and an amount of time and budget resources, these optional tuned factors have to be checked against the available ones. This can be regarded as a top-down process, where information and - what may be easier to comprehend - the possibility of a good, user-adapted interface decreases with every new restriction or non-performance.

On the other hand, chapter 3.2.1 gives guidelines to enable the achievement of a good interface, by means of investigation of special development principles. This can be regarded as a bottom-up process. As with every new fulfilled principle, the probability of a good interface increases.

Now these two processes meet and many conflicts arise. E.g., a non-available colour representation of application data hinders ease of learning and self-descriptiveness if no adequate simulation is possible. The prospective application, together with the desired model of learning and practice for the user, requires a multi-viewport technique which is not possible with the given hardware and software resources. For conflict solving, the following strategy is possible:

A. See if the conflict can be released by a change of primary resources (hardware equipment, software products, etc.) or a change is possible of application development principles (e.g. a more complex user's model, another type of problem solving for application problems, other dialogue leading methods, etc.). If so, check again. Otherwise:

B. See if simulation is possible. Decisions can be very crucial because simulation costs time and resources, and often has side-effects on development principles (e.g. simulation of sample input in GKS is time consuming and changes model of input tool usage; see example discussed further on). Every simulation makes the user interface worse, but this is inevitable. In this case, the designer must document the influence on performance and accepta- bility, in order to locate failures in the whole system.

If simulation is impossible, either because the user cannot be expected to work with that simulation, or because the realisation is impossible due to missing resources, the design process must be terminated and a new one begun.

Remember that every compromise is a possible contributory factor which can lead to bad performance or lack of acceptability. We will confirm this with a detailed example:

A graphics editor (GEDIT) was developed, with which the pictures in this tutorial were produced. It is a menu-driven editor on a vector refresh display for the generation, manipulation and storage of graphical objects such as polylines, markers, circles, arcs, rectangles and many other more complex objects, together with various kinds of text and object attributes which can be chosen. The users were involved in the design process. Soon, a disadvantage about which many users complained, appeared: the transformation of objects. Analysis showed the reason for this.

The user's model of transforming an object was to identify
that object by pick, and announce the required operation
(shift, scale, rotate) by menu pick. Then for rotation, for
example, a function knob or a mouse would be the appropriate
input tool for sampling the required transformation angle
and direction. Unfortunately, however, the graphical kernel
system used on that machine could not support sample input.
Therefore, sample input had to be simulated. The chosen
method later showed the restriction to the designers of the
underlying graphical kernel system, because they forced the
user to arrange a transformation matrix by menu selection,
to be applied to the desired object. Many users complained
because they did not get a model of this. (There were no
programmers on the graphical system.)

Other simulation methods, like input of changing coordinates
for every little movement, turned out to be too time
consuming and boring. To settle the conflict, each new user
was personally instructed on these critical parts of the
application.

Here is an example from our experiences so far; once again,
it should be made clear that no general strategy for solving
all problems in the design of user interfaces can ever
exist. The main point is the carefully addressed conscious-
ness to those problems described above. But sometimes,
things are not quite so bad and problems can be overcome by
use of tricks.

Example:

For a special application, the common surface for application output and interaction input/output (here: a menu),
should be strictly represented. No system support is available for this problem, i.e. different background colours.
What can be done? From the user's point of view, a visual
reparation can be achieved by displaying "boxes", each
indicating an independent area of usage. Therefore, an
application and a dialogue leading area were established by
framing each area with a rectangular thin white line.

Another trick is to display intermediate messages, if the computing time for some problem increases above a time limit of ca. three seconds, and/or engaging the user in some operations, meaningless to normal computation, but attracting his attention.

3.3.2. Examples of "Bad" and "Good" Design

It is hard to decide on "good" or "bad" examples in man-machine dialogue. There are several reasons for this, which should up until now, have been made clear. Neverthe-less, some criteria must be found in order to judge an actual dialogue. The aim of criticism is a constructive proposal for improvement.

We use the following strategy - a product of our own experience - which has been shown to work quite well in the past. Two lists have to be established; one indicating the "good" elements which have been recognised and one indica-ting the "bad" elements. An evaluation then has to take place, analysing the correlation between the lists, i.e. whether the design of a "good" element has led to a "bad" element (side-effect). Within this analysis, the compromises in the design process will be uncovered. After this, the implementation can be judged, leading to exact findings like whether a design failure took place, or, taking all circum-stances into consideration, whether the best compromise - however bad it may look - has been achieved. Constructive proposals can then lead to improvements.

Example:

Let us consider a SIEMENS computer with a BS 2000 operating system. System error messages are of the following form:

        % E018 COMMAND NOT FOUND
        % E076 DO YOU WISH A PDUMP? REPLY (Y=YES;N=NO)
        % E749 COMMAND RECEIVED

With this system, a "HELP" facility is available. Giving the command "/HELP" without the error number will display a long form, if a short form has already been displayed, or else a German version of the long form. The command "/HELP E749" will display the message for that error. On studying the instruction manual for the operating system, you may read that all help information is stored in files. Although it would be possible to edit messages in this form, in most cases, the system error message manual has to be consulted. E.g. for E749 the manual explains that the "/TEXEC" command has been accepted and the user is asked to wait for the next message. In this case, no general design error has been made, "only" not enough care has been taken in editing the system error messages.

On the other hand, the BS 2000 operating system totally rejects every incorrect input (that are in most cases caused by typing errors). No analysis of the determining error and partial recovery is performed.

Example:

The command

/CATALOG FILE1,FILE2,STATE=I

will cause an error, because STATE=I is not a valid option. In this case "I" was the next character to "U" on the keyboard. A correct support would be to ask the user to respecify the "STATE=" option. In this case, a design fault may be recognised.

4. Tools and Techniques

4.1. System Model

4.1.1 Design Principles

Generally accepted principles for designing software systems
are:

- Modularity: the system is composed of independent parts
  called modules accessing each other through well-defined
  interfaces, which allow for separate implementation and
  validation of each module; modularity is a prerequisite
  for extendability, i.e., new modules can be easily added.

- Portability: the system program can be installed on
  different computers with minimal effort.

- Device independence: the exchange of different peripheral
  devices has no major effect on the programs and their
  usability.

The method of achieving portability and device independence,
is to isolate device and installation specifics in modules
and to minimise their number and size. Changing the installation only results in the changing or re-writing of these
modules. However, this method works rather well with regard
to the software system, but the use of highly interactive
programs can be influenced by minimal device changes. This
problem will be discussed later on.

4.1.2. System Components

To begin with, a model of an interactive system is derived
from a system implementor's point of view, taking into
account the above-mentioned principles. A task of the
application area is accomplished, using a computer interactively. Part of the work is done by the machine, and part
by man. The knowledge is distributed between both partners,
the task thus being able to be performed with dialogue
between man and machine (see fig. 4.1).

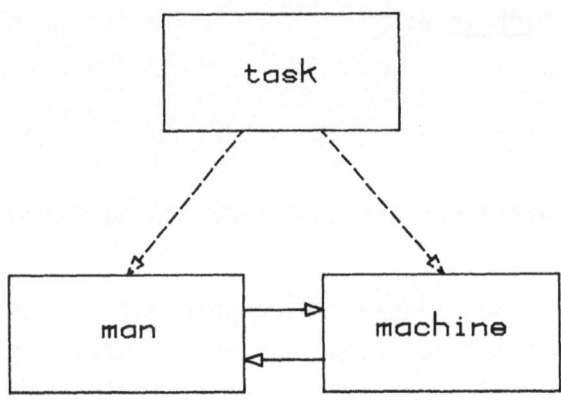

Figure 4.1:   Man and Machine

Communication with the user is via input and output devices. In order to enable comfortable dialogue, tools for device control and software support are needed. The dialogue instance handles all aspects of communication with the user. This includes support of the user by appropriate input methods, the selection of application algorithms and the data being delivered to them (fig. 4.2).

The application is represented in the computer by data structures, i.e. objects and their connections and inter-relations, and algorithms which manipulate these objects. Some algorithms generate graphical objects which visualise the data structure and results of other algorithms. Therefore, we call them data presentation algorithms.

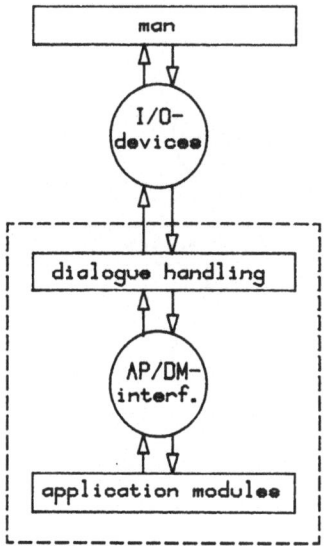

Figure 4.2:   Global System Structure

In   accordance with the above-mentioned design principles, a
first step in providing such a tool is the use of a graphics
system;   it   handles   input   from and output to the physical
devices   on   an   abstract   level. The standardised Graphical
Kernel   System (GKS) /GKS82/ defines the interface to such a
system. (In /FND83/ a detailed explanation of GKS is given).
It provides input and output functions which are used by the
dialogue   instance   to   communicate   with the end user. This
stage of refinement is shown in figure 4.3.

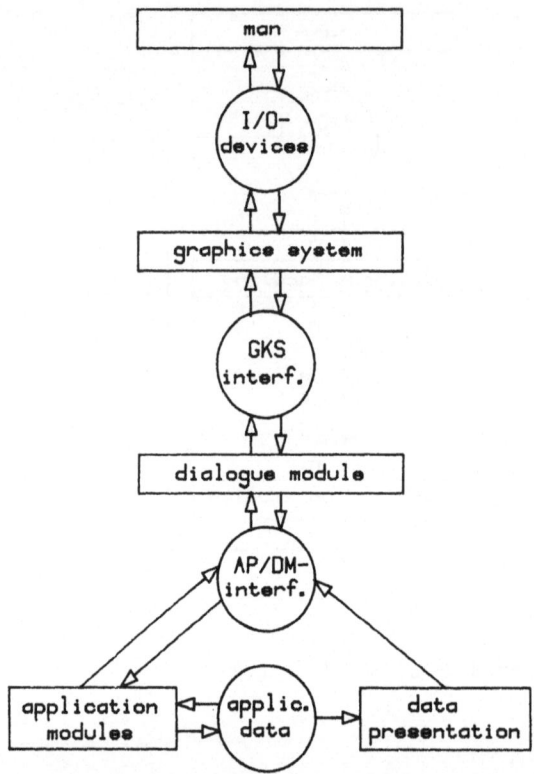

Figure 4.3: Refined System Structure

For output in GKS, five primitives are available: POLYLINE,
POLYMARKER, TEXT, FILL AREA, and CELL ARRAY and appropriate
attributes. The input devices are grouped into 6 classes:
LOCATOR, STROKE, VALUATOR, CHOICE, PICK, and STRING. Such a
"logical device" (often also called "abstract" or "virtual"
device) may be implemented on various hardware devices.

By abstraction from special device properties, the prerequi-
sites for device independence are given and an extension for
new devices - and especially new types - can be undertaken
using this higher interface. In the following, GKS is
regarded as "the" graphics system.

4.1.3. Abstract Devices and User Interface

Using GKS as a standardised system, portable interactive systems can be realised.

From a programmer's point of view, the portability problem is thus solved. But, as indicated above, the usability of a software system may change drastically when a terminal is replaced by one of a different type, because the user interface is very much determined by hardware properties and device drivers. Here is an example of how a minimal change makes a program useless (Ref. /ANS79/):

Imagine a program which requests some points to create a symbol; these points are entered by a locator device which has a crosshair echo. Now this device is replaced by another one which does not provide a crosshair but only a small symbol to indicate the current input device position. The users enter the points in horizontal and vertical correspondence to already entered points, which could be done precisely with a crosshair echo; this is not so with the new device; but the application is exactly the correlation of points.

From this example, we learn that logical devices should not only be seen from the implementor's point of view, but the implications of special device properties also have a great impact on the work a user can perform with the whole system. Therefore, the classification of input devices in GKS is insufficient with regard to the user interface. In /BUX83/ such pragmatic considerations are discussed and as an example of further classification, a tableau of continuous devices is presented. The properties regarded as being relevant are:

- number of dimensions (1, 2, or 3)
- what is sensed (position, motion or pressure)

A further subdivision is whether the sensing is mechanically or touch sensitive. By this taxonomy he explains which device types can be replaced by others. But depending on the application requirements, the range of devices which can be replaced by others differs.

4.1.4. The Dialogue Module

The dialogue module - together with the input functions of
the graphics system - define the user interface, in so far
as it is software determinable. This module is also called
the "user interface manager", abbreviated as "UIM". A level
concept is used as the basis for further explanation, which
is similar to the one Foley and van Dam give (/FOL82/):

- conceptual (task)
- semantic
- syntactic
- lexical

The lexical level corresponds largely with the data types,
values of which the GKS input functions can deliver. These
can be regarded as lexems. Several of them will be combined,
in order to represent a semantic item; the ordering of
lexems is a syntactical matter. The semantic items indicate
objects and terms of the application domain; a collection of
them allows the user to perform an application task. At each
level, prompts and echoes should be generated for user
guidance; at the task level, this is the notification of the
results of the application algorithms.

The tasks of the dialogue module are:

- control of the GKS input devices: selection of the
  appropriate device, prompt/echo type, initial values and
  operation mode.

- deriving compound and structured values from entered data.

- passing this prepared data to the application modules.

- generation of prompts and echoes corresponding to the
  compound data.

- providing detailed information about the usage of the
  system and its devices.

- checking for correctness or plausibility at the appropriate level and performing an error reaction.

- enabling the user to correct wrong values easily.

- providing status information.

- controlling the screen layout; both the areas used for dialogue purposes and those used for the display of application data.

Further on the dialogue module should comprise features for statistics, which are the basis for analysing the quality of the provided user interface. E.g., monitoring the input and output functions on some levels can be used to select the input technique most appropriate for the user (see previous chapter).

4.1.5. The Data Flow

The data flow from the user to the application modules and back is presented, taking into account the application interface.

A series of prompts is displayed, showing possible alternative values and their meanings on the above-mentioned levels. While on the lowest level, GKS performs prompting and echoing, on the next higher one the entered values are checked for correctness - i.e. fitting in the syntax - and echos are produced indicating their syntactic correlation.

When a correct syntactic description of a semantic item is entered, a semantic echo is produced, e.g., some points and other data lead to a graphical symbol which directly corresponds to an application object. When some semantic items are derived and acknowledged by the user, they are passed to the application. This means the algorithm is selected and its input parameters are set. The result can be seen through pictures which are produced by the data representation algorithms, using output and attribute functions of the graphics system. Notice that the location on the display surface is controlled by the dialogue module.

Not every interaction results in the handing over of data to an application module, but correction loops should be handled in the dialogue module. Data correction at the different levels should be possible without the need to enter data twice. The main purpose of the various echos is the user's support in correcting entered data. Simple correction facilities are often directly provided in the hardware (e.g. character string editing). At each level, an implicit or explicit user's acknowledgement will result in continuing the dialogue.

During the creation of graphical objects, information must be gathered which allows for further interaction with the results of the application algorithms. The user must be able to identify displayed objects (picture segments) and from this, reference application specific data; then the user can change this data and make it the basis for further algorithms.

The graphics system must provide features to perform this identification (e.g. pick input); deriving the application objects from the identifier of the graphics objects (segment number) is part of the application domain. E.g. the correspondence between segment numbers and the application objects is part of the application data structure. However, a layer on top of GKS can partly unburden the application modules; e.g. when tree-like structured graphical objects are available, often, a direct correspondence to the application objects will be possible, because most applications use hierarchically-structured objects.

The data which passes the application/dialogue interface can now be classified. It can be grouped in:

- control information, comprising
  - identification of the application module to be executed
  - feedback about its successful or erroneous execution
  - control parameters, which allow for modifications of control flow

- providing data to the application module which is directly passed over, or by a pointer; the latter is especially advantageous for large amounts of data

- inquiring of the application data structure for
  - giving information to the user
  - getting the correspondence between graphics objects and
    application objects.

4.2. Describing a Dialogue System

4.2.1. Implementation Concepts

In order to implement a user interface, an environment supporting this task is needed. Two approaches are possible, tackling the problem from different points of view:

(a) Let us call the first one the "language approach". The communication between man and machine is performed via an input and an output language. Here, the input language is defined via a meta-language, e.g. by expressions over terminal and non-terminal symbols (production systems, represented in Backus-Naur Form). The operators of the meta-language are the known ones of regular expressions, but they may also be extended by operators which do not fix the input sequence, but allow for parallelism and arbitrary sequence /SHA80, SHA78/. From this description, a parser is derived, processing user input according to the language specification. In this concept, the problem is how to specify and connect the semantic actions to the input language specification and how to describe the interrelations between input and output language. Further problems are the provision of initial values depending on the context and controlling the maintenance of the current device value between the activations.

(b) In the second approach, interactions are described through "abstract input devices", also called "interaction units" /GUE80/. Each one can accept input values, perform a reaction (e.g. echoing, semantic action) and deliver a derived value to a higher level device. The dialogue is described by a hierarchy of abstract input devices, the highest one passes a structured value to the application program. The devices can operate in request mode, i.e. one at a time, a higher device requests a structured value from a lower one and by this, it sets itself in a wait state, until the value is delivered or an error is indicated.

When realising this concept in a direct manner, no parser is needed, but each interaction unit can be implemented as a subprogram or a task (the two possibilities do not exclude each other, e.g. some subprograms may be combined to one task).

A parallel implementation is also possible; then several devices work simultaneously. The data transfer to higher level devices can be accomplished via reading a register, in which a valid value is always to be kept, via queues, or by a message system. A problem in this concept arises when several abstract devices work in parallel and two or more of them want to get data from the same lower device. As a solution, the same value could be provided to all requesting ones, but may not lead to the effects the user expects. Another possibility is the delivery of the value to one receiver; this one must be selected by a rule (e.g. priority).

The first approach is a top-down strategy, the second one a bottom-up one; however, when realising a dialogue system often a combination of both will be advantageous.

4.2.2. Control Structure

The components explained in the previous chapter can be organised in several ways. Joining these parts to a system depends on the features of the available computer and the languages used for implementing the system. A very important point is whether multiprocessing is available or only monoprocessing; new problems arise when there is a multi-processor system without automatic distribution of the task on the processors, though some problems decrease. There are some interrelations between the processor and the language features; e.g., whether a "normal" programming language is used for realising the dialogue module, or co-routines are available (SIMULA) or the realisation is performed in an object-oriented language, e.g., SMALLTALK /KAY80/ or Star Graphics /XER82/.

Possible structures are:

- External control structure: There exists no application program but several independent modules; they were initiated by a supervisor which is part of the user interface manager (dialogue instance, see figure 4.4).

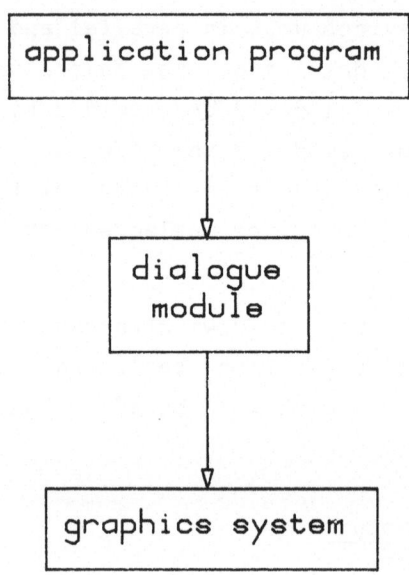

Figure 4.4:   External Control

- When using the internal control model the control instance is the application program which requests the data from the dialogue instance or directly from the graphics system (traditional method, see figure 4.5).

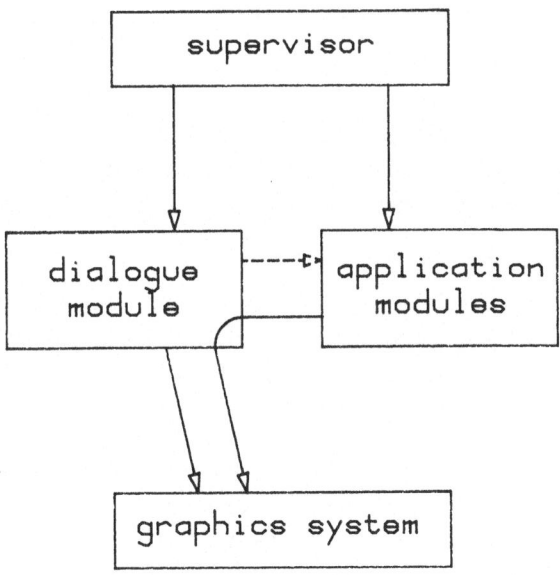

Figure 4.5:   Internal Control

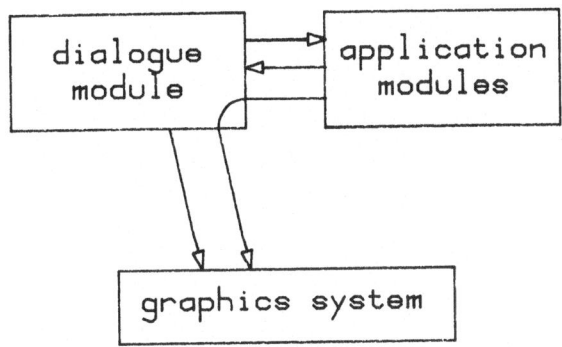

Figure 4.6:   Alternate Control

- Other control models allow for changing the control instance during the time depending on the current stage of the task and the user interface manager (figure 4.6).

The advantage of the external control model is:

- easily extendable by new modules

- a facility for defining dialogue sequences can be provided
  which gives the user a tool for adapting the dialogue to
  his own wishes and may reduce the number of values to be
  entered.

But if a abnormal conditon occurs in the application module
it is not allowed (and not possible) to request help from
the human user directly, as would be possible in the internal control model.

Also, in the internal control concept there are benefits
from a powerful dialogue module. Only prepared data blocks,
sufficient for performing a task, are handed over to the
application program. Note that the differences between both
concepts decrease if the application program is not overly
restrictive in the sequence of the single tasks (e.g., when
it only selects the task to be performed, the application
program is just the supervisor).

While the above concepts also work well for monoprocessing
systems the change of initative would require parallel
processing facilities (if it is realised in a direct
manner); at least the UIM and the application program would
run in parallel. The natural communication would be through
messages.

4.2.3. Existing Concepts

Now some existing concepts for describing and specifying the
man-machine interface are presented.

4.2.3.1. The Command Language Grammar

Moran presents the Command Language Grammar /MOR81/ as a
tool for describing and presenting user interfaces; it may
be also used as a basis for analysation under cognitive
aspects. It starts with a **conceptual model** of a system; it
corresponds to the user model - i.e. which the system

designer has about the user and his way to achieve a task.
This model should be in accordance with the end user's model
of the system.

Three hierarchical components are identified, each of which
are made up of several levels. In a refinement process each
level is mapped to the lower one by describing the upper one
in more detail, using a formal grammar.

The components and levels are:

    Conceptual component (abstract concepts)
      - task level
      - semantic level

    Communication component
      - syntactic level
      - interaction level

    Physical component
      - spatial layout
      - devices

The CLG focuses on the first and second component which
build up a hierarchy, while the physical component does not
fit in, but has impacts on the other components.

Within each level a set of entities (objects), tasks,
procedures, and methods are specified, where the procedures
are operations manipulating the objects and defining the
relation of the tasks at the task level. Methods define how
the tasks are accomplished by using the operations, in lower
levels they specify the connection to the tasks of the task
level. In the CLG-approach the user actions are also
formalised and described.

In the task level the tasks are described in an almost
informal way and their interrelations (hierarchy). In the
semantic level conceptual objects and corresponding operations are defined, giving the functional capabilities of the
system. The syntactiacal level is used for embedding the
conceptual model in a command language structure, which is
built out of a few syntactic elements: commands, arguments,
contexts which indicate the valid context in which the

command can be used, and state variables. From the semantic methods the syntactic level commands are derived.

At the **interaction level** the dialogue actions are fixed;
i.e., the prompt, keystroke or another device action necessary for initiating a command, the resulting response
(echo), the terminating action (if necessary), and the
interpretation of the entered value. In the "Body" the
syntax of the arguments are specified which can repeatedly
consist of the above syntactic elements (i.e., a hierarchy
may be so defind). The "When" constituents allow for
specifying conditions for time sequences of the other
constituents. At the interaction level using these elements
the interactions are described by rules. E.g.:

"when" in the "specification" of a "specific command" -->
time condition; or:

"prompt" in the specification of "argument 1" --> DISPLAY
message ....; or:

"action" for "specific command" --> KEY "identifier" for
initiating command.

The physical level is not yet investigated in detail; some
problems arise like the display layout of the various
viewports for which no adaequat level has been found because
some others are related and it is difficult to fit it in the
hierarchical structure.

In the context of user interface design and implementation
CLG covers the range from the conceptual domain down to the
devices. It belongs to the command language approaches but
does not support facilities for implementation nor focuses
graphics systems which provide abstract input devices.

4.2.3.2. Input Tools

In /PLA81/ the Input Tool Model (ITM) is presented. This
concept allows for describing the user interface in terms of
input tools which are a form of abstract input devices.
The user can trigger such a tool by a certain input
sequence. The entered input string (not only text strings)

called the input sequence, is checked to see if it fulfills the **input rule** of each active device. This rule specifies which input sequence is accepted by the device. In case of such a **match** the action defined in the tool body is executed. Here, the input data can be used in algorithmic constructions, e.g. for producing prompts and echoes. After finishing the actions, a value is generated to be delivered to higher level tools to be handled as input.

An input rule is defined by an expression over lower level tools, thus creating a tool hierarchy. At the lowest level, predefined tools correspond to physical devices which are triggered by user actions; the highest one is a **tool program.** Each tool activates all lower tools which could accept input at that specific moment. Note that normally, several tools are active simultaneously.

The operators available for definition of the input rule are:

A + B   A or B,   wait for completion of A or B

A & B   A and B, wait for completion of A and B (arbitrary sequence)

A ; B   A followed by B, wait for completion of A, then for B

/T/:A   if T then A else empty, matched if T is true and A is completed, prefix test

A:/T/   A; if T then matched else failed, postfix test

A%   while A not empty do A, infinite repetition, at least one A

A*   zero or more A's, (Keene Star)

Hereby A and B mean input expressions, T a boolean function. Note that the failing of a match results in an empty input rule; no empty rule can be matched.

Because of the above input expressions, several tools may be active at the same time. Inherently, there is ambiguity for selecting the matching input rule. The strategy is: catch the first one which fulfills the expression. However, some combinations of operations still lead to ambiguities (e.g., the Keen Star at the end of a rule, A;B*); these are forbidden.

Other problems arise with the failure of a high-level input rule in conjunction with actions of the tool body. The matching of lower level input rules results in actions which may produce global effects (e.g. picture changes) which cannot be withdrawn. The user interface designer is requested to pay attention to these effects.

In order to provide correction facilities to the user, an escape mechanism is introduced. The escape event tool is a tool which is always active and directly related to a physical device (e.g. key). Its triggering sets the system in the escape mode. Inside the tool body, an escape tool may be defined, to which all input entered during the escape mode is sent. Thus, the correction of values can be carried out. When the escape tool has finished, the system is set back into the normal state.

4.2.3.3. Sites, Modes, and Trails

The approach undertaken by Nievergelt /NIF80/ is mainly concerned with user guidance. He comes up with the questions:

- **Where am I?**
- **What can I do here?**
- **How did I get here? Where can I go? How do I get there?**

When a user is interrupted during a dialogue session and then is going to continue his work, the following information should be provided:

- the context currently accessible,
- currently available commands,
- what he has done before the interrupt.

Further on he needs to know the possible actions and the way leading to them.

For fulfilling these requirements the model of **sites**, **modes**, and **trails** has been developed. A **site** defines the part of the data accessible at the moment. A **mode** similarily is the subset of the available commands in a specific system status. **Sites** and **modes** are connected to other **sites and modes** and build up hierarchies. On **modes** operations are available like enable, disable, and protect.

A **trail** is a feasible time sequence of pairs which consist of a **site** and a **mode**. It is created during a dialogue session reflecting the history of user actions and accessed data. **Trails** are objects which can be manipulated, e.g., stored, edited, inspected, and re-invoked. Thus beside the history of a dialogue, they can represent the available alternatives for proceeding from the current dialogue status.

From a **trail** the trace of **sites** can be extracted which delivers the accessed data; the trace of Modes consists of the executed commands.

This concept provides powerful facilities for telling the user the current status, its past and possibilities for the future. Allowing the modification and re-use of **trails**, a tool for dialogue control is given to the user.

4.2.3.4. The Device Model

The **Device Model** described in /ANS79, ANS82/ sets up a specification language to define abstract devices. A device is specified by a combination of the elements **state**, **event** and **action**.

A **state** is a variable of any type and structure; part of it may be **transparent** to other devices, or **external**, which means that a transparent state of another device is used to derive it, other parts of the state are **hidden**, i.e. it is only accessible inside the device. External states may be defined as functions of transparent and hidden states.

Events are discrete elements of communication between devices. Each event is caused by an action and may trigger an action in one or more other devices; parameters may be sent in conjunction with an event.

Actions occur in response to events. Typically, an action will alter the internal state, signal an event and then terminate immediately.

Each abstract device can be described to the outside in terms of the events it responds to, its transparent state upon completion of any action and the events caused by each action. Hierarchies of devices can thus be built. The linking of devices is specified separately, allowing late binding and changes to the set of devices used, without necessitating their modification.

4.3. Dialogue Cells

Now a dialogue specification language shall be explained in more detail and the implementation aspects discussed. The Dialogue Cells (DC), described in /GEP82/, are a tool for defining and implementing man-machine dialogues; i.e., a user interface of a system is specified. A collection of them, together with a runtime system, builds a dialogue module in the sense of chapter 4.1.

First the concepts are presented, then the syntax of cells is described.

4.3.1. Semantics of Dialogue Cells

4.3.1.1. Basic Elements

There are four basic elements of which each dialogue between a human user and a computer consists. These are the **prompt** as indication of the type of data to be entered, the **symbol**, which is fed in by the user, the **echo** which shows the interpretation of the entered symbol, and the **value** which is derived from the symbol for further use. All these elements can appear in several forms and extensions. They can also influence each other in various ways.

A **dialogue cell** is a unit which completely specifies the actions of a step in a dialogue. The actions involved in each step are the following:

(1) A structured value offered by the application program (or a higher level cell) for processing in this step is elaborated (initial value V_i).

(2) The user receives all information necessary to perform his part of the action (prompt P).

(3) The gaining of user input (Symbol S).

(4) For each input the reaction sent to the user is executed as described by echo (E).

(5) The mapping from user inputs to values is performed (V_e).

(6) Upon termination of the user input, the resulting value is delivered (V_o).

(7) The cell echo is produced, all other local effects in terms of prompts, echoes and values are removed (E_o).

The actions correspond to the statements of dialogue cells and to the global order in which all the parts are elaborated. Each cell may contain all or part of them. P, S, V_e, E can be combined in several ways. Initial values V_i influence all other parts, thus universal cells may be designed.

Dialogue cells can be organised in a hierarchy; a means for this is the SYMBOL statement. Its execution results in an activation of a subcell which handles a subdialogue. Parameters may be passed which are used as initial values inside the subcell. The value derived by the subcell as a consequence of the subdialogue is passed via output parameters to the activating cell. This cell then treats it as an input symbol (which may be complex and structured). The behaviour of all elements in conjunction with a cell hierarchy are explained in detail after the explanation of the prompt, symbol, and echo features. The basic cells correspond to GKS-input functions, for creation of prompts and echoes, GKS-output and attribute functions are available.

4.3.1.2. Objects

In order to specify prompts and echoes and evaluation parts, variables of several types are needed. Because of the graphical nature of the dialogue aimed at, the usual data types (integer, real, boolean, string) are not sufficient. They are extended by **point**, **picture**, **menu**, and **viewport**.

Points are equivalent to two reals; variables of type picture, menu and viewport are references (or pointers) to the corresponding objects. Pictures can be created during the initialisation of a cell in the body, i.e. its shape is defined by user input. The GKS-output and -attribute functions are available for picture definition.

A menu defines a numbered set of alternatives, each of which is visualised via a text string or a picture. Normally, it is displayed by a prompt function and a subsequent symbol statement requests the user to select and input one alternative. Further on, text objects may be generated, but only implicitly, by prompt and echo functions, as opposed to pictures and menus.

All variables can serve as input or output parameters - including picture, menu and viewport type. Variables exist, at most, as long as the cell in which they are declared remains active. Pictures and menus may be deleted explicitly. Viewports are explained in the next chapter.

4.3.1.3. Viewports

The screen layout is defined by means of **viewports.** The screen is subdivided into several areas, called viewports, each of which is identified by name. Inside each cell, new viewports may be defined; they exist from cell activation until cell end. Viewports may overlap and they may be defined in relation to others; but no dynamic change is allowed.

By assigning priorities to them, graphical elements displayed within them may take precedence over information contained in overlapping viewports having less priority. The priority is especially relevant for input. In conjunction with locator input, the viewport with the highest priority in which the position lies, is in addition delivered back.

Viewports - and the screen - are divided into two classes. **dialoge viewports** are reserved for that purpose; no appliction module is allowed to send data to them. Inside **application viewports,** the application may produce graphics output as well as the dialogue module.

4.3.1.4. Prompt

A **prompt** is a means of user guidance and preparation for
input action. It may be displaying a cursor, a message, a
picture, or a menu indicating the possible alternatives.
There may be combined prompts like displaying the text
"please select object" and two menus, one of them giving
graphical representations of the choices, the other giving
keywords (descriptors). It is the responsibility of the
dialogue author to select a proper subset from the set of
possible prompts, which may be reduced by hardware limitations and/or screen-layout problems.

The semantics of all these prompt functions are defined by
attribute setting for input (e.g. echo type), (re-) defining
input symbol sets allowed (e.g. enable locator, extend
menu), or by generation of graphics output.

Through a prompt function, an object of type text, menu, or
picture may be placed in a viewport, or an existing object
may be modified; e.g., a picture already used as prompt may
be highlighted or transformed.

The lifetime of prompt objects may be defined in relation to
the appearance of other objects (e.g. till next echo) and
may be bound to the prompt viewport (e.g. till next prompt
in the same viewport). The maximum lifetime lasts till cell
end.

4.3.1.5. Echo

Echo informs the user of the system's understanding of the
values entered. Echoes may be (similar to prompts) messages
or output of picture elements or even modifications of the
previously defined output. Echoes are also related to
specific viewports, which may overlap other ones.

Two aspects must also be distinguished here. One is the echo
as implied by the symbol produced. The other is the echo
to show what has happened to the symbols on that level
(e.g., how they are interpreted). The latter echoes build
the effect of the cell as a whole.

The disappearance of the echo is defined in the same way as for prompts; but one exception is made: The effect of echoing may still exist after the cell has been closed, if the environment has prepared to maintan it. In this way complicated interactions for setting up a dialogue are possible. This can be achieved by creating a picture, echoing it and passing it as a parameter to a higher instance, which may be an application module. Implicitly it is done by defining: "till next echo" which may be beyond the cell end.

4.3.1.6. Value

Input symbols will generally not be the exact data requested by the application program or by other dialogue parts. Usually some conversions and/or computations are necessary. The result of these operations are the output parameters of a dialogue cell, referred to as value. The value part does not include new input actions. They can be exclusively in the symbol part.

4.3.1.7. Constructs

The actions of a cell may be combined to form action sequences or conditional executions.

Constructs are needed for concatenation (i.e. sequential execution), repeated and conditional execution, whereas a selection construct is advantageous because it corresponds directly to the user's selection of different alternatives. The same constructs are desirable for defining picture objects.

4.3.1.8. Hierarchical Organisation

Tools for defining hierarchical dialogue structures are absolutely essential for building more complex systems. Consequently, dialogue cells can be organized in this way. Via the SYMBOL statement a subcell activation can be specified. Similar to a procedure call, cells may have parameters for the passing of data. These parameters may influence all of the elements of the subcell; in most cases, they will be used as initial values and, in the output parameters, The results of the subdialogue are delivered back.

In this way, an easy mapping of top-down dialogue design to dialogue cells can be performed. By having a library of already defined dialogue cells, new systems can be configured very easily. Some problems however will arise with scope rules and lifetimes of prompts and echoes. Next is described how these can be solved.

4.3.1.9. Hierarchy of Prompts

Prompts are related to the task being performed just now. Hence this task may be decomposed into simpler ones, the prompts are also refined. Nevertheless it is often useful on a basic level to know - by the still visible global prompt - in which context a certain action takes place. On the other hand, previous prompts of the same hierarchical level are no longer meaningful if the action required has resulted in a symbol-expression and an echo. Thereby the two basic prompt scope rules are:

(P1) the lifetime of a prompt ends (in general), if the requested input action is performed and the echo is generated;

(P2) more than one prompt may be active on different hierarchical levels;

(P3) prompts may use pictures and menus, and they may modify them; prompts may generate text objects;

(P4) prompts must not use objects already used as echoes.

If the situation occurs, that more than one prompt (or echo) is associated with the same viewport, precedence rules may require the temporary switching off of some prompts. Automatically, only prompts of the same type (menu or text) may cause the disappearance of prompt objects; a prompt text may also lead to the disappearance of an echo text. For picture objects no such mechanism is advantageous, because in most cases several pictures should appear in the same viewport.

When a lower level prompt has caused the switching off of a higher level prompt or echo, and the prompt lifetime ends, the higher level object is made visible again. Dialogue leading going beyond these features should be controlled explicitly by the dialogue designer.

4.3.1.10. Hierarchy of Echoes

Echoes cause, with respect to hierarchy, similar problems as prompts. Echoes indicate the system reaction on user input. With finishing subcells, echoes on a higher level are possible and thereby

(E1) the lifetime of an echo ends at the latest, when the echo of the next higher level is performed, (if not passed by parameter),

(E2) more than one echo may be active,

(E3) echoes may use pictures, and they may modify them; echoes may generate text objects.

(E4) Echoes must not use objects already used as prompts.

(E5) In case of passing the echoed picture as a parameter to a higher level cell, this cell controls its longer lifespan.

For echoes the corresponding overwriting rules are valid, as they are for prompts; so the echoed text objects may cause the disappearance of other text objects.

4.3.2. Realisation

4.3.2.1. Implementation Aspects

The implemention of the outlined dialogue concept consists of several tasks, described in the following:

- the embedding of the dialogue elements in a programming or specification language to be used by a dialogue designer (respectively dialogue implementor).

- the implemenatation of a basis for the dialogue module,
  i.e. the runtime system and basic cells; an installation
  of the Graphical Kernel System (GKS) is prerequisited.

- building an interpreter or compiler, which maps the
  language constructs to the functions of the runtime
  system;

- fixing the format of the interface between application
  program and dialogue system.

When this is implemented, a given application can use the
dialogue system by adapting its input and output functions
to the interface, and by defining a command language by
means of dialogue cells.

4.3.2.2. Language Embedding

For the dialogue elements a syntax has to be defined by
which the author can specify dialogue cells. Therefore, a
new language must be designed or an existing one has to be
extended in some way. Such a language should include the
following facilities or, if not, building them should be a
simple task:

- syntactic expressions for dialogue cells and elements,

- constructs for building a hierarchy of dialogue cells,

- parameter passing between cells (e.g. via a procedure
  concept),

- control structures for combining the elements.

The question was whether the syntax should look like a
programming language or like production rules, e.g., as the
regular expressions. In the second case, the control structures would be expressed in terms of operators over symbols.
But if doing so there is still the need to specify
algorithmic parts (e.g. for defing pictures); the problem
how to connect input symbols to prompts and echoes and
object arises, as well as the parameter passing.

Furthermore the language should be easily learnable and its
rules should be simple and consistent. Therefore, we decided

on a programming language type.

The realisation should support a decentral solution. E.g., the dialogue processing occurs on an intelligent satellite, while the application modules are executed on a mainframe computer.

The selection of implementation language was forced by the need for portability and device independence, to be achieved by choosing GKS. In order to fulfil these requirements FORTRAN is used as the implementation language because a GKS implementation in FORTRAN was early available on several machines.

The next question was whether an interpreter should be developed or FORTRAN be extended. Arguments against an interpreter solution are the runtime efficiency which is necessary for good dialogues especially when the interpretation of extensive calculations is needed (e.g. for the generation of pictures) and concepts such as parameter passing. Designing a totally new language and implementing it is a very hard task, especially when only a few new constructs are needed; therefore available resources should be used. Thus a language extension of FORTRAN was aimed at.

FORTRAN fulfils some but not all the needs of a language for designing dialogues. Hierarchies can be built by subroutines, the language is widely distributed, well known and has no complicated rules. But two points oppose its direct use: the common control structures are only rudimentarily available (no while-loops, no if-then-else construct). A subroutine package would be possible for dialogue definitions, but there would be no progress because the dialogue author should be supported as well as possible.

Thus FORTRAN was extended by control constructs and constructs for dialogue programming. These are compiled to FORTRAN by a preprocessor.

4.3.3. A Dialogue Example

Before describing the implementation of the preprocessor,
a simple example is given. Assume the entering of a line
depending on previous input; in our example we assume the
line to be the tangential continuation of an arc.

The following screen layout, shown in figure 4.7, forms the
basis:

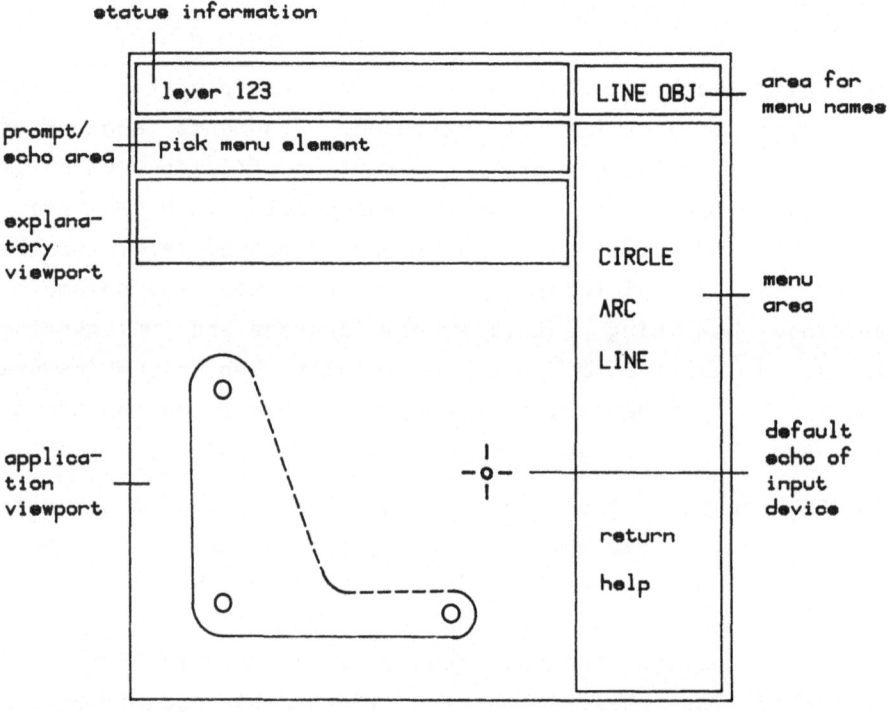

Figure 4.7: Screen Layout of the Example

The task context shall be to construct a lever from some
lines and arcs. The solid line in application viewport
indicates the current state of progress, the dashed one the
user's imagination.

The user sits in front of a screen which shows the
figure 4.7. As input hardware an alpha-numeric keyboard,

some function keys, and a tablet with a pen should be
available. The pen position is shown by an echo symbol on
the screen (e.g. tracking cross). Moving the pen on (or near
above) the tablet moves the echo symbol. Pressing the pen to
the tablet surface triggers a switch inside the pen. This is
interpreted as entering the position - respectively, the
symbol or picture element displayed near the echo position.

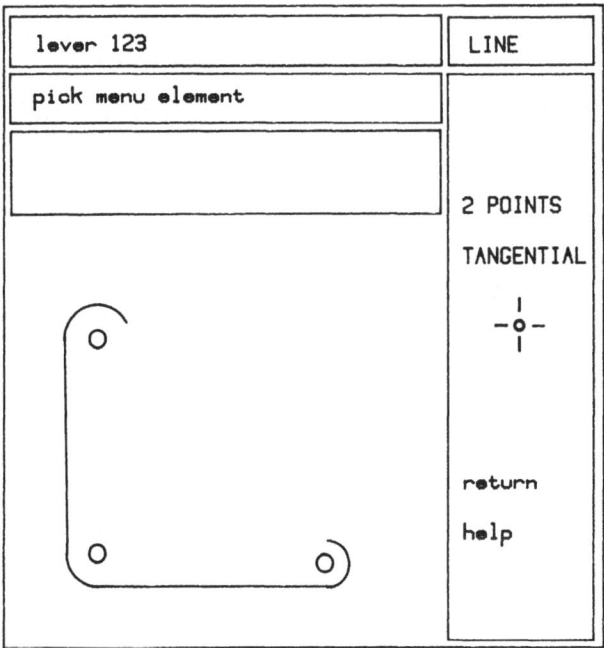

Figure 4.8:   Selection of Operation from Menu

In this example the user is provided with information about
the current state of the dialogue by texts inside a
viewport showing the application context (lever number)
In the prompt/echo area, the next expected action is
indicated. The menu area provides the visualisation of the
current alternatives. Above this viewport the menu name is
given, or the previously picked menu item.

Let us assume the user moves the tracking cross on the
"Line"-text and presses the pen down for a moment; thus this
alternative is selected and the generation of a line

is initiated. This leads to the appearance of the next menu
(figure 4.8), giving the choice of the supported input
techniques: define line by two points or by a tangential
line to an arc.

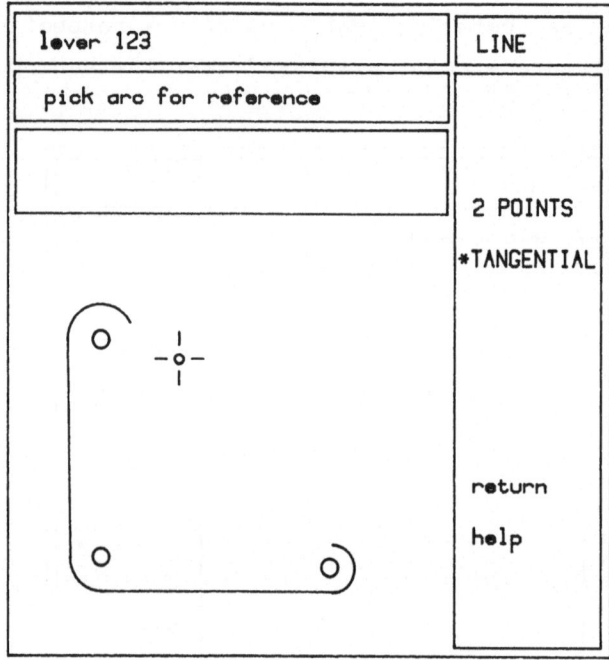

Figure 4.9: Selection of Input Technique

The user chooses the second technique by picking the text
"tangential"; performed in the same way as explained above
(figure 4.9).

The tracking cross disappears, the menu element "tangential"
is marked by an asterisk, the string "pick menu element" is
replaced by "pick arc for reference".

Now let us look when the user makes an error: he moves
the tracking cross on the small circle which marks the
centre of the arc; he enters this position wrongly (see
figure 4.10).

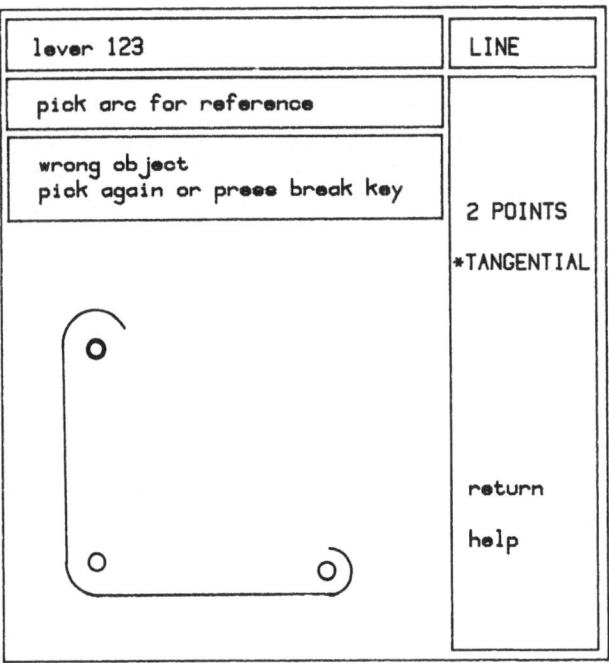

Figure 4.10: Reaction to an Errorneous Input

This leads to an error message in the explanatory viewport
(figure 4.10). The user is requested to pick an arc object
or to terminate the subdialogue by pressing the break key.
As a general feature, pressing the break key shall always be
allowed; it should result in removing the local effects
(e.g. echoes) and in a restart on a higher dialogue level
(e.g., returning to the menu shown in the first picture of
our example).

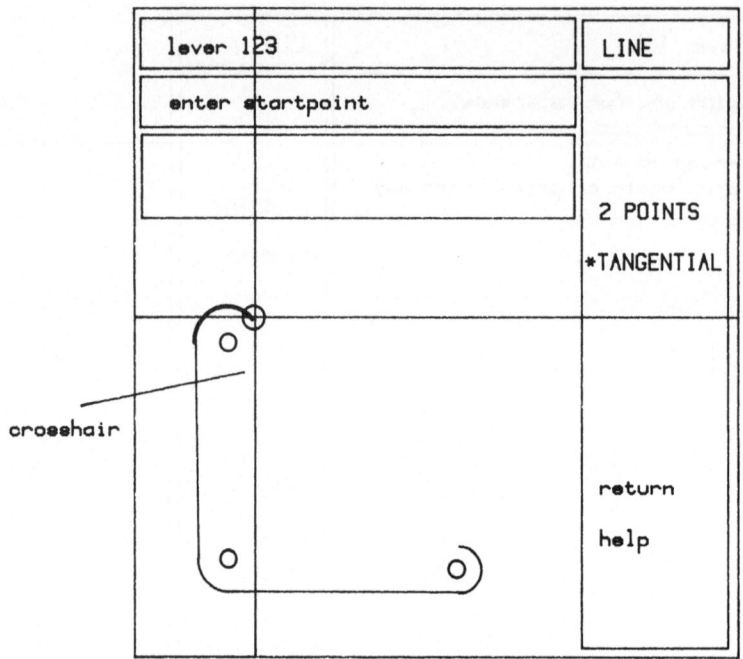

Figure 4.11: Picking a Valid Object

Back to our example: Let us assume the user identifies the
upper arc by picking it.

The arc is highlighted by blinking for a short period of
time (in figure 4.11 indicated by doubling the linewidth).

Now the user is prompted by the text "enter start position";
the tracking cross is exchanged by a crosshair.

The user moves the crosshair to the right end of the arc
which is in the application viewport, and enters this
position.

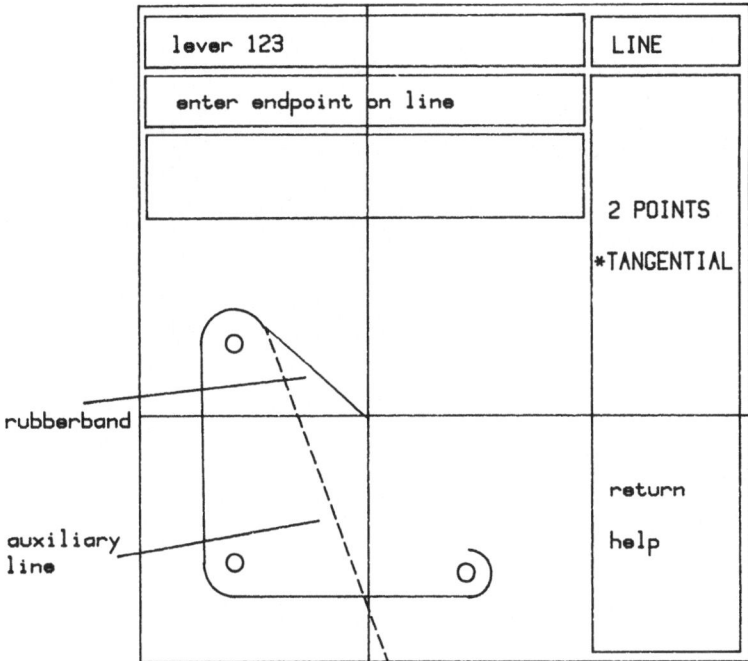

Figure 4.12: Auxiliary Line as Echo

This position is marked by a small circle for a few
seconds (i.e. ackowledging the position, see figure 4.11).
In consequence a tangential line is drawn starting from the
end of the arc and reaching to the viewport boundary (figure
4.12). The text "enter end point on the line" appears in the
prompt/echo viewport.

The user enters the end point in the same way as the first
point, but now an additional echo is provided: a rubberband
line which starts from the first point and is always
drawn to the current position of the crosshair.

The entered point is orthogonally projected on the tangent,
and thus, the end point of the line is found. As a result of
this dialogue sequence, the line is drawn (as an echo). At
the cell end local prompts and echoes are removed. Giving
control back to the activating cell, the first menu appears
again (figure 4.13).

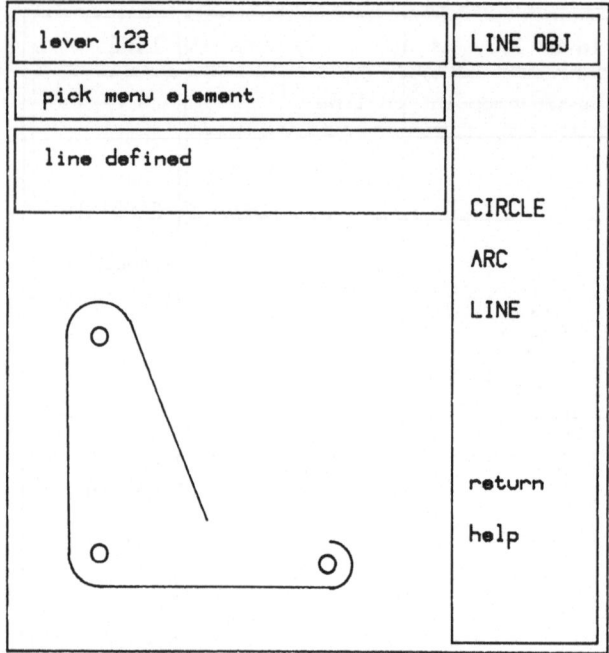

Figure 4.13:   End of Subdialogue "tangential line"

In this dialogue example we want to show the user guidance
by menus, texts, and different echoes of the GKS-devices.
Note also, that for value entering, it may be necessary to
refer to other objects and its data.

4.3.4. The Syntax of a Dialogue Cell

Now it is demonstrated, how this example may be implemented
using dialogue cells. By means of this example, the syntax
of dialogue cells is explained. We start after the selection
of the input technique "tangential" line.

Each dialogue cell is a unit in which a subdialogue is
described; it is identified by unique name. In the headline
the cell name is defined and its parameters:

DIACELL tangentialline (startp, endp, echopic, break)

Words in upper case letters are keywords, in lower case ones
identifiers; identifiers consists of letters and digits and
start with a letter. The end of a line normally identifys
the end of a statement. Comments can be appended to each
statement starting with slash asterisk /* and terminating
with the line end.

After the headline, the parameter specification follows,
separated into input, transient, and output ones.

```
OUT  POINT     startp          /* start point
               endp            /* end point
     PICTURE   echopic         /* picture id. for the line
     LOGICAL   break           /* termination indicator
```

Next the access to global variables is specified. In our
example we assume the viewports to be global. A dialogue
cell may access several global areas; therefore they are
identified by name.

```
GLOBAL /viewports/
     VIEWPORT  vpstatus        /* status information
               vppromptecho    /* prompt/echo area
               vpexplain       /* for additional explanations
               vpmenuname      /* previous selected menu
                               /* alternative
               vpappl          /* application picture area
               vpmenu          /* menu area
```

Variables needed only in the current cell are declared in
the LOCAL statement.

```
LOCAL VIEWPORT  vpout          /* viewport delivered back
                               /* from locator
      PICTURE   tangentpic     /* picture of tangent
                pickpic        /* picked picture identifier
      LOGICAL   ok             /* end of loop indicator
                clwise         /* indicates direction of beam
      CHARACTER objtype        /*  object type
      POINT     initpos        /* dummy position
```

                p(3)   /* point array of length 3

In the initialisation part, default values can be assigned to variables (including output parameters); pictures and menus may be defined.

INIT

    ok = FALSE   /* end of loop indicator
    initpos = (0., 0.)   /* set dummy position

After the INIT-section in the cell BODY, the sequence of prompting, requesting input and echoing is defined. First a prompt text is generated.

BODY

PROMPT VIEWPORT vppromptecho   /* in prompt/echo area
      TILL ECHOPRO SVIEW   /* lifetime last until the next
                             /* echo or prompt is generated
                             /* in the same viewport
      TEXT 'pick arc for reference' /* prompt text
PROMPT END

Now an object identifier is requested via a subdialogue from a pick input device; the default echo type is "highlighted by blinking".

SUBDIALOGUE pick ('default', pickpic, break)

The "pick"-subdialogue corresponds to the GKS-functions INITIALISE PICK and REQUEST PICK; however some parameters are hidden to facilitate designer's task; e.g., the workstation identifier; the mapping to the GKS-input devices is once set when initialising the whole dialogue system.

Each GKS-input device provides a break facilitiy, e.g., a special key on the keyboard. Its triggering is reported in the parameter "break"; no valid values are delivered in the other parameter (e.g., no valid object). Therefore in our example the triggering of the break key results in a

termination of the subdialogue "tangentialline" with removal of the resulting effects of previously entered data.

```
IF (break) terminate_cell            /* call macro
```

For termination a makro is called which ensures a correct
display and thus ensures a correct dialogue continuation.
The macro is defined at the end of the cell.

The data belonging to the identified object is fetched and
testetd to see, whether an arc has been picked. If true, in
the parameter array "p" the centre point (in "p(1)"), and
the start and endpoint of the arc (in "p(2)" and "p(3)" in
this sequence) are contained. The arc is defined counter-
clockwise from start to end point.

```
REPEAT
     IF (objtype='arc')          /* check for arc object
     THEN ok = TRUE              /* arc: terminate loop
     ELSE
        PROMPT VIEWPORT vpexplain  /* no arc
             TILL NEXT PROMPT      /* further prompt text
             TEXT 'no arc object, pick again, or' ,
                  'press break key for termination'
        PROMPT END
        SUBDIALOGUE pick ('default', pickpic, break)
                                   /* request object id again
        IF (break) terminate_cell
     FI
UNTIL (ok OR break)
```

Next the user is prompted and the start point is requested.

```
PROMPT VIEWPORT vppromptecho       /* in prompt/echo area
        TILL ECHOPRO SVIEW         /* lifetime last until the next
                                   /* echo or prompt is generated
                                   /* in the same viewport
        TEXT 'enter start position' /* prompt text
PROMPT END
```

SUBDIALOGUE locator

('crosshair', initpos, startp, vpappl, vpout, break)

IF (break) terminate_cell   /* call macro

The parameter "initpos" may be used to define the initial
position of the echo; in our example it is just a dummy
because a tablet device gives an absolute position and,
combined with the crosshair echo, the initial position
will immediately change to that corresponding to the pen on
the tablet.

The "locator"-subdialogue corresponds to the GKS-functions
INITIALISE LOCATOR and REQUEST LOCATOR (as the "pick"-sub-
dialogue"). In the parameter "startp" the entered position
is delivered back. The possible position may be restricted
to a viewport on a srceen (by the parameter "vpappl"). In
case of the viewport being undefined, the viewport in which
the position lies is given back ("vpout").

The entered position is used for selecting the endpoint of
the arc to be used as start point of the line. This is done
by choosing the nearest point. Therefore the distances are
computed using the function "dist" which input parameters
consisting of two points.

IF (dist(p(1),startp) **LESS** dist(p(2),startp))
THEN
        startp = p(1)   /* set start point
        clwise = **TRUE**   /* angle is clockwise
ELSE
        startp = p(2)   /* other point
        clwise = **FALSE**   /* counterclockwise
FI

Next, the tangent is computed by a subroutine.

CALL comptangent (p(1), startp, clwise, vpappl, endp)

A tangential beam is aimed at to illustrate the possible

endpoint of the line. The parameter "p(1)" is the arc centre point, "startp" the start point, while "clwise" controls the direction of the beam. The routine delivers the intersection between the beam and a viewport boundary in the parameter "endp".

Next the beam can be prompted; note, inside a picture definition calculations and flow constructs are allowed.

```
CREATE PICTURE tangentpic        /* picture containing the beam
        p(1) = startp
        p(2) = centrep
        SET LINETYPE ('dashed')
        POLYLINE (2,p)
END PICTURE


ECHO  VIEWPORT vpappl            /* in application area
        TILL NEXT ECHO SVIEW     /* lifetime last until the next
                                 /* echo in the same viewport
        PICTURE tangentpic       /* picture of the beam
ECHO END
```

The generation of pictures and their prompting or echoing is separated because pictures can be used several times as echoes or prompts. Additionally, pictures may be transferred as parameters.

Now the second line position to be on the beam is requested.

```
PROMPT VIEWPORT vppromptecho     /* in prompt/echo area
        TILL ECHOPRO SVIEW       /* lifetime last until the next
                                 /* echo or prompt is generated
                                 /* in the same viewport
        TEXT 'enter end point'   /* prompt text
PROMPT END


SUBDIALOGUE locator ('rubberband', startp, endp, vpappl, vpout, break)
```

The prompt/echo type is set to rubberbanding, which uses the initial position as fixpoint; it is set to the previously entered point. Further parameters correspond to the above subdialogue.

Because of the break facility the check for break is needed.

IF (break) terminate_cell

Now the entered position is orthogonally projected to the beam line, because now exact positioning on the beam can be expected. This is done by a subroutine which obtains the points defining the line ("p(1), p(2)") and the point to be mapped ("endp"); in the last parameter the resulting position on the line is delivered back. (The variable "endp" is also used for this purpose.)

CALL projection (p(1), p(2), endp, endp)

Now the final echo can be generated: the entered line.

```
CREATE PICTURE echopic          /* picture containing the line
     p(2) = endp                /* to be transferred as parameter
     POLYLINE (2,p)
END PICTURE


ECHO  VIEWPORT vpappl
     PICTURE echopic            /* echo of the line
ECHO END
```

The default echo lifetime is used which means "until next echo in same viewport"; thus the lifetime is extended beyond the cellend.

Just before the end of the cell the macro is defined to ensure a proper continuation in case of a break.

```
TO terminate_cell
     DELETE ALL ECHOES          /* removes the visible echoes
     EXIT CELL                  /* jumps immediately to the
                                /* cellend
FIN
```

Prompts are always removed at the cell end and thus need not be explicitly deleted. Pictures which are declared locally are also deleted implicitly because of the scope rules.

DIACELL END /* end of cell

At the cellend all local prompts, echoes, and pictures are deleted. The parameters are passed to the calling cell. By extending the lifetime of echoes and passing the corresponding pictures to the activating cell, this cell controls the further lifetime.

This subdialogue specification causes the user to identify a reference object and a start point always, when the input method of the example is used. When connected line segments are entered in the sequence of connection, the system has in principle the necessary information. The doublicated entering can be avoided by a slight change of the dialogue cell; provide the lastly entered object and point as defaults. Realising this, the parameter list of the cell has to be extended by a picture and a point input parameter. Extra user action to decide for the defaults or for others can be avoided by just use the passed data as initial values for the basic cells.

The benefits of the dialogue cells are the author's support by encouraging a structured programming style and by providing scope rules and semi-automatic control of graphics objects. The generation of temporal prompts and echoes is especially facilitated. The designer can control the screen layout by defining viewports which may depend on others and on user input.

By allowing the embedding of FORTRAN statements and subroutine calls existing non-graphical routines for calculations can be used. Introducing control constructs (also between FORTRAN statements) the control flow can be specified in an easy way.

4.3.5. Generating a Dialogue Processor

Here the implementation concept is described in more detail,
and how a dialogue module, also called dialogue processor,
is generated out of the dialogue cell description.

Each cell is preprocessed separately to a subroutine which
is then compiled by the normal FORTRAN-compiler. The resulting object modules, together with the dialogue cell runtime
system and GKS, build the dialogue module; additionally,
linking is necessary on most computers (see figure 4.14).

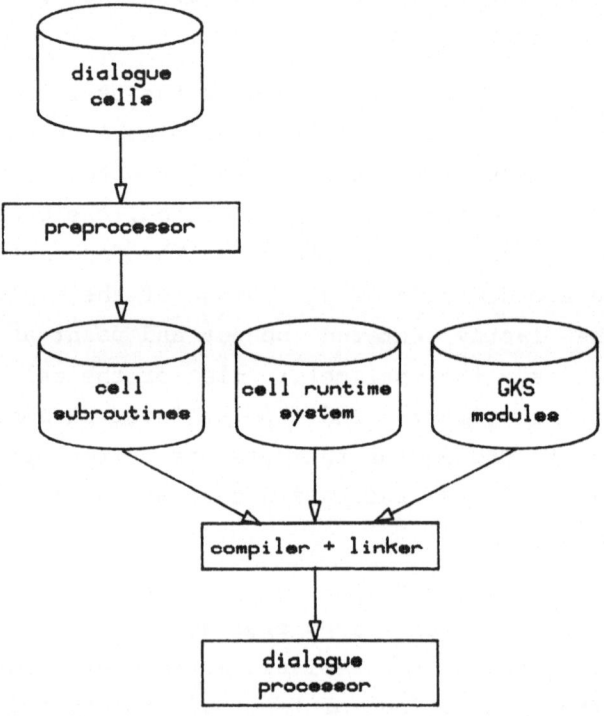

Figure 4.14: Generation of the Dialogue Module

This generation process is a separate phase; preproces-
sing and even the compilation may be carried out on a
machine different from the destination computer which provides major resources. The efficiency of the generated code
is important, while the efforts for gaining this code are of
minor interest. Because of the limitations on many mini-
computers (restricted address space) the code resulting from

a cell should not be overly large. This is prevented by isolating functions to be performed often in many cells and assigning its tasks to the runtime system. In the generated code just calls to the runtime system are inserted.

The runtime system manages the screen layout and the graphics objects; it controls input and output devices and maintains status information about the dialogue cells. Mapping to GKS-functions is performed and the correlation of dialogue cell objects to GKS-segments and other GKS-objects (e.g. viewports). A stack of active dialogue cells is used to control the relation between objects and cells.

4.3.6. The Preprocessor

The preprocessor consists of two major parts:

- the parser (inclusive code-generator)
- utilities

The utility modules comprise functions needed for parser support. They undertake the condensation of the input strings and form **tokens** and deliver them to the parser. They support the generation of the destination and listing files, and ease the error handling inside the parser. Portability and device independence are ensured. The parser structure is shown in figure 4.15.

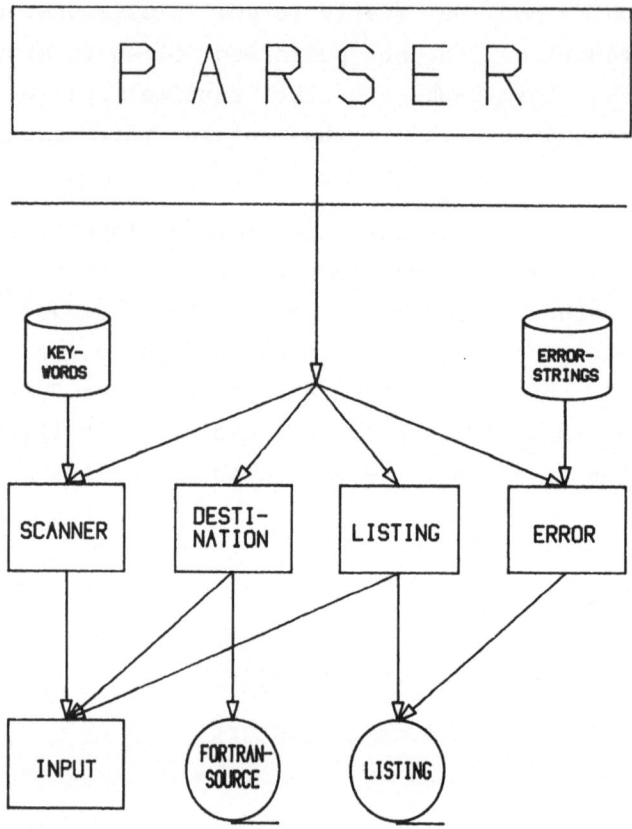

Figure 4.15: Parser Utilities

The INPUT-module delivers one character at a time to the
scanner. On encountering the end of a line it reads
the next one. By using variables as constants placed in a
FORTRAN-COMMON the input line length can be chosen, preceding and succeeding columns can be fade out; these may be
used for other purposes (e.g., numbering the statements).
Installation dependent parts are isolated in subroutines and
marked explicitly thus being easily change able.

The SCANNER derives tokens form the input stream provided by
the input module in a line-independent manner. It fetches
characters one at a time, so long as a character sequence is
recognised as a token. Three classes of tokens exist:

- predefined tokens: special signs such as + - * / , % (
  and FORTRAN-operations such as .EQ., .TRUE. ....

- integer and real numbers and text strings (enclosed in
  apostrophes '...')

- identifiers which start with a letter and contain letters
  and digits.

Identifiers are split into two groups: keywords are read in
from a keyword file just after starting the preprocessor; a
recognised identifier is checked to see if it occurs in the
keyword table. When the search is successful the related
code is delivered to the parser; otherwise the code for a
nonkeyword identifier is passed. This method of providing
keywords allows the change of spellings and different words
may represent the same token; thus long and short forms may
be provided.

The DESTINATION module provides routines for code generation
on the FORTRAN-source file which is to be compiled.
Functions are available for copying total or partial lines
from the source to the destination file, insertion of
substrings and the generation of new lines are possible. The
continuation lines, caused by FORTRAN-conventions, are
generated automatically when a destination line exceeds the
preset line length (which is provided in the same way as
input line length).

Using the LISTING module a listing file is produced from the
input lines. The nesting depth of the statement structures
is shown by indenting. Some statistics may also be output at
the end of each preprocessed dialogue cell and at the end of
the file.

The ERROR module allows the parser to address an error,
recognised in an input line, by an error code. The associated error texts are read in from a file. The number and the
text are written to the listing above the erroneous line and
the error position is marked with an asterisk; additionally
errors are protocolled on an error listing file.

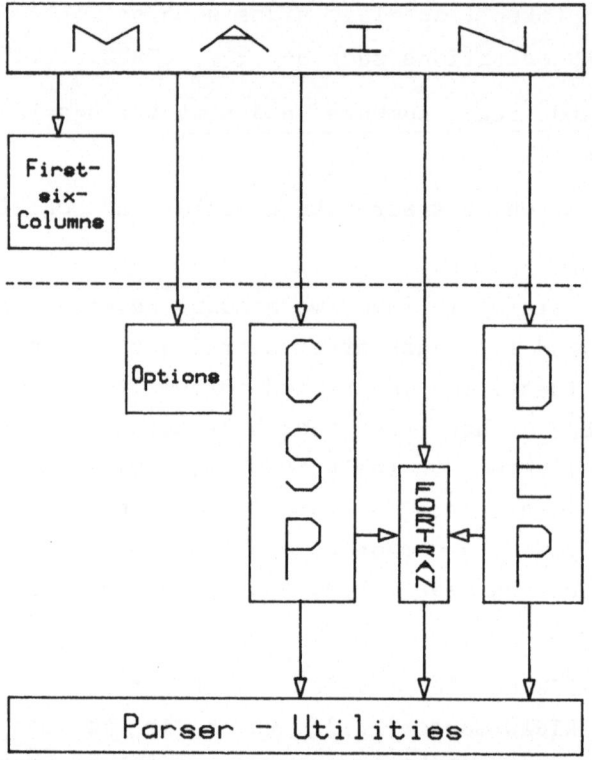

Figure 4.16: Parser Structure

The parser consists of several modules as illustrated in figure 4.16

The global control is centralised in the part MAIN which parses each input line separately (because of the FORTRAN line structure of statements). A "pre-parsing" analyses the first six columns and the first token after column six (FORTRAN!). Depending on this pre-parsing the statements are divided into the following classes:

- comment and blank lines
- options
- control flow constructs
- dialogue statements

While comment and blank lines are immediately processed, the last three classes are each handled in a separate module.

The control instance is realised by a finite state automaton. After parsing the first six columns, the next tokens are clustered - mostly one token is sufficient to do so. Depending on the cluster code and the current automaton status, an action and the succeeding status are selected. Thus the execution is controlled in a simple and changeable way. Most errors are recognised by the automaton thus the continuation is ensured after its occurrance.

Several options are available, controlling the production of the listing (on or off), the type of the generated code (FORTRAN IV or FORTRAN 77), and copying the comment lines to the destination file (copy or suppress).

The dialogue element parser (DEP) uses subautomaton to control the exact sequence of statements. It produces subroutine calls to the runtime system using the above mentioned utilities.

The control structure parser (CSP) uses a stack to remember the nesting depth and the correspondence between statements which together form a construct (e.g. IF...THEN... ELSE...FI, while several statements may be between THEN and ELSE and between ELSE and FI). The generated code results in FORTRAN statements.

The parser itself is written in extended FORTRAN (i.e. the above mentioned control constructs are used), thus being readable and easily changeable. Special efforts were made to ensure its portability.

4.3.7. The Runtime System

As mentioned above, the runtime system establishes the connection to GKS and manages the dialogue objects. In the former domain, the major task is the device control. It is carried out via a table which contains the mapping to the GKS devices:

- the workstation identifier, the connection identifier, and

the   type of the workstation used during the dialogue session

- the   correlation to the devices used in the dialogue cells
  and the corresponding   hardware   devices,   selected by the
  input device number

- properties   of   the   input   devices,   inquired   of via GKS
  inquiry functions

Information   about   the   dialogue   objects   to be managed is
stored   in   the   "object   table".   Information   about   every
picture,   text   and menu is generated by a create, prompt or
echo statement. For each one, its identifier, type (picture,
text,   menu),   the related viewport, lifetime, whether it is
used   as   an   echo   or   a prompt and others are kept. Access
functions   allow for insertion, inquiry, deletion and change
of these entries.

At the top of these tables and using GKS, "handlers" perform
the   generation   of   graphics   objects   and   fit   them   into
viewports.   In   addition, they solve conflicts occuring when
several   objects   are   to be displayed in the same viewport.
They ensure deletion when the object lifetime ends.

During   runtime,   a stack of dialogue cells is maintained to
control the calling hierarchy and the resulting hierarchy of
prompts   and   echoes;   especially,   the observation of scope
rules is ensured.

5. Conclusion

"Specification Tools and Implementation Techniques" - they alone turned out to be not sufficient enough to garantee a "good" machine-user interface. One of the reasons may be that up to now less incorporation of human factors has been undertaken.

Our approach in settling design conflicts is the requirement of an adaptive design strategy which involves several models, goals, and guidelines, each of them sufficient for one special class of problems. Furthermore we confirmed that in many cases the raising of awareness to human factors will lead to a more effective and "user-friendly" interface. Although much effort has been investigated onto this area, success can only be discovered with difficulty. New strategies and further concentration on both, man and machine, will probably lead to success in future.

6. Literature

/ANS79/ E. Anson, "The Semantics of Graphical Input,"
Computer Graphics, XIII, 2(1979), 113-120. (Proc.
of SIGGRAPH 79)

/ANS82/ E. Anson, "The Device Model of Interaction,"
Computer Graphics, XVI, 3(1982), 107-114.

/BLA83/ A. Blaser and M. Zoeppritz (ed.), "Enduser Systems
and Their Human Factors," (Berlin: Springer, 1983).
(Proc. of the Scientific Symposium of IBM, Heidelberg)

/BOR83/ H.G. Borufka, H. Hanusa, H. Kuhlmann, G. Pfaff,
"Wenschdorf III, Workshop on Universal Interface
Managers," (Darmstadt: Technische Hochschule, 1983).
(Research and Development Report GRIS 83-9)

/BOS82/ J. van den Bos, "Introduction to Man-Computer Communication," Computer Graphics Forum, I, 4(1982),
194-203.

/BUX83/ W. Buxton, "Lexical and Pragmatic Considerations of
Input Structures," Computer Graphics, XVII,1(1983)
31-37.

/CAK80/ A. Cakir, D.J. Hart, T.F.M. Stewart, "The VDT Manual," (London: John Wiley & Sons. Ltd., 1980).

/CAR82/ J.M. Carroll, "The Adventure of Getting to Know a
Computer," IEEE Computer, XV, 11(1982), 49-58.

/DAV83/ E. Davis and R.W. Swezey, "Human Factors Guidelines
in Computer Graphics: a case study," Int. J. Man-
Machine Studies, 18(1983), 113-133.

/DIN83/ DIN 66234,"Bildschirmarbeitsplätze - Teil 8: Dialog-
gestaltung," (Berlin: Deutsches Institut für Norm-
ung). (Internal proposal, 15.7.1983; only for internal use)

/DZI78/ W. Dzida, S. Herda, W.D. Itzfeld, "User - Perceived Quality of Interactive Systems," IEEE Transactions on Software Engng., IV, 4(1978), 270-276.

/ENC82/ J. Encarnacao, "An Approach for CAD-System Simulation," Computer Graphics Forum, I,3(1982),116-123.

/ENC83/ J. Encarnacao and L.A. Messina, "A System Simulation Technique for the Technical Evaluation and Economic Justification of CAD-Systems," (Berlin: AMK Berlin, to be published in 1983). (Proceedings of CAMP ´83, Berlin)

/ENC83b/ J. Encarnacao, H.G. Borufka, H. Hanusa, H.W. Kuhlmann, G. Pfaff, H.R. Weber, "An Integrated Concept for Generating Graphics Dialogues Processors," (Amsterdam: North-Holland, 1983), 643-658.(Proceedings of CAPE ´83, Amsterdam)

/END83/ G. Enderle, K. Kansy, G. Pfaff, "Computer Graphics Programming. GKS - The Graphics Standard," (Berlin: Springer, 1983).

/FAB83/ F. Fabian and C.Rathke, "Menüs: Einsatzmöglichkeiten eines Fenstersystems zur Unterstützung der Mensch-Maschine Kommunikation," Office Management, spec. issue, (1983), 42-44. (in German)

/FOL81a/ J. Foley, "How to Design User-Computer Interfaces," Tutorial held at SIGGRAPH/81.

/FOL81b/ J.D. Foley, V.L. Wallace, P. Chan, "The Human Factors of Graphics Interaction; Tasks and Techniques," (Washington: The George Washington University, Dep. of Elec. Engng. and Comp. Science, 1981). (Report GWU-IIST-81-3)

/FOL81c/ J.D. Foley, "Tools for the Designer of User Interfaces," (Washington: The George Washington University, Dep. of Elec. Engng. and Comp. Science, 1981). (Report GWU-IIST-81-7)

/FOL82/   J.D. Foley and A.van Dam, "Fundamentals of Interactive Computer Graphics," (Reading, Mass.: Addison-Wesley Publ. Comp., 1982).

/GEP82/   H.G. Borufka, H.W. Kuhlmann, H.R. Weber, "GEP - Generator von Eingabeprocessoren," (Darmstadt: Technical University, 1982). (Research and Development Report GRIS 82-13; in German)

/GKS82/   International Standard Organisation (ISO), "Information Processing - Graphical Kernel System (GKS) - Functional Description," (New York: ISO, 1982). (Document-No. ISO DIS 7942)

/GUE80/   R. Guedj, ed. "Methodology of Interaction," Amsterdam: North-Holland Publishing Company, 1980. (= IFIP Workshop on Methodology of Interaction, Seillac, France).

/HAN82/   H. Hanusa, H.W. Kuhlmann, G.E. Pfaff, "On Constructing Interactive Graphics Systems," EUROGRAPHICS '82, ed. D.S. Greenaway and E.A. Warman, (Amsterdam: North-Holland, 1982), pp. 237-248. (Proceedings of EUROGRAPHICS '82)

/HAN83a/   H. Hanusa and H.R. Weber, "Entwicklung eines Monitor-Modelles zur Evaluierung der Leistungsfähigkeit und der Benutzerfreundlichkeit interaktiver Systeme," In: "Measurement, Modelling and Evaluation of Computersystems", ed. P.J. Kühn and K.M. Schulz (Berlin: Springer, 1983), 382-396. (Proceedings of the 2nd GI/NTG Technical Conference, Feb. 21-23, 1983, Stuttgart)

/HAN83b/   H. Hanusa, "Tools and Techniques for the Monitoring of Interactive Graphics Dialogues," accepted for publication in Int. J. Man-Machine Studies.

/HLN83/   E. Hollnagel, "What We Do Not Know about Man-Machine Systems," Int. J. Man-Machine Studies, 18(1983), 135-143.

/HOL83/ F.L. Holl, B. Klutmann, H.Peschke,"Arbeitsumfeld und Mensch-Maschine Kommunikation," Office Management, spec. issue, (1983), 14-17. (in German)

/KAY80/ A. Kay, "Smalltalk," In: /GUE80/, 7-11.

/KER83/ K.W. Kerber, "Attitudes Towards Specific Uses of the Computer," Behaviour and Inform. Technology, II, 2(1983), 197-209.

/KNA83/ J.M. Knapp, "The Ergonomic Millenium," Computer Graphics World, VI, 6(1983), 86-92.

/LEF72/ G.R. Lefrancois, "Psychological Theories and Human Learning: Kongors Report,"(Belmont/Calif.: Wadsworth Publ. Corp., 1972).

/MAR83/ F. Margulies, "User Participation in Systems Development - a Case Study," "Computer Applications in Production and Engineering," ed. E.A. Warman (Amsterdam: North-Holland, 1983), pp.117-127.

/MOR81/ T.P. Moran, "The Command Language Grammar: A Representation for the User Interface of Interactive Computer Systems," Int. J. Man-Machine Studies, XV, 1(1981), 3-50.

/NIE80/ J. Nievergelt and J. Weydert, "Sites, Modes, and Trails: Telling the User of an Interactive System Where He Is, What He Can Do, and How To Get To Places," In: /GUE80/, 327-338.

/PFA82/ G.E. Pfaff, H.W. Kuhlmann, H. Hanusa, "Constructing User Interfaces Based on Logical Input Devices," IEEE Computer, XV, 11(1982), 62-68.

/PLA81/ M.J. Plasmeijer, "Input Tools - A Language Model for Interaction and Process Communication," PhD Thesis, Katholieke Universiteit Nijmegen, 1981.

/SHA78/ A.C. Shaw, "Software Description with Flow Expressions," IEEE Trans. Software Engng., IV, 3(1978), 242-254.

/SHA80/ A.C. Shaw, "On the Specification of Graphics Command Languages and their Processors," In: /GUE80/, pp. 377-392.

/SHN83/ B. Shneiderman, "Human Factors of Interactive Software," In: /BLA83/, pp. 9-29.

/STE83/ G.C. Stevens, "User-Friendly Computer Systems? A Critical Examination of the Concept," Behaviour and Inform. Technology, II, 1(1983), 3-16.

/STR82/ D.H. Straayer, "A Methodology for Populating Default Color Maps," In: EUROGRAPHICS '82, ed. D.S.Greenaway and E.A. Warman, (Amsterdam: North-Holland, 1982), 311-319. (Proceddings of EUROGRAPHICS '82)

/THI83/ H. Thimbleby, "What You See is What You Have Got - A User Engineering Principle for Manipulative Displays?," "Software-Ergonomics", ed. H. Balzert (Stuttgart: Teubner, 1983), pp. 70-84. (Berichte des German Chapter of the ACM, Bd. 14)

/WEB81/ H.R. Weber, "Entwicklung eines Modells zur Messung und Bewertung von Benutzerverhalten für die Anpassung des Mensch-Maschine Dialoges interaktiver Systeme," Diploma-Thesis, (Darmstadt: Technische Hochschule, Nov. 1981). (In German)

/XER82/ D.E. Lipkie, et al., "Star Graphics: An Object-Oriented Implementation," Computer Graphics, XVI, 3(1982), 115-124.

VI. The Graphical Kernel System

J. Schönhut

1. Introduction

The Graphical Kernel System GKS /1/ has been developed in a long
process since 1976 and finally evolved as the internationally
recognized sound standard for computer graphics it is today. The
original design was done by the German Standards Institute DIN
subcommittee NI 5.9. It was accepted by ISO as work item covered
by ISO working group ISO TC97/SC5/WG2 Graphics. During the process of international reviewing GKS was refined and improved. The
actual status of GKS is ISO Draft International Standard (ISO/DIS
7942) and is expected soon to become International Standard.
During this last step from ISO DIS to IS only editorial but no
more technical changes are possible.

In the following a summary of the major milestones in the
development of GKS is given:

- 1975 foundation of DIN NI 5.9
- 1976 Seillac I workshop on graphics standards
- 1977 foundation of ISO TC97/SC5/WG2 Graphics;
       July: first version of GKS published
- 1980 GKS version 6.2 becomes ISO work item
- 1981 GKS version 7.0 becomes ISO Draft Proposal
- 1982 GKS is processed to its final version 7.2 and becomes ISO
       DIS 7942; support by national delegations as national
       standards as well as internations standard.
- 1983 GKS is expected to become ISO DIS as well as national
       standard in various countries.

2. GKS Overview

GKS provides a functional interface for computer graphics
programming. It is a set of functions which can be used by a
majority of graphics applications that produce computer generated
two dimensional pictures on vector or raster graphics devices. As
a functional standard GKS is also independent of a particular
programming language.

There are three main motives for introducing the GKS standard:

- easy portability of application programs between different
  installations with different computers and different graphics
  devices;

- to aid portability of programmers by providing an accepted
  understanding of terms and methods used in computer graphics;

- to serve computer graphics equipment manufacturers as a guideline in providing useful combinations of graphics functionality in a device.

GKS contains two dimensional vector and raster graphics output primitives, graphical input and output on one or more graphics workstations, facilities to store and modify graphical information in device independent manner during program execution, and means for adapting programs to device characteristics. GKS consists of serveral upward compatible levels of increasing functionality.

GKS itself only defines a language independent nucleus, which is embedded in a language dependent layer, providing the means by which GKS is accessed from that particular programming language.

The layer model represented in figure 1 illustrates the role of GKS in a general graphical system.

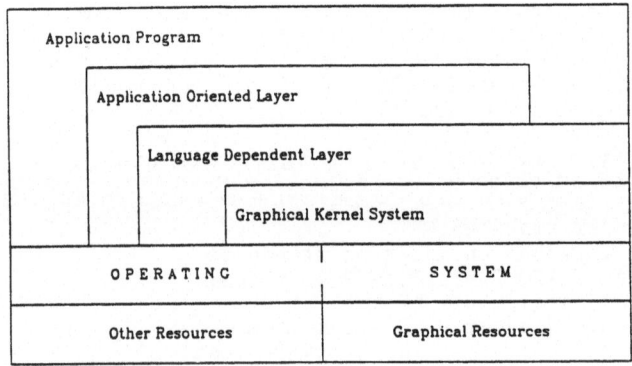

Figure 1: Layer model of GKS

3. Concepts and Programming of GKS

This Chapter explains the basic concepts of GKS. A selected set of examples show how they are utilized when programming with GKS.

3.1 Graphical Output

One of the basic tasks of graphics systems is to build up pictures from the set of functions available on a certain device. The graphical output generated by GKS is built up from two groups of basic elements, called output primitives and primitive attributes. These output primitives are mapped by GKS to the available functions of a device. The visual appearance of these output primitives is controlled by a set of attributes.

GKS contains the following output primitives:

POLYLINE   - GKS generates a set of connected lines defined by
                a sequence of points.
POLYMARKER   - GKS generates symbols centered at the given posi-
                tions.
TEXT   - GKS generates a character string at a given posi-
                tion.
FILL AREA   - GKS generates a polygon which may be hollow or
                filled with a uniform colour, a pattern or a hatch
                style.
CELL ARRAY   - GKS generates an array of rectangualar cells
                filled with individual colours which are mapped to
                pixels on the output device. However the cells need
                not map one-to-one to the pixels.
GENERALIZED DRAWING PRIMITIVE (GDP)
                - GKS addresses special geometrical output capabili-
                ties of a workstation (e.g. drawing a spline curve,
                a circular arc, etc.)

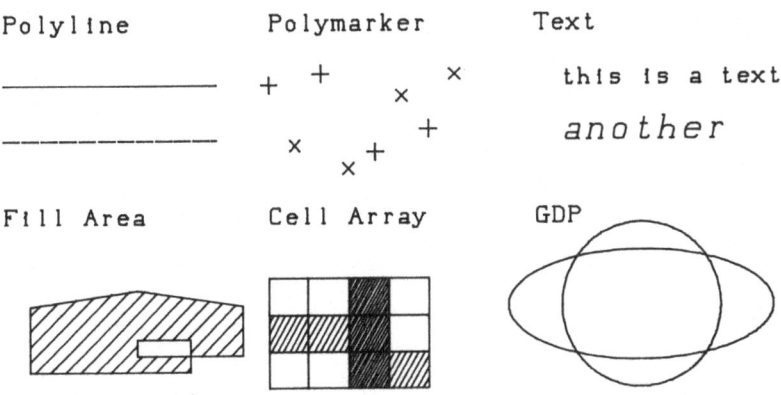

Figure 2: Output Primitives available in GKS

An output primitive potentially has three types of attributes.
Two of them control the appearance of the output primitive; the
third is used in connection with input.

Attributes of the first type control geometric aspects of primitives, e.g. character hight for text. Attributes of that type are
workstations independent and where appropriate expressed in world
coordinates.

Attributes of the second type control the non-geometric aspects
of primitives; these are aspects which do not affect the shape or
size of the primitive but only affect its appearance (e.g. line-
type for POLYLINE, colour index for all primitives except CELL
ARRAY). Non-geometric aspect of a primitive may be specified

individually or via a bundle. For individual specification of aspects there is a separate attribute for every non-geometric aspect. For specification of aspects via bundle there is one attribute per primitive called the primitive index except for GENERALIZED DRAWING PRIMITIVE and CELL ARRAY (e.g. polyline index or polymarker index). This index points into a bundle table which contains all the non-geometric aspects of that particular primitive type. The values of these aspects are workstation dependent. Each workstation has its own set of bundle tables. The values in a particular bundle (or bundle table entry) may be different on different workstations, so that the facilities on different devices may be used efficiently.

For a given non-geometric aspect of a primitive, the values are the same that can be assigned to the particular bundle table entry and to the attribute for individual specification.

As already mentioned GENERALISED DRAWING PRIMITIVE and CELL ARRAY do not have associated bundle tables nor corresponding individually set attributes. The GDP uses the most appropriate bundle or sets of individual attributes for each GDP function. CELL ARRAY has color indices as part of its function specification and has no other non-geometric aspects.

The use of bundled or individually set attributes may be chosen for each aspect separately. A further set of attributes (one for each aspect) called ASPECT SOURCE FLAGS (ASF, values bundled or individual) specify the choice.

There is one attribute of the third type per primitive, which is the PICK IDENTIFIER. It is used for identifying a group of primitives in a segment when this segment is picked.

The following list gives all attributes applying to each output primitive.

POLYLINE:
    POLYLINE INDEX
    LINETYPE
    LINEWIDTH SCALE FACTOR
    POLYLINE COLOUR INDEX
    LINETYPE ASF
    LINEWIDTH SCALE FACTOR ASF
    POLYLINE COLOUR INDEX ASF
    PICK IDENTIFIER

POLYMARKER:
    POLYMARKER INDEX
    MARKER TYPE
    MARKER SIZE SCALE FACTOR
    POLYMARKER COLOUR INDEX
    MARKER TYPE ASF
    MARKER SIZE FACTOR ASF
    POLYMARKER COLOUR INDEX ASF
    PICK IDENTIFIER

TEXT:
    TEXT INDEX
    TEXT FONT AND PRECISION
    CHARACTER EXPANSION FACTOR
    CHARACTER SPACING

```
        TEXT XOLOUR INDEX
        TEXT FONT AND PRECISION ASF
        CHARACTER EXPANSION FACTOR ASF
        CHARACTER SPACING ASF
        TEXT COLOUR INDEX ASF
        CHARACTER HEIGHT
        CHARACTER UP VECTOR
        TEXT PATH
        TEXT ALIGNMENT
        PICK IDENTIFIER

FILL AREA:
        FILL AREA INDEX
        FILL AREA INTERIOR STYLE
        FILL AREA STYLE INDEX
        FILL AREA COLOUR INDEX
        FILL AREA INTERIOR STYLE ASF
        FILL AREA STYLE INDEX ASF
        FILL AREA COLOUR INDEX ASF
        PATTERN SIZE
        PATTERN REFERENCE POINT
        PICK IDENTIFIER

CELL ARRAY
        PICK IDENTIFIER

GENERALISED DRAWING PRIMITIVE:
        zero, one or more of the sets given before, except that PICK
        IDENTIFIER is always an attribute
```

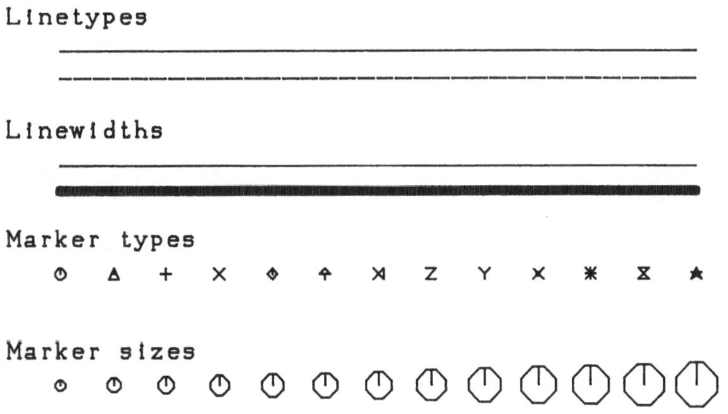

Linetypes

Linewidths

Marker types

Marker sizes

Figure 3:Examples for polyline and polymarker attributes

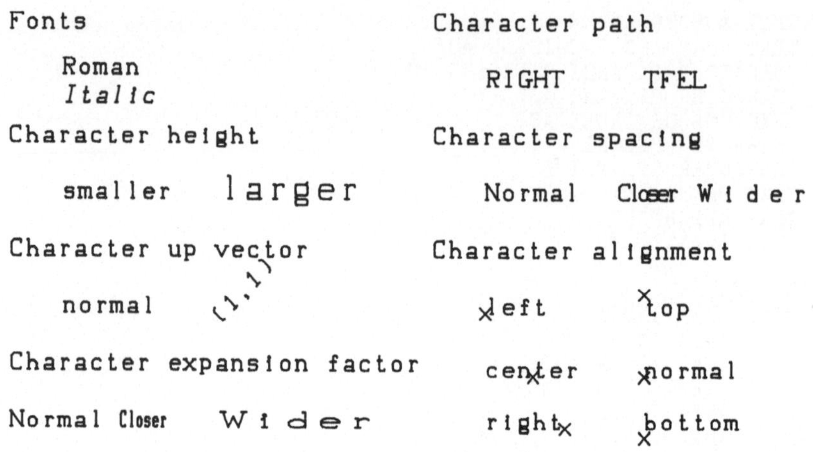

Fonts   Character path

     Roman   RIGHT   TFEL
     Italic

Character height   Character spacing

      smaller   larger   Normal   Closer Wider

Character up vector   Character alignment

      normal   (1,1)   left   top

Character expansion factor   center   normal

Normal Closer   W i d e r   right   bottom

Figure 4:Examples for text attributes

Hollow   Solid   Hatched

Pattern Array   Patterned

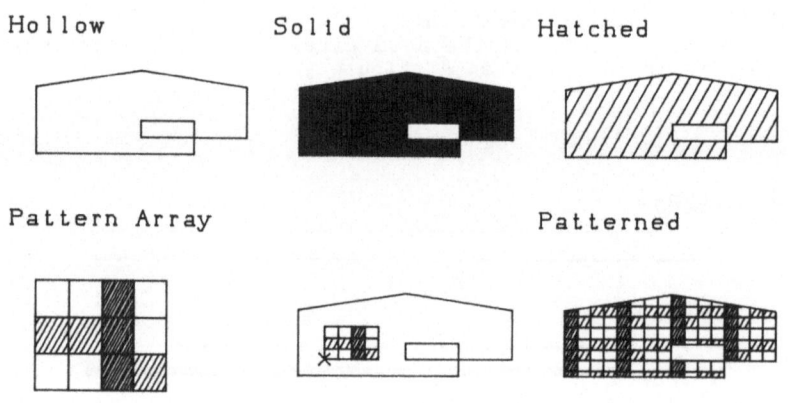

Figure 5:Examples for fill area attributes

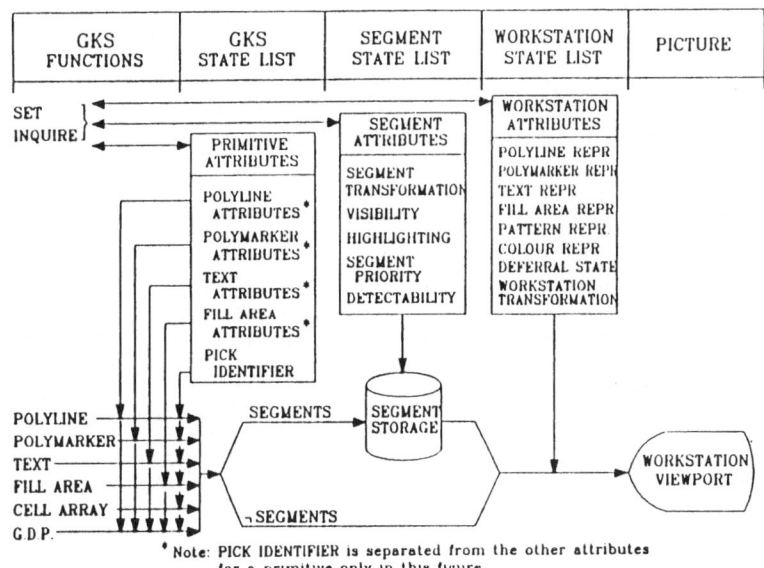

GKS FUNCTIONS	GKS STATE LIST	SEGMENT STATE LIST	WORKSTATION STATE LIST	PICTURE

Figure 6: Attribute binding in GKS

3.2 Workstation Concepts

GKS utilizes the concept of abstract graphical workstations, providing a logical interface by which the application program can control physical devices.

A fully equipped GKS workstation consists of
- one adressable display surface
- several linetypes, text fonts, character sizes, etc.
- one or more logical input devices for each input class
- REQUEST, EVENT and SAMPLE input
- facilities for segment creation and manipulation.

A "real" workstation may not be equipped with all of these capabilities. Each workstation belongs to one of six categories:
- output workstation
- input workstation
- output/input workstation
- workstation independent segment storage (WISS)
- GKS metafile output
- GKS metafile input

GKS allows output primitives to appear differently on different workstations to make optimal use of the device capabilities. The appearance of output primitives is controlled by the following workstation dependent information (if the corresponding aspect source flags are set to bundled):
- polyline representation
- polymarker representation
- text representation
- fill area representation
- colour representation
- deferral state
- workstation transformation

A GKS workstation is selected for input by the function OPEN WORKSTATION, for output by the function ACTIVATE WORKSTATION; the deselection is done by DEACTIVATE WORKSTATION and CLOSE WORKSTATION respectively.

The following example illustrates the selection and deselection of workstations.

```
OPEN GKS;                                    start working with GKS
   OPEN WORKSTATION ( W1 , ..... ) ;         open workstations
   OPEN WORKSTATION ( W2 , ..... ) ;
      ACTIVATE WORKSTATION ( W1 ) ;          allow output on W1
         output functions ;                  possible on W1
         input functions ;                   possible on W1 and W2
      ACTIVATE WORKSTATION ( W2 ) ;          ouput also on W2
         output functions ;                  output on W1 and W2
      DEACTIVATE WORKSTATION ( W1 ) ;        no more output on W1
         output functions ;                  output on W2 only
         input functions ;                   possible from W1 and W2
      DEACTIVATE WORKSTATION ( W2 ) ;        no more output
   CLOSE WORKSTATION ( W2 ) ;                close workstations
   CLOSE WORKSTATION ( W1 ) ;
CLOSE GKS;                                   end working with GKS
```

The picture displayed on a workstation should as far as possible reflect the actual state of the picture requested by the application program. To use the capabilities of a workstation efficiently, picture changes which may be necessary during program execution may be deferred by GKS; deferring picture changes is controlled by the workstation dependent deferral mode (as soon as possible, before next input on this workstation, before next input globally, at some time) and the implicit regeneration mode (suppressed or allowed). Application programs can change deferral state (SET DEFERRAL STATE); however reasonable default values are supplied by the implementation, depending on the characteristics of the device associated with this workstation, e.g. a vector refresh display should be updated as fast as possible, whereas on a storage tube erasing the screen and redrawing the picture may be optimized by deferring. The updating of the picture can be forced by the application program using the UPDATE WORKSTATION function.

In addition to these facilities a message function is provided to inform the operator at the specified workstation.

3.3 Coordinate Systems and Transformations

In GKS the application programmer defines his pictures in his own world coordinate systems (WC). The relative positioning of different parts of pictures is done via a single normalized device coordinate (NDC) space ranging in the interval 0 to 1. Primitives are not clipped to that region in NDC, as clipping is postponed to the workstation; they may well extend over this area e.g. in transformed segments. This NDC space can be seen as a workstation independent viewing surface.

The mapping between WC and NDC is done by a set of normalization transformations which are defined by their window (in WC) and their viewport (in NDC). Application programs can define them by use of the functions SET WINDOW (in WC) and SET VIEWPORT (in NDC). Multiple such normalization transformations may be present. The current normalization transformation for output primitives is

selected by an invocation of the function SELECT NORMALISATION
TRANSFORMATION giving the index of the selected transformation.

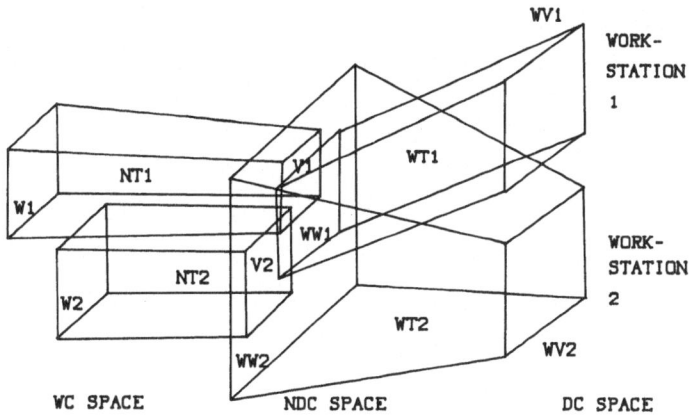

Figure 7: Normalisation and workstation transformation

The viewport associated with a particular normalization transformation may be used to define a clipping rectangle. Clipping to
this viewport boundary may be enabled or disabled (if disabled
the clipping rectangle is the default (0..1) x (0..1)) by use of
the function SET CLIPPING INDICATOR. Clipping does not take place
when the normalization transformation is performed but is delayed
until output primitives are to be displayed on a view surface of
a workstation.

To perform the mapping from the device independent NDC system to
the workstation dependent device coordinate system (DC) the workstation transformation is used. It is defined on a workstation by
workstation basis utilizing SET WORKSTATION WINDOW (in NDC) and
SET WORKSTATION VIEWPORT (in DC) which specify rectangles parallel to the coordinate axes in NDC and DC. The aspect ratio of the
picture in NDC is preserved by the workstation transformation.
This workstation transformation can be used to zoom in on a
picture or to have a complete picture on one workstation and a
zoomed section on a second workstation.

For locator input the inverse of the workstation transformation
is applied to the DC coordinates to give NDC values; then the
inverse normalization transformation is selected from the list of
normalization transformations by checking in which viewport the
point lies; overlapping of viewports is resolved by a viewport
input priority associated with each viewport. The data returned
to the application consists of the coordinate values and the
index of the normalisation transformation used for inverse transformation of the point from NDC to WC.

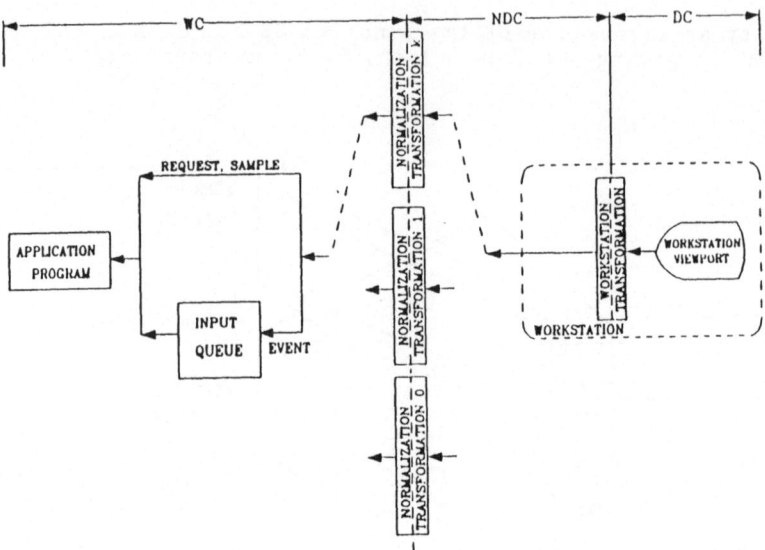

Figure 8: Transformations used for Locator Input

3.4 Segment Concept

In GKS output primitives may be grouped in segments as well as being generated outside segments. All output primitives generated between function calls to CREATE SEGMENT and CLOSE SEGMENT are collected in a segment. Segments are identified by a unique segment name specified by the application program in the CREATE SEGMENT function. The following actions may be performed with segments; segments may be
- transformed,
- made visible or invisible,
- ordered front to back (impacts overlapping primitives),
- deleted,
- renamed,
- inserted into the open segment or into the stream of output primitives.

Besides the identification by a unique segment name there is an arbitrary pick identifier associated with a single primitive or a group of primitives inside segments; this pick identifier is used for identification purposes only and cannot be used for manipulation. There is no restriction on pick identifiers regarding uniqueness; the same pick identifier may be chosen for disjoint groups of primitives even of the same segment. The following sequence of functions shows the use of pick identifiers together with segment names:

```
SET PICK IDENTIFIER ( 7 ) ;
CREATE SEGMENT ( 1 ) ;
   output functions ;          (* segment = 1; pick id = 7 *)
SET PICK IDENTIFIER ( 3 ) ;
   output functions ;          (* segment = 1; pick id = 3 *)
CLOSE SEGMENT ;
output primitives ;           (* unpickable ; pick id = 3 *)
```

```
SET PICK IDENTIFIER ( 5 ) ;
output primitives ;                (* unpickable ; pick id = 5 *)
CREATE SEGMENT ( 2 ) ;
   output functions ;              (* segment = 2; pick id = 5 *)
SET PICK IDENTIFIER ( 3 ) ;
   output functions ;             (* segment = 2; pick id = 3 *)
CLOSE SEGMENT ;
```

Segment attributes affect all primitives in a segment. Segment attributes are:
- segment transformation
- visibility
- highlighting
- segment priority
- detectability

Segment attributes are unique for each segment and do not vary between workstations. The attributes may be altered for any existing segment.

The segment transformation takes place after the normalisation transformation and maps segments from NDC to NDC. The segment transformation is specified by the SET SEGMENT TRANSFORMATION using a 2x3 transformation matrix. Succesive calls to that function are not accumulated. Locator input data is not affected by any segment transformation.

If parts of segments overlap (e.g. FILL AREA or PIXEL ARRAY), the segment with the higher priority will be used to generate the picture; the segment priority is also used for resolving overlap for pick input; the segment with the higher priority (if it is detectable) is selected.

Normally segments are stored in a workstation dependent segment store (WDSS). To permit segments to be transferred from one workstation to another or to be inserted into the open segment, one device independent segment store (WISS) is available. There segments can be stored for use by the functions COPY SEGMENT TO WORKSTATION, ASSCOCIATE SEGMENT WITH WORKSTATION and INSERT SEGMENT.

When inserting a segment, this segments transformation and the insert transformation are applied in this sequence. The clipping of primitives (inside and outside segments) is postponed until the workstation transformation is applied. When inserting a segment, the clipping rectangle associated with the stored segment is discarded; instead the actual clipping rectangle (either the viewport of the current normalisation transformation if the clipping indicator is on, or $(0..1)x(0..1)$) is associated with the inserted primitives.

COPY SEGMENT TO WORKSTATION copies the primitives of the specified segment from WISS to the specified workstation without retaining the segment information on that workstation.

ASSOCIATE SEGMENT WITH WORKSTATION copies the full segment information available from WISS to the WDSS of that workstation.

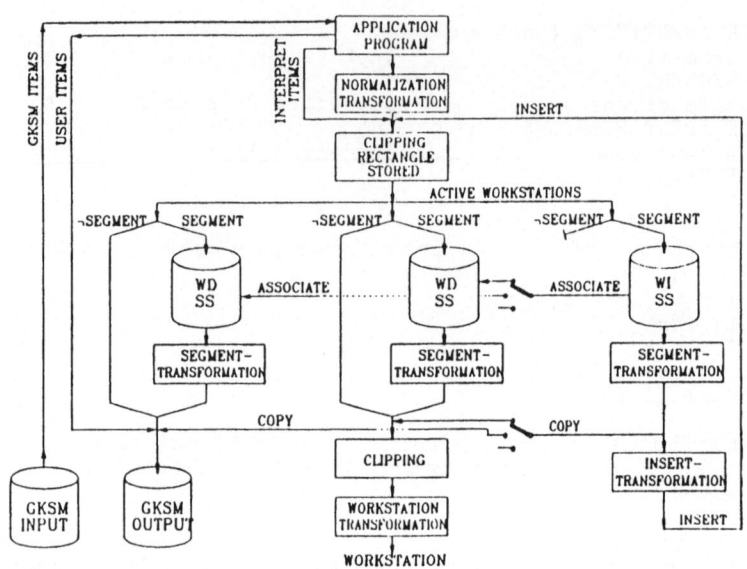

Figure 9:GKS data flow graph

Utility functions SET TRANSFORMATION MATRIX and ACCUMULATE
TRANSFORMATION MATRIX are supplied for setting up the transformation matrices.

3.5 Graphical Input

Graphical input in GKS uses the concept of logical input devices.
GKS controls one ore more logical input devices and delivers
logical input values back to the application program.

A logical input device is characterized by a workstation identifier (specifying the workstation, this input device is connected
with), an input class and a device number (distinguishing different logical input devices of the same class on the same workstation).

The input class defines the type of value received by the application program. The following five input classes are supported by
GKS:
- locator: provides a position in world coordinates and a
                normalization transformation number;
- stroke: provides a sequence of positions in world
                coordinates and a normalisation transformation
                number;
- valuator: provides a real number;
- choice: provides a nonnegative integer choice number;
                a zero value indicates no choice;
- pick: provides a pick status, a segment name and a
                pick identifier;
- string: provides a character string.

Each logical input device can be operated in three modes. At any
time an input device is in exactly one mode. The modes supported
are:
- request: an invocation of a REQUEST <input class> func-
              tion causes the attempt to read a logical
              value from the specified device (which must be
              in request mode); GKS waits until the input is
              entered or a break action is performed by the
              operator; if a break has occurred, the logical
              input value is invalid;
- sample: an invocation of a SAMPLE <input class> func-
              tion returns the current logical input value
              from the specified logical input device (must
              be in sample mode) without waiting for opera-
              tor action;
- event: GKS maintains one input queue of temporally
              ordered event reports; an event report con-
              tains the identification of the logical input
              device and its logical input value; event
              reports are created by operator action only
              from input devices in event mode. The applica-
              tion program can remove the event reports in
              the order they were created; it can also flush
              all event reports from a specific logical
              input device.

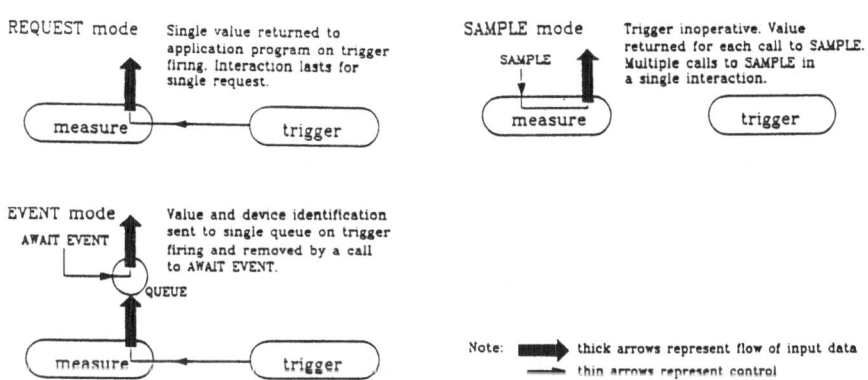

Figure 10: Relationship between measure and trigger for different
           operating modes

The relationship between logical and physical input devices is
described using the concept of measure and trigger. Each logical
input device contains a measure, a trigger, an initial value, a
prompt/echo type, an echo area and a data record defining details
of the echo type. Initial value and prompt/echo data can be set
via the INITIALISE <device class> function. A measure can be
regarded as the state of an active process (the measure process).
The current state of this measure process is available to GKS as

a logical input value. One single physical device can have more than one simultaneously associated logical devices, and hence more than one associated measure processes and measures. The measure process is in existence while an interaction with the logical input device is taking place.

The trigger of a logical input device is a physical input device, with which the operator can indicate the significant moment in time to take over the measure value. At these moments a trigger is said to fire. A single operator action can cause several triggers to fire. A trigger can be seen as an active process (the trigger process) sending a message to one or more logical input devices when it fires. The trigger process is in existence as long as there is at least one receiving measure process in existence.

The availability of a logical input device is signalled to the operator by a prompt. The currrent value of the measure is signalled to the operator by the echo of the logical device. Upon firing of a trigger the operator receives an acknowledgement.

3.6 GKS Metafile Interface

GKS provides facilities for long term storage of graphical information through its metafile interface. The GKS metafile (GKSM) can be used for transporting graphical information between systems or between applications, and for storing non-graphical information with the graphical data.

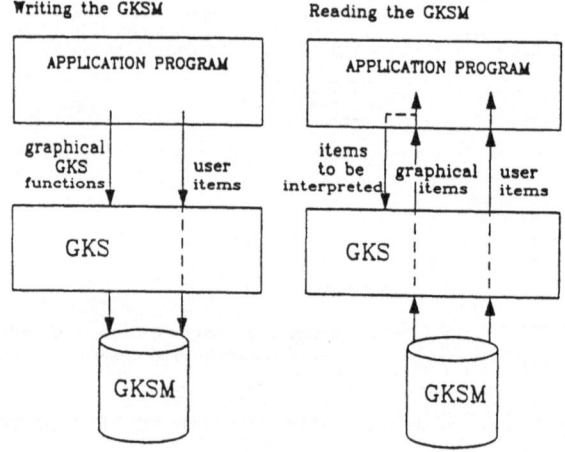

Figure 11: Relationship between GKS and GKSM

GKS supplies means for output as well as for input of metafiles using the workstation concept. On GKSM output workstations all GKS functions referring to output workstations except inquiries are recorded; besides that the user may record user items on the GKSM (function WRITE ITEM TO GKSM). GKSM input workstations are supported via the functions GET ITEM TYPE FROM GKSM, READ ITEM

FROM GKSM and INTERPRET ITEM.

The functionality is integral part of the proposed ISO standard. The format of the GKSM is not part of the standard, but is contained in an appendix.

3.7 GKS Level Structure

GKS was constructed to be used by a wide range of applications. Therefore it is desirable to permit GKS implementations with certain upward compatible levels of increasing functionality. GKS has a level concept that allows for varying capabilities in two different axes: input and all other functions (called 'output').

The output levels are:
- 0: minimal output (among other restictions only one work-station active at a time, not all attributes controllable);
- 1: full output capabilities with basic segmentation;
- 2: full segmentation capabilities with device independent segment store.

The input levels are:
- a: no input;
- b: request input only;
- c: full input (including sample and event input).

Output Level	Input Level		
	a	b	c
0	No input, minimal control, only predefined bundles, multiple normalization transformation facilities but minimum settable required is 1, and all output functions; metafile workstations optional	REQUEST input, mode setting and initialise functions for logical input devices, no PICK, and set viewport input priority	SAMPLE and EVENT input, no PICK.
1	Full output including full bundle concept, multiple workstation concept, basic segmentation (everything except Workstation Independent Segment Storage); metafile workstations required	REQUEST PICK, mode setting and initialise for PICK	SAMPLE and EVENT input for PICK
2	Workstation Independent Segment Storage.		

Figure 12: Level diagram of GKS

Besides these nine levels 0a (minimal output, no input) up to 2c (full input, full segmentation and output) GKS specifies minimal requirements for a GKS implementation regarding ranges of parameters.

3.8 State of GKS

The internal state of GKS is defined by state variables grouped in lists. The following informations are available:
- operating state (see figure 13);
- GKS state list;
- segment state list for every existing segment;
- input queue;
- workstation state list for every open workstation;
- workstation description table for every workstation type known to the system;
- GKS error state list.

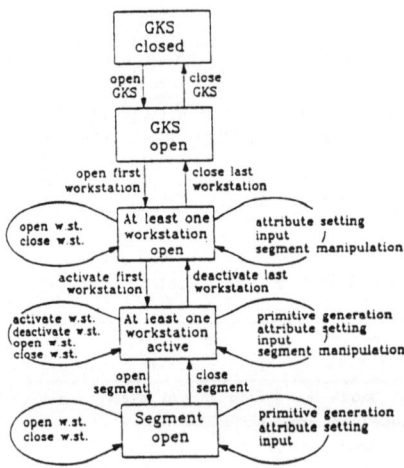

Figure 13: Transition diagram of GKS operating states

All information contained in the state lists can be inquired from the application program.

3.9 Error Handling

The GKS document specifies with each function a set of error situations which must be recognized by a GKS implementation. Besides the standard error reaction it is possible to supply a user error handling procedure with the application program; this routine is called every time an error is recognized. It may inquire the state lists using the INQUIRY functions, but it may not alter them. Thereby an optimal user reaction on errors is possible.

A special provision is made to recover from difficult error situations with as little loss of information as possible; the GKS function EMERGENCY CLOSE GKS is an implementation dependent facility to save as much information as possible, clean up files and environment, and close GKS in a save way.

3.10 Special Interfaces

GKS specifies a "standard way of being non-standard" by supplying
uniform access to installation or hardware dependent features.
This obviously reduces portability of application programs, but
it does this in an easily identifyable manner. The functions
available for that purpose are ESCAPE for non geometrical information and the GENERALISED DRAWING PRIMITIVE (GDP) for geometrical output (such as splines, circular or elliptic arcs etc.).

4. GKS Interfaces

GKS is a nucleus which needs further specification in several
aspects:

- it defines abstract functions and data types in a language
  independent way;
- it provides these functions in a device independent way;
- its functions shall serve a large constituency of users and
  applications.

To make GKS a practical vehicle for computer graphics programming, several interfaces have to be specified through which
communication between GKS and other system components are
achieved; these interfaces are:

- the functional interface;
- the language interface;
- the device interface;
- the operator interface.

The functional interface is described in the standard GKS
document ISO DIS 7942 and in chapter 3 of this report. The
operator interface is based on the logical input device model,
the device interface mainly on the workstation concept given in
GKS. For language interfaces the GKS document specifies several
language binding rules.

4.1 GKS Language Interfaces

As GKS is defined as an abstract functional standard, it needs
complementation with a concrete binding to a language for use in
a practical programming environment. In parallel with the definition of the standard have been around implementations of the
variaous stages of GKS mostly in FORTRAN. This is also the
language with the most commonly accepted binding for GKS. Besides
there is work going on to integrate a low level of GKS into the
new BASIC standard. On the other hand there are implementation
efforts in C and PASCAL, which are developed on a more private or
institutional basis.

The FORTRAN interface /2/ was designed by DIN and refined in
cooperation mainly with ANSI and BSI. The FORTRAN language binding is defined for full FORTRAN 77 including functions different
for the FORTRAN 77 subset. In the following the language binding
rules given in GKS are applied to the FORTRAN binding and the
decisions taken are explained.

Rule L1: GKS functions are mapped to FORTRAN SUBROUTINEs on a one to one correspondence, except for special situations in inquiries. This means a GKS function has a unique FORTRAN name and can be invoked by a FORTRAN CALL.

Rule L2: All FORTRAN SUBROUTINE names start with the sentinel character "G"; the remaining letters are chosen by deriving a unique abbreviation of the single words of the function names. For example, ACTIVATE becomes AC, workstation becomes WK; hence the FORTRAN SUBROUTINE name of ACTIVATE WORKSTATION becomes GACWK. A complete list of the FORTRAN names is given in annex 1.

Rule L3: The GKS standard uses abstract data types, most of which have no immediate equivalent in FORTRAN. Annex 2 shows the correspondence between the abstract data types in GKS and their representation in FORTRAN. Also a list of identifiers is given (annex 3) for the FORTRAN mapping of enumeration type values in GKS; these names are not required to be used; nevertheless this is a convenient means for writing application programs if these mnemonics can be used by an application via a include statement.

Rule L4: As all GKS functions are represented as FORTRAN SUBROUTINEs, their invocation is done via CALL statement; the parameters are passed according to FORTRAN parameter passing conventions.

Rule L5: For internal communication a GKS implementation may need reserved global names; these global names shall start with the letters "GK" to avoid conflicts in usage with application program defined procedures. Therefore application programs should avoid names starting with "GK". GKS installations should provide means for renaming globally known internal names when necessary.

5. Acknowledgement

This presentation is based on the work of many individuals who contributed to the development of GKS and its international reviewing process. The GKS document /1/ and the GKS FORTRAN binding document /2/ have been basic sources for this paper.

6. References

/1/ Graphical Kernel System (GKS)
    Version 7.2
    ISO/DIS 7942 - 1982

/2/ FORTRAN Interface of GKS 7.2
    ISO TC97/SC5/WG2 N165
    NI-5.9/11-83
    Erlangen, May 1983

/3/ G. Enderle, K. Kansy, G. Pfaff
    GKS - The Graphical Standard
    Berlin - Heidelberg - New York
    Springer 1983

Annex 1: GKS FORTRAN SUBROUTINE names

The GKS functions are appearing in the order of the GKS document
together with their level and a hyphenated form showing their
construction.

```
GOPKS    OP-KS       OA    OPEN GKS
GCLKS    CL-KS       OA    CLOSE GKS
GOPWK    OP-WK       OA    OPEN WORKSTATION
GCLWK    CL-WK       OA    CLOSE WORKSTATION
GACWK    AC-WK       OA    ACTIVATE WORKSTATION
GDAWK    DA-WK       OA    DEACTIVATE WORKSTATION
GCLRWK   CLR-WK      OA    CLEAR WORKSTATION
GRSGWK   R-SG-WK     1A    REDRAW ALL SEGMENTS ON WORKSTATION
GUWK     U-WK        OA    UPDATE WORKSTATION
GSDS     S-D-S       1A    SET DEFERRAL STATE
GMSG     MSG         1A    MESSAGE
GMSGS    MSG-S       1A    MESSAGE (FORTRAN 77 SUBSET)
GESC     ESC         OA    ESCAPE
GPL      PL          OA    POLYLINE
GPM      PM          OA    POLYMARKER
GTX      TX          OA    TEXT
GTXS     TX-S        OA    TEXT (FORTRAN 77 SUBSET)
GFA      F-A         OA    FILL AREA
GCA      C-A         OA    CELL ARRAY
GGDP     G-D-P       OA    GENERALIZED DRAWING PRIMITIVE
GSPLI    S-PL-I      OA    SET POLYLINE INDEX
GSLN     S-LN        OA    SET LINETYPE
GSLWSC   S-LW-SC     OA    SET LINEWIDTH SCALE FACTOR
GSPLCI   S-PL-C-I    OA    SET POLYLINE COLOUR INDEX
GSPMI    S-PM-I      OA    SET POLYMARKER INDEX
GSMK     S-MK        OA    SET MARKERTYPE
GSMKSC   S-MK-SC     OA    SET MARKER SIZE SCALE FACTOR
GSPMCI   S-PM-C-I    OA    SET POLYMARKER COLOUR INDEX
GSTXI    S-TX-I      OA    SET TEXT INDEX
GSTXFP   S-TX-F-P    OA    SET TEXT FONT AND PRECISION
GSCHXP   S-CH-XP     OA    SET CHARACTER EXPANSION FACTOR
GSCHSP   S-CH-SP     OA    SET CHARACTER SPACING
GSTXCI   S-TX-C-I    OA    SET TEXT COLOUR INDEX
GSCHH    S-CH-H      OA    SET CHARACTER HEIGHT
GSCHUP   S-CH-UP     OA    SET CHARACTER UP VECTOR
GSTXP    S-TX-P      OA    SET TEXT PATH
GSTXAL   S-TX-AL     OA    SET TEXT ALIGNMENT
GSFAI    S-F-A-I     OA    SET FILL AREA INDEX
GSFAIS   S-F-A-I-S   OA    SET FILL AREA INTERIOR STYLE
GSFASI   S-F-A-S-I   OA    SET FILL AREA STYLE INDEX
GSFACI   S-F-A-C-I   OA    SET FILL AREA COLOUR INDEX
GSPA     S-PA        OA    SET PATTERN SIZE
GSPARF   S-PA-RF     OA    SET PATTERN REFERENCE POINT
GSASF    S-A-S-F     OA    SET ASPECT SOURCE FLAGS
GSPKID   S-PK-ID     1B    SET PICK IDENTIFIER
GSPLR    S-PL-R      1A    SET POLYLINE REPRESENTATION
GSPMR    S-PM-R      1A    SET POLYMARKER REPRESENTATION
GSTXR    S-TX-R      1A    SET TEXT REPRESENTATION
GSFAR    S-F-A-R     1A    SET FILL AREA REPRESENTATION
GSPAR    S-PA-R      1A    SET PATTERN REPRESENTATION
GSCR     S-C-R       OA    SET COLOUR REPRESENTATION
GSWN     S-WN        OA    SET WINDOW
GSVP     S-VP        OA    SET VIEWPORT
GSVPIP   S-VP-I-P    OB    SET VIEWPORT INPUT PRIORITY
GSELNT   SEL-N-T     OA    SELECT NORMALIZATION TRANSFORMATION
```

```
GSCLIP   S-CLIP      OA   SET CLIPPING INDICATOR
GSWKWN   S-WK-WN     OA   SET WORKSTATION WINDOW
GSWKVP   S-WK-VP     OA   SET WORKSTATION VIEWPORT
GCRSG    CR-SG       1A   CREATE SEGMENT
GCLSG    CL-SG       1A   CLOSE SEGMENT
GRENSG   REN-SG      1A   RENAME SEGMENT
GDSG     D-SG        1A   DELETE SEGMENT
GDSGWK   D-SG-WK     1A   DELETE SEGMENT FROM WORKSTATION
GASGWK   A-SG-WK     2A   ASSOCIATE SEGMENT WITH WORKSTATION
GCSGWK   C-SG-WK     2A   COPY SEGMENT TO WORKSTATION
GINSG    IN-SG       2A   INSERT SEGMENT
GSSGT    S-SG-T      1A   SET SEGMENT TRANSFORMATION
GSVIS    S-VIS       1A   SET VISIBILITY
GSHLIT   S-HLIT      1A   SET HIGHLIGHTING
GSSGP    S-SG-P      1A   SET SEGMENT PRIORITY
GSDTEC   S-DTEC      1B   SET DETECTABILITY
GINLC    IN-LC       OB   INITIALISE LOCATOR
GINSK    IN-SK       OB   INITIALISE STROKE
GINVL    IN-VL       OB   INITIALISE VALUATOR
GINCH    IN-CH       OB   INITIALISE CHOICE
GINPK    IN-PK       1B   INITIALISE PICK
GINST    IN-ST       OB   INITIALISE STRING
GINSTS   IN-ST-S     OB   INITIALISE STRING (FORTRAN 77 SUBSET)
GSLCM    S-LC-M      OB   SET LOCATOR MODE
GSSKM    S-SK-M      OB   SET STROKE MODE
GSVLM    S-VL-M      OB   SET VALUATOR MODE
GSCHM    S-CH-M      OB   SET CHOICE MODE
GSPKM    S-PK-M      1B   SET PICK MODE
GSSTM    S-ST-M      OB   SET STRING MODE
GRQLC    RQ-LC       OB   REQUEST LOCATOR
GRQSK    RQ-SK       OB   REQUEST STROKE
GRQVL    RQ-VL       OB   REQUEST VALUATOR
GRQCH    RQ-CH       OB   REQUEST CHOICE
GRQPK    RQ-PK       1B   REQUEST PICK
GRQST    RQ-ST       OB   REQUEST STRING
GRQSTS   RQ-ST-S     OB   REQUEST STRING (FORTRAN 77 SUBSET)
GSMLC    SM-LC       OC   SAMPLE LOCATOR
GSMSK    SM-SK       OC   SAMPLE STROKE
GSMVL    SM-VL       OC   SAMPLE VALUATOR
GSMCH    SM-CH       OC   SAMPLE CHOICE
GSMPK    SM-PK       1C   SAMPLE PICK
GSMST    SM-ST       OC   SAMPLE STRING
GSMSTS   SM-ST-S     OC   SAMPLE STRING (FORTRAN 77 SUBSET)
GWAIT    WAIT        OC   AWAIT EVENT
GFLUSH   FLUSH       OC   FLUSH DEVICE EVENTS
GGTLC    GT-LC       OC   GET LOCATOR
GGTSK    GT-SK       OC   GET STROKE
GGTVL    GT-VL       OC   GET VALUATOR
GGTCH    GT-CH       OC   GET CHOICE
GGTPK    GT-PK       1C   GET PICK
GGTST    GT-ST       OC   GET STRING
GGTSTS   GT-ST-S     OC   GET STRING (FORTRAN 77 SUBSET)
GWITM    W-ITM       OA   WRITE ITEM TO GKSM
GGTITM   GT-ITM      OA   GET ITEM TYPE FROM GKSM
GRDITM   RD-ITM      OA   READ ITEM FROM GKSM
GIITM    I-ITM       OA   INTERPRET ITEM
GQOPS    Q-OP-S      OA   INQUIRE OPERATING STATE VALUE
GQLVKS   Q-LV-KS     OA   INQUIRE LEVEL OF GKS
GQEWK    Q-E-WK      OA   INQUIRE LIST element OF AVAILABLE WORKSTATION TYPE
GQWKM    Q-WK-M      1A   INQUIRE WORKSTATION MAXIMUM NUMBERS
GQMNTN   Q-M-N-T-N   OA   INQUIRE MAXIMUM NORMALIZATION TRANSFORMATION NUMBE
```

```
GQWKCA    Q-WK-CA       OB    INQUIRE WORKSTATION CATEGORY
GQWKCL    Q-WK-CL       OB    INQUIRE WORKSTATION CLASSIFICATION
GQMDS     Q-M-D-S       OA    INQUIRE MAXIMUM DISPLAY SURFACE SIZE
GQDWKA    Q-D-WK-A      1A    INQUIRE DYNAMIC MODIFICATION OF WORKSTATION ATTRIB
GQDDS     Q-D-D-S       1A    INQUIRE DEFAULT DEFERRAL STATE VALUES
GQPLF     Q-PL-F        OA    INQUIRE POLYLINE FACILITIES
GQPPLR    Q-P-PL-R      OA    INQUIRE PREDEFINED POLYLINE REPRESENTATION
GQPMF     Q-PM-F        OA    INQUIRE POLYMARKER FACILITIES
GQPPMR    Q-P-PM-R      OA    INQUIRE PREDEFINED POLYMARKER REPRESENTATION
GQTXF     Q-TX-F        OA    INQUIRE TEXT FACILITIES
GQPTXR    Q-P-TX-R      OA    INQUIRE PREDEFINED TEXT REPRESENTATION
GQFAF     Q-F-A-F       OA    INQUIRE FILL AREA FACILITIES
GQPFAR    Q-P-F-A-R     OA    INQUIRE PREDEFINED FILL AREA REPRESENTATION
GQPAF     Q-PA-F        OA    INQUIRE PATTERN FACILITIES
GQPPAR    Q-P-PA-R      OA    INQUIRE PREDEFINED PATTERN REPRESENTATION
GQCF      Q-C-F         OA    INQUIRE COLOUR FACILITIES
GQPCR     Q-P-C-R       OA    INQUIRE PREDEFINED COLOUR REPRESENTATION
GQEGDP    Q-E-G-D-P     OA    INQUIRE LIST element OF
                              AVAILABLE GENERALIZED DRAWING PRIMITIVES
GQGDP     Q-G-D-P       OA    INQUIRE GENERALIZED DRAWING PRIMITIVE
GQLWK     Q-L-WK        1A    INQUIRE MAXIMUM LENGTH OF WORKSTATION STATE TABLES
GQSGP     Q-SG-P        1A    INQUIRE NUMBER OF SEGMENT PRIORITIES SUPPORTED
GQDSGA    Q-D-SG-A      1A    INQUIRE DYNAMIC MODIFICATION OF SEGMENT ATTRIBUTES
GQLI      Q-L-I         OB    INQUIRE NUMBER OF AVAILABLE LOGICAL INPUT DEVICES
GQDLC     Q-D-LC        OB    INQUIRE DEFAULT LOCATOR DEVICE DATA
GQDSK     Q-D-SK        OB    INQUIRE DEFAULT STROKE DEVICE DATA
GQDVL     Q-D-VL        OB    INQUIRE DEFAULT VALUATOR DEVICE DATA
GQDCH     Q-D-CH        OB    INQUIRE DEFAULT CHOICE DEVICE DATA
GQDPK     Q-D-PK        1B    INQUIRE DEFAULT PICK DEVICE DATA
GQDST     Q-D-ST        OB    INQUIRE DEFAULT STRING DEVICE DATA
GQASWK    Q-AS-WK       1A    INQUIRE SET member OF ASSOCIATED WORKSTATIONS
GQSGA     Q-SG-A        1A    INQUIRE SEGMENT ATTRIBUTES
GQPXAD    Q-PX-A-D      OA    INQUIRE PIXEL ARRAY DIMENSIONS
GQPXA     Q-PX-A        OA    INQUIRE PIXEL ARRAY
GQPX      Q-PX          OA    INQUIRE PIXEL
GQIQOV    Q-I-Q-OV      OC    INQUIRE INPUT QUEUE OVERFLOW
GEVTM     EV-T-M        1A    EVALUATE TRANSFORMATION MATRIX
GACTM     AC-T-M        1A    ACCUMULATE TRANSFORMATION MATRIX
GECLKS    E-CL-KS       OA    EMERGENCY CLOSE GKS
GERHND    ER-HND        OA    ERROR HANDLING
GERLOG    ER-LOG        OA    ERROR LOGGING
GPREC     P-REC         OA    PACK DATA RECORD
GUREC     U-REC         OA    UNPACK DATA RECORD
```

```
GQOPWK    Q-OP-WK     OA   INQUIRE SET member OF OPEN WORKSTATIONS
GQACWK    Q-AC-WK     1A   INQUIRE SET member OF ACTIVE WORKSTATIONS
GQPLI     Q-PL-I      OA   INQUIRE POLYLINE INDEX                    -PRIM ATTR
GQPMI     Q-PM-I      OA   INQUIRE POLYMARKER INDEX                  -PRIM ATTR
GQTXI     Q-TX-I      OA   INQUIRE TEXT INDEX                        -PRIM ATTR
GQCHH     Q-CH-H      OA   INQUIRE CHARACTER HEIGHT                  -PRIM ATTR
GQCHUP    Q-CH-UP     OA   INQUIRE CHARACTER UP VECTOR               -PRIM ATTR
GQTXP     Q-TX-P      OA   INQUIRE TEXT PATH                         -PRIM ATTR
GQTXAL    Q-TX-AL     OA   INQUIRE TEXT ALIGNMENT                    -PRIM ATTR
GQFAI     Q-F-A-I     OA   INQUIRE FILL AREA INDEX                   -PRIM ATTR
GQPA      Q-PA        OA   INQUIRE PATTERN SIZE                      -PRIM ATTR
GQPARF    Q-PA-RF     OA   INQUIRE PATTERN REFERENCE POINT           -PRIM ATTR
GQPKID    Q-PK-ID     OA   INQUIRE PICK IDENTIFIER.                  -PRIM ATTR
GQLN      Q-LN        OA   INQUIRE LINETYPE                          -INDIVID ATTR
GQLWSC    Q-LW-SC     OA   INQUIRE LINEWIDTH SCALE FACTOR            -INDIVID ATTR
GQPLCI    Q-PL-C-I    OA   INQUIRE POLYLINE COLOUR INDEX             -INDIVID ATTR
GQMK      Q-MK        OA   INQUIRE MARKERTYPE                        -INDIVID ATTR
GQMKSC    Q-MK-SC     OA   INQUIRE MARKER SIZE SCALE FACTOR          -INDIVID ATTR
GQPMCI    Q-PM-C-I    OA   INQUIRE POLYMARKER COLOUR INDEX           -INDIVID ATTR
GQTXFP    Q-TX-F-P    OA   INQUIRE TEXT FONT AND PRECISION           -INDIVID ATTR
GQCHXP    Q-CH-XP     OA   INQUIRE CHARACTER EXPANSION FACTOR        -INDIVID ATTR
GQCHSP    Q-CH-SP     OA   INQUIRE CHARACTER SPACING                 -INDIVID ATTR
GQTXCI    Q-TX-C-I    OA   INQUIRE TEXT COLOUR INDEX                 -INDIVID ATTR
GQFAIS    Q-F-A-I-S   OA   INQUIRE FILL AREA INTERIOR STYLE          -INDIVID ATTR
GQFASI    Q-F-A-S-I   OA   INQUIRE FILL AREA STYLE INDEX             -INDIVID ATTR
GQFACI    Q-F-A-C-I   OA   INQUIRE FILL AREA COLOUR INDEX            -INDIVID ATTR
GQASF     Q-A-S-F     OA   INQUIRE ASPECT SOURCE FLAGS               -INDIVID ATTR
GQCNTN    Q-C-N-T-N   OA   INQUIRE CURRENT NORMALIZATION TRANSFORMATION NUMBE
GQENTN    Q-E-N-T-N   OA   INQUIRE LIST element OF
                                  NORMALIZATION TRANSFORMATION NUMBERS
GQNT      Q-N-T       OA   INQUIRE NORMALIZATION TRANSFORMATION
GQCLIP    Q-CLIP      OA   INQUIRE CLIPPING INDICATOR
GQOPSG    Q-OP-SG     1A   INQUIRE NAME OF OPEN SEGMENT
GQSGUS    Q-SG-US     1A   INQUIRE SET member OF SEGMENT NAMES IN USE
GQSIM     Q-SIM       OC   INQUIRE MORE SIMULTANEOUS EVENTS
GQWKC     Q-WK-C      OA   INQUIRE WORKSTATION CONNECTION AND TYPE
GQWKS     Q-WK-S      OA   INQUIRE WORKSTATION STATE
GQWKDU    Q-WK-D-U    OA   INQUIRE WORKSTATION DEFERRAL AND UPDATE STATES
GQEPLI    Q-E-PL-I    1A   INQUIRE LIST element OF POLYLINE INDICES
GQPLR     Q-PL-R      1A   INQUIRE POLYLINE REPRESENTATION
GQEPMI    Q-E-PM-I    1A   INQUIRE LIST element OF POLYMARKER INDICES
GQPMR     Q-PM-R      1A   INQUIRE POLYMARKER REPRESENTATION
GQETXI    Q-E-TX-I    1A   INQUIRE LIST element OF TEXT INDICES
GQTXR     Q-TX-R      1A   INQUIRE TEXT REPRESENTATION
GQTXX     Q-TX-X      OA   INQUIRE TEXT EXTENT
GQTXXS    Q-TX-X-S    OA   INQUIRE TEXT EXTENT (FORTRAN 77 SUBSET)
GQEFAI    Q-E-F-A-I   1A   INQUIRE LIST element OF FILL AREA INDICES
GQFAR     Q-F-A-R     1A   INQUIRE FILL AREA REPRESENTATION
GQEPAI    Q-E-PA-I    1A   INQUIRE LIST element OF PATTERN INDICES
GQPAR     Q-PA-R      1A   INQUIRE PATTERN REPRESENTATION
GQECI     Q-E-C-I     OA   INQUIRE LIST element OF COLOUR INDICES
GQCR      Q-C-R       OA   INQUIRE COLOUR REPRESENTATION
GQWKT     Q-WK-T      OA   INQUIRE WORKSTATION TRANSFORMATION
GQSGWK    Q-SG-WK     OA   INQUIRE SET member OF SEGMENT NAMES ON WORKSTATION
GQLCS     Q-LC-S      OB   INQUIRE LOCATOR DEVICE STATE
GQSKS     Q-SK-S      OB   INQUIRE STROKE DEVICE STATE
GQVLS     Q-VL-S      OB   INQUIRE VALUATOR DEVICE STATE
GQCHS     Q-CH-S      OB   INQUIRE CHOICE DEVICE STATE
GQPKS     Q-PK-S      1B   INQUIRE PICK DEVICE STATE
GQSTS     Q-ST-S      OB   INQUIRE STRING DEVICE STATE
GQSTSS    Q-ST-S-S    OB   INQUIRE STRING DEVICE STATE (FORTRAN 77 SUBSET)
```

Annex 2: Correspondence of GKS data types and FORTRAN data types

GKS Data Type	FORTRAN Data Representation
INTEGER	INTEGER
INTEGER ARRAY	INTEGER giving the length of the INTEGER array INTEGER array(length)
REAL	REAL
REAL ARRAY	INTEGER giving the length of the REAL array REAL array(length)
const x REAL	List of REALs, OR REAL array (const) in Inquiry functions where const > 3.
STRING	INTEGER giving the number of characters (for output string argument only) CHARACTER*(*) containing the string (In a FORTRAN 77 Subset implementation: INTEGER giving the number of characters input INTEGER giving the number of characters returned (for output string argument only) CHARACTER*const containing the string)
POINT	REAL,REAL giving the X- and Y-values
POINT ARRAY	INTEGER giving the length of the POINT ARRAY REAL array1(length) containing the X-values REAL array2(length) containing the Y-values
NAME	INTEGER
ENUMERATION	INTEGER Note: All values are mapped to the range zero to N-1, where N is the number of enumeration alternatives. Except for null values, the order of the enumeration alternatives is the same as in the GKS document: null values always appear in the first position.
RECORD	Represented as a set of scalar values and an array of CHARACTER*80 containing the remainder of the data Note: The set of scalar values is empty, except where the data record contains values which are compulsory in GKS. Data can be written into the data record with the FORTRAN READ and WRITE statements. Special utility functions are defined to pack INTEGER, REAL, and CHARACTER data into the data record and to unpack the data record to the individual data items (GPREC, GUREC).

The representation of CELL ARRAY, PIXEL ARRAY, and PATTERN allows the user of the routines requiring a cell array parameter to store his data in either a one or two dimensional array, and pass any portion of the array as an argument. Two examples should make this clear. Note however that passing only part of the array relies on call-by-address parameter passing and the FORTRAN standard array storage convention.

Certainly the user can pass an entire two-dimensional array. In this case the number of columns of the cell array is the same as the first dimension of the FORTRAN array:

```
INTEGER DX, DY, CELLS (DX,DY)
CALL GCA (X1, Y1, X2, Y2, DX, DY, DX, CELLS)
```

```
!                                                                    !
!   (1,1)    (2,1)    (3,1)    . . .            (DX,1)               !
!   (1,2)    (2,2)    (3,2)    . . .            (DX,2)               !
!     .        .        .                         .                 !
!     .        .        .                         .                 !
!     .        .        .                         .                 !
!   (1,DY)   (2,DY)   (3,DY)   . . .           (DX,DY)              !
!                                                                    !
```

To use an arbitrary portion of an array the user passes the upper left corner of the portion as starting address and the first dimension of the entire array for the right treatment of addresses. The area inside the asterisks is the cell array being passed:

```
INTEGER DX, DY, DIMX, DIMY, CELLS (DIMX,DIMY)
DATA DX/2/, DY/3/
CALL GCA (X1, Y1, X2, Y2, DX, DY, DIMX, CELLS(3,6) )
```

```
!                                                                        !
!   (1,1)    (2,1)    (3,1)    (4,1)     . . . (DIMX,1)                  !
!   (1,2)    (2,2)    (3,2)    (4,2)     . . . (DIMX,2)                  !
!     .        .        .        .                .                     !
!     .        .    ********************           .                    !
!   (1,6)    (2,6)  * (3,6)    (4,6)  * . . . (DIMX,6)                   !
!   (1,7)    (2,7)  * (3,7)    (4,7)  * . . . (DIMX,7)                   !
!   (1,8)    (2,8)  * (3,8)    (4,8)  * . . . (DIMX,8)                   !
!     .        .    ********************           .                    !
!     .        .        .        .                .                     !
!   (1,DIMY) (2,DIMY) (3,DIMY) (4,DIMY) . . . (DIMX,DIMY)              !
!                                                                        !
```

Annex 3: GKS FORTRAN enumeration type mnemonics

Mnemonic FORTRAN names and their values for GKS ENUMERATION type values

```
C   aspect source                 bundled, individual
        INTEGER     GBUNDL,GINDIV
        DATA        GBUNDL,GINDIV/
        *             0,    1/
C
C   clear control flag            conditionally, always
        INTEGER     GCONDI,GALWAY
        DATA        GCONDI,GALWAY/
        *             0,    1/
C
C   clipping indicator            noclip, clip
        INTEGER     GNCLIP,GCLIP
        DATA        GNCLIP,GCLIP/
        *             0,    1/
C
C   colour available              monochrome, colour
        INTEGER     GMONOC,GCOLOR
        DATA        GMONOC,GCOLOR/
        *             0,    1/
C
C   coordinate switch             WC, NDC
        INTEGER     GWC,GNDC
        DATA        GWC,GNDC/
        *             0,   1/
C
C   deferral mode                 asap, bnil, bnig, asti
        INTEGER     GASAP,GBNIL,GBNIG,GASTI
        DATA        GASAP,GBNIL,GBNIG,GASTI/
        *             0,    1,    2,    3/
C
C   detectability                 undetectable, detectable
        INTEGER     GUNDET,GDETEC
        DATA        GUNDET,GDETEC/
        *             0,    1/
C
C   device coordinate units       metres, other
        INTEGER     GMETRE,GOTHU
        DATA        GMETRE,GOTHU/
        *             0,    1/
C
C   display surface empty         notempty,empty
        INTEGER     GNEMPT,GEMPTY
        DATA        GNEMPT,GEMPTY/
        *             0,    1/
C
C   dynamic modification          irg,imm
        INTEGER     GIRG,GIMM
        DATA        GIRG,GIMM/
        *             0,   1/
C
C   echo switch                   noecho, echo
        INTEGER     GNECHO,GECHO
        DATA        GNECHO,GECHO/
        *             0,    1/
C
```

```
C  fill area interior style    hollow, solid, pattern, hatch
      INTEGER     GHOLLO,GSOLID,GPATTR,GHATCH
      DATA        GHOLLO,GSOLID,GPATTR,GHATCH/
     *                0,    1,    2,    3/
C
C  highlighting                    normal, highlighted
      INTEGER     GNORML,GHILIT
      DATA        GNORML,GHILIT/
     *                0,    1/
C
C  input device status         none, ok, nopick
      INTEGER     GNONE,GOK,GNPICK
      DATA        GNONE,GOK,GNPICK/
     *                0, 1,   2/
C
C  input class : none, locator, stroke , valuator, choice, pick, string
      INTEGER     GNCLAS,GLOCAT,GSTROK,GVALUA,GCHOIC,GPICK,GSTRIN
      DATA        GNCLAS,GLOCAT,GSTROK,GVALUA,GCHOIC,GPICK,GSTRIN/
     *                0,    1,    2,    3,    4,    5,    6/
C
C  implicit regeneration mode  suppressed, allowed
      INTEGER     GSUPPD,GALLOW
      DATA        GSUPPD,GALLOW/
     *                0,    1/
C
C  level of GKS : L0a, L0b, L0c, L1a, L1b, L1c, L2a, L2b, L2c
      INTEGER     GLOA,GLOB,GLOC,GL1A,GL1B,GL1C,GL2A,GL2B,GL2C
      DATA        GLOA,GLOB,GLOC,GL1A,GL1B,GL1C,GL2A,GL2B,GL2C/
     *               0,  1,  2,  3,  4,  5,  6,  7,  8/
C
C  new frame action necessary  no, yes
      INTEGER     GNO,GYES
      DATA        GNO,GYES/
     *               0,  1/
C
C  operating mode                  request, sample, event
      INTEGER     GREQU,GSAMPL,GEVENT
      DATA        GREQU,GSAMPL,GEVENT/
     *                0,    1,    2/
C
C  operating state value        GKCL, GKOP, WSOP, WSAC, SGOP
      INTEGER     GGKCL,GGKOP,GWSOP,GWSAC,GSGOP
      DATA        GGKCL,GGKOP,GWSOP,GWSAC,GSGOP/
     *                0,    1,    2,    3,    4/
C
C  presence of invalid values  absent, present
      INTEGER     GABSNT,GPRSNT
      DATA        GABSNT,GPRSNT/
     *                0,    1/
C
C  regeneration flag               suppress, perform
      INTEGER     GSUPP,GPERFO
      DATA        GSUPP,GPERFO/
     *                0,    1/
C
C  relative input priority     higher, lower
      INTEGER     GHIGHR,GLOWER
      DATA        GHIGHR,GLOWER/
     *                0,    1/
C
```

```
C   simultaneous events flag    nomore, more
        INTEGER    GNMORE,GMORE
        DATA       GNMORE,GMORE/
        *               0,    1/
C
C   text alignment horizontal   normal, left, center, right
        INTEGER    GAHNOR,GALEFT,GACENT,GARITE
        DATA       GAHNOR,GALEFT,GACENT,GARITE/
        *               0,    1,    2,    3/
C
C   text alignment vertical     normal, top, cap, half, base, bottom
        INTEGER    GAVNOR,GATOP,GACAP,GAHALF,GABASE,GABOTT
        DATA       GAVNOR,GATOP,GACAP,GAHALF,GABASE,GABOTT/
        *               0,    1,    2,    3,    4,    5/
C
C   text path                   right, left, up, down
        INTEGER    GRIGHT,GLEFT,GUP,GDOWN
        DATA       GRIGHT,GLEFT,GUP,GDOWN/
        *               0,    1,  2,    3/
C
C   text precision              string, char, stroke
        INTEGER    GSTRP,GCHARP,GSTRKP
        DATA       GSTRP,GCHARP,GSTRKP/
        *               0,    1,    2/
C
C   type of returned values     set,realized
        INTEGER    GSET,GREALI
        DATA       GSET,GREALI/
        *               0,    1/
C
C   update state                notpending, pending
        INTEGER    GNPEND,GPEND
        DATA       GNPEND,GPEND/
        *               0,    1/
C
C   vector/raster/other type    vector,raster,other
        INTEGER    GVECTR,GRASTR,GOTHWK
        DATA       GVECTR,GRASTR,GOTHWK/
        *               0,    1,    2/
C
C   visibility                  invisible, visible
        INTEGER    GINVIS,GVISI
        DATA       GINVIS,GVISI/
        *               0,    1/
C
C   workstation category        output, input, outin, wiss, mo, mi
        INTEGER    GOUTPT,GINPUT,GOUTIN,GWISS,GMO,GMI
        DATA       GOUTPT,GINPUT,GOUTIN,GWISS,GMO,GMI/
        *               0,    1,    2,    3,  4,  5/
C
C   workstation state           inactive, active
        INTEGER    GINACT,GACTIV
        DATA       GINACT,GACTIV/
        *               0,    1/
C
C   list of GDP attributes
        INTEGER    GPLBND,GPMBND,GTXBND,GFABND
        DATA       GPLBND,GPMBND,GTXBND,GFABND/
        *               0,    1,    2,    3/
C
```

```
C  line type
      INTEGER      GLSOLI,GLDASH,GLDOT,GLDASD
      DATA         GLSOLI,GLDASH,GLDOT,GLDASD/
     *                1,    2,    3,     4/
C
C  marker type
      INTEGER      GPOINT,GPLUS,GAST,GOMARK,GXMARK
      DATA         GPOINT,GPLUS,GAST,GOMARK,GXMARK/
     *                1,    2,    3,    4,     5/
C
C  GKS functions - These names are used for error handling. The names
C                  are the same as the GKS function names except that
C                  the sentinel character 'G' is replaced by 'E'.  The
C                  same function identification is used for both full
C                  FORTRAN 77 and FORTRAN 77 Subset.
      INTEGER EOPKS , ECLKS , EOPWK , ECLWK , EACWK , EDAWK , ECLRWK
      DATA    EOPKS , ECLKS , EOPWK , ECLWK , EACWK , EDAWK , ECLRWK/
     *          0   ,  1    ,  2    ,  3    ,  4    ,  5    ,  6/
      INTEGER ERSGWK, EUWK  , ESDS  , EMSG  , EESC  , EPL   , EPM
      DATA    ERSGWK, EUWK  , ESDS  , EMSG  , EESC  , EPL   , EPM  /
     *          7   ,  8    ,  9    ,  10   ,  11   ,  12   ,  13 /
      INTEGER ETX   , EFA   , ECA   , EGDP  , ESPLI , ESLN  , ESLWSC
      DATA    ETX   , EFA   , ECA   , EGDP  , ESPLI , ESLN  , ESLWSC/
     *          14  ,  15   ,  16   ,  17   ,  18   ,  19   ,  20/
      INTEGER ESPLCI, ESPMI , ESMK  , ESMKSC, ESPMCI, ESTXI , ESTXFP
      DATA    ESPLCI, ESPMI , ESMK  , ESMKSC, ESPMCI, ESTXI , ESTXFP/
     *          21  ,  22   ,  23   ,  24   ,  25   ,  26   ,  27/
      INTEGER ESCHXP, ESCHSP, ESTXCI, ESCHH , ESCHUP, ESTXP , ESTXAL
      DATA    ESCHXP, ESCHSP, ESTXCI, ESCHH , ESCHUP, ESTXP , ESTXAL/
     *          28  ,  29   ,  30   ,  31   ,  32   ,  33   ,  34/
      INTEGER ESFAI , ESFAIS, ESFASI, ESFACI, ESPA  , ESPARF, ESASF
      DATA    ESFAI , ESFAIS, ESFASI, ESFACI, ESPA  , ESPARF, ESASF /
     *          35  ,  36   ,  37   ,  38   ,  39   ,  40   ,  41 /
      INTEGER ESPKID, ESPLR , ESPMR , ESTXR , ESFAR , ESPAR , ESCR
      DATA    ESPKID, ESPLR , ESPMR , ESTXR , ESFAR , ESPAR , ESCR/
     *          42  ,  43   ,  44   ,  45   ,  46   ,  47   ,  48/
      INTEGER ESWN  , ESVP  , ESVPIP, ESELNT, ESCLIP, ESWKWN, ESWKVP
      DATA    ESWN  , ESVP  , ESVPIP, ESELNT, ESCLIP, ESWKWN, ESWKVP/
     *          49  ,  50   ,  51   ,  52   ,  53   ,  54   ,  55/
      INTEGER ECRSG , ECLSG , ERENSG, EDSG  , EDSGWK, EASGWK, ECSGWK
      DATA    ECRSG , ECLSG , ERENSG, EDSG  , EDSGWK, EASGWK, ECSGWK/
     *          56  ,  57   ,  58   ,  59   ,  60   ,  61   ,  62/
      INTEGER EINSG , ESSGT , ESVIS , ESHLIT, ESSGP , ESDTEC, EINLC
      DATA    EINSG , ESSGT , ESVIS , ESHLIT, ESSGP , ESDTEC, EINLC /
     *          63  ,  64   ,  65   ,  66   ,  67   ,  68   ,  69 /
      INTEGER EINSK , EINVL , EINCH , EINPK , EINST , ESLCM , ESSKM
      DATA    EINSK , EINVL , EINCH , EINPK , EINST , ESLCM , ESSKM /
     *          70  ,  71   ,  72   ,  73   ,  74   ,  75   ,  76 /
      INTEGER ESVLM , ESCHM , ESPKM , ESSTM , ERQLC , ERQSK , ERQVL
      DATA    ESVLM , ESCHM , ESPKM , ESSTM , ERQLC , ERQSK , ERQVL /
     *          77  ,  78   ,  79   ,  80   ,  81   ,  82   ,  83 /
      INTEGER ERQCH , ERQPK , ERQST , ESMLC , ESMSK , ESMVL , ESMCH
      DATA    ERQCH , ERQPK , ERQST , ESMLC , ESMSK , ESMVL , ESMCH /
     *          84  ,  85   ,  86   ,  87   ,  88   ,  89   ,  90 /
      INTEGER ESMPK , ESMST , EWAIT , EFLUSH, EGTLC , EGTSK , EGTVL
      DATA    ESMPK , ESMST , EWAIT , EFLUSH, EGTLC , EGTSK , EGTVL /
     *          91  ,  92   ,  93   ,  94   ,  95   ,  96   ,  97 /
      INTEGER EGTCH , EGTPK , EGTST , EWITM , EGTITM, ERDITM, EIITM
      DATA    EGTCH , EGTPK , EGTST , EWITM , EGTITM, ERDITM, EIITM /
     *          98  ,  99   ,  100  ,  101  ,  102  ,  103  ,  104 /
      INTEGER EEVTM , EACTM , EPREC , EUREC
```

```
    DATA    EEVTM , EACTM , EPREC , EUREC/
*           105   , 106   , 107   , 108/
```

VII. Case Study of GKS Development

C. D. Osland

A B S T R A C T

This paper describes some aspects of the GKS
implementation project undertaken jointly by ICL and
RAL. It concentrates on the problems of the system as
a whole and thereby seeks to explore in some detail
various aspects of GKS that are not immediately
obvious. It is broken into chapters on the output
system (both primitives and attributes), the input
system, the methods used to implement segments and
finally metafiles. There is a detailed analysis of the
basic design, since this differs from most existing
graphics systems as a result of the fresh ideas
embodied in GKS.

Chapter 1

INTRODUCTION

1.1   OUR REQUIREMENTS

The Rutherford Appleton Laboratory (Rutherford) is the largest of the institutes run by the Science and Engineering Research Council (SERC) of Great Britain: about 2000 people work there. The SERC provides extensive computing facilities to about 3500 research workers throughout Great Britain. The computer power is provided by a number of mainframes located at Rutherford and another laboratory:

    1 IBM 3081
    1 IBM 3032
    1 ICL Atlas 10 (alias Fujitsu M380)
    1 NAS 7000

and a network of smaller machines that cover the whole country:

    15 Prime 400/550/750
    25 GEC 4000
     8 VAX 11/780

The computers are all connected by an X25 network which provides terminal access, file transfer, job transfer and mail facilities to almost all other computers on the network. Access to the computers is mostly from online terminals distributed throughout the country, connected to their nearest computer. A wide range of terminals is used; approximate figures are:

    1000 text-only ASCII screens
     250 Tektronix 4006/4010/4012/4014 storage tube terminals
     200 black/white raster refresh terminals (Sigma 5670)
      25 IBM (or lookalike) 327x screens
      20 colour raster refresh terminals (Sigma 5660)
      16 Imlac vector refresh terminals
      14 image processing displays (Sigma ARGS 7000)

In addition, there are about 30 1 metre drum plotters (Benson) and a number of desktop A3 plotters (Hewlett-Packard, Calcomp and Zeta). Finally, a central service is provided by Rutherford on an (offline) III FR80 film recorder that produces film (black/white and colour), hardcopy and microfiche. A rough idea of the network is given in figure 1.

Computing Division at Rutherford is responsible for system and basic application software on all these machines. Included in the 'basic application software' are statistical packages, graphics packages and text processing systems. There is a general policy that a subset of the software will be common across all machines so that:

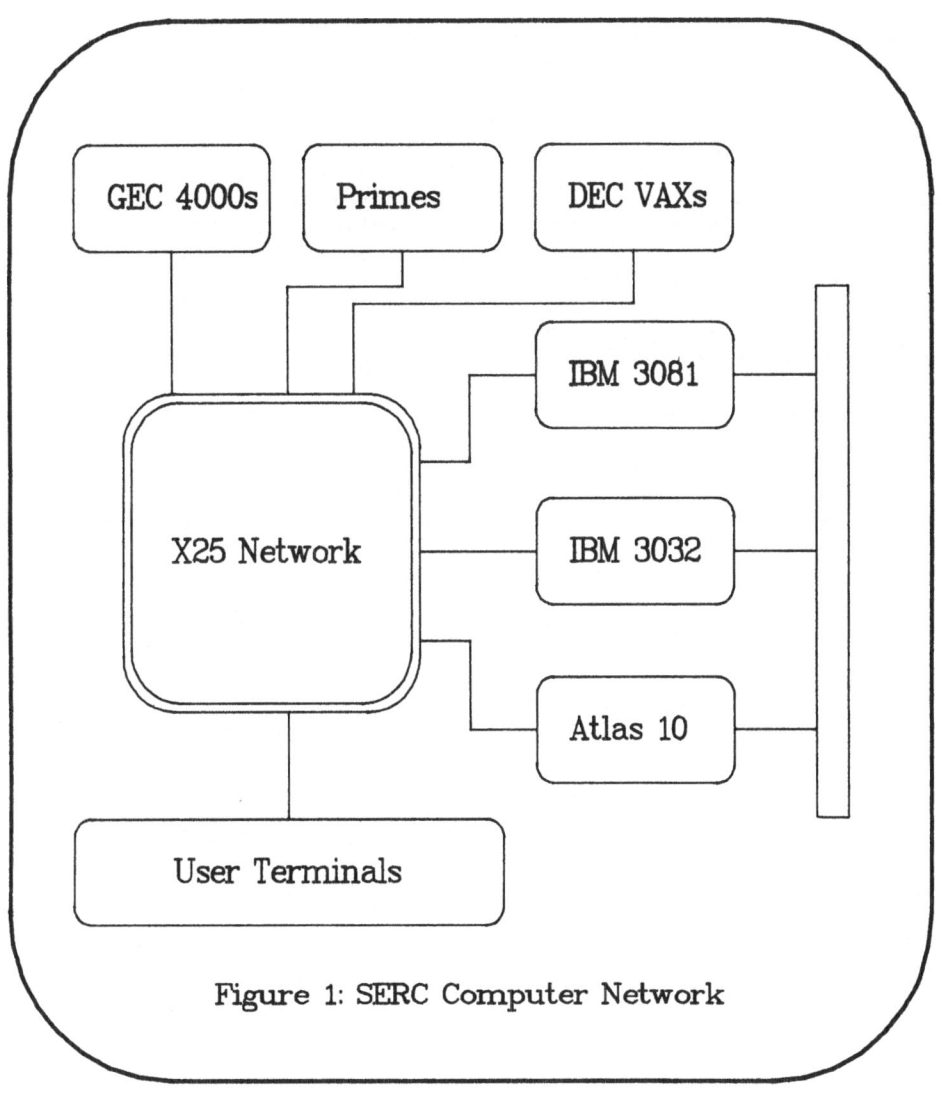

Figure 1: SERC Computer Network

(a) users may move from one machine to another as the scale or nature
     of their workload changes;

(b) Computing Division can minimize the effort required to support all
     this software.

     In the last two years, a 'Common Base Policy' has been evolved, taking
the idea of a common software subset a stage further and applying it to

hardware and communications as well. The policy is that, for all suitable applications, research workers will be encouraged to use single-user computers (like PERQ, Apollo, SUN: SERC's choice is PERQ), to write in Fortran 77 or Pascal and to use GKS as their graphics system. In addition, local communication between these single-user systems will be by high-speed link (Cambridge Ring or Ethernet: SERC's choice is Cambridge Ring) and more distant communication will by via X25. At present, SERC possesses just over 100 PERQs. These present enormous potential for graphics work because of the very fast rate at which the screen can be updated (30 MHz) and large local Winchester disk (24 Mbyte).

Rutherford currently provides a number of graphics packages on the machines it supports; these are shown in figure 2.

It can be seen from this background that SERC have a requirement for a GKS implementation with various constraints:

* it must be transportable to about six different operating systems with minimal effort and affected as little as possible by operating system changes; the computers range from 1 MIP personal computers to 15 MIP mainframes;

* it must handle a very wide range of devices, encompassing almost all those considered as being serviceable by GKS;

* it must exploit the devices it drives to the full, since a majority of the user population currently uses SERC computers over relatively slow communications links;

* it must be highly reliable and have very few faults, since the user population would overload the support team if this was not so;

* it must be designed in a way that allows future devices (with new features) to be fully supported;

* it must be small and fast enough to be attractive to research workers who just wish to add graphics to their (already large) applications programs.

We had to decide what language the system should be written in. The main possibilities were Fortran and Pascal (as they were the two encouraged by the Common Base Policy). C was also considered but was not available on a sufficient number of our machines.

Experience had shown that it was in general possible to call Fortran from Pascal but not the other way round; the reason for this was usually associated with the Pascal stack. For this reason, Fortran 77 was chosen as the implementation language. Once the system is fully operational, a natural interface to it from Pascal will be provided.

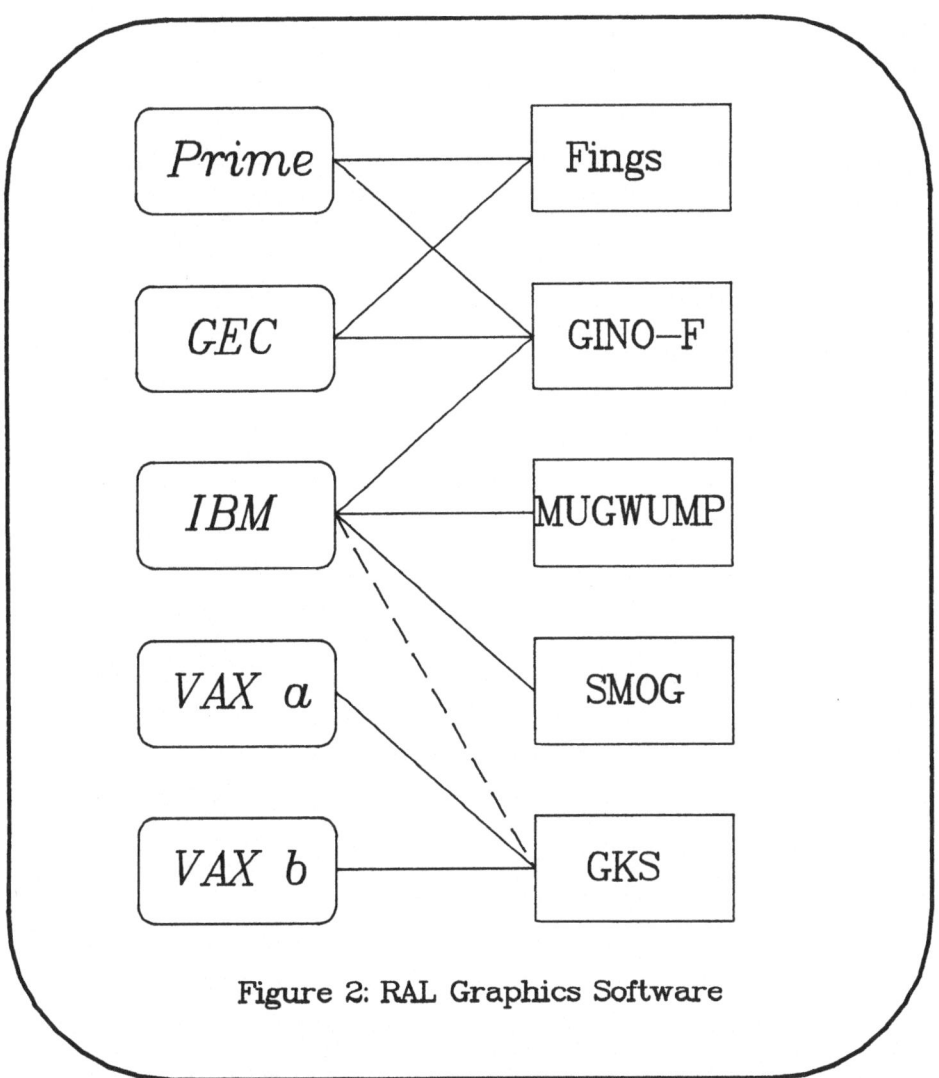

Figure 2: RAL Graphics Software

1.2 OBJECTIVES OF GKS

The objectives of GKS are fully given in Chapter 0 of the GKS document. Some of them do not need to be reviewed since they are aims shared by most software systems: efficiency, robustness, compactness. Others do contribute a particular flavour to GKS and it is up to an implementation to honour these.

"GKS shall include all the capabilities that are essential for the
whole spectrum of graphics, from simple passive output to highly
interactive applications; ... the whole range of graphics devices
... shall be controllable from GKS in a uniform way"

This is crucial to the aim of GKS; it is what distinguishes GKS from
most existing graphics systems: it sets out to use an unpredictable range
of graphics devices fully, not just to be able to drive them. This is
restated in the GKS document as follows:

"richness: a rich set of functions offers an extensive range of
facilities that stretches beyond the basic functions and includes
higher order capabilities"

This encourages the implementor to strive for a maximum exploitation of
each device's capabilities; it also encourages device manufacturers to
configure their next generation of devices according to the philosophy of
GKS. This is already happening - eg the Sigma 6100 - and we had to take
account of this in our design.

1.3   DESIGN PHASES

The team that was available to implement GKS consisted of two groups of
people:

   *   those who had helped with the development of the GKS standard for
        two or three years, or were involved with the maintenance of an
        implementation of GKS 6.2;

   *   those who had extensive knowledge of other graphics systems but
        effectively knew nothing about GKS.

There was therefore a period of education before the project as a whole
could get started.

There was then a long period (about 4 months) when the main design
members of the team discussed the data structures that were necessary for
GKS. Naively it might seem as though all this work has been done and that
clause 6 of the GKS document is all you need; this is however a small
fraction of what is needed.

This initial phase of designing the data structures concentrated on the
relationships between each data item and the code that would access it; for
each (class of) data item, a 'life history' was written that indicated when
it came into existence, what modified it, what updated it and when it
ceased to exist. It was found feasible to break down the system into
separate 'pipelines', one for each of the output primitives. In addition,
the data structures for input and segments were specified at this stage.

The work was then split into smaller areas of responsibility:

1   polyline and polymarker pipelines;
2   text pipeline;
3   fill area and cell array pipelines;
4   control functions;
5   transformation functions;
6   a workstation driver;
7   library and documentation management.

Most of this organization appears to have been a good idea. The only change from this intended structure was that the person working on transformations took over the design and implementation of all routines between the user interface and the workstation interface except those directly called by the user.

Once the design stage was complete, work on the coding was started and it only took about three weeks for a sort of GKS to draw lines, markers and a little text. That was about 10 months ago. Since then the output system has been completed, but more work has been necessary on the input design before coding could start on that and the same applied to segments.

1.4   OVERALL STRUCTURE OF OUR GKS SYSTEM

Let us define a few terms that will be necessary for the discussion of the structure we decided upon:

workstation
    the graphics device wrapped up by a layer of device-dependent software;

workstation driver
    the device-dependent software; it brings the device up to the level of a GKS workstation;

front-end
    the code between the user-level interface and the workstation drivers;

workstation interface
    the interface between the front-end and the workstation drivers;

utilities
    code that may be used by more than one workstation driver.

You will understand from the list of requirements given in 1.1 above that we were liable to have a problem: we had to support both dumb and intelligent devices and yet we wanted a system that would really use most of the functions available on the intelligent ones. In addition, we wanted to do this in a small and fast system.

Our main design decision came from these requirements: it was that the
front-end would be as 'thin' as possible. In most cases the workstation
driver would have to react to all requests passed to it from the
user-level.

This approach was one of about six that were considered.   Others were
rejected for the following reasons:

1   mapping all GKS functions to simple device functions

         rejected because it would prevent use of the intelligence in
         modern terminals;

2   having a front-end that knew about the capabilities of
     workstations from a data file

         rejected because a number of characteristics are very
         difficult or expensive to describe by means of data, but can
         be implemented quite simply in code;

3   allowing a workstation driver to refuse requests for action and
     leave the front-end to emulate the function for it

         rejected as the main way of working because it increases the
         number of calls across the workstation interface, but
         reserved in case it proved the best method for some special
         aspect of GKS: in the end we decides to use a modified form
         of this method for segments.

The decision to have the workstation interface very close to the
user-level interface was only taken when we were convinced that it was
economic to write a large number of utility routines that could be used by
workstation drivers for functions that particular devices could not do
directly. Unless this had been true, the effort required to write each new
workstation driver would have been too great. As it is, we believe that
the effort involved in writing a new workstation driver is the minimum that
could be expected if the device is to be driven fully. The overall
structure is shown in figure 3 on the next page.

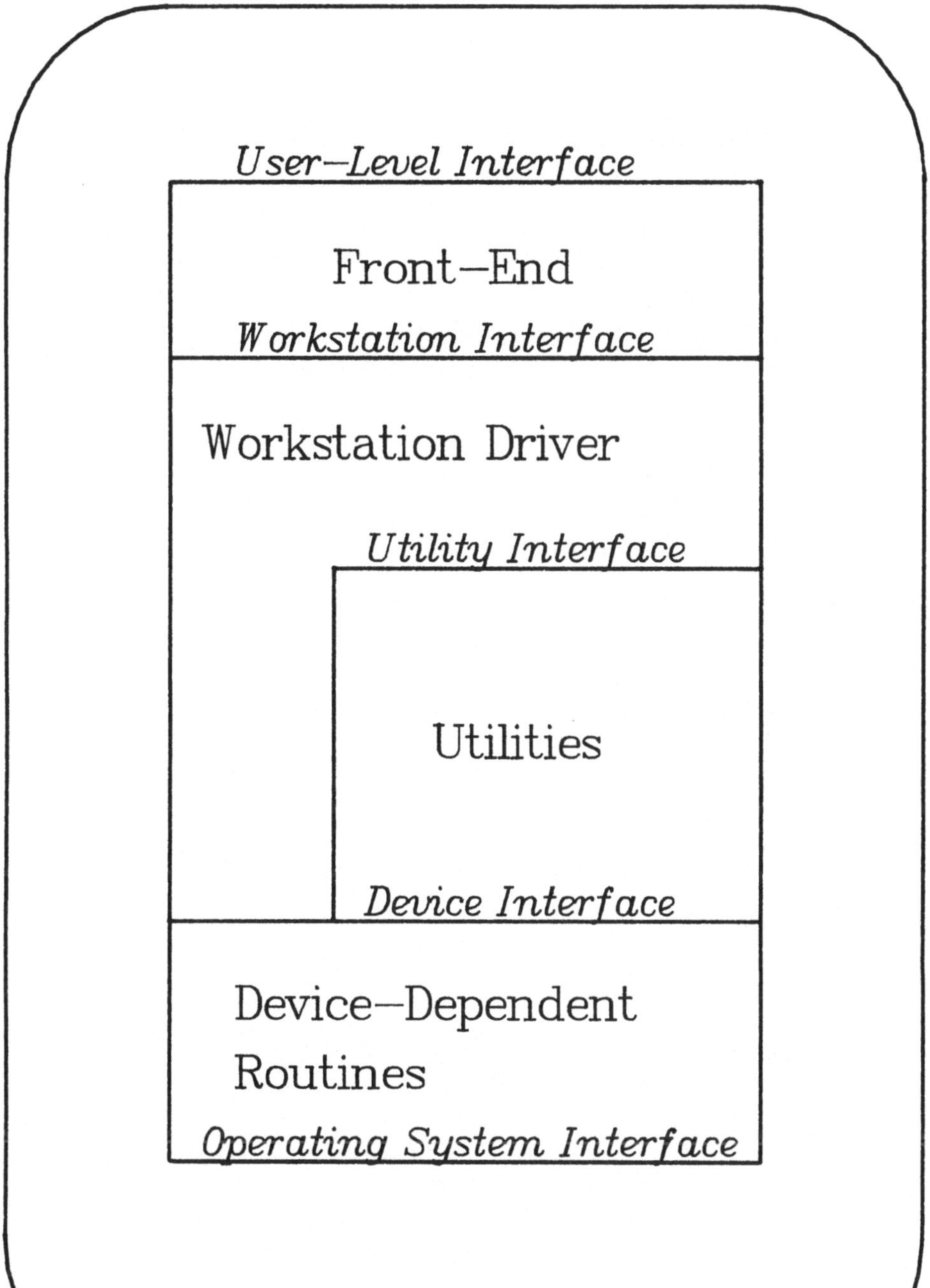

Figure 3: Overall GKS system structure

Chapter 2

OUTPUT AND ATTRIBUTES

2.1   THE WORKSTATION INTERFACE

As noted above, the workstation interface is very 'high' in our
implementation; most GKS functions are either passed through the front-end
directly to the relevant workstations or are handled entirely within the
front-end.

The first decision was how data from the front-end would be passed to
the workstations.   After discussion, it was agreed that three paths were
required:

1   a path to a single workstation;

2   a path to all active workstations;

3   a path to all open workstations.

This organization is shown in figure 4 and meant that the front-end handled
GKS functions as follows:

attribute setting functions:
      workstation-independent changes are accumulated in the front-end
      and not passed to workstations; workstation-dependent changes are
      passed directly to the specific workstation;

output primitives:
      if the attributes have been changed, a workstation routine is
      called that will update the workstation aspects; whether or not
      this is the case, the output primitive is then passed to the
      workstation;

functions that change transformations:
      normalization transformation changes are remembered in the
      front-end in rather the same way as attributes
      workstation-independent attributes; workstation transformation
      changes are passed straight to the workstation;

inquiry functions
      passed straight to workstation if workstation-dependent; otherwise
      replied to directly by the front-end;

control functions
      most of the required action is in the front-end but workstation
      routines are called when a particular workstation needs to react
      (eg DEACTIVATE WORKSTATION);

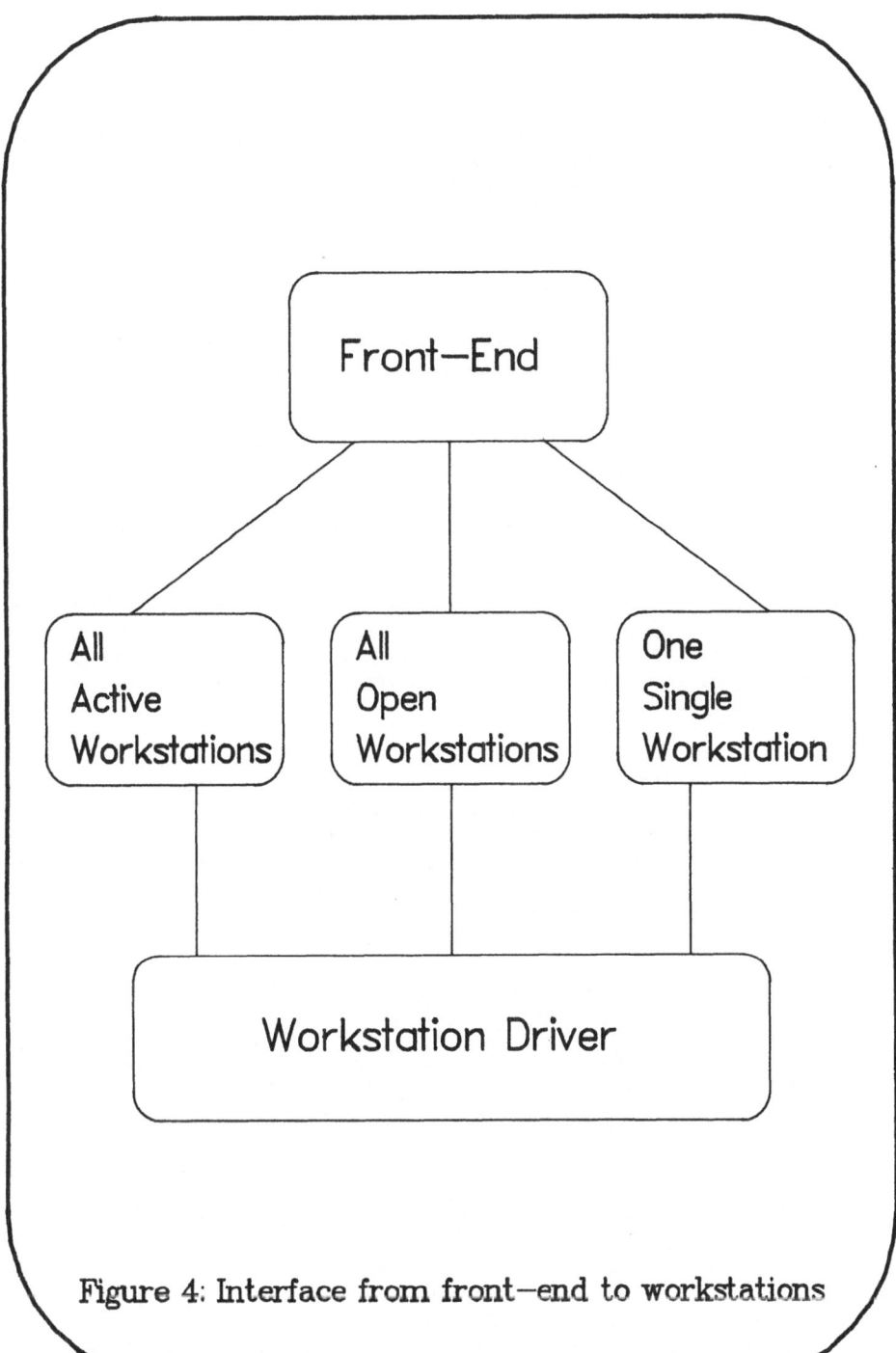

Figure 4: Interface from front—end to workstations

input functions
>   passed through the front-end straight to the workstation;

segment functions
>   passed to the workstation, which may respond that it is incapable of handling the request and that it should be stored in the Common Segment Store - see chapter 4;

metafile functions
>   passed straight to the metafile input or output workstation as appropriate - see chapter 5.

2.2   HANDLING OF ATTRIBUTES

Originally, our design passed requests for attribute changes straight through to the workstation. One advantage of this is that the function always takes the same time. However, this appeared to be a problem when text attributes were being changed. It was more than likely that a user would want to change more than one text attribute (eg font and size) simultaneously but GKS provided separate functions. If the attribute changes were passed through to the workstation as each function was called, the workstation might have to do a large amount of work twice, since a request to change font would probably involve disk access and calculation of width tables; this work would be redundant if the text size was changed before any text was output.

Then we noticed that this situation could occur in other pipelines and also that the same situation could easily occur when the end user was using a package above GKS: if well written, the package would be very likely to stack and restore attributes so that any graphics produced directly by the user was not affected by any after-effects of calling the package. However, if the user did not do any graphics directly, the attributes might be repeatedly stacked and restored, the ones used for any drawing never actually varying.

For this reason, it was seen to be essential that the front-end reacted to all attribute changes and only asked the workstation to change attributes when an output primitive was called that needed them to be up-to-date. Each pipeline is therefore implemented by two entry points at the workstation interface; one is for the primitive and one requests that the workstation makes its attributes for the primitive correct.

2.3   HANDLING OF TRANSFORMATIONS

The same philosophy is used to handle transformations. GKS describes transformations in terms of World Coordinates (WC), Normalized Device Coordinates (NDC) and Device Coordinates (DC). A set of Normalization Transformations may be set up from different WC systems to NDC and each workstation has its own mapping from NDC to DC.

For GKS primitives outside segments, the result can be implemented by a single transformation matrix and clipping rectangle. In our implementation, all data is passed through the system in WC, accompanied by a transformation index, so that each workstation may achieve the desired result in the way that is simplest for it. This allows workstations that can perform complex transformations internally to be driven properly.

2.4   ORGANIZATION OF 'PIPELINES'

Each of the output primitives is logically handled by a separate pipeline and all the pipelines are designed the same way. Recall that each output primitive may have two types of attributes: workstation-dependent and workstation-independent:

	Independent	Dependent
POLYLINE	Index	Linetype
		Linewidth Scale Factor
		Polyline Colour Index
POLYMARKER	Index	Marker Type
		Marker Size Scale Factor
		Polymarker Colour Index
TEXT	Index	Text Font and Precision
	Character Height	Character Expansion Factor
	Character Up Vector	Character Spacing
	Text Path	Text Colour Index
	Text Alignment	
FILL AREA	Index	Fill Area Interior Style
	Pattern Size	Fill Area Style Index
	Pattern Reference Point	Fill area Colour Index

All of the pipelines are affected by the setting of the ASPECT SOURCE FLAGS.

It can be seen that, except for devices that would react directly to GKS attributes, there would usually need to be some form of derivation of workstation aspects from the supplied attributes. This work is localised into one routine per pipeline, and is called the 'catch-up' routine; after any number of attribute changes have been made (since the last use of the output primitive and just before its next use) the front-end calls the 'catch-up' routine to ensure that all derived aspects are up-to-date.

There is a complication with TEXT and FILL AREA in that they both have attributes that are interpreted with respect to the current coordinate system and so changes to the normalization transformation require the derived values of these aspects to be recalculated. This is simply dealt with by the front-end setting the 'must-catch-up' flag for TEXT and FILL AREA whenever the normalization transformation is changed.

2.5   DESIGN OF OUTPUT UTILITIES

At first, it appeared simple to define a set of utilities that could be
called from any workstation driver to emulate functions of which the
workstation was incapable. However, it soon became apparent that only
experience of writing some workstation drivers would produce a really
useful set: each person had different ideas.   The problem was in the
different level of function available from the different devices.

It was finally decided that each person implementing a particular
pipeline could define the interface from any utility to a device-dependent
routine (eg 'Draw a Line') and the project would occasionally review the
interfaces that had been assumed by each person and see whether any saving
could be achieved. This approach seems to have worked.

We also had to decide whether utilities should return the results of
their emulation (eg a set of polylines as emulation of a TEXT call) or
whether they should themselves call the device-level routines to achieve
the output. It was decided that they should call the device-level routines
since there might not be sufficient space available for the result.   For
this reason, the utilities that actually send output to a device are
invoked with the name of a device-level routine that will actually perform
the output.   The routines defined so far at this level output a polyline,
set colour, set linestyle, set linewidth, set clipping parameters and
output a raster scan line.

There now exists a large range of utilities, arranged roughly as
follows:

POLYLINE

The attributes that can modify a POLYLINE are not complex, but still
require emulation on unintelligent devices. The utility routines provided
deal with

* emulating linestyle
* emulating linewidth
* transforming coordinates
* software clipping

Many of these utilities are re-used by other pipelines. They finally call
a device-dependent polyline routine. A utility to perform vector to raster
conversion will be added for unintelligent raster printers at a later date.

POLYMARKER

A single extra utility is required for polymarkers:

* simulate polymarker type and size

The rest of its pipeline is very similar to POLYLINE.

TEXT

At present, the only utilities provided use vector definitions (the Hershey characters) to emulate text. There are four top level utilities:

* Inquire Text Extent for CHAR precision
* Inquire Text Extent for STROKE precision

* Generate CHAR text
* Generate STROKE text

These share a large number of lower level utilities, typically

* determine text start point from ALIGNMENT and text extent
* determine concatenation point
* determine centre of character
* determine character extent
* draw character using device-dependent polyline routine

The system rests on top of a font database from which definitions of characters are read. The drawing of characters is performed by calling the same device-dependent routines as are used for POLYLINE.

FILL AREA

Filled areas are a little complex to deal with because

(a) the number of vertices may grow as a result of clipping;

(b) patterns and hatching need to be supported.

As a result of this, most of the utilities for FILL AREA do not overlap with the previous ones; there is one top level utility:

* emulate FILL AREA

which deals with both patterns and hatching and in turn this calls on utilities for:

* clipping polygon to clip rectangle
* constructing new edge table
* selecting a pattern
* selecting a hatch style

Finally, device-level routines for output of either raster scan lines or vectors are invoked.

CELL ARRAY

Little simulation of this is possible, although the transformation of the reference points is common to most devices. A single utility deals with the mapping of a cell array to a screen raster that mismatches it.

2.6   PROBLEMS WITH ERROR HANDLING

When the project was well advanced, one member of the team noticed that recursion had crept into the implementation. This was not in any code we had written (or we might have noticed!). The problem lay with error handling, as defined in the GKS document.

The document states that the user may provide his own error handling routine and that this may issue GKS inquiry functions. As we had designed the system, calls to the error routine were being made throughout code. Graphically the situation was as in figure 5.

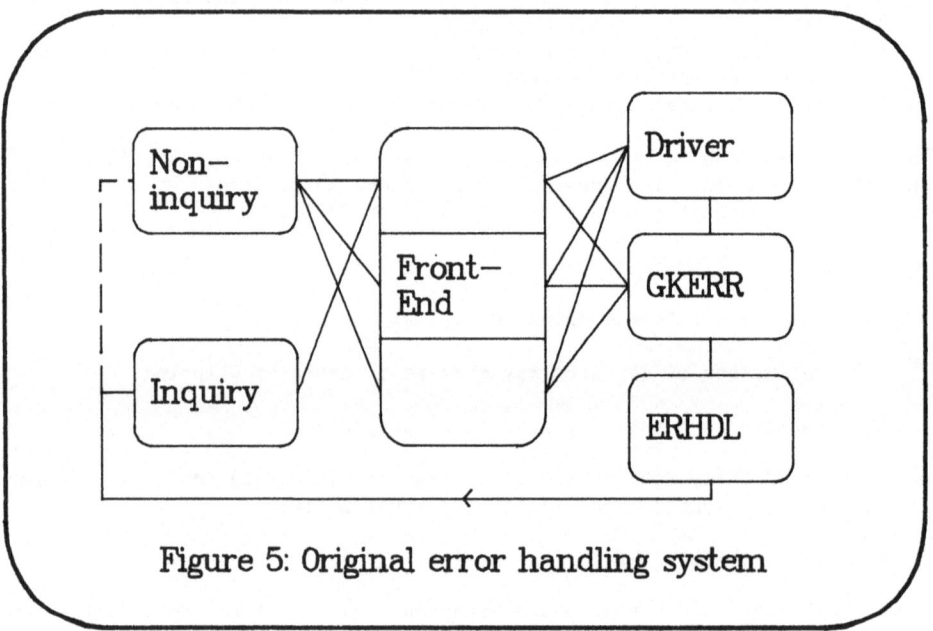

Figure 5: Original error handling system

A variety of solutions to this were proposed; the solution adopted was that the error handler would only be called from user callable routines. This solves the problem, although it took some effort to change all the existing code to conform to this new convention. The result is shown in figure 6 (on the next page).

2.7   GENERAL UTILITIES

From the earliest days of the design phase, it was apparent that the generality of GKS would mean that some parts of the system would need variable amounts of working storage to accomplish their tasks. This was particularly true for metafiles (somewhere to read a record perhaps

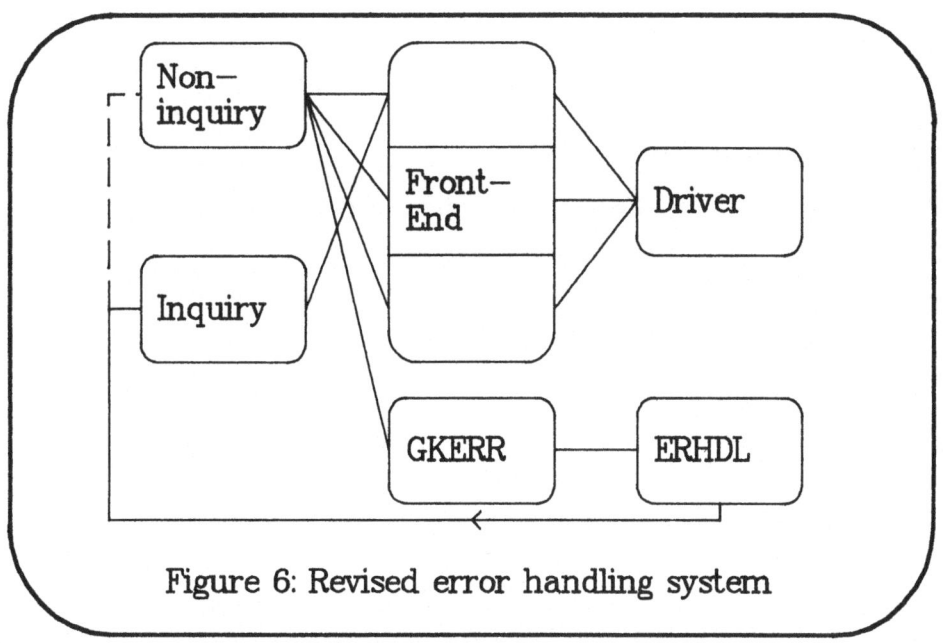

Figure 6: Revised error handling system

produced by a totally different system), FILL AREA (where space was needed to handle clipping the pattern to a many-sided polygon) and STROKE precision TEXT (where a polygon set would be produced per character).

Other parts of the system need a more permanent form of storage, whose size will only be known when a program executes. This applies to the various workstation-specific lists that the user can set.

For this reason - and because Fortran has no facilities for these types of storage management - the implementation includes both STACK and HEAP storage packages. For both, there are the obvious functions:

* initialize
* allocate
* deallocate
* close down

For the heap, there is a garbage collection system and it is also possible to inquire how much space is available available without doing a garbage collection.

In the early days of the project, we had assumed that a general purpose store (capable of holding large amounts of data like a few fonts) would be needed, but the amount of store required for any purpose has (so far) not exceeded the amount that can readily be held in the stack or on the heap.

Chapter 3

INPUT SYSTEM

3.1 PROBLEMS WITH LEVEL 'C' INPUT

GKS organizes its input functions into six classes:

* LOCATOR
* STROKE
* VALUATOR
* CHOICE
* PICK
* STRING

and three modes:

* REQUEST
* SAMPLE
* EVENT

REQUEST mode is provided at input level 'b' (with PICK only available at or above '1b'); SAMPLE and EVENT are only available at input level 'c'. We considered implementing level 'c' input as part of the project, but decided that it was not feasible to write any significant amount of transportable code for level 'c'. The range of operating systems we have to support seemed to rule this out. One of them is not multi-tasking from the user's point of view (CMS on the IBMs); two are fairly normal (VAX/VMS and Prime/Primos), one relies on message passing (GEC/OS4000) and Unix has yet another set of rules.

This does not mean we will not be providing level 'c' input; however it does mean that we will initially write different support for level 'c' for each separate operating system. Once we have done this, it may become obvious that some of the code is transportable (for instance the input queue manager). We expect that the difficult code will always be system-dependent.

3.2 ORGANIZATION OF INPUT SYSTEM

Because we were only tackling level 'b' input (REQUEST) it was logically unnecessary to consider how the input queue would be organized. The overall structure for input resembles that for output quite closely. The work could be split into:

* reverse transformation for positional data;

* extensions to the front-end to deal with input requests;

* definition of the workstation-independent data structures for input;

* utilities to simulate various input devices on devices with no actual input mechanism corresponding to GKS logical input devices;

* implementation of PICK input.

It was decided that we should only support a reasonable number of logical input devices initially, although some devices like the PERQ tempted us to provide a very rich system. Those chosen were:

LOCATOR a   native locator on the device; triggered by key or button as appropriate for the device; data record would specify alternate cursor identifier, colour and pattern;

STROKE a   native locator on the device; data record would specify the same data as for LOCATOR (see above) and also any thinning criteria (eg sample speed) and the attributes to be used for any connecting lines or markers;

STROKE b   possibly the keyboard (!) or cursor moving keys;

VALUATOR a   native locator on the device, moving against scale, bar or dial; data record selects attributes of scale, bar or dial and the cursor attributes (as for LOCATOR);

VALUATOR b   native valuator on device (eg thumbwheel on Tektronix) moving against scale; data record would specify frequency of subdivisions on the scale;

VALUATOR c   number typed by user; data record controls range of allowed values;

CHOICE a   button box; data record would provide menu to be displayed for PROMPT/ECHO type 2;

CHOICE b   menu item selected by user typing its name; data record would provide list of allowed strings;

CHOICE c   keyboard used like a button board; data record much as for type 'a';

CHOICE d   menu selection by cursor hit; data record as for type 'a';

PICK   still under discussion at time of writing lecture notes!

STRING a   user types string at keyboard; data record controls handling of the text string on the display surface.

All of these would, of course, not be provided on every workstation capable of input - only a relevant subset.

3.3   INPUT DATA RECORDS

Although the most recent updates to the GKS document have resulted in all mandatory control of input being passed as separate parameters of the input functions, the data record remains as the way of controlling less standard aspects of the input devices.   These records are, for this reason, implementation-dependent. However, it was our intention to make programs as compatible between devices as possible, and this meant that data records passed to input devices had to be very well-behaved.

   To support the various functions expected of the input devices, it was decided to organize data records into individual entities; each distinct entity (eg 'cursor pattern', 'lower bound of value range') would be assigned a 'Parameter Identifier' ('PID').   A set of routines would be provided that allowed the user to inquire about the existence of a PID, to examine its value and to set its value. Workstation drivers would be written using the same set of routines. By this means, access to the data structures would remain symbolic and the user would not have to know the details of the data record structure.

3.4   TWO PROBLEMS WITH INPUT

1. At input level 'c', there is no problem in one trigger (say the hitting
    of a key) producing two input records (say one for a LOCATOR and one
    for CHOICE). This provides a convenient and well-organized formal
    mechanism for reacting to the common form of input from display
    terminals, where hitting a key when the cursor is displayed returns the
    position of the cursor and the code for the key that was hit.

    At input level 'b', this is not possible because INQUIRE MORE
    SIMULTANEOUS EVENTS is a level 'c' function. Since it was thought
    undesirable for the implementation to lack an interface to this
    facility - it would make exact conversion of existing programs
    impossible - a method of providing access to it was sought.   The only
    method that appeared safe and in conformance with GKS was for an ESCAPE
    to be defined with effectively the same parameter list as REQUEST
    LOCATOR apart from an extra CHARACTER*1 parameter.

2. While discussing segments, a question was raised about PICK input.   It
    had been assumed that boundary boxes (ie the limits of a rectangle in
    which all the primitives fitted) would be maintained for each segment
    and that these would be available in storage so that the PICK utilities
    could quickly exclude any segments that were completely missed by the
    picking device. However, it was realized that POLYLINE, POLYMARKER and
    TEXT (at least) had workstation-dependent attributes which could affect
    the size of the output primitive on the display surface. Thus there
    was a different boundary box for each segment on each workstation. For
    POLYLINE and POLYMARKER this can be allowed for (by adding the nominal
    size to the expected area covered by the primitive) but for text this
    is difficult since the workstation may (at a low precision) have
    ignored the TEXT PATH parameter and drawn text to the right when the
    user requested that it go down.

Chapter 4

SEGMENTS

4.1   DIFFERENT POSSIBLE DESIGN STRUCTURES

A number of possibilities existed for the implementation of segments. They were as follows:

1. Restrict the implementation to output level '0' and do not implement them.

    This was ruled out since it would not provide a GKS system that could replace existing packages like GINO-F.

2. Provide the segment functions entirely within the front-end.

    This would rule out the possibility of using segment facilities available in devices and so was not satisfactory as a long-term solution. Since it would have taken a major effort to take it out of the front-end once it had been written this way, this was not thought adequate.

3. Provide utilities that workstation drivers can use if the workstation cannot store segments.

    This would make the structure the same as for output and input. The problem is that all workstations which cannot support segments want the same information stored for them, but since they would all independently use the utilities to store the segment for them, it would be stored several times if more than 'incapable' workstation was active.

4. Add a 'phantom workstation' to the end of the active workstation list and let it store segment instructions if any active workstation is incapable of doing so.

    This is attractive because it ensures that only one copy of the instructions in each segment are stored even when more than one active workstation needs this support.   It makes scanning the active workstation list slightly more complicated but is easily justified in terms of performance.

It was this last solution that was adopted.   Whenever a segment is created, any workstation may report back to the front-end that it cannot support segments. If so, the front-end will add a 'phantom' Central Segment Store workstation (CSS) to the list of active workstations and initialize it. When any functions are called that contribute to the segment, each incapable active workstation will ignore the function but CSS will store it.

4.2   COMMUNICATION WITH CENTRAL SEGMENT STORE

Once this strategy had been adopted, the only remaining issues were:

* *   how would segment data be read back from CSS; and

* *   where would information about the correspondence between workstations and segments be kept.

The CSS solution does require two lists to be maintained; one gives the list of workstations on which each segment exists and the other the list of segments associated with each workstation.

For the present these are held in heap storage; on small systems it may be necessary to page these out to disk.   Both lists are held in the front-end and only the front-end ever reads data back out of the CSS.   The list of segments per workstation is only stored for workstations that cannot handle segments, since they are not needed by workstations that can.

4.3   DESIGN OF WORKSTATION-INDEPENDENT SEGMENT STORAGE

Although the project was only committed to producing a system to level '1b', it has become obvious that CSS could provide all the code required for Workstation-Independent Segment Storage (WISS).   WISS is the only feature that distinguishes output levels '1' and '2'.

The curious fact is that the simplest way of implementing WISS is for it to appear to the front-end as though it is INCAPABLE of handling segments; in this case, the front-end will use CSS to store the information and the functionality is perfect.   Naturally, the other functions required for WISS also have to be added, but they are confined to the front-end by this solution.

Chapter 5

METAFILES

5.1 DEVELOPMENTS IN METAFILE STANDARDS

Since the days when GKS was purely a DIN paper, the document has defined an interface to a graphics metafile system and has included an example of a format that is sufficient for the purpose. In the GKS document, this is in annex E and is provided purely as an example, since it is not part of the formal standard.

In the last couple of years, there has been an increasing amount of work done on graphics metafiles and interfaces for virtual graphics devices. In particular, ANSI have done a great deal of work in this area and a proposal from them concerning a standard graphics metafile is currently under review by both ANSI and ISO. It is almost certain that a standard for graphics metafiles based on this proposal will be agreed in the near future.

It was therefore necessary to implement the workstation functions in such a way that other metafile formats could easily be added to the system later, without changing the front-end code.

5.2 REQUIREMENTS OF GKS METAFILE INTERFACE

The GKS document describes a number of routines that are provided specifically for metafile support; in addition, since a metafile output workstation is effectively the same as any other output workstation, the majority of (non-inquiry) routines will cause records to be written to any active output metafile.

The routines that are provided for metafile support are:

GET ITEM TYPE FROM GKSM
> obtains the type of the next metafile item and other information necessary for the item to be readable;

READ ITEM FROM GKSM
> reads the next metafile item into user storage;

INTERPRET ITEM
> takes appropriate action according to the item type;

WRITE ITEM TO GKSM
> allows the user to add records to the metafile that will be fitted to the metafile format and can be read back but which have no interpretation in GKS.

5.3   SOME PROBLEMS WITH METAFILES

At first glance metafiles seem a simple enough concept and   one   that   will
not take much effort.   However, there are several aspects of metafiles that
cause problems.

1.   Conceptually, attributes are bound to every output primitive

     This means that when an output attribute is interpreted, it   should   be
     supplied   to   its   pipeline   together with the attributes it had in the
     metafile, not the   current   attributes.   As   a   result   of   this,   the
     pipelines are quite badly disturbed when a metafile is read.

2.   Although the parameter lists of functions dealing with metafiles do not
     contain   any   reference   to   a particular metafile, it is necessary for
     this information to be available so that INTERPRET ITEM can work.

3.   Since a variety of metafile formats may be supported in the fullness of
     time,   all   have   to   be translated to some common format in order that
     INTERPRET ITEM can remain unchanged as new metafile input   workstations
     are   added   to   the   system.   This   can   cause   quite   an   overhead in
     processing a metafile.

4.   The format of the GDP record given in annex E of the GKS document makes
     it   exceptionally   hard   even   to   skip, since length fields are stored
     after variable length data records.

     The task of implementing the metafile functions was split into:

     1.   metafile output workstation
     2.   metafile input workstation
     3.   INTERPRET ITEM

The first and second tasks were relatively simple.   The last showed up   the
problems of metafile items not containing any indication of the workstation
from which it came.   The final structure is nearly the same as would result
if   INTERPRET ITEM was implemented above the user-level interface, although
some of the checking that is performed is different.

5.4   FUTURE DEVELOPMENTS IN METAFILE SUPPORT

Our implementation decided that initially only   a   single   metafile   format
(that   given   in   annex   E)   would   be supported both for output and input.
Since the ANSI/ISO metafile document is finding   broad   acceptance   amongst
those   who have worked on, prototype output and input metafile workstations
for that metafile will be provided when effort permits.

     GKS will become the main supported graphics system on   SERC   computers;
therefore   it will tend to be GKS that has the best support of new devices.
For this reason, it will increasingly become attractive for metafile   input
workstations to be added for the metafiles produced by other packages.

Chapter 6

CONCLUSIONS

6.1 SURVEY OF PROBLEMS

The problems may be split into those that were self-inflicted and those that are intrinsic to GKS.

The type of GKS system we decided to implement was determined by the wide range of user applications, operating systems and device types which the GKS system would have to support. Other implementations may not need this great generality and may therefore be able to avoid a few of the problems we hit, but not many.

The greatest challenge was to design and implement a system that appeared reasonable on both unintelligent systems and systems that implemented more or less of GKS in firmware. It meant that design of the interface to the utilities was considerably harder than would be the case if the system only had to deal with dumb terminals.

A few technical problems were encountered and have been dealt with above: in summary they were as follows.

1. It is essential to optimize the attribute-changing paths of the system to avoid unnecessary calls to the workstation driver.

2. A design where all routines call through one interface has to be avoided since a user written error handler may call user-level inquiry functions.

3. Emulation of some functions can make large demands for temporary storage.

4. It appears difficult to design a level 'c' input system that is transportable; this is due to operating system constraints, not any unusual requirements imposed by GKS.

5. Level 'b' GKS cannot directly support cursor+key responses from terminals; the only 'clean' solution appears to be the use of ESCAPE.

6. Boundary boxes, useful as a performance enhancement when simulating PICK input, are workstation-dependent.

7. Metafiles are surprisingly difficult to implement because of their definition in the GKS document.

6.2   SURVEY OF TARGETS ACHIEVED

At the time of writing, the project is continuing, although much   more   is
complete than still remains to be done.   The output system has been
demonstrated on three operating systems:

*   POS on the PERQ, to the PERQ screen;

*   PNX (Unix) on the PERQ, to the PERQ screen;

*   VMS on the VAX, to a Sigma 5674.

All output primitives and output attributes work, correctly as far as we
know!

Metafile output and input are both working but relatively untested
since INTERPRET ITEM is still being tested. This took much longer than
expected because of editorial changes introduced in GKS 7.2.

Work on input and segments is continuing but should soon be complete;
the main delay with input was not the input model but the handling of the
data records.

The size of the system is much as we expected; the current total
library size on the VAX is of the order of 120 kbytes.

The speed of the system is difficult to measure since on the VAX there
is lots of storage (so little paging) but slow devices (typically running
at 4800 baud) and on the PERQ there is no lack of speed in the display but
some penalty in working through a window manager. In general we are
pleased with the speed of the system.

The time taken for the project has been about 30% more   than
anticipated, but some of this has been caused by the changes made to GKS at
Eindhoven: not because we had to redesign our implementation but because
two members of the project were responsible for editing the GKS document
and so were lost to the project for some months.

6.3   FUTURE DEVELOPMENTS

The joint project had as its aim to develop a complete GKS 7.2 system to
level 1b which worked on PERQ under Unix and VAX under VMS. However the
reason for contemplating this massive task in the first place was so that
Rutherford could provide GKS on all its computers under all of their
operating systems. Therefore our immediate task is to transport the system
to all our other machines.

We are committed to supporting a rather wide range of graphics devices
and so will, in parallel with the migration to other machines and operating
systems, be increasing the number of workstation drivers available.

Although we limited ourselves to level 1b for reasons given above, it is essential that on almost all the machines we provide support for SAMPLE and EVENT input. Similarly, we anticipate that the method by which we have simulated workstation segments for workstations that cannot support GKS segments will make it very simple to go to output level 2 (adding Workstation Independent Segment Storage).

Since GKS is a much richer basic graphics system than its predecessors, there will be extensions to do within GKS, such as a more extensive marker/font library, new ESCAPEs and GDPs and, in particular, revision of the ways in which segments are handled on devices. Perhaps the most urgent task here is to provide a segment handling system on high-speed bitmap devices (like the PERQ) where each segment is held on an area of virtual storage (as well as in normal segment store) and segment transformations can be implemented by slipping segments around the screen by means of RasterOp.

The set of utility routines will have to be extended to deal with unintelligent raster printers, where vector to raster conversion must be done by the package.

At present the font database that is used to provide STROKE precision text only uses vector font definitions. However, the structure of the database is such that raster and filled area definitions can also be added. With a few extra utility routines, the text emulation package could be extended to provide much better text output on raster workstations.

We have already converted a large number of applications-oriented routines so that they use GKS 6.2. These provide functions like graph drawing, contour plotting, curve-fitting and 3D histogramming. With very little change these will run above GKS 7.2. There is also, by now, quite a backlog of routines and utility programs which we want to write or rewrite but have held back from doing until we had GKS available; these include a presentation plotting system and the foil making program that produced the foils for this talk and the illustrations in the lecture notes.

R E F E R E N C E

ISO/DIS 7942 Information Processing: Graphical Kernel System (GKS): Functional Description.

VIII. Surface Design Foundations

W. Böhm and G. Farin

Abstract. The tutorial covers all major surface design methods, including the underlying curve schemes. Tensor product surfaces are described in the forms of Bézier, Coons, and B-Spline surfaces. These methods are also carried over to triangular surface patches. Where appropriate, interpolation aspects are treated as well as approximations.

NOTE

The following notes are a transcript of the slide originals as they were presented and discussed at the tutorial. They are not intended to be a self-contained text but should rather be used as a concise orientation aid in connection with other sources. An expanded version has now appeared as a survey article: Böhm, W., Farin, G., Kahmann, J.: A Survey of Curve and Surface Methods in CAGD, Computer Aided Geometric Design 1 (1984).

CONTENTS   page

1. LOCAL COORDINATES

Curves: map $\mathbb{R}^1 \longrightarrow \mathbb{R}^2$ or $\mathbb{R}^3$

domain $\longrightarrow$ range

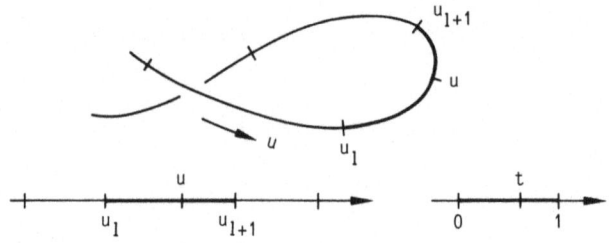

global coordinates   u; $u \in [u_1, u_{1+1}]$
local coordinates   t; $t \in [0, 1]$

$$u = u_1 \cdot (1 - t) + u_{1+1} \cdot t$$

Rectangular patches: $\mathbb{R}^2 \longrightarrow \mathbb{R}^3$

Rectangular partition of domain

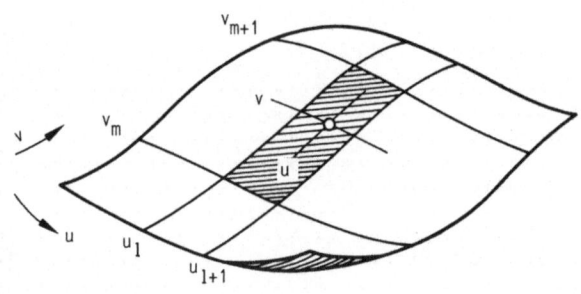

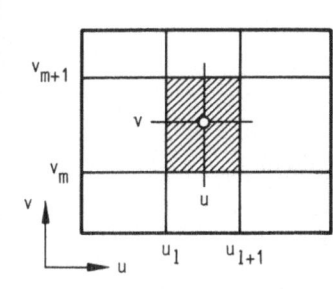
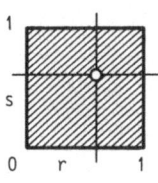

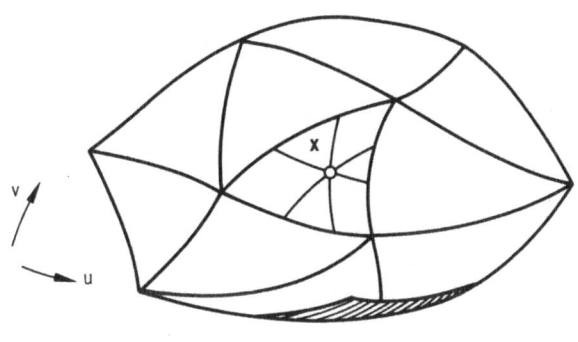

Triangular patches: $\mathbb{R}^2 \longrightarrow \mathbb{R}^3$

triangulation of domain

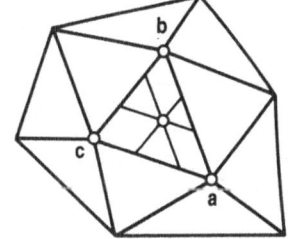
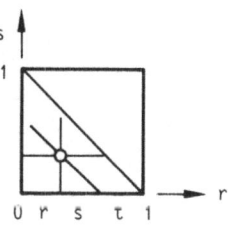

$\mathbf{u} = \mathbf{a}r + \mathbf{b}s + \mathbf{c}t$

local coordinates (r,s,t): barycentric coordinates

Linear Interpolation

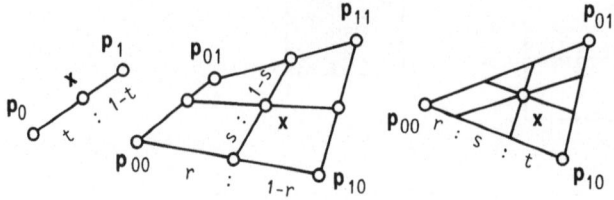

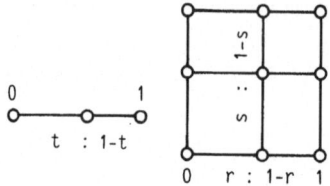 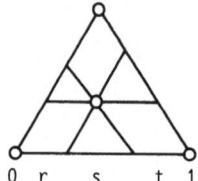

$$\mathbf{x}(t) \quad = \mathbf{p}_0(1-t) + \mathbf{p}_1 t \qquad\qquad \text{linear}$$

$$\mathbf{x}(r,s) \quad = (\mathbf{p}_{00}(1-r) + \mathbf{p}_{10}r)\,(1-s)$$

$$+\;(\mathbf{p}_{01}(1-r) + \mathbf{p}_{11}r)\cdot s \qquad \text{bilinear}$$

$$\mathbf{x}(r,s,t) = \mathbf{p}_{10}r + \mathbf{p}_{01}s + \mathbf{p}_{00}t \qquad\qquad \text{planar}$$

● Affine invariance

---

2. POLYNOMIAL CURVES

Monomial form:

$$\mathbf{x}(u) = \mathbf{a}_0 + \mathbf{a}_1 t + \mathbf{a}_2 t^2 + \mathbf{a}_3 t^3$$

⊕ fast evaluation; Horner's scheme
⊖ $\mathbf{a}_i$ are not geometric
⊖ not affinely invariant

Lagrange form:

$$\mathbf{x}(u) = \mathbf{p}_0 L_0^3(u) + \mathbf{p}_1 L_1^3(u) + \mathbf{p}_2 L_2^3(u) + \mathbf{p}_3 L_3^3(u)$$

$$L_i^3(u_k) = \delta_{i,k} = \begin{cases} 1 & i = k \\ 0 & i \neq k \end{cases}$$

⊕ $\mathbf{p}_i$ on curve
⊕ affine invariance ($\sum_i L_i^3 \equiv 1$)
⊖ oscillations

Hermite form:

$$\mathbf{x}(u) = \mathbf{p}_0 H_0^3(t) + D_t \mathbf{p}_0 H_1^3(t)$$

$$+ D_t \mathbf{p}_1 H_2^3(t) + \mathbf{p}_1 H_3^3(t)$$

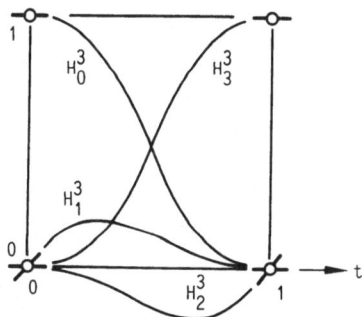

⊕ Affine invariance
⊕ Smooth piecewise curves
⊖ Tangent vector magnitudes

Bernstein Polynomials

$$\mathbf{x}(u) = \mathbf{b}_0 B_0^3(t) + \mathbf{b}_1 B_1^3(t) + \mathbf{b}_2 B_2^3(t) + \mathbf{b}_3 B_3^3(t)$$

$$B_i^3(t) = \binom{3}{i} (1-t)^{3-i} t^i$$

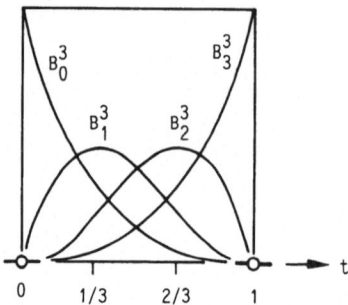

$\mathbf{b}_i$: Bézier points $\longrightarrow$ Bézier polygon

partition of unity: $\quad \sum\limits_{i=0}^{3} B_i^3(t) \equiv 1$

positivity: $\quad B_i^3(t) \geq 0; \quad t \in [0,1]$

recursion: $\quad B_i^n(t) = (1-t) B_i^{n-1}(t) + t B_{i-1}^{n-1}(t)$

De Casteljau Algorithm

Start: $\quad \mathbf{b}_i^0(t) = \mathbf{b}_i$

repeated linear
interpolation: $\quad \mathbf{b}_i^k(t) = (1-t) \mathbf{b}_i^{k-1} + t \mathbf{b}_{i+1}^{k-1}$

result: $\quad \mathbf{x}(u) = \mathbf{b}_3^3(t)$

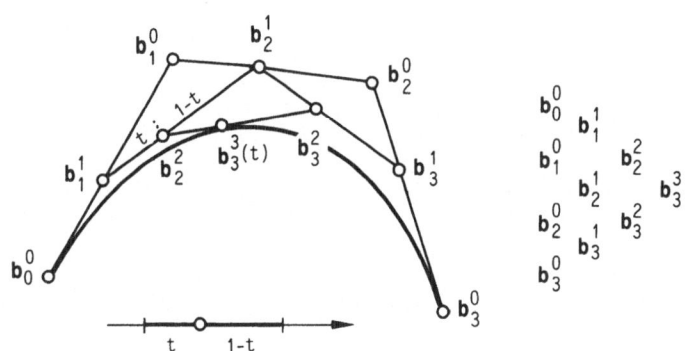

Subdivision: $\mathbf{b}_3^3$ splits curve segment

left $\mathbf{b}_0^0$ $\mathbf{b}_1^1$ $\mathbf{b}_2^2$ $\mathbf{b}_3^3$

right $\mathbf{b}_3^3$ $\mathbf{b}_3^2$ $\mathbf{b}_3^1$ $\mathbf{b}_3^0$

Derivatives

$$D_u\mathbf{x}(u) = 3 \cdot \frac{1}{\Delta u_0} (\Delta\mathbf{b}_0 B_0^2(t) + \Delta\mathbf{b}_1 B_1^2(t) + \Delta\mathbf{b}_2 B_2^2(t))$$

$$D_u^2\mathbf{x}(u) = 6 \cdot \frac{1}{(\Delta u_0)^2} (\Delta^2\mathbf{b}_0 B_0^1(t) + \Delta^2\mathbf{b}_1 B_1^1(t))$$

Δ: difference operator $\Delta\mathbf{b}_i = \mathbf{b}_{i+1} - \mathbf{b}_i$

$\mathbf{x}(u)$ is quadratic if $\Delta^3\mathbf{b}_0 = \mathbf{0}$

Also:

$$D_u\mathbf{x}(u) = 3 \cdot \frac{1}{\Delta u_0} \Delta\mathbf{b}_2^2(t); \quad D_u^2\mathbf{x}(u) = 6 \cdot \frac{1}{(\Delta u_0)^2} \Delta^2\mathbf{b}_1^1(t)$$

at $t = 0$:

$$D\mathbf{x}(u_0) = 3\Delta\mathbf{b}_0, \quad D^2\mathbf{x}(u_0) = 6\Delta^2\mathbf{b}_0$$

Endpoint derivatives depend only on nearby Bézier points.

$\longrightarrow$ Conversion to monomial (Taylor) form:

$$\mathbf{x}(u) = \mathbf{a}_0 + \mathbf{a}_1 t + \mathbf{a}_2 t^2 + \mathbf{a}_3 t^3$$

$$\mathbf{a}_0 = \mathbf{b}_0; \quad \mathbf{a}_1 = 3\Delta\mathbf{b}_0; \quad \mathbf{a}_2 = 3\Delta^2\mathbf{b}_0; \quad \mathbf{a}_3 = \Delta^3\mathbf{b}_0$$

Degree Elevation

$$\mathbf{x}(u) = \mathbf{b}_0 B_0^3 + \mathbf{b}_1 B_1^3 + \mathbf{b}_2 B_2^3 + \mathbf{b}_3 B_3^3$$

$$\quad = \hat{\mathbf{b}}_0 B_0^4 + \hat{\mathbf{b}}_1 B_1^4 + \hat{\mathbf{b}}_2 B_2^4 + \hat{\mathbf{b}}_3 B_3^4 + \hat{\mathbf{b}}_4 B_4^4$$

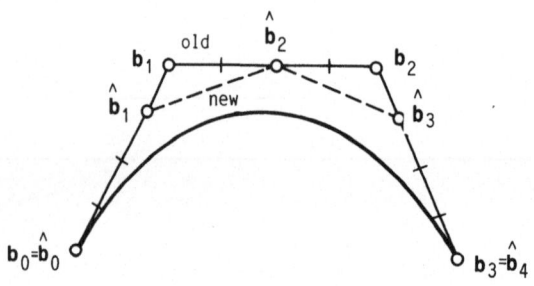

$$\hat{\mathbf{b}}_i = \alpha_i \mathbf{b}_{i-1} + (1 - \alpha_i)\mathbf{b}_i; \quad \alpha_i = \frac{i}{4}$$

Repeated degree elevation: polygons converge to curve.

Degree reduction usually not possible!

Composite Bézier Curves

Two intervals: $u_0 < u_1 < u_2$

local parameters: t in $[u_0, u_1]$, s in $[u_1, u_2]$

two segments: $\mathbf{x}(t)$, $\mathbf{y}(s)$ defined over $[u_0, u_2]$

Conditions for c^1, c^2, ... continuity:

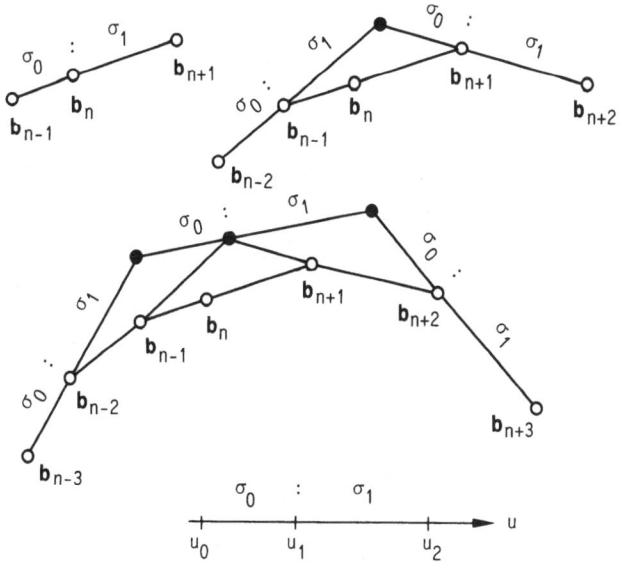

Composite cubic c^1 curve:

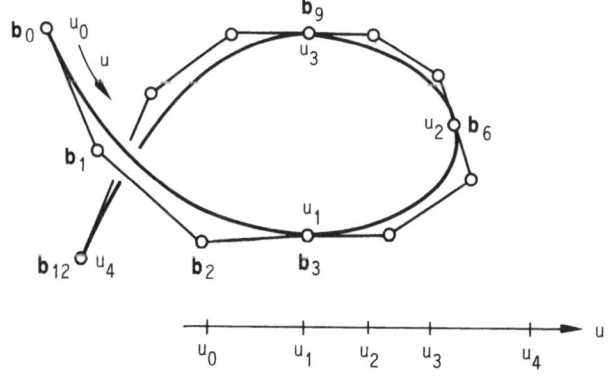

Smooth Interpolation by Piecewise Cubics

Given: points $\mathbf{p}_0, \mathbf{p}_1, \ldots, \mathbf{p}_n$

knots $u_0, u_1, \ldots, u_n$

Find: Interpolating curve $\mathbf{x}(u)$ with

1. $\mathbf{x}(u_k) = \mathbf{p}_k$
2. $\mathbf{x}(u)$ is C^1

Solution in two steps:

a) find slopes $\mathbf{s}_k = D_u\mathbf{x}(u_k)$ at each point $\mathbf{p}_k$

b) find tangent lengths at each $\mathbf{p}_k$

$\mathbf{x}(u)$ is composite Bézier curve: $\mathbf{p}_k = \mathbf{b}_{3k}$

b) becomes: find $\mathbf{b}_{3k\pm 1}$

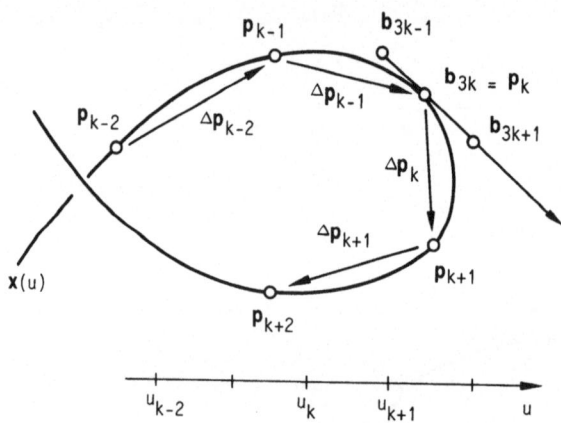

Make slopes $\mathbf{s}_k$ linear combinations of chords:

$$\mathbf{s}_k = (1 - \alpha_k)\,\mathbf{c}_{k-1} + \alpha_k\mathbf{c}_k \,;\quad \mathbf{c}_k = \Delta\mathbf{p}_k/\Delta u_k$$

Bessel/(Overhauser):

$$\alpha_k = \frac{\Delta u_{k-1}}{\Delta u_{k-1} + \Delta u_k}$$

i.e. s_k is slope of parabola through $p_{k-1}p_kp_{k+1}$;

use this for endpoint slopes: $s_0 = 2c_0 - s_1$

$$s_m = 2c_{m-1} - s_{m-1}$$

● Affine invariance

Akima/Pochop-Renner:

$$\alpha_k = \frac{|\Delta c_{k-2}|}{|\Delta c_{k-2}| + |\Delta c_k|}$$

endpoint slopes s_0, s_1, s_{n-1}, s_n from BESSEL (e.g.)

● Straight line through three points is reproduced.
No affine invariance (only eucledean).

Fmill:

$$s_k = \frac{1}{\Delta u_{k-1} + \Delta u_k} \Delta p_{k-1} + \frac{1}{\Delta u_{k-1} + \Delta u_k} \Delta p_k$$

i.e. s_k parallel to $p_{k-1}'p_{k+1}$

endpoint slopes s_0, s_n from BESSEL

● Affine invariance

Step b) (tangent lengths) is the same for all methods:

$$b_{3k-1} = p_k - \frac{1}{3} \Delta u_{k-1} s_k$$

$$b_{3k+1} = p_k + \frac{1}{3} \Delta u_k s_k$$

PARAMETRIZATION:

Simple and fast: *equidistant*

$$\Delta u_k = c \qquad c = \text{arb. const.}$$

drawback: possible oscillations

more geometric: *chord lengths*

$$\Delta u_k = c \cdot |\Delta \mathbf{p}_k|$$

Nonparametric Bézier Curves

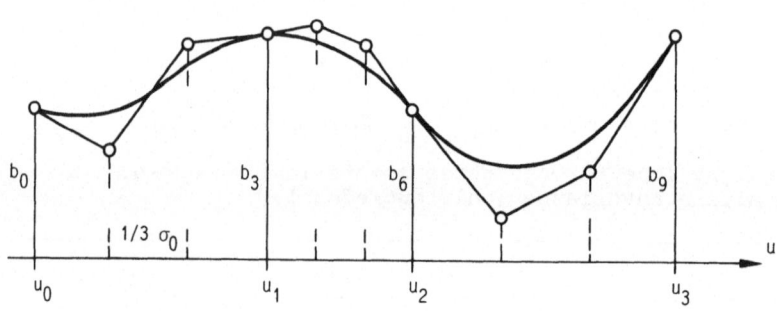

Nonparametric: functions $y = f(u)$

Instead of Bézier points $\mathbf{b}_i$ now: Bézier ordinates b_i
with abscissae:

$$v_i = u_0 + \frac{i}{3} \Delta u_0$$

Degree elevation: evaluate polygon at $\hat{v}_i = u_0 + \frac{i}{4} \Delta u_0$

3. B-SPLINE CURVES

Recall C^2 conditions:

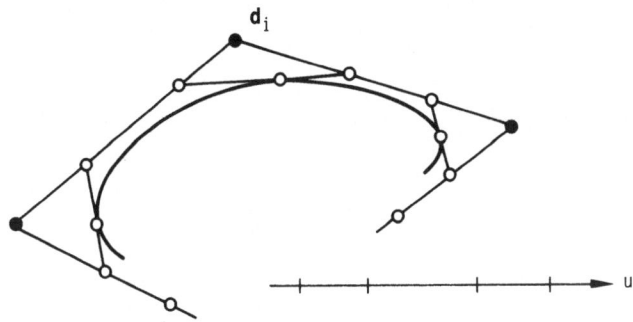

$\mathbf{d}_i$ are constructed from $\mathbf{b}_i$.

Reverse: *construct* $\mathbf{b}_i$ *from* $\mathbf{d}_i$.

$\mathbf{d}_i$: de Boor points

Write whole curve as

$$\mathbf{x}(u) = \sum \mathbf{d}_i N_i^3(u)$$

N_i^3: cubic B-splines

Properties of the N_i^3:

- partition of unity: $\sum\limits_i N_i^3(u) \equiv 1$

- positivity: $N_i^3(u) \geq 0$

- local support: $N_i^3(u) = 0$ for $u \notin [u_i, u_{i+4}]$

- continuity: N_i^3 is twice diff.

• recursion:

$$N_i^r(u) = \frac{u - u_i}{u_{i+r} - u_i} N_i^{r-1}(u) + \frac{u_{i+r} - u}{u_{i+r+1} - u_{i+1}} N_{i+1}^{r-1}(u)$$

$$N_i^0(u) = \begin{cases} 1 & u \in [u_i, u_{i+1}] \\ 0 & u \notin [u_i, u_{i+1}] \end{cases}$$

(Mansfield, de Boor, Cox)

recursion, geometric:

N_i^3

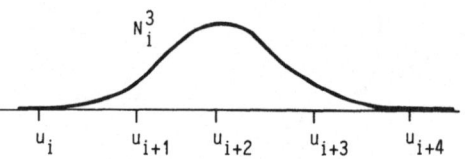

$$= N_i^2 \frac{u - u_i}{u_{i+3} - u_i}$$

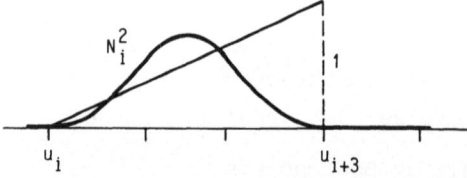

$$+ N_{i+1}^2 \frac{u_{i+3} - u}{u_{i+4} - u_{i+1}}$$

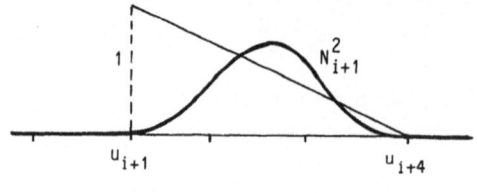

De Boor Algorithm

Start: $\qquad\qquad d_i^0(u) = d_i$

repeated linear $\quad d_i^k(u) = (1 - \alpha_i^k) d_{i-1}^{k-1} + \alpha_i^k d_i^{k-1}$
interpolation:

$$\alpha_i^k = \frac{u - u_i}{u_{i+4-k} - u_i}$$

result: $\qquad\qquad s(u) = d_3^3(u)$

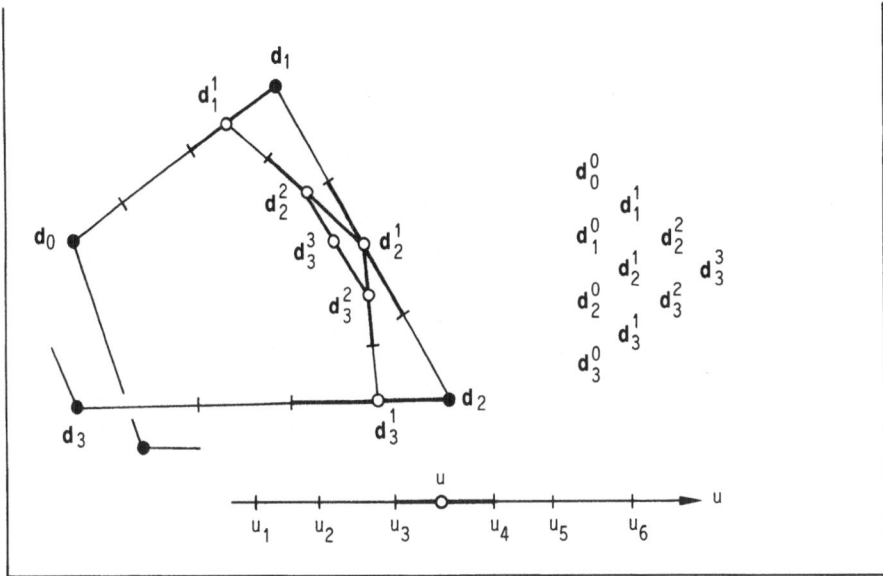

Derivatives

B-spline curves of degree n:

$$\mathbf{s}(u) = \sum_i \mathbf{d}_i \, N_i^n(u)$$

over partition $\{u_k\}$ has derivative that is B-spline curve of degree n-1 over same knots:

$$D_u \mathbf{s}(u) = \sum_i \mathbf{d}_i^{(1)} \, N_i^{n-1}(u)$$

$$\mathbf{d}_i^{(1)} = n \, \frac{\Delta \mathbf{d}_{i-1}}{u_{i+n} - u_i}$$

Higher derivatives: higher differences, can be used for Taylor expansion.

Inserting New Knots

"Pseudo"-knot $\hat{u} \in [u_1, u_{1+1}]$

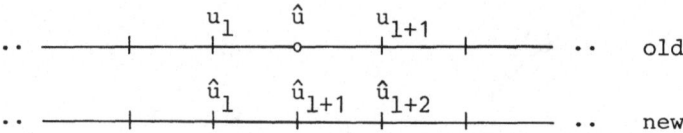

Corresponding new de Boor points: first row of de Boor scheme for $s(\hat{u})$, i.e. replace $\mathbf{d}_{1-2}, \mathbf{d}_{1-1}$ by $\mathbf{d}_{1-2}^1, \mathbf{d}_{1-1}^1, \mathbf{d}_1^1$.

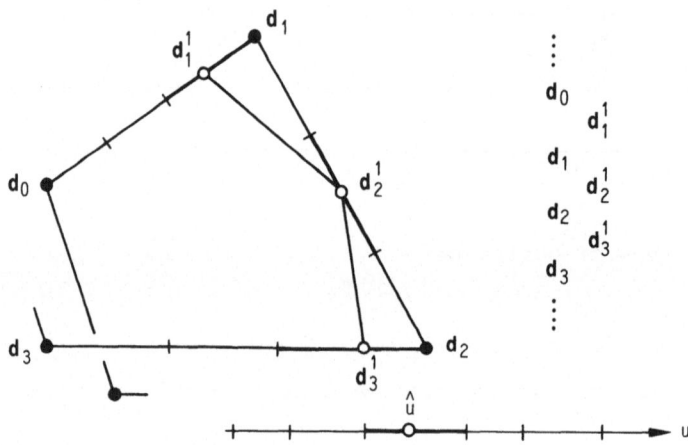

Multiple insertion also possible.

Bézier Points of B-Splines

Insert every knot twice. The resulting de Boor points are
the Bézier points.

Double knot insertion:

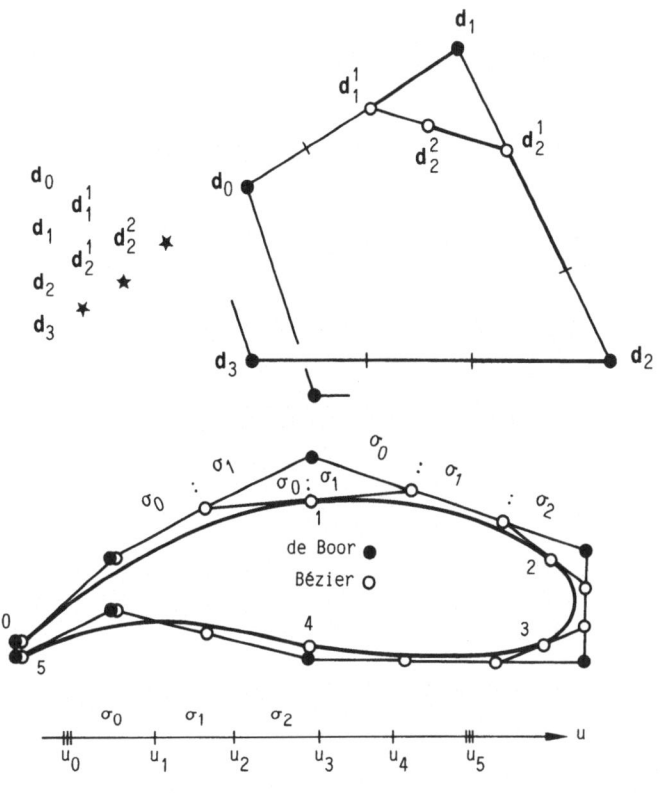

In general: assign multiplicity 3 to end knots.

Spline Interpolation

Given: points $\mathbf{p}_i$ and knots u_i; $i = 0,\ldots,r$

Find: interpolating cubic B-spline curve:

$$\mathbf{s}(u_i) = \sum_k \mathbf{d}_k N_k^3(u_i) = \mathbf{p}_i ; \qquad i = 0,\ldots,r$$

Recall relation between $\mathbf{d}$'s and $\mathbf{b}$'s:

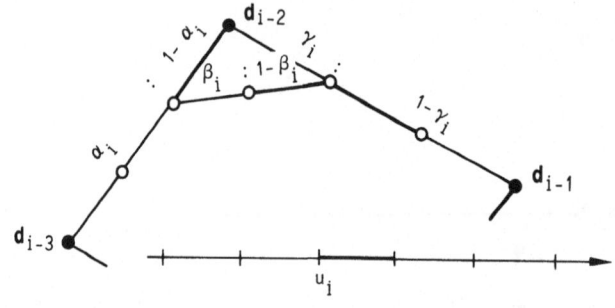

$$(1 - \gamma_i)\, \mathbf{d}_{i-2} + \gamma_i\, \mathbf{d}_{i-1} \qquad\qquad = \mathbf{b}_{3i+1}$$

$$(1 - \beta_i)\Big((1 - \alpha_i)\, \mathbf{d}_{i-3} + \alpha_i\, \mathbf{d}_{i-2}\Big) +$$

$$\beta_i \Big((1 - \gamma_i)\, \mathbf{d}_{i-2} + \gamma_i\, \mathbf{d}_{i-1}\Big) \qquad = \mathbf{b}_{3i} = \mathbf{p}_i \qquad *$$

$$\alpha_i = \frac{u_i - u_{i-2}}{u_{i+1} - u_{i-2}}, \qquad \beta_i = \frac{u_i - u_{i-1}}{u_{i+1} - u_{i-2}}, \qquad \gamma_i = \frac{u_i - u_{i-1}}{u_{i+1} - u_{i-2}}$$

left end knot has multiplicity 3:

$$u_0 = u_{-1} = u_{-2} \quad\longrightarrow\quad \mathbf{d}_{-3} = \mathbf{p}_0, \quad \mathbf{d}_1 = \mathbf{b}_1$$

same for right end:

$$u_r = u_{r-1} = u_{r-2} \quad\longrightarrow\quad \mathbf{d}_{r-2} = \mathbf{b}_{r-1}, \quad \mathbf{d}_{r-1} = \mathbf{p}_r$$

From this and (✱) linear system:

$$
\begin{bmatrix}
1 & 0 & & & & \\
0 & 1 & 0 & & & \\
& * & * & * & & \\
& & \cdot & \cdot & \cdot & \\
& & \cdot & \cdot & \cdot & \\
& & \cdot & \cdot & \cdot & \\
& & 0 & 1 & 0 & \\
& & & 0 & 1 &
\end{bmatrix}
\begin{bmatrix}
\mathbf{d}_{-3} \\
\mathbf{d}_{-2} \\
\mathbf{d}_{-1} \\
\vdots \\
\mathbf{d}_{r-2} \\
\mathbf{d}_{r-1}
\end{bmatrix}
=
\begin{bmatrix}
\mathbf{p}_0 \\
\mathbf{b}_1 \\
\mathbf{p}_1 \\
\vdots \\
\mathbf{b}_{3r-1} \\
\mathbf{p}_r
\end{bmatrix}
$$

Solve by LU-factorization.

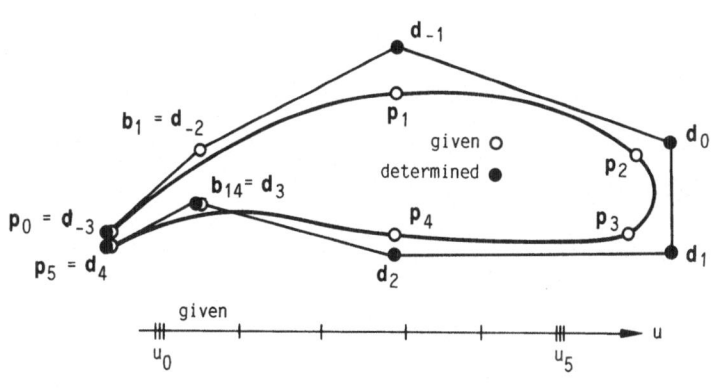

Spline Approximation

Given: *many* points $\mathbf{p}_i$ and knots u_i

Find: approximating B-spline curve

$$\mathbf{s}(u_i) = \sum_k \mathbf{d}_k N_k^3(u_i) \approx \mathbf{p}_i \qquad \text{✱}$$

knots:

given u_i :

(✲) is overdetermined linear system for **d**'s:

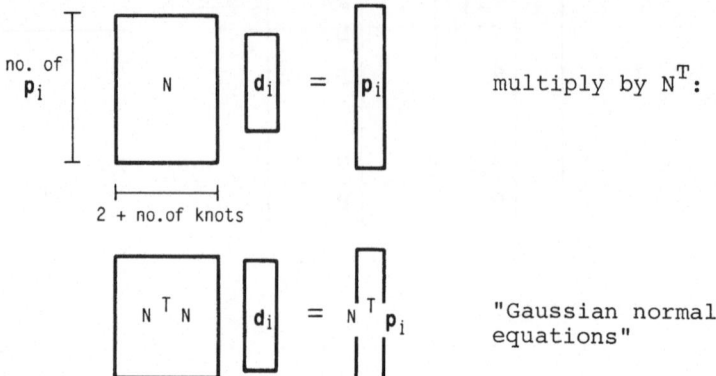

multiply by N^T:

"Gaussian normal equations"

Solution is optimal in the least-square sense.

Nonparametric Splines

$$s(u) = \sum_k d_k N_k^3(u)$$

Note:

$$u = \sum_k v_k N_k^3(u) \; ; \qquad v_k = \frac{1}{3}(u_{k+1} + u_{k+2} + u_{k+3})$$

v_k are abscissae for de Boor ordinates d_k.

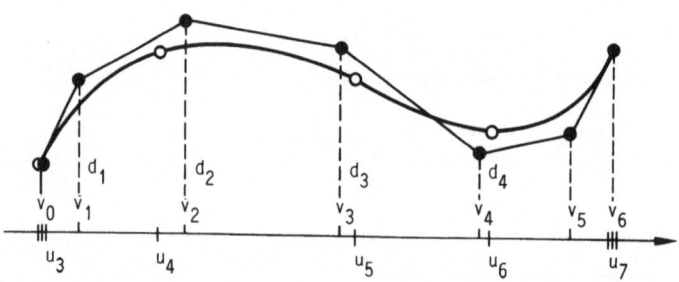

Knot insertion: determine new $\hat{v}_k$ and evaluate polygon there.

4. RATIONAL CURVES

- invariance under projective transformations
- include conic sections

$$\mathbf{r}(u) = \frac{\beta\mathbf{x}(t)}{\beta(t)} = \frac{\beta_0\mathbf{b}_0 B_0^3(t) + \ldots + \beta_3\mathbf{b}_3 B_3^3(t)}{\beta_0 B_0^3(t) + \ldots + \beta_3 B_3^3(t)}$$

all β_i of one sign $\longrightarrow$ curve in convex hull of $\mathbf{b}_i$

↑   ↑

weights   Bézier polygon

It is possible to write the denominator as quadratic polynomials (rational linear parameter transformation). Then
$t = {}^1\!/_2$ is called shoulder point.

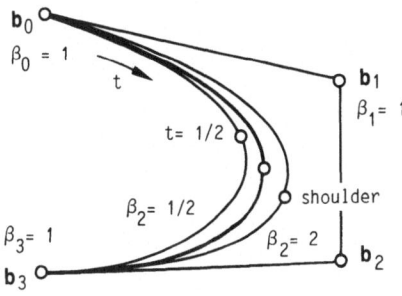

Conic Sections

Rational quadratics are conic sections:

$$\mathbf{q}(u) = \frac{\beta_0\mathbf{b}_0 B_0^2(t) + \beta_1\mathbf{b}_1 B_1^2(t) + \beta_2\mathbf{b}_2 B_2^2(t)}{\beta_0 B_0^2(t) + \beta_1 B_1^2(t) + \beta_2 B_2^2(t)}$$

Usually one sets $\beta_0 = \beta_2 = 1$.

Shoulder point $\mathbf{s} = \mathbf{q}(\frac{1}{2})$:

$$\mathbf{s} = \mathbf{m}\cdot(1-s) + \mathbf{b}_1\cdot s ;$$

$$\mathbf{m} = \frac{1}{2}(\mathbf{b}_0 + \mathbf{b}_2)$$

$$s = \beta_1/(1+\beta_1)$$

Choice of β_1 determines $\mathbf{q}$.

$s = \frac{1}{2}$: parabola (nonrational)

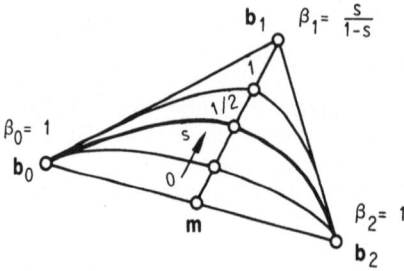

Special case: circular arc

$$|\mathbf{b}_1 - \mathbf{b}_0| = |\mathbf{b}_1 - \mathbf{b}_2|$$

$$\beta_1 = \cos\varphi$$

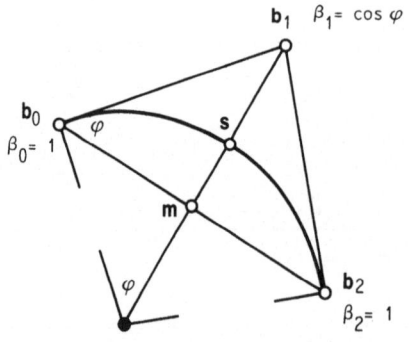

Ball's Rational Cubics

= generalized conic sections:

Define straight line through $\mathbf{1}_0, \mathbf{1}_1$.

Make $\mathbf{b}_1$ (from conic section) function of t (= local parameter on line *and* curve):

$$\mathbf{b}_1 = \frac{\beta_1 \mathbf{b}_1(t)}{\beta_1(t)} = \frac{\lambda_0 \mathbf{1}_0 (1-t) + \lambda_1 \mathbf{1}_1 \cdot t}{\lambda_0 (1-t) + \lambda_1 \cdot t}$$

t = 0: curve passes through $\mathbf{b}_0$, tangent $= 2 \dfrac{\beta_1}{\beta_0} (\mathbf{1}_0 - \mathbf{b}_0)$

t = 1: " " " $\mathbf{b}_2$, " $= 2 \dfrac{\beta_1}{\beta_2} (\mathbf{b}_2 - \mathbf{1}_1)$

shoulder $\mathbf{s}$:

$$\mathbf{s} = \frac{\beta_0 \mathbf{b}_0 + \beta_1 (\mathbf{1}_0 + \mathbf{1}_1) + \beta_2 \mathbf{b}_2}{\beta_0 + 2\beta_1 + \beta_2}$$

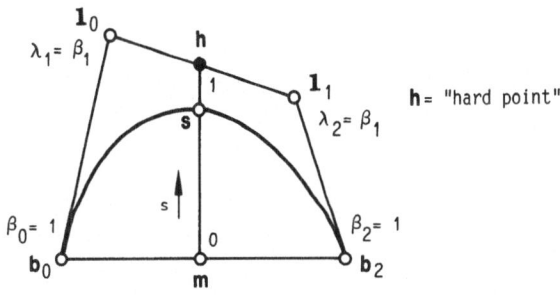

h = "hard point"

"Generalized conic segment":

Given $\mathbf{b}_0, \mathbf{b}_2$ & tangents there.

Find $\mathbf{1}_0, \mathbf{1}_1$: dist $\mathbf{b}_0, \mathbf{1}_0$ = dist $\mathbf{b}_0, \mathbf{1}_1$;

dist $\mathbf{b}_3, \mathbf{1}_0$ = dist $\mathbf{b}_3, \mathbf{1}_1$

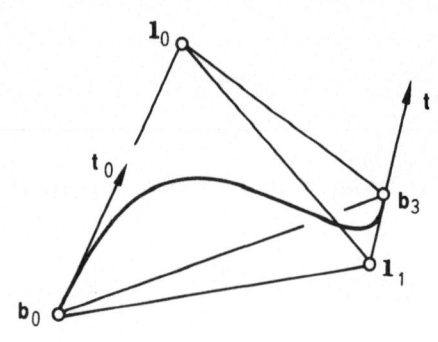

5. TENSOR-PRODUCT POLYNOMIAL SURFACES

Surface = points swept out by moving curve.

$$\mathbf{x}(u) = \sum_{i=0}^{3} \mathbf{c}_i \, f_i(u)$$

Let $\mathbf{c}_i$ vary on curves:

$$\mathbf{c}_i(v) = \sum_{k=0}^{3} \mathbf{a}_{i,k} \, g_k(v)$$

Inserting:

$$\mathbf{x}(u,v) = \sum_i \mathbf{c}_i(v) \, f_i(u) = \sum_i \sum_k \mathbf{a}_{i,k} \, f_i(u) \, g_k(v)$$

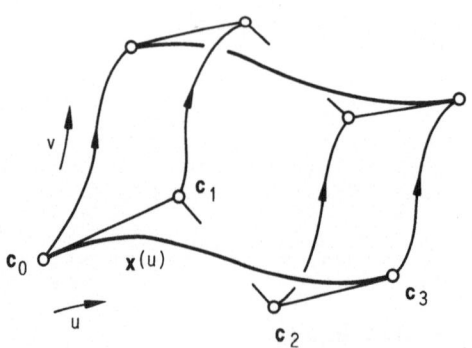

One could also start with lines $\mathbf{x}(v)$.

Standard Examples:

- $\mathbf{x}(u,v) = \sum\limits_{i=0}^{3} \sum\limits_{k=0}^{3} \mathbf{a}_{i,k}\, u^i v^k$ monomial

- $\mathbf{x}(u,v) = \sum\limits_{i=0}^{3} \sum\limits_{k=0}^{3} \mathbf{p}_{i,k}\, L_i^3(u)\, J_k^3(v)$ Lagrange

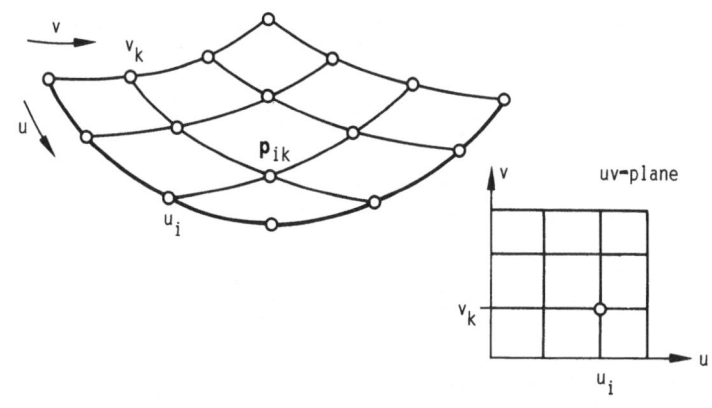

Bézier Patches

$$\mathbf{x}(u,v) = \sum\limits_{i=0}^{3} \sum\limits_{k=0}^{3} \mathbf{b}_{i,k}\, B_k(s)\, B_i(r)$$

$\mathbf{b}_{i,k}$: Bézier points $\longrightarrow$ Bézier net

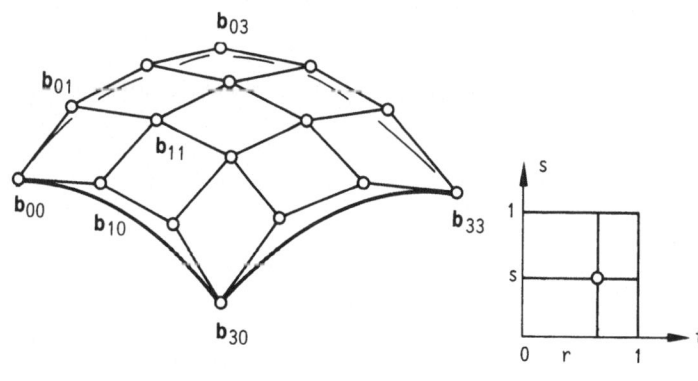

- lines of constant v (i.e. u-lines): Bézier points

$$\mathbf{b}_i(v) = \sum_{k=0}^{3} \mathbf{b}_{i,k} B_k^3(s)$$

- Cross-boundary derivative:

$$D_u \mathbf{x}(u_0, v) = \frac{3}{\Delta u_0} \sum_{k=0}^{3} \Delta^{1,0} \mathbf{b}_{0,k} B_k^3(s)$$

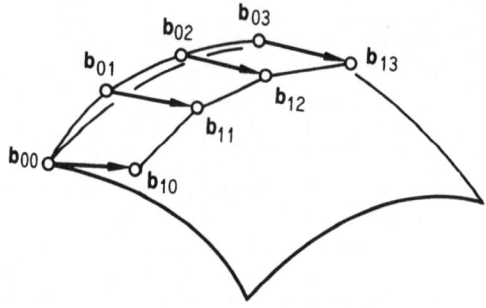

- de Casteljau algorithm: For given (u,v), i.e. (r,s):

  1. Find: $\mathbf{b}_k(r) = \sum_{i=0}^{3} \mathbf{b}_{i,k} B_i^3(r)$; $k = 0,1,2,3$

  2. $\mathbf{x}(r,s) = \sum_{k=0}^{3} \mathbf{b}_k(r) B_k^3(s)$

  Use de Casteljau for 1. and 2.

- Evaluation of many points: convert to monomial form.

- Subdivision:
  Subdivide all rows of Bézier points.

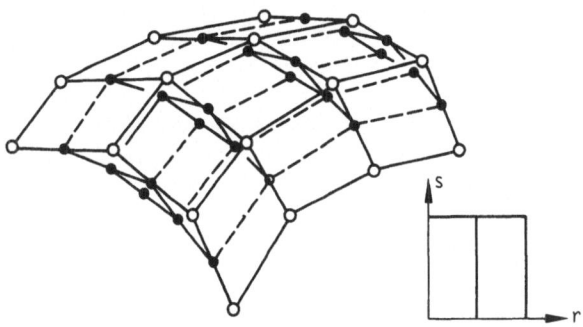

- Degree elevation:
  Elevate degree of all rows of Bézier points:

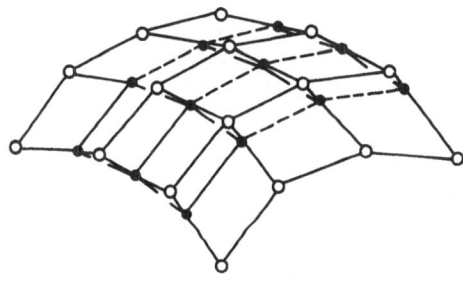

For degree elevation in other direction, elevate degree of
all new rows.

Composite Bézier Surfaces

c^1 (c^2) continuity condition for two adjacent patches: all rows of Bézier points form Bézier polygons of c^1 (c^2) curves.

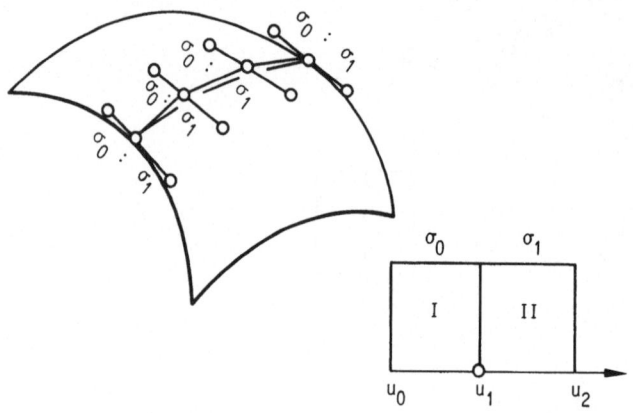

Common twist at (u_1, v_0):

$$\mathbf{x}_{u,v}(u_1, v_0) = \frac{9}{\Delta u_1 \Delta v_0} \Delta^{1,1} \mathbf{b}_{3,0} = \frac{9}{\Delta u_0 \Delta v_0} \Delta^{1,1} \mathbf{b}_{2,0}$$

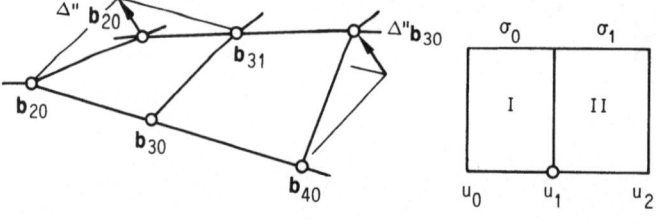

Smooth Interpolation by Piecewise Bicubics

Given: $(p+1)(q+1)$ array of points $\mathbf{p}_{i,k}$

Find: Interpolating C^1 surface, consisting of pq bicubic
         patches

1. Apply curve scheme (e.g. BESSEL) to all $p+1$ rows of
   points. Obtain $3(q+1)+1$ Bézier points for each row.

2. Apply curve scheme to all $3(q+1)+1$ columns. This gives
   the final net.

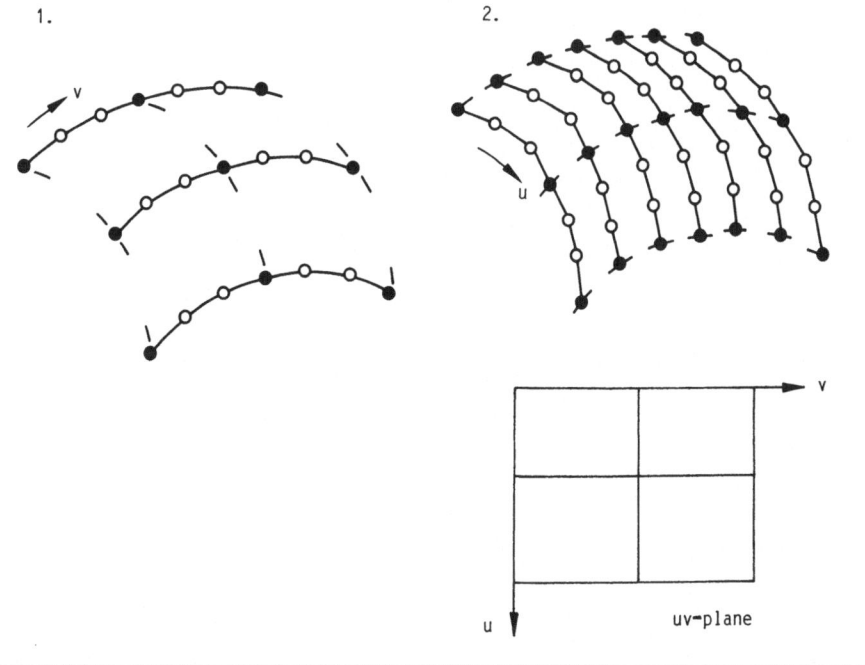

Twists

If the curve scheme is FMILL, the twists of the interpolating surface are:

$$t_{i,k} = \frac{P_{i+1,k+1} - P_{i-1,k+1} - P_{i+1,k-1} + P_{i-1,k-1}}{(\Delta u_{i-1} + \Delta u_i) \cdot (\Delta v_{k-1} + \Delta v_k)}$$

For schemes like AKIMA tensor products do not exist. These schemes yield a network of C^1 curves, and the twists must be determined otherwise. One method:

ADINI's twist (= twist from "bilinearly blended Coons patch")

$$t_{i,k} = \frac{1}{\Delta u_{i-1} + \Delta u_i} \, (D_v \, P_{i+1,k} - D_v \, P_{i-1,k})$$

$$+ \frac{1}{\Delta v_{k-1} + \Delta v_k} \, (D_u \, P_{i,k+1} - D_u \, P_{i,k-1})$$

$$- \, t_{i,k} \, \text{(FMILL)}$$

(Note: $u_{i-1} = u_i$ etc. allowed!)

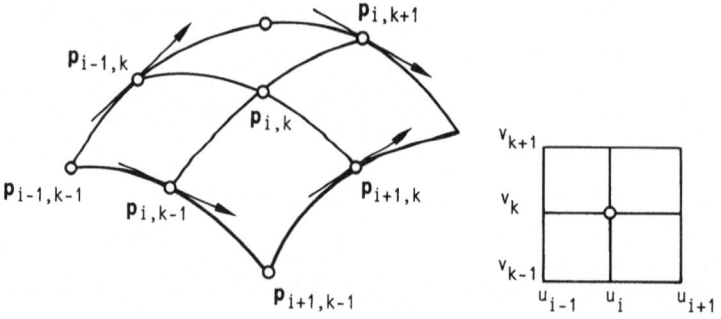

Find inner Bézier points from twists:

$$b_{3i-1,3k+1} = b_{3i,3k+1} + b_{3i-1,3k} - P_{i,k} + \Delta u_{i-1} \Delta v_k \, t_{i,k}$$

6. B-SPLINE SURFACES

$$\mathbf{s}(u,v) = \sum_i \sum_i \mathbf{d}_{i,k} M_k^3(v) N_i^3(u)$$

Basis functions: products of B-splines:

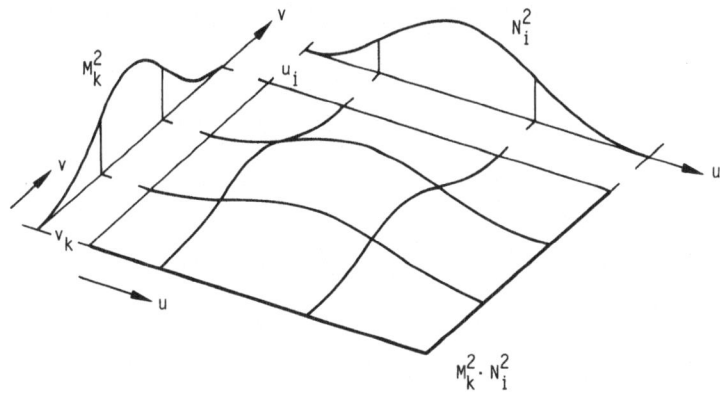

$\mathbf{d}_{i,k}$: de Boor points $\longrightarrow$ de Boor net

All properties from tensor product principle (as for Bézier).

Spline Surface Interpolation

Given: $(p + 1)(q + 1)$ array of points $\mathbf{P}_{i,k}$; u_i, v_k

Find: Interpolating B-spline surface (cubic)

1. Apply B-spline interpolation (univariate) to all $p + 1$ rows of points. Obtain $q + 1$ de Boor points for each row.

2. Apply B-spline interpolation to all $q + 1$ columns of de Boor points. This gives the final net.

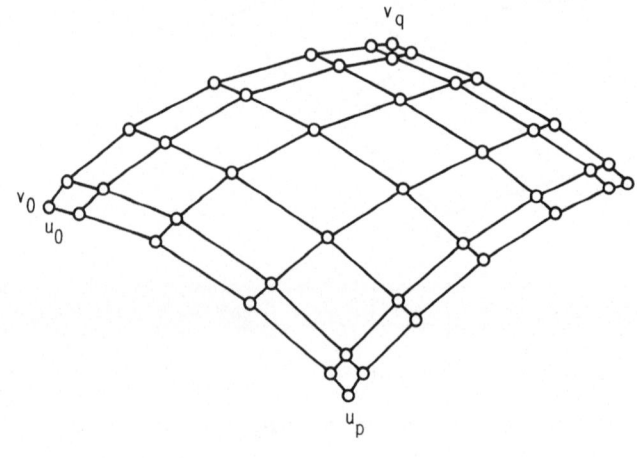

Spline Surface Approximation

Given: q + 1 lines of scattered data:

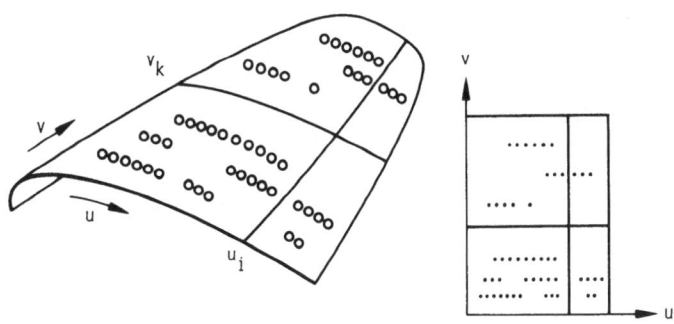

Find: approximating B-spline surface

1. Apply (univariate) B-spline approximation to all rows.
   Obtain, say, p de Boor points per row.

2. Apply (univariate) B-spline approximation (or interpolation)
   to all p rows.

Note: Order of rows/columns is important!

For points that are not arranged in rows or columns, tensor
product methods are not possible: Each point $\mathbf{p}_j$ with parameters
u_j, v_j gives one equation:

$$\mathbf{p}_j = \sum_r \sum_s \mathbf{d}_{r,s} \, N_r^3(u_j) \, M_s^3(v_j)$$

The resulting linear system is *large*. It does not always have
solutions if the data has "holes".

7. TRIANGULAR POLYNOMIAL PATCHES

Bernstein Polynomials

$$\mathbf{x}(u,v) = \sum_{\substack{i+j+k=3 \\ i,j,k \geq 0}} \mathbf{b}_{i,j,k} B^3_{i,j,k}(r,s,t)$$

← 10 terms

$$B^3_{i,j,k}(r,s,t) = \frac{3!}{i!j!k!} r^i s^j t^k \; ; \qquad r,s,t: \text{barycentric coordinates}$$

↑
Bernstein polynomials

$\mathbf{b}_{i,j,k}$: Bézier points ⟶ Bézier net

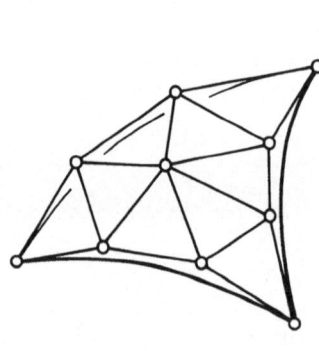

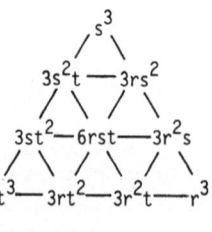

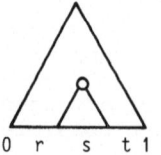

0   r   s   t 1

- partition of unity $\sum_{i,j,k} B^3_{i,j,k}(r,s,t) \equiv 1$

- positivity $B^3_{i,j,k}(r,s,t) \geq 0 \; ; \qquad r,s,t > 0$

- recursion $B^n_{i,j,k} = r\,B^{n-1}_{i-1,j,k} + s\,B^{n-1}_{i,j-1,k} + t\,B^{n-1}_{i,j,k-1}$

- Boundary curves of $\mathbf{x}(r,s,t)$ are univariate Bézier curves. Note:

$$B^n_i(t) = B^n_{i,n-i}(t,1-t)$$

- Straight line in domain ⟶ cubic curve in range.

De Casteljau Algorithm

Start: $\qquad \mathbf{b}^0_{i,j,k}(r,s,t) = \mathbf{b}^0_{i,j,k}$

repeated
linear $\qquad \mathbf{b}^1_{i,j,k}(r,s,t) = r\,\mathbf{b}^{1-1}_{i+1,j,k} + s\,\mathbf{b}^{1-1}_{i,j+1,k} + t\,\mathbf{b}^{1-1}_{i,j,k+1}$
interp.:

result: $\qquad \mathbf{x}(u,v) = \mathbf{b}^3_{0,0,0}(r,s,t)$

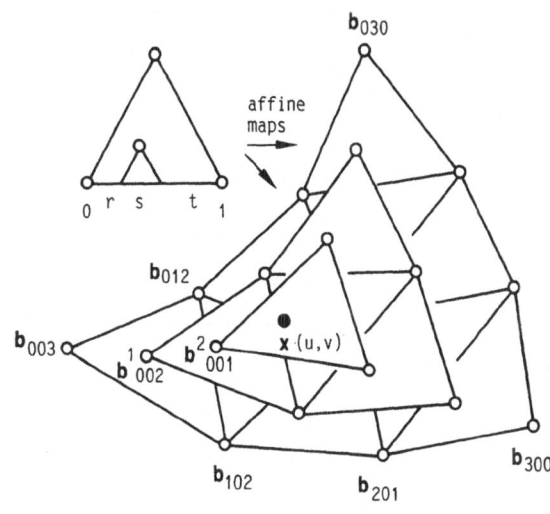

Derivatives

Partial derivatives have no geometric meaning since $r + s + t = 1$.
Hence:

directional derivatives:

$\quad \tau$ – local parameter of straight line
$$\mathbf{r}(\tau) = (1 - \tau)\,\mathbf{r}_0 + \tau\,\mathbf{r}_1 \;; \qquad \mathbf{r} = (r,s,t)$$

$$D_c\mathbf{x}(u(\tau),v(\tau)) = 3 \sum_{i+j+k=2} \mathbf{c}_{i,j,k}\, B^2_{i,j,k}(\mathbf{r}(\tau))$$

$$\mathbf{c}_{i,j,k} = \Delta r_0\,\mathbf{b}_{i+1,j,k} + \Delta s_0\,\mathbf{b}_{i,j+1,k} + \Delta t_0\,\mathbf{b}_{i,j,k+1}\;;$$
$$i + j + k = 2$$

Note:

$$\Delta r_0 + \Delta s_0 + \Delta t_0 = 0$$

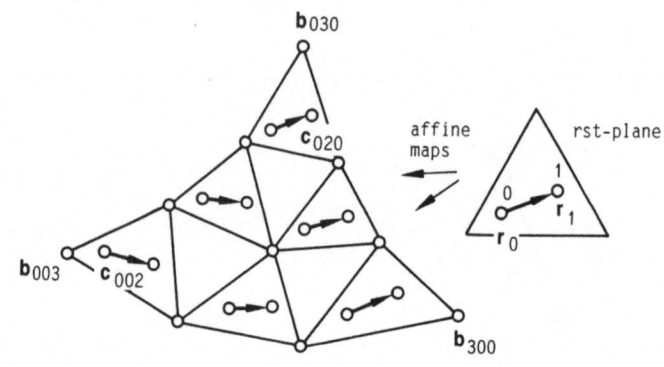

Subdivision

Point **r** subdivides domain triangle. **x(r)** subdivides patch.
Bézier points for subpatches = intermediate (de Casteljau)
points from construction of **x(r)**:

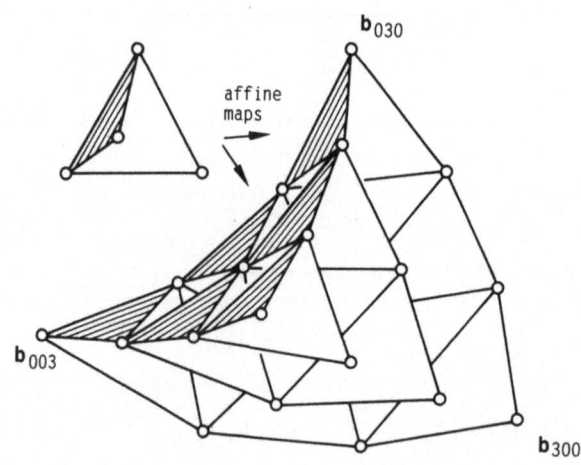

Degree Elevation

$$\mathbf{x}(u,v) = \sum_{i+j+k=3} \mathbf{b}_{i,j,k} B^3_{i,j,k}(\mathbf{r})$$

can be written as quartic:

$$\mathbf{x}(u,v) = \sum_{i+j+k=4} \hat{\mathbf{b}}_{i,j,k} B^4_{i,j,k}(\mathbf{r}) ;$$

$$\hat{\mathbf{b}}_{i,j,k} = \frac{i}{4} \mathbf{b}_{i-1,j,k} + \frac{j}{4} \mathbf{b}_{i,j-1,k} + \frac{k}{4} \mathbf{b}_{i,j,k-1} ; \quad i+j+k = 4$$

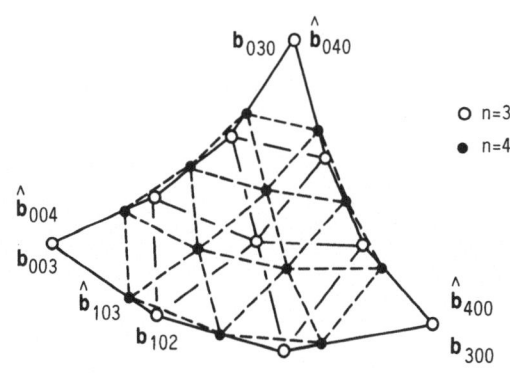

○ n=3
● n=4

Composite Surfaces

General c^1 condition:

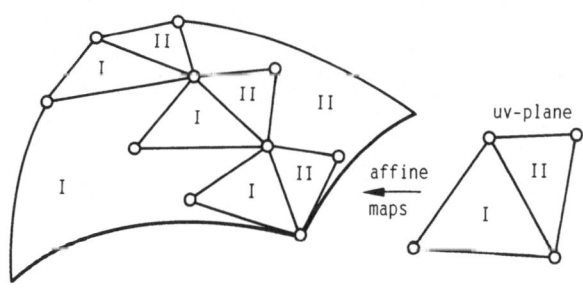

C^1 condition at a vertex:

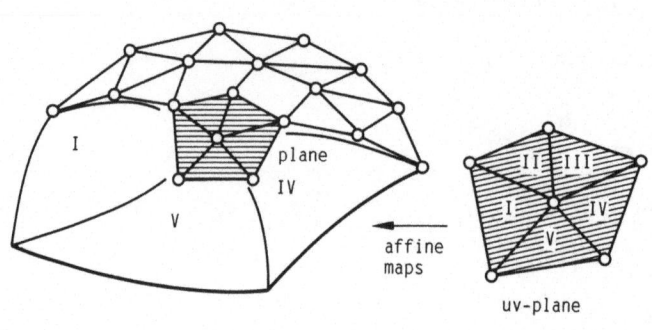

Nonparametric Patches

$$x(r,s,t) = \sum_{i+j+k=3} b_{i,j,k} B^3_{i,j,k}(r,s,t)$$

$b_{i,j,k}$: Bézier ordinates

$\mathbf{r}_{i,j,k} = [\frac{i}{3}, \frac{j}{3}, \frac{k}{3}]$: abscissae

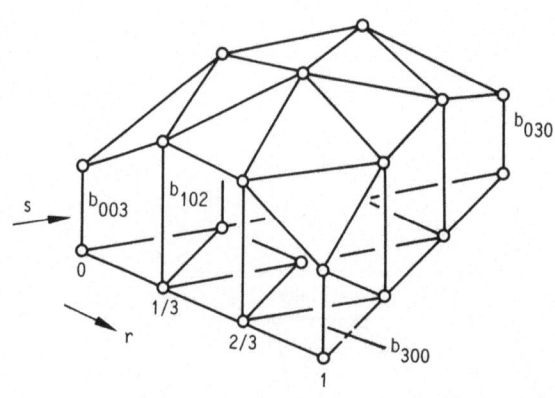

Splines over Triangles (Regular Triangulations)

$$\mathbf{s}(u,v) = \sum_{i,j} \mathbf{d}_{i,j} S^n_{i,j}(u,v) \qquad \mathbf{d}_{i,j}: \text{de Boor points}$$

Examples for $S^n_{i,j}$:

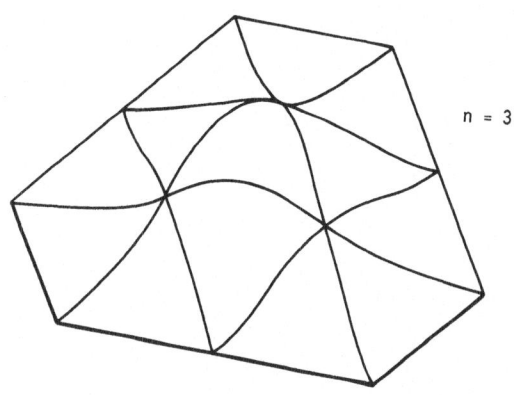

$n = 3$

Continuity class C^r of $S^n_{i,j}$: $\quad r < \frac{2}{3}(n-1)$

(compare with tensor products!)

Bézier Points of Triangular Splines

de Boor points $\mathbf{d}_{i,j}$ form regular nets. Recall univariate
case:

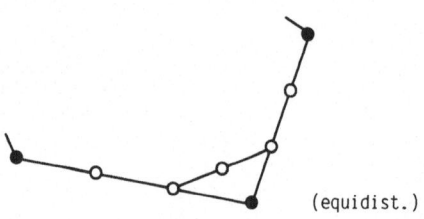

(equidist.)

a)
Cubic splines :

b)
Quartic splines :

Bézier points
○

mask

8. SCATTERED DATA INTERPOLATION

Shepard Methods

Given: abscissae (u_i, v_i) + arbitrary function values P_i

Find: smooth function $p(u,v)$ that interpolates:

$$p(u_i, v_i) = P_i$$

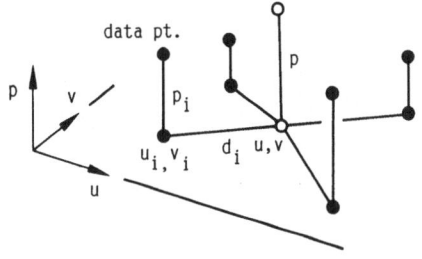

$$d_i = \sqrt{(u - u_i)^2 + (v - v_i)^2}$$

$$\rightarrow d_i = d_i(u,v)$$

One possible solution:

$$p(u,v) = \sum_i \frac{P_i}{d_i} \bigg/ \sum_i \frac{1}{d_i}$$

Drawback: slope discontinuities at P_i

Improvement: square distances:

$$p(u,v) = \sum_i \frac{P_i}{d_i^2} \bigg/ \sum_i \frac{1}{d_i^2}$$

Drawback: flat spots at P_i

Generalization: replace P_i by planes:

$$P_i(u,v) = P_i + (u - u_i)\, a_i + (v - v_i)\, b_i$$

Gradient estimation!

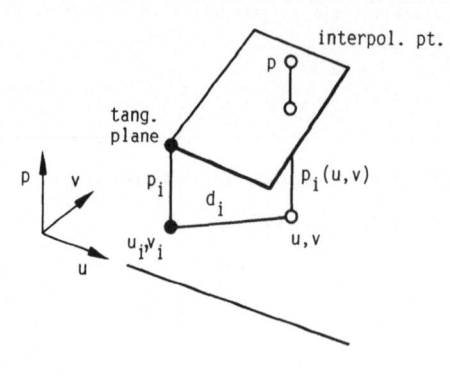

Methods Based on Triangulation
================================

1. triangulate (u_i, v_i)

2. construct interpolant over each triangle

Triangulation:

    1. Find arbitrary triangulation.

    2. Optimize by switching diagonals in convex quadri-
       laterals according to a geometric criterion
       (e.g. maximize min. angle).

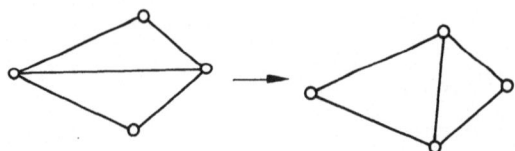

Repeat 2. until no more switches are possible.

Examples for interpolants:

● NINE PARAMETER CUBIC

   Input: position & tangent plane data at u_i, v_i

   Output: c^0 surface, piecewise cubic

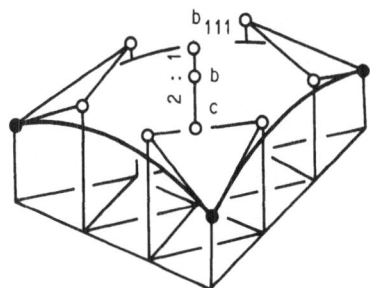

                                     b: centroid of "o"

                                     c: centroid of "●"

Bézier ordinates of boundary curves: univariate problem

Interior $b_{1,1,1}$:

$$b_{1,1,1} = \frac{3}{2} b - \frac{1}{2} c$$

● CLOUGH-TOCHER SCHEME

   Input: position & tangent plane data at u_i, v_i
              + cross-boundary deriv. at edge mid-points

   Output: c^1 surface, piecewise cubic

   Idea: subdivide each triangle, subtriangles are only c^1

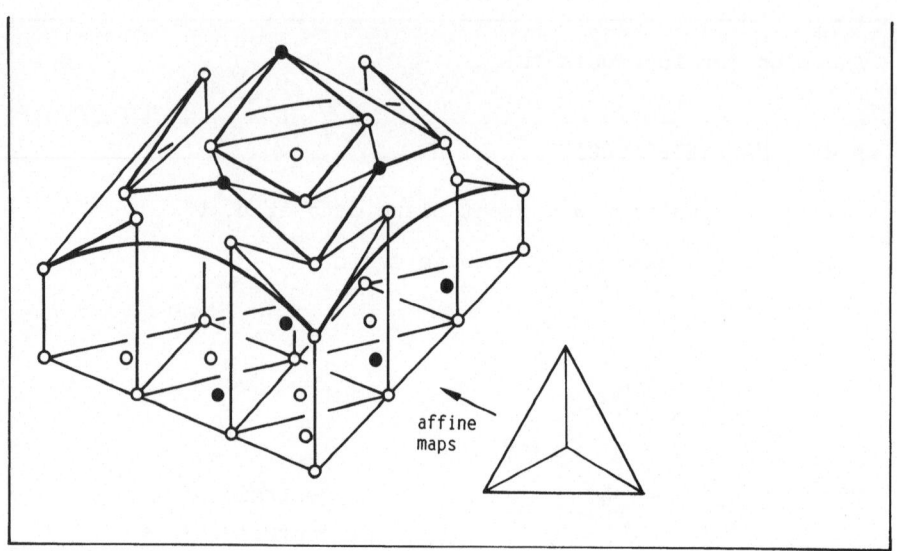

affine
maps

9. TRANSFINITE METHODS

Bilinearly Blended Coons Patch

Given: four boundary *curves*

Find: surface between them

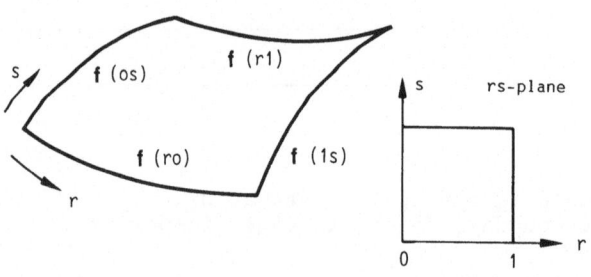

Lofting operators P_1, P_2:

$$P_1 \mathbf{f} = \mathbf{f}(0,s) \, L_0^1(r) + \mathbf{f}(1,s) \, L_1^1(r)$$

$$P_2 \mathbf{f} = \mathbf{f}(r,0) \, L_0^1(s) + \mathbf{f}(r,1) \, L_1^1(s)$$

$P_1 \mathbf{f}, P_2 \mathbf{f}$: ruled surfaces

$P_1 P_2 \mathbf{f}$ = bilinear interpolant

Coons patch $P\mathbf{f}$:

$$P\mathbf{f} = P_1 \mathbf{f} + P_2 \mathbf{f} - P_1 P_2 \mathbf{f}$$

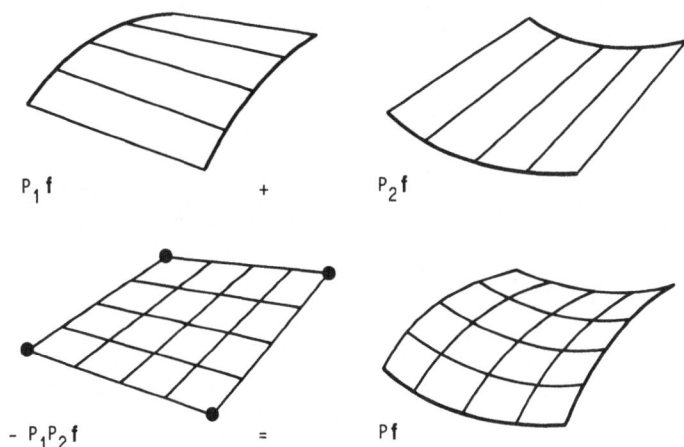

$P_1 f$ + $P_2 f$

$- P_1 P_2 f$ = Pf

L_i^1: "blending functions"

L_i^1 are linear $\longrightarrow$ "bilinearly blended"

Note: bilinearly blended $\neq$ bilinear!

Coons notation:

$$(r,s) := \mathbf{f}(r,s), \quad (r,1) := \mathbf{f}(r,1), \ldots, \quad L_0 s := L_0^1(s)$$

$$(r,s) = -[-1, \, L_0 r, \, L, \, r]
\begin{bmatrix}
0 & r0 & r1 \\
0s & 00 & 01 \\
1s & 10 & 11
\end{bmatrix}
\begin{bmatrix}
-1 \\
L_0 s \\
L_1 s
\end{bmatrix}$$

twist in Coons notation:

$$D_{rs}P_1\mathbf{f} = (1s - 0s)_s + (r1 - r0)_r - (00 - 01 - 10 + 11)$$

$\longrightarrow$ Adini's twist

Remark:

$$P_1 \oplus P_2 = P_1 + P_2 - P_1P_2$$

is called "Boolean sum".

Bicubically Blended Coons Patch

Drawback of last scheme: adjacent patches are only C^0. Now:

Given: four boundary curves
         + cross-boundary derivatives

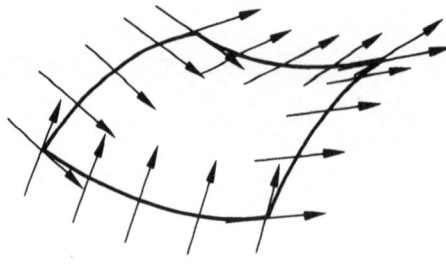

Hermite operators Q_i:

$$Q_1\mathbf{f} = \mathbf{f}(0,s)\, H_0^3(r) + \mathbf{f}_r(0,s)\, H_1^3(r)$$

$$+ \mathbf{f}_r(1,s)\, H_2^3(r) + \mathbf{f}(1,s)\, H_3^3(r)$$

$Q_2\mathbf{f}$ = dual

Bicubically blended patch $Q\mathbf{f}$:

$$Q\mathbf{f} = Q_1\mathbf{f} + Q_2\mathbf{f} - Q_1Q_2\mathbf{f} \qquad \text{(Boolean sum)}$$

Different derivation (Coons):

$Q(P\mathbf{f}) = P\mathbf{f}$,   hence

$Q\mathbf{f} = P\mathbf{f} + Q(\mathbf{f} - P\mathbf{f})$

    ↑   ↑

    bilin.   "correction
    blended   surface"

Coons' matrix form:

$$Q\mathbf{f} = -[-1, L_0 r, L_1 r, H_1 r, H_2 r] \begin{bmatrix} 0 & r0 & r1 & r0_s & r1_s \\ 0s & 00 & 01 & 00_s & 01_s \\ 1s & 10 & 11 & 10_s & 11_s \\ 0s_r & 00_r & 01_r & 00_{rs} & 01_{rs} \\ 1s_r & 10_r & 11_r & 10_{rs} & 11_{rs} \end{bmatrix} \begin{bmatrix} -1 \\ L_0 s \\ L_1 s \\ H_1 s \\ H_2 s \end{bmatrix}$$

"twist partition"

Problem: Twists are required as input data, but not supplied.

"Solution": Compute

$$\mathbf{f}_{rs}(0,0) = D_s \mathbf{f}_r(0,s)\big|_{s=0} \quad \text{etc.}$$

But:

$$\mathbf{f}_{sr}(0,0) = D_r \mathbf{f}_s(r,0)\big|_{r=0} \quad \text{is different!}$$

i.e. cross-boundary data is *incompatible*.

Solution: "Gregory's square" (rational)

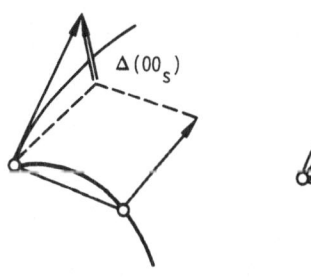

$\Delta(00_s)$

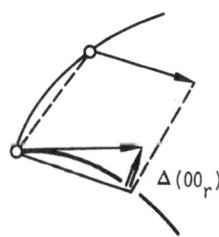

$\Delta(00_r)$

Gordon Surfaces

Given: network of curves

$$\mathbf{f}(u_i, v); \quad i = 0, \ldots, n$$

$$\mathbf{f}(u, v_k); \quad k = 0, \ldots, m$$

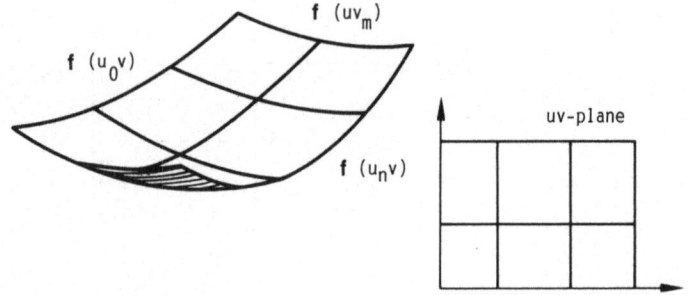

Define operators:

$$P_1\mathbf{f} = \sum_{i=0}^{n} \mathbf{f}(u_i, v) \, L_i^n(u)$$

$$P_2\mathbf{f} = \sum_{k=0}^{m} \mathbf{f}(u, v_k) \, J_k^m(v)$$

Lagrange polynomials

Each operator interpolates to one family of curves. The Boolean sum interpolates to both families:

$$P\mathbf{f} = P_1\mathbf{f} + P_2\mathbf{f} - P_1 P_2 \mathbf{f}$$

Interpolation over Triangles

Given: three boundary curves

$$\mathbf{f}(o, s, t), \quad \mathbf{f}(r, o, t), \quad \mathbf{f}(r, s, o)$$

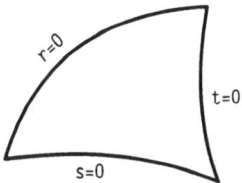
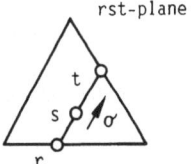

Define

$$P_1 \mathbf{f} = \mathbf{f}(r,o,t) \, L_0^1(\sigma) + \mathbf{f}(r,s,o) \, L_1^1(\sigma)$$

where σ = local coordinate on r = const:

$$\sigma = \frac{s}{s+t}$$

Define P_2, P_3 analogously. The Boolean sum of any two inter-polates:

$$P\mathbf{f} = (P_1 \oplus P_2)\mathbf{f} = \ldots$$

This scheme is only C^0. For a C^1 version, one also needs cross-boundary derivatives. Define

$$Q_1 \mathbf{f} = \mathbf{f}(r,o,t) \, H_0^3(\sigma) + D_\sigma \mathbf{f}(r,o,t) \, H_1^3(\sigma)$$

$$+ \, D_\sigma(r,s,o) \, H_2^3(\sigma) + \mathbf{f}(r,s,o) \, H_3^3(\sigma)$$

Q_2, Q_3 analogously.

Boolean sums interpolate:

$$Q\mathbf{f} = (Q_1 \oplus Q_2)\mathbf{f} = \ldots$$

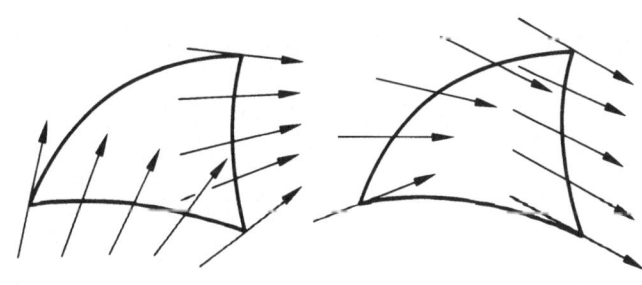

10. References

Ball, A.A.: Consurf I-III. Computer-Aided Design, Vol. 6, No. 4 (1974); Vol. 7, No. 4 (1975); Vol. 9, No. 1 (1977)

Barnhill, R.E.: Representation and Approximation of Surfaces. Mathematical Software III (ed. J.R. Rice). New York: Academic Press (1977)

Barnhill, R.E.: Computer-Aided Surface Representation and Design. Surfaces in CAGD, Proceedings Oberwolfach (eds. R.E. Barnhill, W. Böhm). North Holland (1983)

Bézier, P.E.: Essai de Définition Numérique des Courbes et des Surfaces Expérimentales. Dissertation, Paris (1977)

Böhm, W., Gose, G.: Einführung in die Methoden der Numerischen Mathematik. Braunschweig: Vieweg (1977)

Böhm, W.: Cubic B-Spline Curves and Surfaces in Computer-Aided Geometric Design. Computing, Vol. 19, No. 1 (1977)

Böhm, W.: Inserting New Knots into B-Spline Curves. Computer-Aided Design, Vol. 12, No. 4 (1980)

Böhm, W.: Generating the Bézier Points of B-Spline Curves and Surfaces. Computer-Aided Design, Vol. 13 (1981)

Böhm, W.: On Cubics: A Survey. Computer Graphics and Image Processing *19* (1982)

Böhm, W.: Generating the Bézier Points of Triangular Splines. Surfaces in CAGD, Proceedings Oberwolfach (eds. R.E. Barnhill, W. Böhm). North Holland (1983)

Böhm, W.: Mathematische Grundlagen der geometrischen Datenverarbeitung. Vorlesung TU Braunschweig (1981)

de Boor, C.: A Practical Guide to Splines. New York: Springer (1978)

de Boor, C.: On Calculating with B-Splines. J. Approximation Theory, Vol. 6, No. 1 (1972)

Breden, D.: Die Verwendung von bikubischen Spline-Flächen zur Darstellung von Tragflügeln und Propellern. Dissertation, Braunschweig (1982)

Brown, J.H.: Conforming and Nonconforming Finite Element Models for Curved Regions. Dissertation, Dundee (1976)

de Casteljau, F.: Courbes et Surfaces à Pôles. Enveloppe 40.040. Institut National de la Proprieté Industrielle, Paris (1959)

Catmull, E.E., Clark, J.H.: Recursively Generated B-Spline Surfaces on Arbitrary Topological Meshes. Computer-Aided Design, Vol. 10, No. 6 (1978)

Chaikin, G.M.: An Algorithm for High Speed Curve Generation. Computer Graphics and Image Processing, Vol. 3 (1974)

Cohen, E., Lyche, T., Riesenfeld, R.F.: Discrete B-Splines and Subdivision Techniques in Computer-Aided Geometric Design and Computer Graphics. Computer Graphics and Image Processing, Vol. 14, No. 2 (1980)

Coons, S.A.: Surfaces for Computer-Aided Design of Space Forms. MIT, Project MAC-TR-41 (1967)

Doo, D.W.H.: A Subdivision Algorithm for Smoothing Down Irregular Shaped Polyhedrons. Proceedings Bologna (1978)

Doo, D.W.H., Sabin, M.A.: Behavior of Recursive Division Surfaces Near Extra-ordinary Points. Computer-Aided Design, Vol. 10, No. 6 (1978)

Farin, G.: Konstruktion und Eigenschaften von Bézier-Kurven und Bézier-Flächen. Diplomarbeit, Braunschweig (1977)

Farin, G.: Subsplines über Dreiecken. Dissertation, Braunschweig (1979)

Farin, G.: A Construction for Visual C^1 Continuity of Polynomial Surface Patches. Computer Graphics and Image Processing (1982)

Farin, G.: Designing C^1 Surfaces Consisting of Triangular Cubic Patches. Computer-Aided Design, Vol. 14 (1982)

Farin, G.: Smooth Interpolation to Scattered 3 D Data. Surfaces in CAGD, Proceedings Oberwolfach (eds. R.E. Barnhill, W. Böhm). North Holland (1983)

Faux, I.D., Pratt, M.J.: Computational Geometry for Design and Manufacture. Ellis Horwood Ltd. (1979)

Forrest, A.R.: The Twisted Cubic Curve: A Computer-Aided Geometric Design Approach. Computer-Aided Design, Vol. 12, No. 4 (1980)

Gordon, W.: Blending-Function Methods of Bivariate and Multivariate Inter-polation and Approximation. SIAM J. Numerical Analysis, Vol. 8 (1971)

Gordon, W.: Distributive Lattices and the Approximation of Multi-Variate Functions. Proceedings Madison, Wisc. (1969)

Gordon, W., Riesenfeld, R.F.: B-Spline Curves and Surfaces. Computer-Aided Geometric Design (eds. R.E. Barnhill, R.F. Riesenfeld). New York: Academic Press (1974)

Gregory, J.A.: A C^1 Triangular Interpolation Patch for Computer-Aided Geo-metric Design. Computer Graphics and Image Processing, Vol. 13, No. 1 (1980)

Gregory, J.A.: C^1 Rectangular and Non-Rectangular Surface Patches. Surfaces in CAGD, Proceedings Oberwolfach (eds. R.E. Barnhill, W. Böhm). North Holland (1983)

Greville, T.N.E.: On the Normalisation of the B-Splines and the Location of the Nodes for the Case of Unequally Spaced Knots. Inequalities (ed. O. Shisha) (Supplement to the paper "On Spline Functions" by I.J. Schoen-berg). New York: Academic Press (1967)

Hosaka, M., Kimura, F.: Synthesis Methods of Curves and Surfaces in Inter-active CAD. Proceedings Bologna (1978)

Kahmann, J.: Krümmungsübergänge zusammengesetzter Kurven und Flächen - Detail-fragen des Computer-Aided Design. Dissertation, Braunschweig (1982)

Kestner, W., Saniter, J., et al.: Einführung in Computer Graphics. TU Berlin (1974)

Lane, J.M., Riesenfeld, R.F.: A Theoretical Development for the Computer Generation of Piecewise Polynomial Surfaces. IEEE Trans. Pattern Analysis and Machine Intelligence, Vol. PAMI-2, No. 1 (1980)

Lee, E.: A Simplified B-Spline Computation Routine. Computing 29, 365-373 (1982)

Little, F.F.: Convex Combination Surfaces. Surfaces in CAGD, Proceedings Oberwolfach (eds. R.E. Barnhill, W. Böhm). North Holland (1983)

Nielson, G.M.: Some Piecewise Polynomial Alternatives to Splines under Ten-sion. Computer-Aided Geometric Design (eds. R.E. Barnhill, R.F. Riesen-feld). New York: Academic Press (1974)

Poeppelmeier, C.C.: A Boolean Sum Interpolation Scheme to Random Data for Computer-Aided Geometric Design. Master's thesis, Salt Lake City (1975)

Sabin, M.A.: The Use of Piecewise Forms for the Numerical Representation of Shape. Dissertation, Budapest (1976)

Schmidt, R.M.: Fitting Scattered Surface Data with Large Gaps. Surfaces in CAGD, Proceedings Oberwolfach (eds. R.E. Barnhill, W. Böhm). North Holland (1983)

Schoenberg, I.: On Spline Functions. Inequalities (ed. O. Shisha). New York: Academic Press (1967)

Schoenberg, I.: On Variation Diminishing Approximation Methods. On Numerical Approximation (ed. R.E. Langer). Madison, Wisc. (1959)

Shepard, D.: A Two-Dimensional Interpolation Function for Irregularly Spaced Data. Proc. ACM Nat'l. Conf. (1965)

see also:

Böhm, W., Kahmann, J.: Grundlagen Kurven- und Flächen-orientierter Modellierung. In: Geometrisches Modellieren, Proceedings of a GI-Conference on CAD at TU Berlin (eds. Gnatz/Nowacki). Berlin: Springer (1983)

Böhm, W., Farin, G., Kahmann, J.: A Survey of Curve and Surface Methods in Computer-Aided Geometric Design. Computer-Aided Geometric Design 1 (1984)

IX. Geometric Modelling – Fundamentals

M. A. Sabin

THE OBJECTIVES OF GEOMETRIC MODELLING

A model is some analogue of an entity of interest, sharing some of its properties. Physical models typically share shape but not size, nor detail.

The purpose of modelling is to enable us to answer questions about the modelled entity more cheaply or more conveniently than referring to the original.

Geometric models represent the shape of some thing, and their recent development has been stimulated by the need in manufacturing engineering

(i) to analyse properties of the part or assembly which are dependent on the shape.

and (ii) to determine certain derived shapes, such as those of tooling or inspection aids, which are needed in manufacture.

Examples of questions which geometric models may be needed to help answer are:-

(i)   What does the shape I am designing look like?

(ii)   What is the engineering drawing of the the shape I have just designed?

(iii)   How much does it weigh?

(iv)   Does this part foul that one as they move?

(v)   Is it strong enough?

(vi)   How do I make it?

- What tools?

- What cutter path?

- What forging press load?

- What risers and feeders for casting?

- Where is the split line?

(vii)   Where is an empty space big enough to mount this extra item?

We discuss here mathematical models, which provide the theory for numerical models, which in turn allow us to compute the properties we are interested in.

In a numerical model, the different aspects of the shape of the object are modelled by numbers, from which the desired properties are computed numerically.

The mathematical model provides the ideas and concepts for a numerical model, and forms the framework which gives us confidence that a numerical modelling system is going to work. In order to understand the way specific numerical models work we examine the mathematics 'underneath'.

Many different numerical models have been proposed and used.

(i)   2D drawing models

(ii)   Sculptured surface models

(iii)   Wire Frames

(iv)   Primitive Instancing

(v)   Constructive Solid Geometry

(vi)   Boundary models

(vii)   Finite Element meshes

(viii) 2.5D machining models.

Each of these has its own mathematical foundation: each is useful for answering certain kinds of question: and each is applicable only to certain kinds of shape. There is no universal method equally good for all questions and all shapes.

EARLY MODELS

2D Drawing model

The model used for most engineering processes before the computer was available (and still today) was the engineering drawing. Lines on paper represent the faces of the object, and the three-dimensional nature of the object is captured by as many views as are necessary.

The mathematical model underlying drawing is the theory of projective geometry, and the art of projection developed by Monge and others in the late 18th century. There is also a large amount of symbolism involved, which is partly standardised in national standards, and partly dependent on local conventions within each company.

The robustness of this theory is evidenced by the possibility of 'draw the third view' exercises for trainee draughtsmen.

The loopholes are evidenced by the fact that it is possible to draw nonsense drawings, which represent no actual shape.

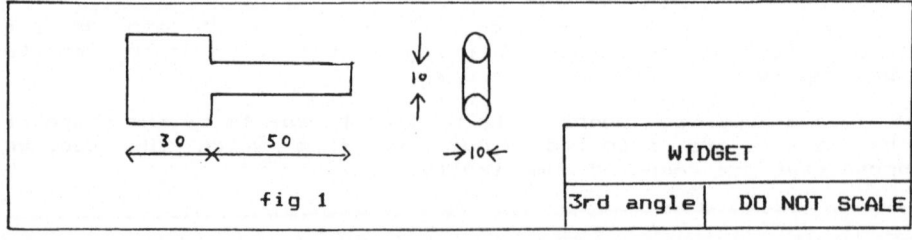

fig 1

When a computer becomes available, with screen and plotter output peripherals, one way of using it is to take over the entire drawing method, and represent the shapes of things indirectly by representing their drawings.

The earliest draughting systems, which became available in the early 1970s did just that. In such a system each piece of line on a drawing was represented by a record holding the coordinates of its end points.

The data structure for a minimal system could be

NL   the number of line segments represented

X1,Y1,X2,Y2   arrays holding the coordinates of the start and end points of the line segments.

The three operations necessary within such a minimal draughting system are:- adding a line segment, deleting a line segment, and plotting out the result.

ADD SEGMENT:

```
begin     NL := NL+1
          INPUT X1(NL),Y1(NL),X2(NL),Y2(NL)
end
```

DELETE SEGMENT I

```
begin     for  J=I to NL-1
          do   X1(J):=X1(J+1)
               Y1(J):=Y1(J+1)
               X2(J):=X2(J+1)
               Y2(J):=Y2(J+1)
          od
          NL=NL-1
end
```

DRAW:

```
begin     for  J=1 to NL
          do   MOVE TO X1(J),Y1(J)
               DRAW TO X2(J),Y2(J)
          od
end
```

Drawing on a screen and drawing on a plotter are not different from the representation point of view.

These code fragments are obviously much oversimplified. Any usable draughting system would need checks in the addition code to make sure that the capacity of the system was not being exceeded, and the deletion code would need a check to make sure that the segment being deleted actually existed. The whole lot would have to be driven by a command interpreter considerably more complex than the code implementing the functions, and some filing system would be needed to retain drawings from one session to the next.

Further, there would typically need to be representations for unbounded construction items (at least points, lines and circles) and algorithms for calculation of incidence and tangency between them. These are outlined in Appendix 1.

None the less, the example above gives a picture of a simple but effective numerical representation of a drawing based on the mathematical model which says that a line segment is represented by the cartesian coordinates of its end points.

The mathematical properties which underpin this representation are that

(i)   Within a given coordinate system, each ordered pair of coordinate values corresponds to only one point, and vice versa.

(ii)   Each pair of end points corresponds to only one line segment, and vice versa. There is an element of imprecision here, as we are storing ordered pairs of points, and each line segment has two of these, so the code must be carefully written not to depend on the order of the two points.

Certain additions to the shape model can make it considerably more effective as a basis for draughting. Specifically, the inclusion of a linestyle field in the representation of each line segment means that a dotted or chain line can be represented by one long line segment instead of many short ones: also the inclusion of a primitive shape selector field allows a circular arc to be stored as such instead of as a large number of approximating chords.

A third change which gives some reduction in the amount of store required, is to use indirection, so that the shape elements themselves hold, not the coordinates of their defining points, but their names, the coordinates themselves being stored separately. The arguments for and against this are outlined by Besant in [2].

The representation now looks like

NL   Number of segments
NP   Number of points

X,Y   Arrays containing the X and Y coordinates of the stored
                points.

T,S,P1,P2,P3   Arrays holding respectively

T   the segment type (e.g. 1=line, 2=clockwise arc etc.)
S   linestyle (e.g. 1=full, 2=dotted etc.)
P1,P2   the subscripts of the coordinates of the end points of
                the line segment.
P3   the subscript of the coordinates of the centre of a
                circular arc.

The operations now needed are

ADD POINT:

```
begin      NP:=NP+1
           INPUT  X(NP),Y(NP)
end
```

This would normally be invoked by the command interpreter as a side effect of instructions to make line, rather than by explicit 'make point' commands.

ADD SEGMENT:

```
begin      NL:=NL+1
           INPUT T(NL),S(NL),P1(NL),P2(NL)
           if   T(NL)=ARC then INPUT P3(NL) fi
end
```

DRAW:

```
begin      for  I=1 to NL
           do   case T(NL) in
                LINE:   CODE TO DRAW FULL, DOTTED OR CHAIN LINE
                ARC:    CODE TO DRAW FULL, DOTTED OR CHAIN ARC
                etc.
                esac
           od
end
```

DELETE SEGMENT:

This is a simple extension of the previous delete code. If you have understood what these representations are doing you will be able to fill it in here for yourself.

A rather more difficult exercise is to decide which of the list of questions on page 2 above can be answered by code accessing this representation of a shape. Because the human engineer can read a drawing and answer all of them, the information must be present in the data: however, only the second of those questions is easily answered by a simple algorithm.

This kind of representation is therefore suitable only for a draughting system. It can be used for other tasks, but only by having a human operator, who looks at the image on the screen and decides what it depicts.

It is suitable only for those shapes which the engineering drawing itself represents adequately.

Sculptured Surface Model

The drawing has always been found least satisfactory as a representation for shapes which are smooth and without obvious equation. Examples of such shapes are the bodies of cars, ship hulls and aircraft.

The drawing technique for such shapes is to use a dense nest of parallel sections in each of three views. From these sections the shapes of other sections can be constructed by manual graphical methods. Robertson [13] is a good textbook. The errors in such constructions tend to build up, however, and so it is necessary to draw at large scale to avoid unacceptable discrepancies.

One of the early successes of CAD, before it was even called that, was to devise specialised numerical equivalents for this lofting process. Two of these are now seen as important, the directrix/generator methods, and the patch methods.

The many individual techniques within the directrix/generator family all share a common structure.

(i)   A number of directrix curves are defined in space. In the earliest versions these were the intersection curves of cylinders whose axes were aligned with coordinate axes, and whose cross sections were second order curves (conic sections).

(ii)   A correspondance structure is set up, so that to each point on any one of the directrices corresponds one point on each of the others. The early conic lofting method used equal distance along the third coordinate axis as the correspondance rule.

(iii)   From each set of corresponding points a generator curve is defined. Again, in conic lofting the generator curves were conic sections. These did not pass through all the directrix points, the tangent intersection point being a favourite way of gettng ergonomic control over the tangent directions. A fullness factor was also used as a parameter for this interpolation which was a scalar function with one value for each correspondance set.

A generator is defined for each point on any of the directrices. As that point slides along its directrix, with the corresponding points sliding along theirs, the generator sweeps out a surface. Such a surface is fully defined, whereas the purely graphical technique defined a finite set of curves lying in the surface with only the definition 'smooth' to constrain what happened in between.

Conic lofting (see Lidbro [8,9] and Walter [16]) was widely used when the computing power available was that of the mechanical desk calculator. Because it needed at most the extraction of square roots to solve typical problems in closed form, it was adequately fast. It required considerable mathematical skill, however, to describe the shapes required.

In the mid 1960s the spline techniques were introduced, which used vector valued parametric splines as both directrices and generators, and which used equal parameter value as the correspondance rule. This resulted in surface equations which were actually simpler than those of conic lofting, but which did not have the special relationship with the axes which made conic lofting quick to compute. Computing speeds were by then adequate for the iterative solutions needed, and the axis-independence of the vector-valued methods gave much greater freedom for interrogation of these shapes. It also became possible for loftsmen rather than mathematicians to define the shapes they were responsible for.

The mathematical model underlying this general method is that there is a mapping from two degrees of freedom, one varying along the directrices, the other along the generators, to position in space of three dimensions.

In its most abstract form this can be written

$$P = F(u,v)$$

where P and F are vectors, represented by triples of coordinates, and u and v are the _parameters_ which, by their variation, sweep out the surface.

A surprisingly large amount of theory needs only this as its knowledge of the surface. For example, the surface normal vector at any point of the surface is just the cross product of the derivatives of the position function with respect to the two parameters. The vector tangent to a plane section is just the cross product of that surface normal with the normal to the plane.

An important result, fundamental to the machining of such shapes by numerically controlled machine tools, is that the surface traversed by the centre of a cutter which is just touching the defined surface is itself a surface of the same abstract form.

The second approach, that of using patches, was also developed in the early to mid 1960s. The concept here was that of using a number of pieces of surface, typically vector-valued parametric bicubics, to cover the shape required. An important patch, not widely used but of great theoretical significance, was the Coons patch (Coons [6]), which could be used to interpolate boundaries of any parametric equation. There is some confusion about Coons patches and bicubics: the Coons patch is the general form, while the bicubic is a special case separately invented and described in publications at about the same time. Ferguson [7]

The patch approach tends to look at the surface being designed piecemeal, the directrix generator method more holistically. The patch idea does have the advantage, though, that it is possible to invent patches which are not four sided, and include them in the patchwork which covers the surface, thus allowing the natural curves of a contorted surface to be used for its definition.

All patches, however, are still mappings from a known two dimensional parameter manifold into space of three dimensions.

Both major classes of sculptured surface methods are thus essentially generative, being able to churn out as many points as you want which are guaranteed to lie on the surface. Neither is capable of answering in closed form the question 'On which side of this surface does this point lie?'

Both deal with a finite extent of surface, because they map a part of the parameter plane to the shape in three dimensions.

A typical sculptured surface system has in its data structure curve and surface entities, as well as such items as points, planes and coordinate systems used to help construct the main items.

The main operations typically provided within such a system are

CREATE SURFACE:

curve := INTERSECTION (surface, plane)

curve := INTERSECTION (surface1, surface2)

curve := SILHOUETTE (surface, viewpoint)

DRAW CURVE (curve, view)

MACHINE CURVE (curve, orientation)

Clearly the detailed functions within CREATE SURFACE depend on the exact form of the equations used. So would EDIT SURFACE.

The calculations of curves from surfaces tend to be much more general, dependent only on the abstract form $P = F(u,v)$.

It is therefore appropriate to regard the procedure which, given u and v, evaluates the corresponding point and its derivatives as the numerical representation of the surface. This needs to be supplemented by information about the ranges over which u and v vary.

In the case of recursive division surfaces (see below) the halving procedure takes a similar role.

There are three main ways of implementing these interrogation algorithms:-

(i)   Marching methods.

        These find first one point on the curve, probably by scanning round the boundary, and then work in curve order from there, using the local derivatives to make a good estimate for the parameter values for the next point, which can be improved by iteration. This then acts as a starting point for the next step, and so on, until the curve either reaches the edge of the surface again, or returns to its starting point.

(ii)   Lattice methods

        These divide the surface up into pieces which are small enough for bilinear interpolation to be adequately accurate. The curve is then traced from cell to cell across the surface, or alternatively each strip of cells is taken in turn.

(iii)   Recursive division methods.

        Some of the more recent surface equations have the properties that each piece of surface lies within the convex hull of a set of points which control it, and that a simple algorithm exists for constructing the control points of each half. If both these properties hold there is a nice algorithm which checks to see if the convex hull intersects: if it does not, there is no intersection: if it does, the surface is divided into two and the procedure is called recursively for each half. At some level of detail simplification takes place to decide that a simple plane facet intersection can be performed instead, which truncates the recursion.

        Marching methods are fast, but are not guaranteed to find all intersections, only all those which intersect the boundary of the surface. They can also be made to calculate curves optimal in the sense that the points calculated along the curve can fit some dynamic spacing criterion.

        Lattice methods are slow because the fineness of the lattice must match the finest wavelength in the surface, and they are still not guaranteed to find all the intersections.

        Recursive division is also adaptive in the sense that it only divides when it needs to, and has the nice property that all intersections will be found. Unfortunately, not all surfaces have the convex hull and subdivision properties. In particular, offset surfaces do not have such properties.

        The three algorithms for calculating plane sections of a surface are outlined in Appendix 4.

352

Wire Frames

During the early 1970s, the graphics community noticed how simple projection of a point in space to a projection on a plane is in computing terms.

They also noticed how easy it would be to enhance the simple drawing model to hold three dimensional coordinates. Merely by adding a Z field to the data holding the coordinates of points and by modifying the DRAW function to

DRAW:

```
begin      for   J=1 to NL
           do    PROJECT X1(J),Y1(J),Z1(J) TO H,V
                 MOVE TO  H , V
                 PROJECT X2(J),Y2(J),Z2(J) TO H,V
                 DRAW TO  H , V
           od
end
```

it becomes possible to hold a single three-dimensional model, and calculate all the separate views.

Suddenly 3D draughting systems became so fashionable that it became very difficult to sell a 2D one.

The operational advantages of this were

(i)   that there can be some economy of input, reflecting the economy of stored data.

(ii)   that it becomes less easy to make a drawing with two views inconsistent.

(iii)   that the system becomes useful, to some extent, for visualisation, thus helping design as well as draughting, since a detailed object description may be viewed from many angles to help understanding of exactly what shape is represented.

The mathematical foundation for this is essentially that:

straight lines map into straight lines under perspective transformations, so that projecting the end points and joining the projections gives the same result as projecting every single point along the line.

The mathematical foundations which are n̲o̲t̲ there are that

(i)   A shape is represented by its edges. Often this is
nearly enough true for practical purposes, but there are a
few counterexamples which show that two or more different
bodies can share the same set of edges. The 2D drawing model
just uses enough separate scrap views to resolve the issue
or the dotted hidden line information, but in a wire frame
system these views would have to be generated from the
single central model, which doesn't have enough information.
The classic counter example is

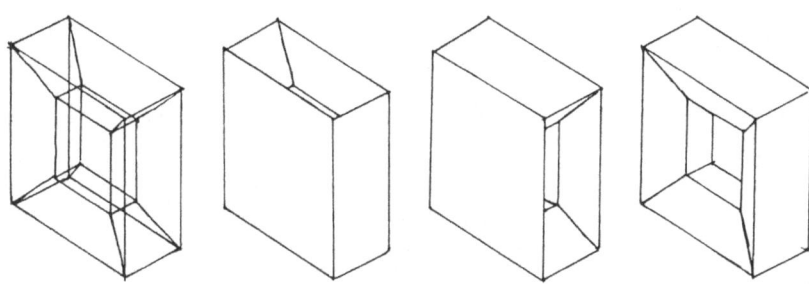

fig 2

(ii)   Evenly spaced linestyles map into evenly spaced
linestyles. Again, if you are using only the three
orthogonal views and perhaps an isometric this is
effectively true, but as soon as there is any significant
perspective in the picture the spacing of the dots and
dashes ought to vary along any line with depth variation.

    As a result of trying to go beyond what the mathematics can
strictly stand, 3D draughting systems with a wire frame model
have tended to be somewhat awkward to drive. Sometimes the model
behaves like a solid object, sometimes like lines on paper. Many
of the systems of this kind that I have seen in use have been
used in strictly 2D mode, the Z coordinate of everything being
left at zero the whole time.

    A few of the representations and algorithms necessary in a
3D constructions package supporting a 3D system are outlined in
Appendix 2.

GEOMETRICALLY COMPLETE MODELS

Geometric Completeness

At about the same time that the draughting system vendors were adding 3D to their products a number of research groups were studying ways of representing shape unambiguously. At the PROLAMAT conference in Budapest in 1973 four groups reported work in this area. Since then their different approaches have become better understood and related to one another. Others have also joined in and it is this type of representation which is commonly referred to now as 'Geometric Modelling'

The properties which are sought for a geometric model are

-    validity   Does every representation have a
                           corresponding shape?

-    uniqueness.   Is there only one representation of a
                           given shape?

-    unambiguity   Is there only one shape with a given
                           representation?

An unambiguous scheme of definition is referred to as being geometrically complete.

There are five general representation techniques which have this property.

(i)   Spatial Enumeration

In this method space is divided into disjoint pieces, the occupancy of each of which is recorded.

(ii)   Primitive instancing

Here standard shapes are regarded as known by the software, and copies of those shapes are placed in the 3D space without overlap.

(iii)   Constructive Solid Geometry (CSG)

Here primitive shapes are again invoked, but they may overlap, and the relationship between two shapes may be more complex.

(iv)   Boundary model

The shape of any object is uniquely defined by the shape of its boundary, and so storing adequate data about all the faces of a body is a geometrically complete model.

(v)   Sweeps

If a well defined area is swept through space along a well defined trajectory, the part of space through which some point of the area passes is also well defined.

We shall consider these one at a time.

Spatial Enumeration

This has two variations, one of which uses a regular division of space, the other an irregular division.

The regular division obviously has the potential to use a very large amount of memory to store a reasonably sized irregular shape to a reasonable resolution. It is not therefore used as a primary representation. As memory sizes increase and memory costs drop it is beginning to be considered as a good indexing method to increase the performance of other models. The Oct-tree method used by Woodwark looks promising as a way of accessing very complex models in acceptable computing times.

The irregular division method is widely used as the basis for Finite Element Analysis of fields (electromagnetic, displacement, temperature, particle flux, etc.) within non-trivial shapes. The description of such a mesh is, however, an extremely tedious and error prone procedure, and one of the current research problems is to seek for a way of generating such a mesh from the other representations. This is not straightforward, as the elements into which the shape is divided have to be well-conditioned for the analysis.

Both the regular and the irregular versions are approximate.

Primitive Instancing

This technique is also used, particularly in the modelling of petrochemical plant, when the primitives are the individual items of plant, the pipes joining them and the structure supporting them. Clearly these will not intersect in fact, and so they do not need to in the model, though modellers of this kind usually provide the facility of detecting unintentional overlaps.

In order to avoid the need for an excessive number of distinct primitives, the primitives are often parametrized, so that a piece of pipe can be called up with a length which is part of the instance, not part of the primitive.

Constructive Solid Geometry

This is the best understood model, since the mathematical model underlying numerical implementations is the sharpest defined.

In this mathematical model objects are modelled by sets of points. Each shape is modelled by the set of all points which lie inside it. Now any set is specified either by enumeration or by the combination of a generator, which can give lots of candidate members, with one or more filters, which are conditions saying whether each one of those candidates is actually a member of the set.

The generator in CSG is just R^3, the whole of Euclidean space, and the filter is some expression which combines conditions which bound the object.

The individual conditions which bound the object can be thought of as corresponding to the surfaces in which the faces lie, and the expression as corresponding to the relationships of the faces.

Any single surface divides space into two parts, that part on the same side of the surface as the stuff of the object, and that part on the other side. This is modelled nicely numerically by the form of surface equation

$$f(P) = 0$$

in which we evaluate some function of position. On one side of the surface $f(P)$ will be positive, on the other negative, and we can use this to model the relationship of the surface to the object.

The simple surfaces that engineering objects are typically made up of do have simple well-behaved equations of this form. The plane has a linear equation: the cylinder and cone, as well as the sphere and the ellipsoid and a few other shapes, have quadratic equations. The torus has a quartic equation which happens also to be well behaved, but there are equations which correspond to self-intersecting surfaces: for these the simple numerical model which uses the sign of the function to distinguish between the two sides would not be quite adequate. The mathematical model, however, would.

The sets of points satisfying conditions of the form

$$f(P) < 0$$

are termed half-spaces.

Boolean Operators

The combination of these basic shapes into objects is made by the Boolean Operators, of Union, Intersection and Set Difference.

Let P be a point and S1 and S2 sets of points.

P is a member of the union of S1 and S2 if P is a member of S1 or of S2 or of both.

P is a member of the intersection of S1 and S2 if P is a member of both S1 and S2.

P is a member of the set difference of S1 and S2 if P is a member of S1 but not of S2.

These definitions map back into corresponding definitions about shapes, by using the basic relationship 'P is a member of the set S if and only if it lies in the shape defined by S.'

Thus we can define the union of two shapes as being the shape containing all the points lying in either of the two shapes and the intersection of the two shapes as being the shape containing all the points that lie in both shapes.

There is some advantage in using rather more complex primitives than simple halfspaces in a CSG implementation. Systems such as PADL and BUILD use primitives such as rectangular bricks and unit lengths of circular cylinder. MODCON (see Knight [4]) uses modified versions of these shapes with draft angles and fillet radii, to make it easy to define the shapes which are actually encountered in heavy forgings.

The first advantage is that if all the primitives are finite point sets, then there is no way of making an infinite one, and so algorithms need not concern themselves with the possibility of the object being too big.

A modification to the data structure outlined above which can be used to improve the speed of evaluation of the model is the adding of a bounding box or bounding sphere to every record. If the test point P is outside the bounding box then the algorithm can immediately return false without exploring the contents of the box in detail.

The second is that some performance can be gained by using primitives which are as complex as possible while remaining convex. It is quicker to have built in code for a complete primitive rather than interpret the corresponding definition in terms of its intersection of half-spaces. Clearly having primitives with ready-defined edges and faces gives the classification technique a head start in computing the sire frame.

These CSG trees usually work out to store a complex shape in a small amount of memory compared with other methods. Related to this is the fact that combining and differencing shapes is a convenient and compact way of describing many machine-like shapes. Store efficiency is best if common subshapes are instanced rather than copied, with a reference to a local coordinate system being included in each reference to an instance. Such instances can be expanded out, with the change of coordinate system being taken into effect, by a single pass through the dense stored form, to give the representation described above.

However, the pure CSG representation suffers from the problem that the edges of the object and even its faces are nowhere explicit, and so there is a fairly time-consuming calculation to be performed before we can draw a picture, for example.

Modellers based on CSG representations usually therefore contain a Boundary File, which is the Boundary representation of the same shape. This is computed, when first required, from the CSG master, and retained until a change to the CSG description makes it out of date. Since recomputing it is costly methods of incremental boundary evaluation are proposed to update a boundary file from changes in the CSG master.

The fundamental algorithm, typical in structure of many others, is the point membership test, which evaluates whether a given point P is inside or outside the defined shape S.

TEST POINT P IN S:

```
begin      if   S IS PRIMITIVE
           then case  PRTYPE of S in
                TYPE1:    first primitive test using PRDATA of S
                TYPE2:    second primitive test using PRDATA of S
                etc.
                esac
           else case OPTYPE of S in
                UNION:     if   TEST POINT P IN LTREE of S
                           or   TEST POINT P IN RTREE of S
                           then true  else false  fi
                INTERSECTION:  if   TEST POINT IN LTREE of S
                           and  TEST POINT IN RTREE of S
                           then true else false fi
                etc.
                esac
           fi
end
```

The recursion is the neatest way to describe any tree search algorithm. Programming in Fortran would require stack and return management to be explicit in the program, which would make it less easy to read.

Another important procedure is the classification test, which divides a curve into three parts:

-    those segmants which lie IN the volume

-    those segments which lie OUT of the volume

and   those segments which lie ON the boundary of the volume

CLASSIFY ray AGAINST S:

```
begin      if  S is primitive
           then classify ray against primitive S
           else Lray := CLASSIFY ray AGAINST LTREE of S
                Rray := CLASSIFY ray AGAINST RTREE of S
                COMBINE ( Lray,Rray,OPTYPE of S )
           fi
end
```

This procedure returns the division of the tested ray. It is used with straight line rays to produce rendered views of an object (ray-casting, one ray per pixel), and to compute such properties as the volume of an object. It also provides one way of evaluating the edges of an object for calligraphic views: all edges of the original primitives and all intersections of primitive faces are classified against the entire object: those parts which lie on the boundary together form the wire frame which can be plotted.

In fact the above procedure is oversimplified: it needs to be a little more complex to cope correctly with a curve segment which lies ON both LTREE and RTREE of a node.

Although this definition of the word <u>intersection</u> summons up a different mental image from that evoked by the discussion of sculptured surfaces above, a little thought will indicate that the two usages are absolutely consistent at the mathematical model level, although they correspond to completely different algorithms at the numerical model level.

A simple example of a CSG definition is that of a unit square

$$x > 0 \;\underline{and}\; y > 0 \;\underline{and}\; x < 1 \;\underline{and}\; y < 1$$

Because this is itself a point set we could define a quadrant by taking the intersection of this with a unit circle, and then more complex shapes by adding (via the union operator) or subtracting other combinations of primitives. Because any point set can be used as an operand for any combination very complex shapes can be described.

The representation of such a collection of nested combinations takes the form of a graph theory <u>tree</u>, and a phrase often encountered is <u>the</u> CSG <u>tree</u>. This just means the compound expression for a shape in terms of unions, intersections and differences of unions, intersections or differences of....of primitive point sets.

The numerical representation of such a mathematical model takes the form of a collection of records, each of which is either a <u>node</u> record, holding

OPTYPE   an integer specifying whether this is a union, intersection or set difference node

LTREE   a pointer to the first operand of the node, which may be a primitive or another node.

RTREE   a pointer to the second operand of the node.

or a <u>primitive</u> record, holding

PRTYPE   an integer specifying which of the standard primitives this one is an instance of.

PRDATA   further data containing the coefficients of a halfspace equation or the parameters of a more complex primitive.

Regular Sets and Regularized Operators

A complication encountered in the set theoretic basis
for CSG models is that sets can be open or closed. A set is
closed if it contains the limit points of all sequences of
members: in this context, a set is closed if it contains its
boundary. For example,

x $\geq$ 0

A set is open if its complement is closed. For example,

x $>$ 0

This distinction is obviously rather subtle, especially
at the numerical level, but is important at the level of deciding
mathematically exactly what the numerical model represents. It
is clearly helpful to have a consistent representation, so that
boundaries are either within a shape or not. This then leads to
problems if two shapes are adjacent with a common boundary. If we
take their intersection, is the result the common face, or
nothing ? If we take their union is the result the 'common-sense'
union or the common-sense union less the common face ?

A regular set is a closed set which is the closure of
its interior. This definition rules out faces and edges as
bodies, and if we take the closure of the interior of the result
of all our boolean operations, we get new operations (called
regularised intersection, regularised union etc.) which do what
we want, giving the common-sense answer every time.

Distinguishing the regularised version is a somewhat
pedantic way, as far as the programmer is concerned, of
justifying doing the right thing. It is possible that using open
sets consistently, but with modified versions of union and set
difference would be equally satisfactory, but as it would lead to
the same code as regularisation there is not a great deal of
point in working through the fine details.

Boundary Models

The boundary of any shape divides space into two parts, that
inside the shape, and that outside. If we know that we are
dealing with finite shapes only one of the two can be the inside,
and so we have an unambiguous definition.

The actual representation of the boundary is typically by
representing all of the faces, each of which is represented by
the surface in which it lies and the set of directed edges which
bound it. Each edge is represented in turn by the curve in which
it lies and the vertices which bound it.

The individual surfaces and curves are not difficult to
represent: the bulk of a boundary model lies in the holding of
all the relationships between the faces and edges.

In principle it is sufficient to know the edges of each surface and the ends of each edge, but for reasonable performance it is helpful to be able to access from any face the neighbouring faces. Most boundary modellers therefore use a data structure holding faces edges and vertices, linked together by pointers. The best known set of pointers is the winged edge structure devised by Baumgart [1]. A minor variation is the half winged edge which overcomes the asymmetry of the original. With either of these structures it is possible to access any of the items incident with a face edge or vertex by means of a small number of pointer followings.

An early alternative not now widely discussed in the literature is to use incidence matrices. This method sets the bit in row I of column J of the face-edge boolean matrix if face I is bounded by edge J. Other boolean matrices hold the body-face and edge-vertex relationships. This representation is very good for determining how many pieces an object consists of, and for looking for isolated loops in a surface (holes), since transitive closure can be computed very fast using bit combination instructions present in most computers. However, the amount of store required tends to rise as the square of the number of faces present in the model, and so it is not really acceptable as a long term archival form for models of realistic complexity.

Even using pointers there is a large amount of data in all these relationships, and Boundary Models tend to require fairly large amounts of both storage for working and backing store for archiving models.

It is also almost inconceivable that anyone would ever describe a shape in terms of all its individual faces and their relationships. Boundary modellers therefore use other representations, usually sweeps and CSG, as the way in which shapes are initially described.

A typical boundary model algorithm is the calculation of a cross section. Each face in turn is intersected with the sectioning plane, giving zero, one or more directed segments of intersection curve. These segments are assembled together to form the cross-section. Their directed nature assists reassembly, since a head must always join to a tail and vice versa. It also distinguishes the inside of the cross section from the outside.

The links between faces available in the winged edge form enable cross sections to be generated to some extent in curve order, thus reducing the assembly task, which would otherwise have a complexity of the square of the number of intersection segments.

Sweeps

Many machined shapes have a thickness constant over large regions which are separated by cliffs following a two dimensional outline. These shapes are very conveniently described by the sweeping of the area inside such an outline through a depth increment. Again, many shapes have rotational symmetry, and any one of these can be described in terms of half its cross section swept around the centre line.

Areal sweeping is thus a convenient description for a class of shapes often enough encountered to justify some special treatment.

Since these shapes are even more common in combination than in their pure form, the sweep form is most valuable as a description method rather than as an internal representation in its own right.

Areal sweeping is, in fact, a special case of a more general operator volume sweeping, in which some volume is swept along some trajectory. All points inside the volume at any time during the course of the sweeping are inside the sweep.

The important practical problem 'does this NC tape make the part defined by this model?' amounts to converting a volume sweep definition to some other form and then comparing for equality. Making the NC tape in the first place may be regarded as converting the difference between the billet and the required workpiece to a volume sweep representation, subject to constraints of access, clamping and tool availability.

A variant of sweeping makes the slight expansion of the domain to those shapes which can be machined on a 3axis NC mill using line contact milling with a tapered cutter. Here the profiles are at a defined height, and the cliffs are tilted at a draft angle. This is still geometrically complete, although it is possible to define nonsense objects if the base profile has too tight a radius anywhere and the height of the cliff so much that at the other extreme from the defined profile those radii have become negative. The basic geometry for the profiles of such a model are described in Appendix 3.

Volume sweeping is in turn a special case of a more general operator still, Geometric Convolution, in which one volume is placed with its datum point at each point inside a second volume in turn. The union of all points inside any of the positions of the moving shape is the convolution.

This operator may be given a concrete image by thinking of the swathe cut out by a moving cutter whose centre visits every point of some second shape.

In this context sweeping may be regarded as an additional boolean operator. As defined it is an infinite union, but it may also be expressed as a finite union provided that primitives are available which have the sweep boundaries among their half spaces. For example, if all our primitives are polyhedra the convolution is also a polyhedron, and it can be expressed in terms of a finite number of primitive polyhedra.

Geometric Modelling - Fundamentals: Eurographics 1983

CONVERSIONS BETWEEN MODELS

We have encountered a few examples above of needing to transform a model from one geometrically complete form to another. This is an important issue, since many of the trade-offs involved in choosing which representation to use depend on the costs of these transformations.

Although any geometrically complete method represents the shape unambiguously, we are not always able to convert from one form to another. There can be two reasons for this:-

(i)   There are shapes describable within the source description which are not representable in the target form.

Each modeller has limits on what it can represent. A boundary modeller cannot represent shapes whose surfaces are not in the set of face equations offered: A CSG modeller cannot represent shapes whose surfaces are not any of the faces of any of its primitives: A CSG modeller with finite primitives cannot represent an infinite object.

The domain of a model is the set of shapes which it can represent, and if we are to convert, not only must the source be unambiguous, but the domain of the target must include that of the source.

(ii)   We don't know how to write reasonably efficient algorithms.

It is always easier to expand data from a terse, sharp, irredundant representation into more voluminous forms than to discover the short form amidst bulky data.

The state of the art at the moment may be summarised as

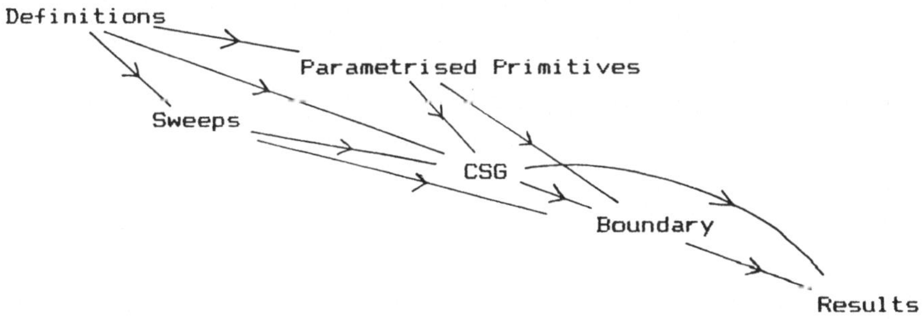

fig 3

The Definition - Representation - Results Spectrum

In looking at different representations we have noted that some are terse but require considerable computation to produce the results which are the purpose of making the model: others are potentially very bulky but can deliver results fast. One way of looking at this is to say that the definition fed in to any modeller is itself a model (It must contain an unambiguous specification of what shape the modeller is to represent). The results produced, taken in all their potential totality are an adequate model, since that is all we are ever going to find out about the model. We may choose to store either extreme or any intermediate form.

Clearly a terse definition is much more usable, because it is shorter to create, and with that goes less likelihood of error. The results, taken in their totality, are going to be very voluminous.

Any partial result determined partway through the calculation which determines results from the initial input could be used as a model for the purposes of internal storage, and the operator of a modelling system should be able to tell which is being used only by the relative speed of the various operations he invokes. If he instructs the model to take the union of two complex bodies and receives a prompt request for the next command, but finds a long delay before any picture starts to appear on the command DRAW, he may guess that a CSG tree is being stored as the model. If the instruction to take the union took a long time, but drawing started instantaneously he could guess that a boundary model was being stored.

Logical separation of Definition from Internal Representation suggests that we could gain the most convenience of definition by allowing a number of different input forms: provided that there is some algorithm for converting from other representations to the one we are going to store, we could talk to the system in whatever terms were appropriate for the shape which needed description today.

Conversion algorithms of all kinds are therefore of major importance in the current development of modelling technology.

We have mentioned two above, the division of a shape into elements, and the creation of a boundary file from a CSG tree definition.

It is also possible to convert linear and rotary sweeps to CSG and directly or indirectly to Boundary form.

The Implicit - Explicit Spectrum

Associated with the spectrum above, though not identical with it, is another, which addresses the semantic content of the representation. A good example here is the handling of fillet surfaces, included in a shape to relieve stresses or to ease manufacture.

In drawing practice these are drawn as circular arcs in cross section, but a fillet along the intersection of two cylinders would be drawn by a convention which merely says 'there is a fillet here'. At the definition stage it is clearly far more acceptable to say 'here put a fillet of radius so-and-so' than to construct carefully the full detail of where the fillet surface is tangential to its neighbours.

Equally, when evaluating the weight of the modelled object, some knowledge of the detailed geometry of that fillet surface is necessary to give an accurate answer. Again, although a rounded cutter of the right radius may be used for finish machining of the fillet, it is important that sharp cornered roughing cutters are not driven through the material which ought to be left uncut.

At some stage, therefore, the implicit 'here is a fillet' has to be converted into the explicit 'this fillet is here'.

Boundary Evaluation

Most modellers use either CSG or the Boundary model as their primary representation. As we have seen, CSG models need to evaluate a boundary in order to draw pictures, and Boundary models need a more convenient description technique: often CSG description is used to drive a Boundary modeller. In both cases a key algorithm is the evaluation of a Boundary representation from a CSG definition.

There are three approaches to this evaluation:-

(i)   Tree following

In this approach each node in the CSG tree is taken in depth first order and the boundary of the combination evaluated in terms of the boundaries of the operands.

BOUNDARY OF S:

```
begin if   S is PRIMITIVE
      then BOUNDARY OF PRIMITIVE S
      else case OPTYPE of S in
           UNION: COMBINE (BOUNDARY OF LTREE of S) diff RTREE of S
                  WITH   (BOUNDARY OF RTREE of S) diff LTREE of S
           INTERSECTION
           etc.
           esac
      fi
end
```

Be warned that this routine is written slightly loosely, since the diff operator is not between two solids, but between a boundary and a solid. A boundary is not a regular set, except in the relative topology. Actual code for this process must take this into account. It must also deal correctly with the case that two subtrees of an operator share some common faces. COMBINE must therefore do a little removal of duplication, and diff must subtract only the interior of its second operand.

(ii)   Classification

Here the potential edges and faces are partitioned into
pieces by their intersections with other faces and edges,
and each piece is compared with the object as a whole to
decide whether it lies inside the object, outside it, or on
the boundary. Those pieces which lie on the boundary are
kept. This process is well explained by Tilove in [15].

Because the algorithm for classification of each curve
against the object is the same, and because all curves are
tested independently, this approach looks a good candidate
for exploiting parallel computing.

(iii)   Oct-tree division

Here space is divided into pieces recursively, a new
object definition being determined for each piece, until
each piece is simple enough for a trivial calculation to
give the boundary. At each stage of the division copies of
the CSG tree are made and then pruned by the logical removal
of any terms which are constant over the entire piece of
space.

For example, if the piece of space we are considering
lies entirely within S1, then within that piece

        S1 intersection S2 is the same set as S2
        S2 diff S1 is empty
    and S1 union S2 is the whole of the piece

Similarly, if the piece of space lies entirely outside
S1

        S1 intersection S2 is empty
        S1 diff S2 is empty
        S2 diff S1 is the same as S2
    and   S1 union S2 is the same as S2

Woodwark[17] suggests that division and simplification
should proceed until each piece contains at most one vertex.
If space is divided by recursive halving many pieces are
found to be either full or empty while still quite large.
Such pieces are not further divided, and so the computation
focusses Warnock-fashion on the places where there is
something to compute. This approach is claimed to be very
fast for very complex models.

Other conversions

(i) Parametrised primitives to CSG or Boundary forms.

The feasibility of this depends entirely on the domains of
the primitives and of the specific boundary or CSG system. If
routines can be written to do point testing and curve
classification against the primitive directly, it can be taken
into a CSG system as a sibling for the more conventional block
and cylinder primitives. The question of conversion then hinges
on the boundary evaluation of the representation which includes
such a primitive.

(ii) Sweeps to CSG

The important special case of linear and rotational sweeps of an area itself compatible with the natural cross sections of the three dimensional primitives used, is fairly straightforward. The area is divided into such cross sections, combined by boolean operators, and the same combination is taken of the parent primitives.

More complex sweeps come up against the domain problem fairly quickly, the polyhedral primitive being swept along a polygonal trajectory or convolving with another polyhedron being about the only easily described domain which is closed under these operations. It is fairly easy to show that the combination of toroidal shapes at any orientation cannot be closed under convolution unless the shapes involved have an unbounded number of terms in their equations.

However, to the extent that routines can be written to do the point testing and classification tasks (possibly by successive approximation) sweep and convolution operators can be taken into a CSG sysem, postponing the problems to the boundary evaluation stage.

(iii)   Sweeps to Boundary form.

Again the important special cases are fairly straightforward. The swept area becomes one face of an object in its initial position and another in its final position. Each of the spans in its boundary becomes a face in the result, and the points where spans abut become edges.

The problem is primarily that of domain. If there are suitable face equations for the shapes generated by a sweep or convolution it is not too difficult to find out which they are.

(iv)   CSG and Boundary to Regular Spatial Enumeration.

If sampling is adequate, point testing solves this problem for the CSG representation, and the hatching of cross sections solves it for Boundary models.

(v)   CSG and Boundary to Irregular Spatial Enumeration.

Experimental software by Wordenweber has demonstrated division of boundary models of considerable topological complexity into tetrahedra. Direct conversion of CSG models is still an open question.

(vi)   Boundary to CSG

Since a ray test can do point testing on a boundary model, boundary models can be taken into a CSG model as primitives. Decomposition of an arbitrary boundary model into a set of predefined primitives does not have a clean solution at the moment.

(vii)   2D or Wire Frame to geometrically complete form.

It was suggested above that this task is impossible, since 2D and wire frame models need not be either valid or unambiguous. However, many object shapes have been captured in 2D or wire frame draughting systems. These descriptions have considerable economic value, and they are not believed to be invalid or ambiguous.   Conversion   techniques   which   would   convert descriptions which happened to be valid and unambiguous, and which would ask for help on those which were not, would be a very valuable practical tool.

Some work has been done by Wesley[11] in this area. It appears likely that the ideas of Waltz from scene recognition are also relevant.

Appendix 1   2D Construction

The drawing board has traditionally used straightedge and compasses for construction work. To create the underlying geometry of 'construction lines' therefore deals with straight lines, circles and their points of intersection and tangency. With appropriate representations, a small number of algorithms provides a rich set of constructions.

A good set of numerical representations is:-

Straight Lines.   The coefficients (a, b and c) of the linear equation for points on the line

$$ax + by - c = 0$$
$$normalised \ so \ that \quad a^2 + b^2 = 1$$

Circles.   The coordinates of the circle centre and its radius. These may be regarded as the coefficients (x, y and r) of the pedal equation

$$c = xa + yb + r$$

Points.   The coordinates (x and y), together with a third, zero field so that the point may be regarded as a circle of zero radius. This allows construction of items passing through a point to use the same code as that for items tangent to a circle.

These numerical representations may all be held in triples of floating point numbers. All are well conditioned, so that single precision storage is likely to be adequate for the representation of engineering parts with respect to a coordinate system whose origin is close by. This precision is certainly much better than that of the lines of an engineering drawing. Double precision may be used within the algorithms if there is serious concern about precise tangency.

A full system will also hold name information, and arrangements for the items to be addressed by name, possibly through a hash table. These aspects apply standard computer science, and will not be laboured here.

Algorithms:

The convention used here is that postfixed variables (x1, b2, r1 etc.) are components of the input items. Unpostfixed variables on the left hand side near the end of each algorithm are the components of the result.

1   Horizontal line at given y value

```
begin    a := 0
         b := 1
         c := y
end
```

2   Vertical line at given x value

```
begin      a := 1
           b := 0
           c := x
end
```

3   Line parallel to a given line and distant a distance d from it.

```
begin      a := a1
           b := b1
           c := c1 + s1*d
end
```

The sign, s1, is a variable of value either +1 or -1, the different signs giving result lines on opposite sides of the original. If directed geometry is used, the result will be on the side to which (a,b) points if s1 is positive. If Aptlike resolution of such ambiguities is used in the control language, it is probably easiest to evaluate both solutions and compare them against the specified choice criterion.

4   Circle concentric with a given circle, and of specified radius.

```
begin      x := x1
           y := y1
           r := r
end
```

This can obviously be used to construct a circle of given centre point and radius also.

5   Circle parallel to a given circle, and distant from it by a specified distance.

```
begin      x := x1
           y := y1
           r := r1 + s1*d
end
```

s1 again resolves the ambiguity. If the fields of each item are addressed by position within the triple, the same code results for this case as for 3 above.

6   Circle tangent to two lines (a1, b1 c1 and a2, b2 c2) and of given radius r.

```
begin      d1 := c1 + s1*r
           d2 := c2 + s2*r
           d  := a1*b2 - a2*b1
           if  d*d < tol then fail. parallel lines
           x := (b2*d1 - b1*d2)/d
           y := (d2*a1 - d1*a2)/d
           r := r
end
```

This code also gives the point of intersection of two lines, by setting r = 0

7   Circle tangent to a line(a1,b1,c1) and a circle(x2,y2,r2),
and of specified radius r.

```
begin      d1 := c1 + s1*r
           t := d1 - x2*a1 - y2*b1
           u := r2 + s2*r
           d := (u-t)*(u+t)
           if d < -tol then fail. no solution
           if d <= 0 then  d := 0
           d := s3*sqrt(d)
           x := x2 + a1*t + b1*d
           y := y2 + b1*t - a1*d
           r := r
end
```

This code also gives the point of intersection of a line and
a circle, and the circle tangent to a given line, and passing
through a given point.

The tolerance used in the first test above avoids spurious
failure due to the inherent imprecision of floating point
representation when the given line and circle are already
tangent. It is still necessary when double precision is used,
though its value can be smaller.

The tolerance throughout these algorithms is of dimension
squared, and should be set to a value slightly greater than the
square of the fractional resolution required.

8   Circle tangent to two given circles(x1,y1,r1 and x2,y2,r2),
and of given radius r.

```
begin      a1 := x2 - x1
           b1 := y2 - y1
           d := sqrt( a1*a1 + b1*b1 )
           d1 := ((x2+x1)*a1    +    (y2+y1)*b1
                  -    (r2+r1+(s2+s1)*r)*(r2-r1) / (2*d)
           a1 := a1/d
           b1 := b1/d
           t := d1 - x2*a1 - y2*b1
           u := r2 + s2*r
           d := (u-t)*(u+t)
           if d < -tol then fail. no solution
           if d <= 0 then  d := 0
           d := s3*sqrt(d)
           x := x2 + a1*t + b1*d
           y := y2 + b1*t - a1*d
           r := r
end
```

This code will also construct the point of intersection of
two circles, the circle tangent to a circle and passing through a
point, and the circle passing through two points.

There is considerable commonality with the previous
construction which could be exploited in implementation.

9   Line tangent to two circles (x1,y1,r1 and x2,y2,r2)

```
begin    dx := x2 - x1
         dy := y2 - y1
         dr := s2*r2 - s1*r1
         d :=  dx*dx +  dy*dy
         if d < tol then fail. concentric circles
         d := sqrt(d)
         a1 := dy/d
         b1 := -dx/d
         t := dr/d
         u := 1
         d := (u-t)*(u+t)
         if d < -tol then fail. no solution
         if d <= 0 then  d := 0 fi
         d := s3*sqrt(d)
         a := a1*t + b1*d
         b := b1*t - a1*d
         c := x2*b - y2*a + r2
end
```

     This code may be used to create the tangent from a point to
a circle or the line joining two points, merely by noting that
the r field for a point is zero. The command processor would
probably set the corresponding s values zero too. Setting the s
value zero gives access to the centre of any circle as if it were
a defined point.

     S3 may be taken as +1 without any loss of generality.

     The commonality of this code with constructions 7 and 8 is
using the duality of lines and points.

Appendix 2   3D Constructions

A modelling system in 3D needs some constructions in order to determine points of intersection etc.

Because there are many more possible shapes in 3D the list of possible intersection/tangency algorithms becomes very large. We list here a few of the simpler ones to indicate how unbounded construction items can be represented and used in such algorithms.

The items needed and considered here are:-

Points   represented by their three coordinates. (x,y,z)

The alternative of representing points by their four homogeneous coordinates is available if projective transformations are likely to be heavily used. For most engineering purposes this is not necessary, just fashionable.

Vectors   represented by their three components. (x,y,z)

If homogeneous coordinates are used for points the distinction between a point and a vector blurs, a vector being a point with a zero fourth component.

Lines   represented by two non-coincident points (P0,P1)

Again there are many alternatives. If homogeneous coordinates are being used for points two rather attractive forms are the 16-number (4*4) outer product matrix, or the 6 numbers of the Cayley form. These give elegant algorithms, but are less obvious geometrically.

Another alternative is to use one point and a unit vector along the line. This is little different from what we use here.

Planes   represented by a point on the plane and a unit normal.
            (P,N)

Alternatives are to hold the four plane coefficients, or to hold a complete coordinate system of which the defined plane is the xy plane.

Coordinate systems   represented by the origin and the three unit axis vectors. (O,X,Y,Z)

Alternatives are to use Euler angles, but these are inconvenient and often ill-conditioned, or axis, shift and rotation (minimal, but not always wellconditioned).

If homogeneous coordinates are used for points the origin and axis vectors fit neatly into a 4*4 matrix, a form which is now conventional in computer graphics.

The term frame will also be used for a local coordinate system, which is becoming standard usage in robotics.

Algorithms

In this appendix the symbol * means either scalar
multiplication, scaling of a vector, or the vector cross product,
depending on immediate context. The symbol . denotes the vector
dot product, andthe vector triple product uses the conventional
notation [A,B,C]

  + means either scalar addition or vector addition, and a
vector written <V> indicates a unit vector. ¦V¦ denotes the
magnitude. Therein lurks a square root.

  Unless otherwise indicated, the symbols O,X,Y,Z are the
origin and axis vectors of the implicit coordinate system

i.e.   O = 0,0,0
        X = 1,0,0
        Y = 0,1,0
        Z = 0,0,1

1   Line L through two points P0,P1

        L(P0,P1):

        begin   P0 of L := P0
                 P1 of L := P1
        end

2   Plane F through three points P0,P1,P2

        F(P0,P1,P2):

        begin   P of F := P0
                 N of F := (P1-P0)*(P2-P0)
                 if N of F = 0
                 then fail. illconditioned geometry
                 else N of F := <N of F>
                 fi
        end

3   Plane through a line and a point

        F(L,P):

        begin   F := F(P0 of L,P1 of L,P)
        end

4   Point of intersection of a Line and Plane

        P(L,F):

        begin   v := P1 of L - P0 of L
                 d := V.N of F
                 if   d = 0
                 then fail. illconditioned geometry
                 else d := (P of F - P0 of L).N of F/d
                      P := P0 of L + d*V
                 fi
        end

5   Point of intersection of three planes

   P(F1,F2,F3):

```
begin      d := [ N of F1 , N of F2 , N of F3 ]
           if d - O
           then fail
           else V1 := N of F2 * N of F3
                V2 := N of F3 * N of F1
                V3 := N of F1 * N of F2
                P := ( ( P of F1 . N of F1 ) * V1
                     + ( P of F2 . N of F2 ) * V2
                     + ( P of F3 . N of F3 ) * V3 )
                     / d
           fi
end
```

6   Line of intersection of two planes.

   L(F1,F2):

```
begin      T := N of F1 * N of F2
           if   T = 0
           then  fail.
           else PO of L := P((O,T),F1,F2)
                P1 of L := PO of L + T
           fi
end
```

7   Evaluation of coordinates of point given coordinates in
local coordinate system

   P(C,PL):

```
begin      P := O of C
              + x of PL * X of C
              + y of PL * Y of C
              + z of PL * Z of C
end
```

8   Evaluation of Vector given representation in local frame

   V(C,VL):

```
begin      V :=  x of VL * X of C
              + y of VL * Y of C
              + z of VL * Z of C
end
```

9   Evaluation of Line given representation in local frame

   L(C,LL):

```
begin      PO of L := P(C,PO of LL)
           P1 of L := P(C,P1 of LL)
end
```

10   Evaluation of Plane given representation in local frame

```
      F(C,FL):

      begin     P of F := P(C,P of FL)
                N of F := V(C,N of FL)
      end
```

Note: this assumes that the frames represent solid body transforms, with an orthonormal axis set. If coordinate systems are being used to introduce shear or differential scaling a more complex algorithm is necessary.

11   Evaluation of local representation of a point

```
      PL(C,P):

      begin     x of PL := (P - O of C) . X of C
                y of PL := (P - O of C  . Y of C
                z of PL := (P - O of C) . Z of C
      end
```

12   Evaluation of local representation of a vector

```
      VL(C,V):

      begin     x of VL := V . X of C
                y of VL := V . Y of C
                z of VL := V . Z of C
      end
```

13   Evaluation of local representation of a plane

```
      FL(C,F):

      begin     P of FL := PL(C,P of F)
                N of FL := VL(C,N of F)
      end
```

14   Evaluation of local representation of a frame

```
      CL(C,C1):

      begin     O of CL := PL(C,O of C1)
                X of CL := VL(C,X of C1)
                Y of CL := VL(C,Y of C1)
                Z of CL := VL(C,Z of C1)
      end
```

Appendix 3   Profile constructions

For machined parts to be made on a 3 axis NC mill using line
contact milling there is a very terse description which uses the
fact that all faces will be either horizontal or vertical. This
has regions which are flat at defined heights, separated from
each other by cliffs based on curves in plan view. This appendix
deals with the representation of such curves.

In the machining context these will for the most part be
made up of straight line segments and circular arcs: and those
which are not can be approximated arbitrarily closely by curves
with such segments.

The representation described here is therefore capable of
describing any closed loop of curve made up of such pieces.

Each curve is represented by an array of triples, one for
each span, together with the length of this array. The three
numbers in each triple are respectively

x   The x-coordinate of the point at the start of the span
y   The y-coordinate of the point at the start of the span
b   The 'bulge factor' of the span.

This third component is the tangent of one-quarter of the
angle turned through by the span, so it is 0 for a straight line
segment, +1 for a semicircle on one side and -1 for a semicircle
on the other side. Within these limits it gives an extremely well
conditioned representation which is also convenient for most
construction and interrogation algorithms.

The triples are in the same order in the array as their
spans are along the curve. Each span can be described completely
by two adjacent triples (or by the last and the first). We may
therefore consider their geometry one span at a time, using the
notation

x0,y0   Coordinates of initial point (together denoted P0)
b   Bulge factor
x1,y1   Coordinates of final point (together denoted P1)

Construction algorithms

Construction of the endpoints of the spans can be done by
use of the algorithms in Appendix 1 above. We concern ourselves
here with calculation of b given various pieces of information.

The pieces of information we might have are:-

PC   The centre of the arc
r   The radius, signed to indicate the sense.
PM   The midpoint of the arc
PG   Some general point on the arc
V0   An initial tangent (pointing into the arc)
V1   A final tangent (pointing out of the arc)
          These need not be unit vectors.
PP   The pole point where the tangents intersect
a   the angle between the initial or final tangent and the chord
s,c   the sine and cosine of a, possibly both multiplied by the
          same factor.

(i)   Given a

        This is the only construction requiring evaluation of
any trigonometric functions.

        b(a):

        begin   b :=   tan(a/2)
        end

(ii) Given s and c

        b(s,c):

        begin   b := -s/(c + sqrt(c*c + s*s))
        end

(iii)   Given V0

        b(V0):

        begin   s := V0 cross (P1-P0)
                     c := V0 dot (P1-P0)
                     b := b(s,c)
        end

    The dot and cross products here are both scalars because the
vectors are two dimensional.

(iv)   Given V1

        b(V1):

        begin   s := (P1-P0) cross V1
                     c := (P1-P0) dot V1
                     b := b(s,c)
        end

(v)   Given PP

    It may be assumed that PP lies on the perpendicular bisector
            of the chord from P0 to P1.

        b(PP):

        begin   V0 := PP-P0
                     b := b(V0)
        end

(vi)   Given PG (or PM which is a perfectly valid general
                                                 point)

        b(PG):

        begin   s := (PG-P0) cross (P1-PG)
                     c := (PG-P0) dot (P1-PG)
                     b := b(s,c)
        end

(vii)   Given PC

    It   may be assumed that the given PC lies   on   the
    perpendicular bisector of the chord from PO to P1

    b(PC):

```
begin      s := (P1-P0) dot (PC-P0)
           c := (P1-P0) cross (PC-P0)
           b := b(s,c)
end
```

(viii)   Given r

    b(r):

```
begin      t := 2*r/dist(P0,P1)
           if   t >1
           or   t < -1
           then    fail. no solution
           b := t/(1 + sqrt((1 + 1/t)*(1 - 1/t)))
end
```

Interrogation algorithms

(ix)   To determine a

    a(P0,P1,b):

```
begin      a := 2*arctan(b)
end
```

(x)   To determine s and c

    s,c(b):

```
begin      d := 1 + b*b
           s := 2*b/d
           c := (1 - b*b)/d
end
```

(xi)   To rotate a vector (x,y) through an angle given by sine
and cosine (s,c).

    ROT((x,y),s,c):

```
begin      x of ROT := x*c + y*s
           y of ROT := y*c - x*s
end
```

(xii)   To determine VO

    VO(P0,P1,b):

```
begin      s,c := s,c(b)
           VO := ROT(P1-P0,s,c)
end
```

(xiii)   To determine V1

V1(P0,P1,b):

```
begin     s,c :=s,c(b)
          V0 := ROT(P1-P0,-s,c)
end
```

(xiv)   To determine PM

PM(P0,P1,b):

```
begin     PM := (P1+P0)/2 - b*ROT(P1-P0,1,0)/2
end
```

(xv)   To determine PC

PC(P0,P1,b):

```
begin     PC := (P1+P0)/2 - (b - 1/b)*ROT(P1-P0,1,0)/2
end
```

(xvi)   To determine r

r(P0,P1,b):

```
begin     r := (b + 1/b)*dist(P0,P1)/4
end
```

(xvii)   To determine PP

PP(P0,P1,b):

```
begin     if   b ≥ 1
          or   b ≤ -1
          then fail. no pole for arc > 180 degrees
          PP := (P0+P1)/2 - ROT(P1-P0,1,0)*b
                   /((1-b)*(1+b))
end
```

(xviii)   To determine whether point P lies to left or right of
the full circle when traversed in the direction of the arc.

f(P,P0,P1,b):

```
begin     s,c := s,c(b)
          f := ( c*(P-P0) cross (P-P1)
              - s*(P-P0) dot (P-P1) )/dist(P0,P1)
end
```

The value f so computed will be approximately the distance
of   P from the nearest point of the full   circle.   This
approximation will be good when f*f << r*r.

(xix)   To determine whether a point P lying close to the full
circle lies near to the arc or near to the other half of the full
circle.

        g(P,P0,P1,b):

        begin   s,c := s,c(b)
                  g := (s*(P-P0) cross (P-P1)
                       - c*(P-P0) dot   (P-P1))
        end

    g will be positive in one case, negative in the other.

(xx)   To determine a sequence of points lying on the arc.
    This algorithm uses a parametric representation to generate
the points. As coded here it is given a scalar parameter, u which
specifies how far along the arc a single generated point is to
be.   The calling program has therefore to manage the loop to
generate as many as are required. To progress from P0 to P1, u
should progress from 0 to 1.

        P(u,P0,P1,b):

        begin   s,c := s,c(b)
                  d0 := 1 + b*b
                  d2 := 4*b*b
                  d1 := -d2
                  N0 := d0*P0
                  N2 := 2*b*(ROT(P1-P0,1,0) + b*(P0+P1))
                  N1 := d0*P1 - N0 -N2

              P := ((N2*u * N1)*u +N0) / ((d2*u + d1)*u + d0)
        end

    The final line of this algorithm is all   that need be
included in any iterative loop. The first   seven lines give
results independent of u.

(xxi)   To find the parameter value u corresponding to a given
           point P.

        u(P,P0,P1,b):

        begin   d := (P1-P0) dot (P1-P0)
                  C := (P0+P1)/2
                  h := 2 * (P-C)dot(P1-P0)/d
                  v := 2 * (P-C)cross(P1-P0)/d
                  u := (1+b*b)*h/((1+b*v)^2 + (b*h)^2)
                  u := (u + 1)/2
        end

(xxii)   Test if a point P near the profile lies within the
            span.

            begin   u := u(P,P0,P1,b)
                      if   u ≥ 0
                      and u ≤ 1
                      then true
                      else false
                      fi
            end

(xxiii)   Find a point Q on the arc near to point P

            Q(P,P0,P1,b):

            begin Q := P(u(P,P0,P1,b) ,P0,P1,b)
            end

(xxiv)   Signed distance d of a point (x,y) from a straight
               line (a1,b1,c1)

            d((x,y),a1,b1,c1):

            begin   d := x*a1 + y*b1 - c
            end

(xxv)   Estimate   e of the distance of point (x,y) from a
               circle (x1,y1,r1)

            e((x,y),x1,y1,r1):

            begin   e := ((x-x1)^2 + (y-y1)^2 -r1^2)/(2*r1)
            end

         This   estimate   has   the   same   approximation
properties as the function f described under (xviii) above..
Its magnitude will be the same when the arc tested there lies in
the circle. The sign, however, may differ, being in one case
positive outside the circle, in the other on the left of the arc.

(xxvi)   Points of intersection of span with a straight
line

```
ni,Q1,Q2(P0,P1,b,a2,b2,c2):

begin      w1 := d(P0,a2,b2,c2)
           w2 := d(PM(P0,P1,b),a2,b2,c2)
           w3 := d(P1,a2,b2,c2)

           t := 2*w2 - (w1+w3)/2
           d := t*t - w1*w3
           if w1*w1<tol and w3*w3<tol and t*t<tol
              then coincidence
           elsf w1*w1<tol and w3*w3<tol
              then ni:=2
                   u1 := 0
                   u2 := 1
           elsf w1*w1<tol and t*w3<0
              then ni := 2
                   u1 := 0
                   u2 := 2*t/(2*t - w3)
           elsf w1*w1<tol
              then ni := 1
                   u1 := 0
           elsf w3*w3<tol and t*w1<0
              then ni := 2
                   u1 := w1/(w1 - 2*t)
                   u2 := 1
           elsf w3*w3<tol
              then ni := 1
                   u1 := 1
           elsf w1>0 and w3>0 and t<-sqrt(w1*w3)
              then ni := 2
                   u1 := (w1-t + sqrt(d))/(w3+w1-2*t)
                   u2 := (w1-t - sqrt(d))/(w3+w1-2*t)
           elsf w1>0 and w3>0
              then ni := 0
           elsf w1<0 and w3<0 and t>sqrt(w1*w3)
              then ni := 2
                   u1 := (w1-t + sqrt(d))/(w3+w1-2*t)
                   u2 := (w1-t - sqrt(d))/(w3+w1-2*t)
           elsf w1<0 and w3<0
              then ni := 0
           else      ni := 1
                   u1 := w1/(sqrt(d)+w1-t)
           fi
           if ni > 0 then Q1 := P(u1,P0,P1,b) fi
           if ni > 1 then Q2 := P(u2,P0,P1,b) fi
     end
```

(xxvii)   Points of intersection of span with a circle

```
ni,Q1,Q2(P0,P1,b,x2,y2,r2):

begin      w1 := e(P0,x2,y2,r2)
           w2 := e(PM(P0,P1,b),x2,y2,r2)*(1+b*b)
           w3 := e(P1,x2,y2,r2)

           t := 2*w2 - (w1+w3)/2
           d := t*t - w1*w3
           if w1*w1<tol and w3*w3<tol and t*t<tol
               then coincidence
           elsf w1*w1<tol and w3*w3<tol
               then ni:=2
                   u1 := 0
                   u2 := 1
           elsf w1*w1<tol and t*w3<0
               then ni := 2
                   u1 := 0
                   u2 := 2*t/(2*t - w3)
           elsf w1*w1<tol
               then ni := 1
                   u1 := 0
           elsf w3*w3<tol and t*w1<0
               then ni := 2
                   u1 := w1/(w1 - 2*t)
                   u2 := 1
           elsf w3*w3<tol
               then ni := 1
                   u1 := 1
           elsf w1>0 and w3>0 and t<-sqrt(w1*w3)
               then ni := 2
                   u1 := (w1-t + sqrt(d))/(w3+w1-2*t)
                   u2 := (w1-t - sqrt(d))/(w3+w1-2*t)
           elsf w1>0 and w3>0
               then ni := 0
           elsf w1<0 and w3<0 and t>sqrt(w1*w3)
               then ni := 2
                   u1 := (w1-t + sqrt(d))/(w3+w1-2*t)
                   u2 := (w1-t - sqrt(d))/(w3+w1-2*t)
           elsf w1<0 and w3<0
               then ni := 0
           else      ni := 1
                   u1 := w1/(sqrt(d)+w1-t)
           fi
           if ni > 0 then Q1 := P(u1,P0,P1,b) fi
           if ni > 1 then Q2 := P(u2,P0,P1,b) fi
end
```

(xviii)   Points of intersection of two spans

ni,Q1,Q2(P0,P1,b,P0a,P1a,ba):

```
begin      w1 := f(P0,P0a,P1a,ba)
           w2 := f(PM(P0,P1,b).P0a,P1a,ba)*(1+b*b)
           w3 := f(P1,P0a,P1a,ba)

           t := 2*w2 - (w1+w3)/2
           d := t*t - w1*w3
           if w1*w1<tol and w3*w3<tol and t*t<tol
              then coincidence
           elsf w1*w1<tol and w3*w3<tol
              then ni:=2
                     u1 := 0
                     u2 := 1
           elsf w1*w1<tol and t*w3<0
              then ni := 2
                     u1 := 0
                     u2 := 2*t/(2*t - w3)
           elsf w1*w1<tol
              then ni := 1
                     u1 := 0
           elsf w3*w3<tol and t*w1<0
              then ni := 2
                     u1 := w1/(w1 - 2*t)
                     u2 := 1
           elsf w3*w3<tol
              then ni := 1
                     u1 := 1
           elsf w1>0 and w3>0 and t<-sqrt(w1*w3)
              then ni := 2
                     u1 := (w1-t + sqrt(d))/(w3+w1-2*t)
                     u2 := (w1-t - sqrt(d))/(w3+w1-2*t)
           elsf w1>0 and w3>0
              then ni := 0
           elsf w1<0 and w3<0 and t>sqrt(w1*w3)
              then ni := 2
                     u1 := (w1-t + sqrt(d))/(w3+w1-2*t)
                     u2 := (w1-t - sqrt(d))/(w3+w1-2*t)
           elsf w1<0 and w3<0
              then ni := 0
           else       ni := 1
                     u1 := w1/(sqrt(d)+w1-t)
           fi
           if ni > 0 then Q1 := P(u1,P0,P1,b) fi
           if ni > 1 then Q2 := P(u2,P0,P1,b) fi
```

```
             case  ni   in
             0:
             1:    if    g(Q1,P0a,P1a,ba)
                   then ni := 0
                   fi
             2:    if    g(Q2,P0a,P1a,ba)
                   then ni := 1
                   fi
                   if    g(Q1,P0a,P1a,ba)
                   then if   ni = 2
                        then ni := 1
                             Q1 := Q2
                        else ni := 0
                        fi
                   fi
             esac
end
```

<u>Appendix 4</u>   Sculptured surface sectioning algorithms.

The most heavily used algorithm in any sculptured surface system is the calculation of the intersection curve of the surface with a plane.   The algorithms which the three approaches (marching, lattice and recursive division) give for this task are:-

1   Step along intersection of surface P(u,v) with plane   (P0,N) by marching method.

This algorithm assumes that a starting point has been found whose parameter values are u,v where

$$(P(u,v) - P0) . N = 0 \quad \text{(or approximately so)}$$

The constant s is the required step length (which will be matched within 10%).   Pu and Pv denote the derivatives of P with respect to u and v respectively, computed within the evaluation routine.

```
begin      EVALUATE P,Pu,Pv(u,v)
           PL :=    P
           du :=    Pv . N
           dv := - Pu . N
           T := Pu * du  +  Pv * dv
           d := sqrt( s*s / T.T )
           until     u := u + d*du
                     v := v + d*dv
                     EVALUATE P,Pu,Pv(u,v)
                     f := (P - P0) . N
                     r := (P - PL) . (P - PL)  - s*s
           f*f < tol
           and   r*r < .04*s*s*s*s
           do        fu := Pu . N
                     fv := Pv . N
                     ru := 2 (P - PL) . Pu
                     rv := 2 (P - PL) . Pv
                     d := 1/(fv*ru - fu*rv)
                     du :=   (fu*r - f*ru)
                     dv :=   (f*rv - fv*r)
           od
           APPEND POINT  P  TO OUTPUT CURVE
end
```

A production algorithm would contain extra tests to avoid the possibility of division by zero, and to ensure convergence of the iterative loop.

This version gives all steps roughly the same size; substitution of more complex expressions for r, ru, and rv , taking into account the angle turned through, can make this method adaptive, so that points are computed more closely together in sharply curved regions of the curve.

Inserting calculation of P0 and N to be an estimate local at P of the tangent plane to a surface f(P) = 0 after every evaluation of P gives the algorithm for intersecting the surface P(u,v) with f(P)=0

2   Step along intersection of surface P(u,v) with plane (PO,N)
by lattice method.

       This   algorithm   assumes   that we have already   evaluated   a
surface point at two parameter pairs,   ul,vl and ur,vr and   that

$$(P(ul,vl)-PO) \cdot N < O$$
and $$(P(ur,vr)-PO) \cdot N \geq O$$

```
begin      ut := ur + vl - vr
           vt := vr + ur - ul
           ft := (P(ut,vt) - PO) . N
           if   ft < O
           then ul := ut
                vl := vt
                fl := ft
           else us := ul + vl - vr
                vs := vl + ur - ul
                fs := (P(us,vs) - PO) .N
                if   fs < O
                then ul := us
                     vl := vs
                     fl := fs
                     ur := ut
                     vr := vt
                     fr := ft
                else ur := us
                     vr := vs
                     fr := fs
                fi
           fi
           u := (fr*ul - fl*ur)/(fr - fl)
           v := (fr*vl - fl*vr)/(fr - fl)
           APPEND POINT  P(u,v)  TO OUTPUT CURVE
end
```

       The precondition is still true at the end, so this procedure
can be called repeatedly to follow a curve until it either leaves
the finite piece of surface, or else returns to the starting
point.

3   Calculate intersection of the surface represented by the
set of control points S with the plane (PO,N) by the recursive
division method.

INTERSECTION (S , (PO,N)):

```
begin      if   all points in S are on the same side of (PO,N)
           then no intersection
           else if   S represents a simple enough surface
                then SIMPLE INTERSECTION ( S , (PO,N) )
                else COMPUTE HALVES   S1, S2  OF  S
                     COMBINE   INTERSECTION (S1 , (PO,N))
                         WITH   INTERSECTION (S2 , (PO,N))
                fi
           fi
end
```

BIBLIOGRAPHY

[1] Baumgart,B.G., Winged Edge Polyhedron Representation, AIM-79 STAN-CS-74-463 Stanford AI Lab, Stanford University 1974

[2] Besant,C.B., Computer Aided Design and Manufacture (Ellis Horwood, 1980)

[3] Braid,I.C., Designing with Volumes, (Computer aided Design Group, University of Cambridge Computer Laboratory, Cambridge, England, 1973)

[4] Chan,Y.K. and Knight,W.A. MODCON: A system for the design of dies and moulds. pp370-381 in proc CAD80 (IPC, Guildford, 1980)

[5] Comba,P.G., A procedure for detecting intersections of three dimensional objects. IBM Corp, New York, 1967

[6] Coons,S.A., Surfaces for computer aided design of space forms. (Project MAC, MIT, Cambridge, Mass, 1967)

[7] Ferguson,J., Multivariable curve interpolation. Journal of ACM vol 11 no 2 pp221-228 April 1964.

[8] Lidbro,N., Modern Aircraft Geometry. Aircraft Engineering pp388-394 November 1956

[9] Lidbro,N., Analytische Formbestimmung van Schiffen. Schiffstechnik heft 42 band 8 pp 91-96 1961

[10] Luh,J.Y.S. and Krolak,R.J., A mathematical model for mechanical part description. CACM vol 8 no 2 pp125-129 1965

[11] Markowsky,G. and Wesley,M.A., Fleshing out wire frames. IBM Journal of R and D, vol 24 no 5 September 1980 pp582-597

[12] Requicha,A.A.G., Representations for Rigid Solids: Theory, Methods and Systems. ACM Computing Surveys Vol 12,No 4 December 1980 pp437-464

[13] Robertson,R.G., Descriptive Geometry (Pitman, London, 1966)

[14] Sabin,M.A., Contouring - Scattered Data. pp63-86 in: Brodlie,K.W. (ed) Mathematical Methods in Computer Graohics and Design (Academic Press, London, 1980)

[15] Tilove,R.B., Set Membership Classification: a Unified Approach to Geometric Intersection Problems, IEEE Transactions on Computers, vol C-29, no 10, October 1980

[16] Walter,H., Computer Aided Design in Aircraft Industry, pp 355-378 in: Vlietstra,J., and Wielinga,R.F.(eds), Computer Aided Design (North Holland, Amsterdam,1973)

[17] Woodwark,J.R. and Quinlan,K.M., The derivation of graphics from volume models by recursive subdivision of the object space. pp335-344 in proc CG80 (Online Publications, Northwood Hills,1980)

X. Solid Modeling: Theory and Applications

M. Mäntylä

1. INTRODUCTION

In his famous article in **Scientific American,** Ivan Sutherland introduced computer graphics by the following:

> "I think of a computer display as a window on Alice's Wonderland in which a programmer can depict either objects that obey well-known natural laws or purely imaginary objects that follow laws he has written into his program. Through computer displays I have landed an airplane on the deck of a moving carrier, observed a nuclear particle hit a potential wall, flown in a rocket at nearly the speed of light and watched a computer reveal its innermost workings." (Sutherland, 1970)

Now, little more than a decade later, similar experiences are within the reach of almost everyone. Ingenious electrical toys use computer graphics to give their user the possibility to fight against enemies from other worlds, to drive a Grand Prix car race, or to hunt savage animals. Popular movies include synthesized scenes that could not be created by other means than computer graphics. In their profession, many people utilize computer graphics as a means to interact with phenomena ranging from simulated mechanical assemblies to office procedures.

The extent to which computers can make use of computer graphics depends mostly on their ability to create a computerized representation of the phenomenon to be visualized. It is the accuracy and completeness of the underlying model that determines the ultimate intelligence of a computer graphics application.

Most strikingly it is so in computer-aided design systems. For instance, a computer-aided design system for mechanical engineering should provide tools for such diverse tasks as model creation by various means, model analysis, drafting, generation of data for computer-aided manufacturing, and data transmission to other information systems in the form of part lists, bills of material, process schedules, and so on. All these operations should be based on a single representation or on multiple but consistent representations created by the user of the computer-aided design system.

Object representations of computer-aided design form the topic of these lectures. Emphasis is put on representations dealing with the geometric shape of the objects designed - geometric models. We will examine various solid representations and their related algorithms. Our goal is to focus attention on the basic properties of each modeling scheme to gain an understanding of what kinds of operations they allow.

2. THE ROLE OF SOLID MODELING IN CAD

2.1. Design Cycle

To appreciate the possibilities offered by a solid modeler, it is instructive to first consider the tasks that must be performed during the design cycle of product. Following Wesley (1980), we list such operations as follows:

(1)   SYNTHESIS: Based on initial specifications for the object, coarse drafts are made and entered into the CAD system. These descriptions include data on the shape of the object and other data such as materials, surface finish, and heat treatment. During the synthesis, these data may be edited to create more detailed specifications.

(2)   ANALYSIS: The technical and economical properties of the object are analyzed by external application programs such as FEM-analysis. Engineering properties such as the strength, stiffness, vibrational characteristics, heat transfer and aerodynamics are derived. In the case of objects assembled from parts or components, relationships between them are investigated. This may include analysis and simulation of static and dynamic interference behavior. Based on the results, the design may be further improved.

(3)   PROCESS PLANNING: When an acceptable level of performance has been reached, data needed for the actual manufacture of the object are produced. These data include technical drawings, bills of material and NC-tapes. For objects to be cast or moulded, the dies are designed and NC-tapes designed. Furthermore, for mechanical objects to be assembled, robot programs for assembly, painting, inspection and quality control are generated.

(4)   DOCUMENTATION: As the product is released to the customer,
      documentation in terms of illustration for instruction and
      service manuals may be generated.

(5)   REDESIGN: Throughout the process the ability to make design
      alterations exists.   This may happen because of changed
      specifications or new manufacturing technology. During the
      life cycle of the product, several redesigns may take
      place. Then all data residing in CAD files may be used as
      a basis for further work.

2.2. Models for CAD

To be capable of supporting the variety of operations listed
above, a CAD system must store the different kinds of data needed
in the form of a structured computational model of the object
designed. In such a model, the geometric properties of an object
seem to play a key role as most tasks require mainly data of the
shape of the object. Thus we may separate between two layers of
computational models - geometric models and object models. Their
distinction lies in that geometric models deal only with the
shape of the object, while object models include additional
problem-dependent data.

Geometric modeling deals with the art of creating data structures
and algorithms that are capable of representing and calculating
data on the three-dimensional physical shape of an object. It is
possible to separate the component dealing with these tasks - a
Geometric Modeling System (GMS) - as an independent component of
a CAD system.

Many current CAD systems are limited in the variety of operations
they can support in an automated fashion. This is so mainly because of deficiencies in the geometric models they are based on.
Solid modeling aims at remedying these deficiencies by focusing
on "informationally complete" representations of solid objects -
representations that (in principle) allow any well-defined opera-

tions or calculations to the performed. In particular, solids can be processed by Boolean set operations to yield new models or to model manufacturing operations. Graphical displays of models can be produced, with hidden lines or surfaces removed. Integral properties such as volume, surface area, center of mass and so on can be automatically calculated.

Solid modeling systems have been an area of active research and development during recent years, and are now entering industrial use. It is therefore appropriate to study the current state of the art in a tutorial like this.

2.3. System Architecture Aspects

While it may well be said that a solid modeler forms a central component of a CAD application, it should be borne in mind that it is just a component, and as such is of limited value. A multitude of other functional components should exist for tasks such as user interface management and command language processing, database management, and data extraction for use in external software packages.

In this environment, a solid modeler can be viewed as a "calculator" that is invoked when specific tasks requiring informationally complete models are performed. It is expected that the modeler is used as well by automata (other programs) as humans; this of course puts heavy requirements on its robustness and its external interface.

Figure 1 (Requicha and Voelcker 1981) summarizes the interfacing issues in a compact form. We expect a geometric modeling system to be able to "understand" definitions of object geometries, and representing them. Based on this, the modeler should be able to answer "geometric questions" such as generation of figures or calculation of properties of the solids represented.

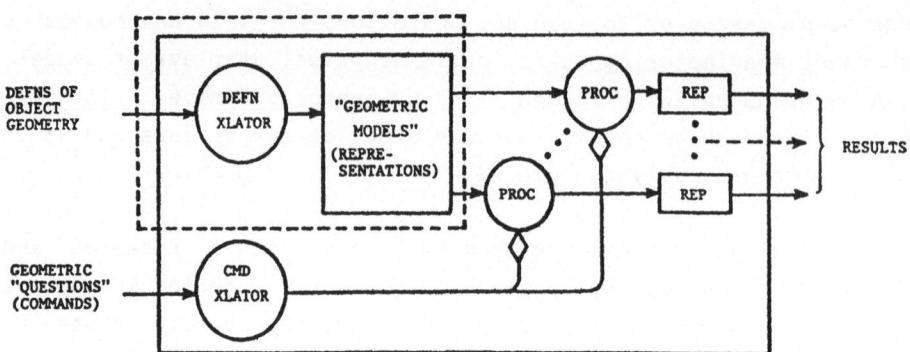

Figure 1. A high-level view of a solid modeler and its external interface.

3. SOLID MODELING TECHNIQUES

As noted in the preceding, solid modeling deals both with data structures and algorithms. It is worthwhile to discuss the main alternatives for representing solid objects.

3.1. Taxonomy of Modeling Schemes

To gain a unified view on various classes of solid modeling techniques, some mathematical terminology is necessary.

We view "solids" as point sets in the three-dimensional Euclidean space E3. To be considered "solid", a point set must satisfy several constraints. Some of them are listed below.

(1)   "THREE-DIMENSIONALITY": Not all point sets satisfy our intuitive notion of "solidity". A set of "separate" points or lines is not a solid, for instance. We may thus require that to be a solid, a point set may not contain "isolated points" or "isolated lines".

(2)   "RIGIDITY": One property that must hold for a solid object is that it remains the same if we move it from one position in the space to the other. A solid object should therefore remain invariant under rigid transformations, i.e. translations or rotations or combinations of these.

(3)   "REPRESENTATIONAL FINITENESS": We have no direct means to represent continuous point sets in a computer. Even while it is physically naive, we must assume that the point set allows some finite indirect representation. For instance, we assume that the surface of the solid is "smooth" and can adequately be modeled by second-order (or like) surfaces. It is in this respect where most differences between various approaches occur.

A collection of such constraints defines the mathematical _model-ing space_ we are interested in. Having (more or less) established the notion of a "solid", the task of solid modeling can be phrased in a more rigorous fashion: A _solid representation_ is a finite collection of symbols (of a finite alphabet) that designates a mathematical entity satisfying the conditions (1) through (3) above. Moreover, the admissible representations of a particular modeling system (i.e. those that can be constructed according to its syntax rules) form its _representation space_. Following Requicha (1980), the pair consisting of a modeling space and a representation space is called a _representation scheme_. In this view, entities of the representation space designate entities of the modeling space, i.e. (abstract) solids.

Many properties of a representation scheme are of theoretical and practical interest. Some of them are listed below.

(1)   RANGE, DOMAIN: Which solids have a representation according to the syntax rules of the representation ?

(2)   VALIDITY: Are all representations valid, i.e. do they
      designate an object that .satisfies the definition of a
      "solid" ? If not, does an algorithm that checks the vali-
      dity of a representation exist ?

(3)   COMPLETENESS: Are all representations "informationally com-
      plete", i.e. does each representation designate a unique
      solid ?

(4)   UNIQUENESS: Are there several representations for a solid ?
      If there are, does an algorithm for "same object detection"
      (SOD) exist ?

(5)   COMPUTATIONAL EFFICIENCY: Which kinds of algorithms can be
      devised for the representation ?

In the following, we briefly discuss some important modeling
schemes.

3.2. Wire Frames

A human being perceives a solid object through its "features".
The sharply bending areas of the surface of a solid certainly belong to these: if somebody is asked to draw a cube, it is likely
that a line drawing of the "edges" of the cube will be produced.

A wire frame model represents a solid object by representing its
"edges" only. The simplest possible wire frame would consist
only of a collection of "lines", represented via six-tuples

        <x1,y1,z1,x2,y2,z2>

that represents the start and end points of a line.

We may immediately note that the expressive power of wire frames
depends only on the complexity of line representations allowed.
However, it is hard to establish the validity of a wire frame: a
collection of lines may or may not represent the edges of a rea-

sonable object. Moreover, a valid wire frame may have many interpretations as depicted in Figure 2 (Wesley 1980). Thus wire frames are informationally incomplete. There exists an algorithm capable of producing all boundary models that correspond to a given wire frame (Markowsky and Wesley 1980).

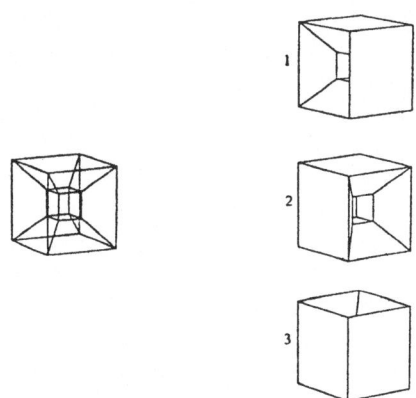

Figure 2. An ambiguous wire frame. Which side of the cube is "open" ?

Turning our attention to algorithms, wire frames do not generally allow automated operations such as generation of figures with hidden lines removed or calculation of mass or other integral properties. Thus solid modeling systems must employ more complete solid representations.

3.3. Boundary Representations

Boundary representations (BR) represent a solid or a surface by a three-level hierarchy of entities face, edge, and vertex. The surface is subdivided into a collection of faces that do not intersect each other except at common edges or vertices. Faces are represented in terms of their bounding edges and vertices. Boundary representations thus represent a point set "indirectly" by its boundary: if the collection of faces "closes", they form a solid model.

Boundary representation, or just boundary model for short, is a generic name covering a wide spectrum of model representations. See the survey of Baer, Eastman, and Henrion (1979) for information on several variations of the basic theme. We employ the convention that faces need not be simply-connected but may include holes; the components of the boundary of a face are then referred to as <u>loops</u>. If faces are planar polygons, one of the loops represents the "exterior" boundary of a face; others (if any) correspond to its holes and will be called <u>rings</u>. We shall use the term "ring" also in the nonplanar case. Furthermore, we allow the surface to be disconnected: the term <u>shell</u> will be used to denote a closed component of the surface. The basic entities of boundary models are depicted by Figure 3.

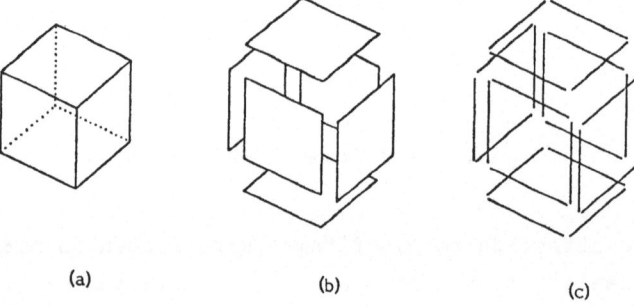

(a)   (b)   (c)

Figure 3 (Mäntylä 1983). Basic entities of boundary models. The surface of the object (a) forms one shell that is subdivided into six planar faces, shown in the exploded hidden surface view of (b). Each face is represented by its bounding edges and vertices, forming one loop, as depicted in the exploded wire-frame view of (c).

While a boundary model might be represented simply as a collection of polygons, boundary modelers frequently also store other explicit data on the connections between elements of the model. For instance, edges can include identifiers of the two loops they belong to and vertices can include identifiers of their attached edges. These connectivity data are usually called the "topology" of a boundary model, while coordinates, surface equations and other similar data are called the "geometry". The modeling space of a boundary modeler then depends on the class of geometries that can be assigned to topological entities face, edge, and vertex.

Not all collections of faces define a physical solid or surface. The topological integrity of a boundary model imposes restrictions on face collections to ensure the validity of the model. For instance, each edge must belong to two loops, and the ordering of edges must remain consistent throughout the whole model. Geometric integrity is satisfied when the shape assigned to faces, edges, and vertices is consistent with the topological information. For instance, faces are not allowed to intersect each other except at common edges or vertices. This excludes self-intersecting objects.

The validity of a boundary model can thus be established by verifying that various constraints are satisfied. This can be computationally expensive, however, and therefore it makes more sense to restrict solid description means in a way that allows large enough expressive power but excludes insensible models. A particular solution to this is explained in the sequel.

Boundary representations are complete. i.e. each valid boundary model designates a unique solid object. They are not unique, however, and same object detection may be complicated. Boundary representations allow rather straightforward algorithms for solid visualization and analysis; we shall return to this in the next chapter.

Boundary representations allow a rich user interface that can be similar to drafting-oriented interfaces typical for current wire-frame systems. They also can support other description methods such as parameterized objects, sweeping by various rules, and Boolean operations. Braid (1979) describes a variety of object description facilities in detail.

3.3.1 Euler Operators

The main problem of boundary models is their complexity: models of practically interesting objects may consist of tens or hundreds of faces, edges and vertices. It is hard to ensure that all required integrity constraints are met.

Fortunately, the modifications of these models can be divided into simple atomic steps that preserve all required topological validity constraints. Let us consider the cube represented by six faces, twelve edges, and eight vertices as shown in Figure 4(a). Consider for a moment the effect of removing the edge marked by an arrow in the figure. In the resulting object, Figure 4(b), the two faces which meet at the edge are united and the remaining collection of five faces, eleven edges and eight vertices is generated. Of course, the geometry of the face created by the uniting operation is no longer planar; however, all topological integrity rules are still met.

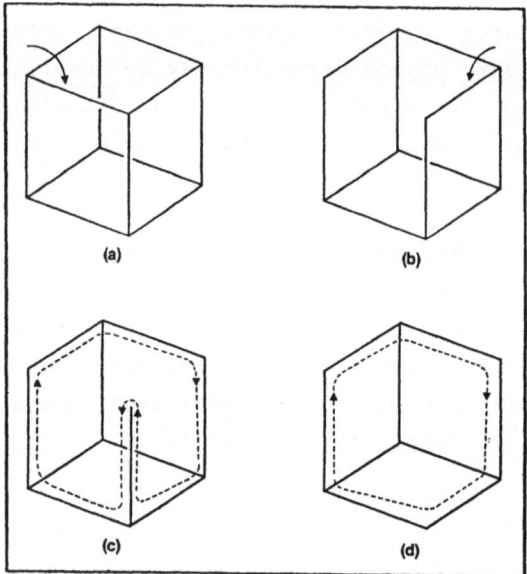

Figure 4 (Mäntylä and Sulonen 1982). A cube (a), after removal of one edge (b), a second edge (c), and a vertex and a third edge (d).

Performing the same operation on the edge marked in Figure 4(b) creates the object in Figure 4(c). It has an edge belonging twice to the loop indicated by dashes. The "upper" vertex of the edge is adjacent to no other edges. Another operation removes such a combination of an edge and a vertex and creates the model in Figure 4(d). These two operations can in fact remove all edges and all vertices except one. A third operation can remove the remaining stripped-down, one-vertex model.

Obviously, each "removal" operation has an inverse "creation" counterpart. While the operations described above can be used to destroy boundary models, these positive operations can be used for the perhaps more interesting purpose of creating boundary models. So the inverse of the third removal operation creates an "initial" object. The inverses of the two other operations add new vertices, edges, and faces to create models of any complexity.

The operations informally described in the preceding are examples of Euler operators. We call the three destructive operators "kef", "kev", and "kvfs", for "kill edge and face", "kill edge and vertex", and "kill vertex, face, and shell". Similarly, their inverses are called "mef", "mev", and "mvfs", where "m" now stands for "make".

Euler operators (Baumgart 1974, 1975) have derived their name from the well-known Euler's Law: in any simple polyhedron, the numbers of faces (f), edges (e), and vertices (v) must satisfy the equation

$$v-e+f = 2. \hspace{6cm} \text{(eq. 1)}$$

Euler's Law may be generalized to arbitrary solid objects by introducing three other parameters, namely (1) the total number of rings (holes in faces, r) in the solid, (2) the total number of holes ("tunnels", h) through the solid, and (3) the number of disconnected components (shells, s) in a solid with a disconnected surface. The general equation is

$$v-e+f = 2*(s-h)+r. \qquad \text{(eq. 2)}$$

A collection of operators that can describe all models satisfying Equation 2 is listed in Table I. It includes the three operators already discussed and two other operator-inverse pairs related to creation of rings (kemr, mekr) and holes (kfmrh, mfkrh).

Operator	Transition Vector	Description
mvfs	1, 0, 1, 0, 1, 0	Make Vertex, Face, Shell
mev	1, 1, 0, 0, 0, 0	Make Edge, Vertex
mef	0, 1, 1, 0, 0, 0	Make Edge, Face
kemr	0,-1, 0, 0, 0, 1	Kill Edge, Make Ring
kfmrh	0, 1,-1, 1, 0, 0	Kill Face, Make Ring, Hole
kvfs	-1, 0,-1, 0,-1, 0	Kill Vertex, Face, Shell
kev	-1,-1, 0, 0, 0, 0	Kill Edge, Vertex
kef	0,-1,-1, 0, 0, 0	Kill Edge, Face
mekr	0, 1, 0, 0, 0,-1	Make Edge, Kill Ring
mfkrh	0,-1, 1,-1, 0, 0	Make Face, Kill Ring, Hole

Table I. Euler operators for closed surfaces. Operators kvfs, kev, kef, mekr, and mfkrh are the exact inverses of operators mvfs, mev, mef, kemr, and kfmrh, respectively.

The fact that all objects satisfying Equation 2 can be modeled is a necessary but not sufficient requirement for a reasonable expressive power. By a more detailed analysis, the following can be shown:

Theorem 1:

> Euler operators are sound and complete (in the class of objects bounded by "ordinary surfaces"), i.e. they create only meaningful models, and every meaningful model can be constructed by them.

To give further clarification on Euler operators, we represent the creation of a cube with a hole in Figure 5. In the figure, the "exterior" cube is created with operations (a) through (f). The "bottom" of the hole to be drilled is created with operations (g) through (i), while its side faces are created by operations (j) through (k). The last operation (kfmrh) "subtracts" a face from another in order to create a hole through the object.

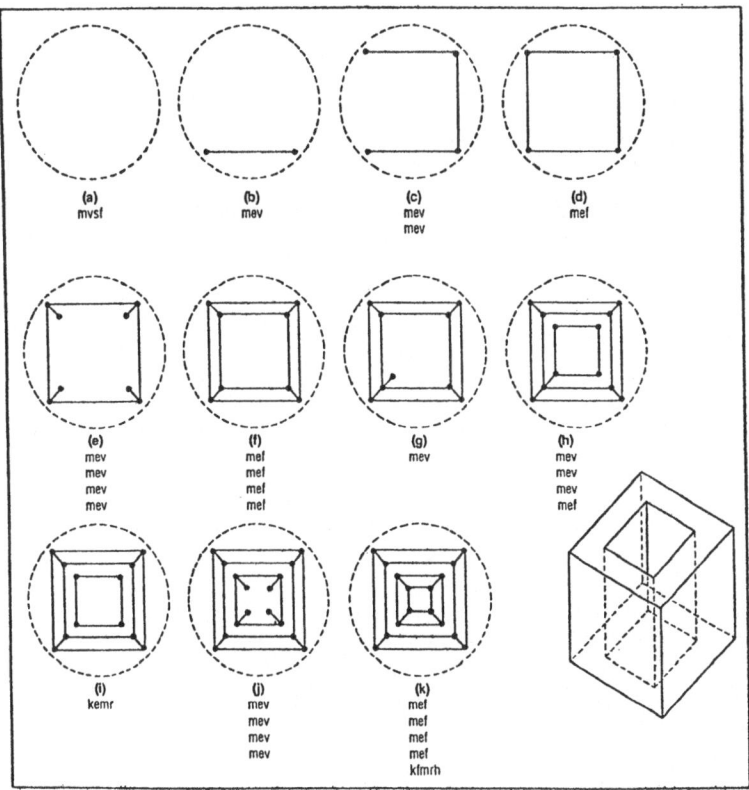

Figure 5 (Mäntylä and Sulonen 1982). Euler operators: a sample definition.

3.4. Constructive Solid Geometry

Boundary representations model point sets indirectly through their boundaries. Another way to represent a point set is to record its construction from simpler point sets that can easily be modeled.

The most general form of this approach is the so-called half-space model. In a half-space model, solids are represented by a combination of a finite number of simple point sets called half-spaces that are combined by Boolean set operations union, intersection and difference. Elementary half-spaces are in turn represented by a real-valued function

F(x, y, z)

that has positive values outside the half-space, is zero on its
boundary, and negative in its interior.

For instance, a solid cylinder may be represented by half-spaces
as depicted in Figure 6.

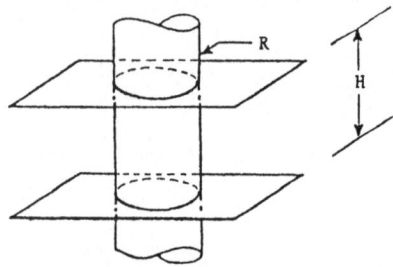

Figure 6. Half-space representation of a cylinder.   The object
is constructed from one (unbounded) cylinder halfspace of form x^2
+ y^2 = R^2, and two planar half-spaces of form z = 0 and z = H.

Half-spaces defined above may be unbounded sets.   (Each of the
three half-spaces of Figure 6 were unbounded.) To avoid this, the
Constructive Solid Geometry (CSG) approach to solid modeling uses
bounded primitive point sets instead of unbounded half-spaces.

CSG adopts the "building block" approach to solid modeling in its
purest form.   The user of a CSG system operates only in terms of
parameterized primitive objects and Boolean operations   that   are
used to create other models.   Nevertheless, it is possible to implement also other types of user interfaces, including   a
"drafting"-type one, but this not not as straightforward as with
BR models.

The strength and user-friendliness of a CSG system depends to a
large extent on the available primitives. Two collections of
primitives are depicted in Figure 7.

Similarly to BR systems, also CSG modelers differ in the way they
construct and represent solid models. The most general variant
of CSG modeling represents solids by a CSG tree that can be de-

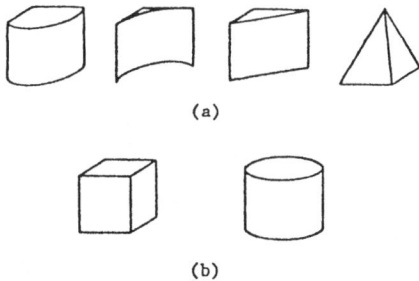

(a)

(b)

Figure 7. Primitives of two CSG modelers.

fined as follows:

```
<CSG tree> ::= <primitive> |
               <CSG tree> <set operation> <CSG tree> |
               <CSG tree> <rigid motion> <motion args>
```

Thus primitives hang in the leaves of the tree; each interior node is marked either by a set operation (union, intersection, or difference) or by a rigid motion (translation, rotation). Often the same subtree can occur multiple times in the tree at different positions to model, for instance, a subassembly. In this case we actually have an acyclic graph instead of a pure tree.

Note that every subtree of a CSG tree models a reasonable solid, being a CSG tree itself. In this respect CSG trees quite naturally lend themselves to stepwise, interactive design.

A sample CSG tree is depicted in Figure 8. Note that objects are shown in an ortographic projection.

The domain of a CSG modeler depends on the variety of half-spaces available in its primitives, on the available rigid motions and on the available set operations. Note that the two collections of Figure 7 have the same domain because the underlying half-spaces are the same. (A CSG model with just one cylinder primitive has the same power as well.)

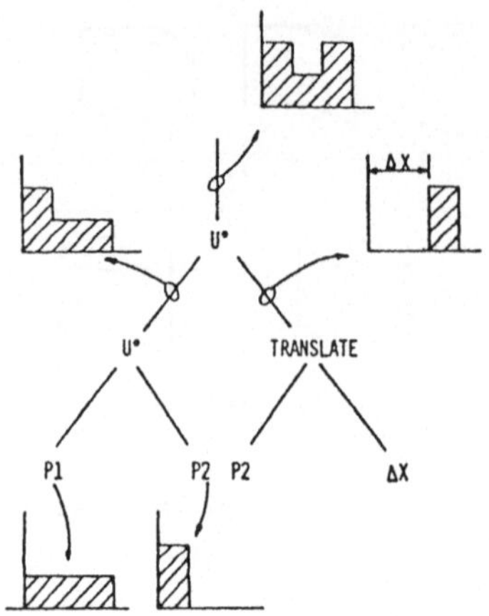

Figure 8. A CSG tree.

Every CSG tree is guaranteed to define a single solid object. Thus CSG representations are complete and always valid, but not unique as a solid usually has many different representations.

3.5. Other Representations

Boundary representations and CSG models form the two main approaches to solid modeling. Some other models are also important, however, and require to be mentioned.

If the general set operations of a CSG model are replaced by one generic "gluing" operation, we end up in a so called Cell Decomposition model. The simplest variant of a CD model has just one primitive being a cube. As all primitives and operations are similar, this variation results in a three-dimensional grid of boxes.

The large storage requirements of a fixed grid can be avoided by employing a variable grid that is dense only at the boundary of the object. This approach results in so-called quadtree and octree models when applied in two and three dimensions, respectively.

A solid or a bounded surface moved along a trajectory defines a volume. Thus another approach to solid modeling would be to represent a solid by the pair (moving body, trajectory), both of which in turn are represented by some suitable representation.

The result of this approach is called a sweeping model. The two mostly used sweeping rules are the linear sweeping, where a (planar) face is swept along a third axis, and rotational sweeping, where a curve is swung around an axis to define a rotational solid. More general sweeping rules would be as useful (to represent, for instance, the region swept by a NC tool in NC simulation) but not well understood.

4. SOLID MODELING APPLICATIONS

Having now discussed the representational problems of solid modeling to some extent, we turn our attention to algorithmic questions. We do this by a collection of case studies that is not aimed to be complete. Emphasis is put on algorithms for the two main classes of representations, namely boundary representations and CSG trees.

4.1. Visualization

The most frequent "question" that a solid modeler must answer is no doubt the generation of a figure of the object modeled. It is therefore important to discuss visualization algorithms of alternative solid representations.

4.1.1 BR Visualization

Boundary representations are directly useful for generating line-oriented images, because faces, edges, and vertices of the model are readily available. (It is probably this why BR models are considered to be "evaluated", in contrast to "unevaluated" CSG models.) Generation of a wire frame figure with hidden lines present is therefore straightforward.

Standard hidden-line removal algorithms work on general on polyhedral models only. Some display devices have efficient "polygon pushers" that are able to process a polyhedral model very rapidly by hardware.

Curved surfaces may pose problems, however. If abovementioned methods are used to generate figures without hidden lines, curved surfaces must first be "faceted", i.e. the model must be converted into a polyhedral model, after which standard methods are applicable again. Facets are useful also to generate shaded color images by (for instance) z-buffer algorithms.

4.1.2 CSG Visualization

CSG models lead to quite different algorithms as those discussed above as faces, edges, and vertices are only implicitly represented. Thus it is necessary to "evaluate" the CSG tree in some sense to display the object modeled.

The most important problem of visualization is the "wire frame problem": given a CSG tree, generate a wire frame corresponding to it. The "brute-force" solution to the wire frame generation problem for CSG is based on the very general "set membership classification" approach (Tilove 1981).

Let us consider a line L and a CSG primitive P. L can usually easily be "classified" into three components LinP, LonP, and LoutP being the parts of L inside P, on the boundary of P, and outside P.

To classify L similarly against a combination S of primitives, a recursive "divide-and-conquer" algorithm is applicable. Now L is first classified with respect to all primitives, the results of which are combined by merge-style rules. The generic wire-frame generation algorithm for CSG is given in Figure 9.

```
/* generate wire-frame of CSG tree S */

procedure WIREFRAME(S)

    /* Generate tentative edges */
    Tentative-list = null list
    for each face, G
        for each face, H
            Tentative-list = Tentative-list U Intersect(G, H)
        end   /* for */
    end   /* for */

    /* classify tentative edges */
    Wire = null list
    for each edge, E, of Tentative-list
        /* classify E against S */
        (EinS, EonS, EoutS) = M(E, S)
        Wire = Wire U EonS
    end /* for */

end /* procedure */

/* set membership classification edge vs. CSG tree */
procedure M(E, S)
    if S is a primitive then return prim-M(E, S)
    else
        A = left-subtree(S)
        B = right-subtree(S)
        <OP> = root(S)
        return combine(M(E, A), M(E, B), <OP>)
    end /* else */
end /* procedure */
```

Figure 9. Wire frame generation algorithm for CSG. Procedure prim-M(E, S) classifies E against one primitive.

To generate shaded pictures of solids modeled by CSG trees, a very general approach is the so-called ray casting approach (Roth 1982). The idea is to send "rays" from the imagined eye location in the three-dimensional space through points of the projection plane. The color of the image point is calculated by finding the point where the ray hits the solid and calculating the color intensities there according to some shading rule.

Again, the set membership classification is applicable.   Now we
classify "rays" against CSG trees, which amounts up to (1) clas-
sifying rays against primitives, and (2) combining results of
primitive classifications.   The ray casting approach easily ex-
tends   to   generation   of   figures   with   shadows   or
transparent/mirroring surfaces.

4.2. Integral Properties

Most basic properties of solid objects (such as volume, center of
mass, moments of inertia) can be calculated by volume integrals
taken with respect to the solid.   Some examples follow.

$$\text{volume V} = \int 1 \, dv$$

$$\text{x-coordinate of center of mass} = 1/V \int x \, dv$$

$$\text{moment of inertia about z} = \rho \int \int x^2 + y^2 \, dv$$

Let us now concentrate only on the calculation of volume;   other
integral properties can ce calculated by very similar algorithms.
The following discussion is based on references (Lee and Requicha
1981) and (Wesley 1980).

4.2.1 Integral Properties of BR Models

Integral properties of solids represented by boundary models may
be evaluated either by direct integration or by using the divergence theorem of integral calculus.

Direct integration is the standard technique discussed in calculus textbooks.   For example, the volume of a polyhedral solid
may be evaluated as

$$\iiint dx \, dy \, dz = -\sum_i \iint_{Fi} z(x, y) \, dx \, dy,$$

where Fi' is the xy projection of face Fi, and z(x,y) is obtained
by solving for z the equation of the plane in which Fi lies. A
similar technique can be used to calculate the contribution of
each edge of Fi' to the double integrals in the right side of the
formula.

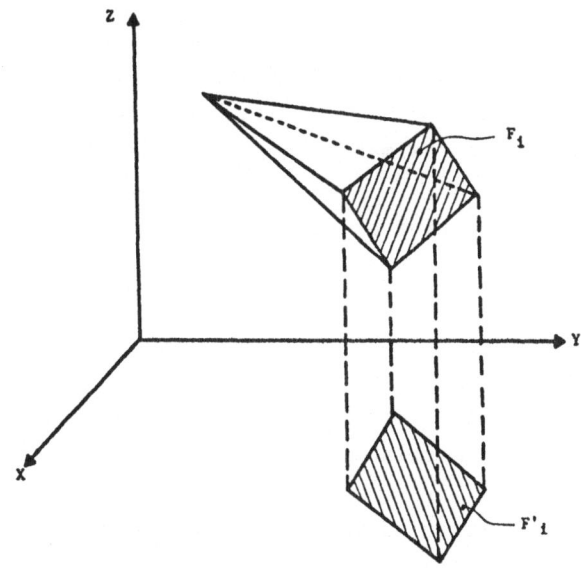

Figure 10. Direct integration method.

While the method of direct integration is quite attractive for
polyhedral models, curved faces pose a problem. Curved faces may
have to be faceted to ensure that z is a one-valued function of x
and y. In addition, it may be hard to solve the surface equation
for z even numerically and the equations of edges of Fi' may not
be available.

The divergence theorem provides an alternative method for the
evaluation of integral properties. Observing that it is always
possible to find a (non-unique) vector function g(x, y, z) such
that **div** g = f for any given continuous function f, it follows
that

$$\int\limits_{S} f \ fv = \int\limits_{S} \textbf{div} \ g \ dv = \sum_{i} \int\limits_{Fi} g \ . \ ni \ dFi,$$

where Fi is a face of the solid, ni is the unit vector normal to Fi, and dFi is the surface differential. If faces Fi are planar polygons, integrals on the right side are easily evaluated. In the general case, approximation techniques are needed.

4.2.2 Integral Properties of CSG Models

Evaluation of integral properties of solids modeled by CSG trees are based on conversion algorithms, that (implicitly) construct a cell decomposition that approximates the solid. Then the evaluation reduces to calculating the contribution of each cell to the total result, being a relatively easy task.

The conversion is again based on the set membership classification principle. Several alternative arrangements of cells present themselves, each arrangement being based on some classification principle. Various alternatives are shown in Figure 11.

Let us describe the simplest case, "spatial occupancy enumeration" (Figure 11 (a)) in more detail. This conversion is based on point classification: given a point P (the center point of a cell), determine whether P is inside, on the boundary, or outside the solid.

CSG is directly useful for answering this question. Classification with respect to each underlying half-space amounts up to substituting P into its defining function. Combination rules are also straightforward: Let P be classified with respect to solids A and B. Then the combination can be performed as indicated in the table below.

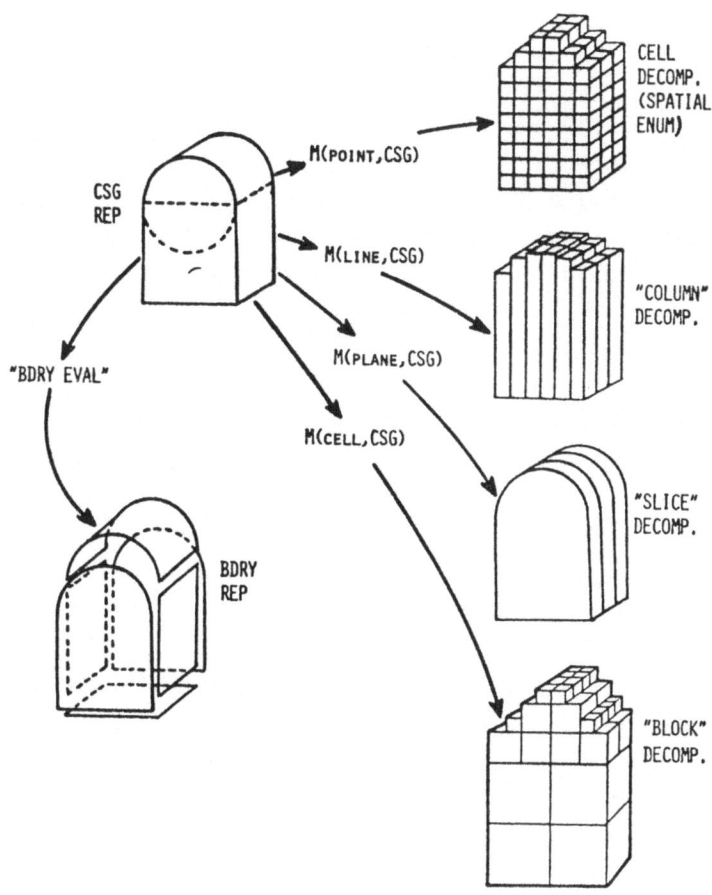

Figure 11. Conversion of CSG representations into cell decompositions by various set membership classification algorithms.

		B		
		in	on	out
	in	in	on	out
A	on	on	on/out	out
	out	out	out	out

The "on/on" case requires a more thorough analysis of the neighborhood of P. The simplest solution is to simply ignore the "on" case and just consider a two-way classification (in/out) that leads to satisfactory results. If more accurate results are needed, it is possible to "perturb" the point P, i.e. to classify other point(s) than the center of the cell. This method is used for instance in the half-space modeler TIPS (Okino et al. 1978).

Calculation of integral properties by "column decomposition" is essentially a ray casting algorithm: a ray is fired through the center of each column. This algorithm is used in Synthavision (Goldstein and Malin 1979), a CSG-based solid modeler.

4.3. Kinematic Analysis

So far we have been investigating very basic algorithms, mainly to illustrate the relative strengths of the main alternative solid modeling techniques. In this section a more high-level analysis capability will be discussed, in order to comprehend the capabilities offered by solid modelers. The section is based on the recent article of Bob Tilove (1983).

All solid modelers allow the creation of models of single parts. If these parts are to be used as components of an assembly, capability to model and analyze a combination of parts is required.

The most straightforward method to this end is to move "manually" (i.e. by basic routines for object translation and rotation) objects in suitable positions. In this approach, each new position requires a complicated series of positioning commands, a tedious and error-prone task.

Kinematic models offer a solution to this. In this approach, components of an assembly and constraints of their relative motion with respect to each other must be modeled. Now the user can examine the operation of the assembly just by modifying the few free parameters of the assembly.

A mechanism cn be viewed conceptually as a collection of rigid solids whose relative positions are constrained. the individual solids are often called "links", and the position constraints "joints". A joint between two solids, S1 and S2, can be viewed as a family of rigid transformations that dictate how S2 may move with respect to S1. Figure 12 depicts a crackshaft assembly and some "legal" configurations of its solids.

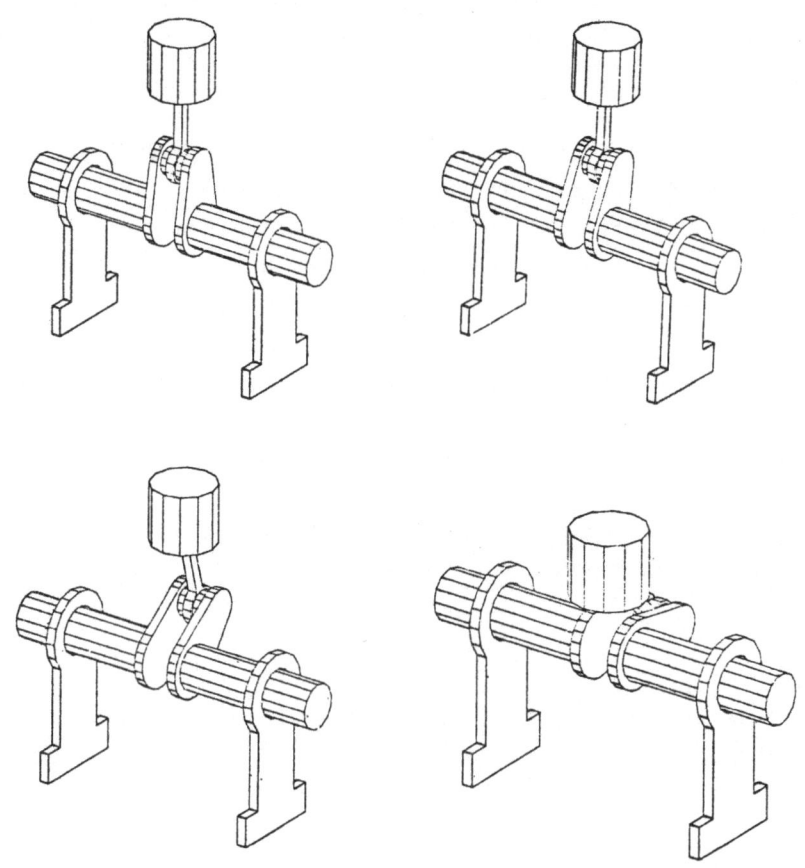

Figure 12. A crankshaft assembly.

An assembly can be represented by a connected, undirected graph whose nodes correspond to the links, and arcs to the joints. If the graph is acyclic, the mechanism is called an "open-loop mechanism". (Cyclic graphs are quite possible to occur; they represent "closed-loop mechanisms". For simplicity, we shall leave them aside.)

If a particular solid is chosen to be "rigid", the graph is converted to a tree. We now proceed as follows: to each solid of
the tree, we attach coordinate systems that are rigidly connected
to each other. Joints can now be modeled as parameterized
transformations from a coordinate system CS1 of one solid to a
coordinate system CS2 of another.

For instance, the fact that the shaft of the assembly can only
rotate around its axis is expressed by stating that the coordinate system CS1 attached to the "holes" of the base can only be
transformed to CS2, a coordinate system attached to the axis of
the shaft, by a "revolute" transformation.

Transformations can easily be represented by 4x4 matrices, if the
homogeneous coordinate representation is used. The revolute
transformation is represented, for instance, by matrix

$$
\begin{array}{llll}
\cos(a) & \sin(a) & 0 & 0 \\
-\sin(a) & \cos(a) & 0 & 0 \\
0 & 0 & 1 & 0 \\
0 & 0 & 0 & 1
\end{array}
$$

where a is the angle of rotation, a free parameter of this assembly. (The crankshaft assembly of Figure 12 has three free parameters determining three revolute transformations.)

A kinematic modeling tool outlined above can be applied in a
variety of problems. One is the graphical simulation and programming of an industrial robot. It is straightforward to model
the mechanisms of a robot arm by the coordinate transformation
idea. Then it is easy to model the operation of a robot by manipulating the free parameters of the kinematic model. (Robot programming, of course, requires more powerful tools for specifying
application-oriented tasks such as "move object X to this location", an operation that is likely to require a series of primitive movements.) Figure 13 exemplifies the simulation of robot
arm movements.

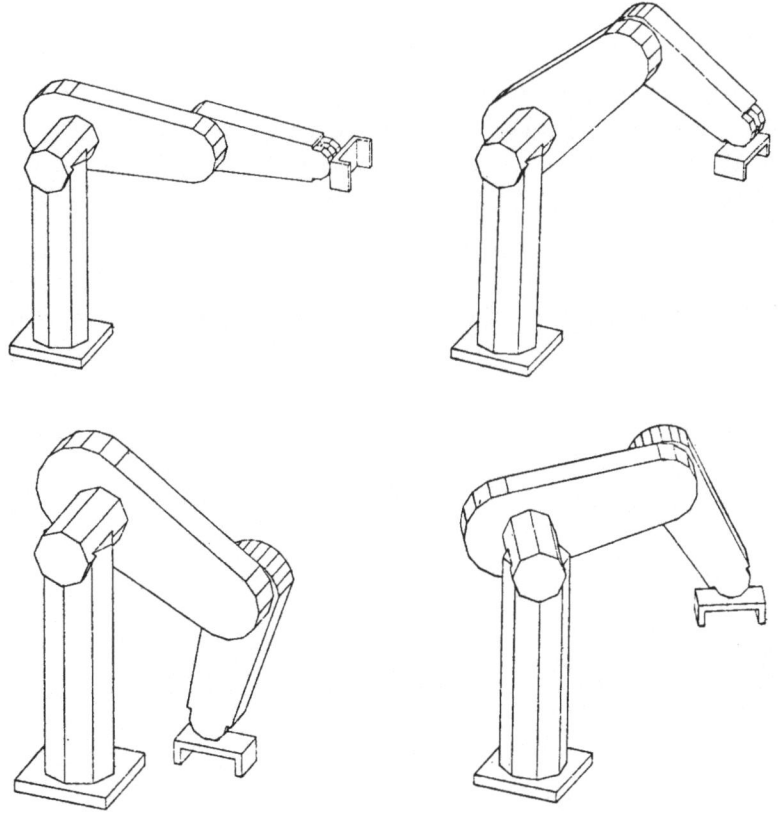

Figure 13. Simulation sequence of the PUMA industrial robot.

Another way to make use of a kinematic modeling package is to integrate it to an kinematic analysis package, several of which are
commercially available. Also the results of such an analysis can
be better visualized by employing the modeling system.

4.4. NC Verification

As the last case study we shall discuss the problem of NC program
verification, mainly to illustrate why there still remains lots
of work to do in solid modeling. This case study is based on
reference (Requicha and Voelcker 1981).

Let us consider a NC program that corresponds to a sequence of
machining operations. The obvious model of each operation is
depicted in Figure 14.

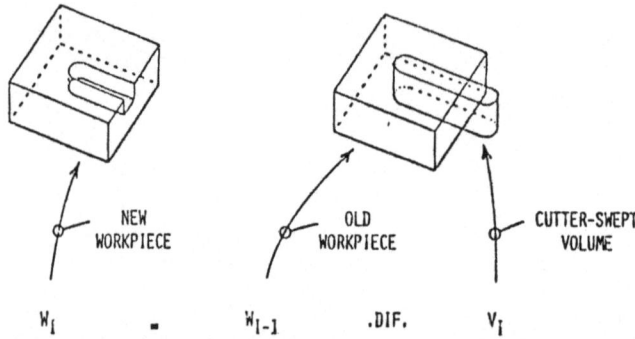

$$W_I \quad = \quad W_{I-1} \quad .DIF. \quad V_I$$

Figure 14. A model for machining.

As the figure suggests, the machining model has the following
components:

- a solid, "old workpiece", that models an object before a
  machining operation,
- a solid, "cutter-swept volume", that models the region occu-
  pied by the cutter as it traverses a trajectory, and
- a solid, "new workpiece", that models the object after
  machining.

The new object is generated as the (regularized) difference of
the old workpiece and the cutter-swept volume. (Regularity is
important to ensure that the new object is still "solid" in the
usual sense.)

Based on the elementary model of machining, one might consider an automatic verification system for NC programs. Given a NC program + information on the initial arrangement of the workpiece, tool, fixtures and so on, the system is expected to either verify that the NC program indeed modifies the workpiece into a desired result, or is invalid. An experimental verifier was implemented along these lines in connection to PADL-1, a CSG solid modeler, by W.A.Hunt (1981).

The simple process model of Figure 14 does not take into account several important conditions that must be embodied in a serious verifier. For instance, the verifier must be able to detect collisions between the tool and fixtures. A more refined process model is given in Figure 15.

```
generate swept-volume V
if          (V .INT. Part = 0        /* invasive machining test */
            and
            V .INT. Fixtures = 0     /* collision test */
            and
            V .INT.Workpiece ≠ 0)    /* effectiveness test */
then        Workpiece <-- Workpiece .DIF. V
            Cutter-position <-- Trajectory-endpoint
else        precondition-error
```

Figure 15. A refined process model.

Let us discuss the computational issues raised by the process model. For each NC command, the verifier is expected to perform two kinds of operations, namely

(1)   represent various objects playing a role in the process model (such as the "effect" V .INT. Part), and

(2)   test nullity of the objects to determine whether preconditions are satisfied (e.g. the test V .INT. Part = 0).

Unfortunately, current state of the art cannot do both tasks efficiently. While nullity testing is easy for boundary models (as the null object has just one representation having no faces at all), it is hard to create models for all desired objects of the process model. In contrast, it is easy to model the objects in

CSG (which amounts to adding leaves in CSG trees), but testing for nullity is hard.

Machining in general offers hard but intellectually attractive problems for developers of solid modelers. For instance, it is not hard to calculate what should be performed to modify a given part ("stock" in Figure 16) into some desired result ("machined part"), but how to select the most appropriate machining operations?

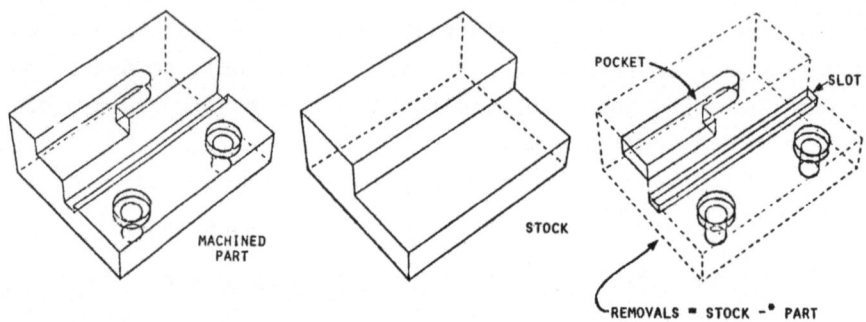

Figure 16. Machining planning problem. How should one select the machining operations?

Figure 16 suggests that a solid modeler should be able to "understand" what kinds of objects it models according to some part classification principle. This would allow the possibility to select for each part type the most efficient operations. This opens a challenging area of research on how to employ methods of artificial intelligence in solid modeling.

5. CONCLUDING REMARKS

As Requicha and Voelcker (1981) state,

> "Geometric modeling will continue to be an active research
> area for the foreseeable future because there are signifi-
> cant gaps in out current knowledge. The most prominent of
> these are centered on applications, which cover a sery broad
> spectrum."

While all solid modelers can produce some sort of graphical
displays and calculate integral properties of solids modeled,
other applications are only emerging. On the other hand, a body
of experience with research and industrial prototype systems exists. It is expected that this will be extended by experience on
true production application during the next few years.

REFERENCES

1. Baer, A., Eastman, C. M. and Henrion, M., Geometric Modeling:
   A Survey. Comput. Aid. Des. 11(1979)5, p. 253-272.

2. Baumgart, B.G., Geometric modeling for computer vision.
   Ph.D. Thesis, Rep. No. CS-463, Computer Science Dept., Stanford Univ., 1974.

3. Baumgart, B.G., A polyhedron representation for computer vision. AFIPS Conf. Proc. Vol. 44, National Computer Conf.,
   1975, p. 589-596.

4. Braid, I.C., Notes on a Geometric Modeller. CAD Group Document No. 101, Computer Laboratory, University of Cambridge,
   Cambridge, England, June, 1979.

5. Goldstein, R. and Malin, L., 3D Modeling with the Synthavision System. Proc. First Ann. Conf. Computer Graphics in
   CAD/CAM Systems, Apr. 9-11, 1979, Cambridge, Mass., p. 244-

247.

6. Hunt, W. A., An exploratory study of automatic verification of programs for numerically controlled machine tools. M.S. thesis, Mechanical and Aerospace Sciences Dept., University of Rochester, 1981.

7. Lee, Y. and Requicha, A. A. G., Algorithms for computing the volume and other integral properties of solid objects. Comm. ACM 25(1982)11.

8. Markowsky, G. and Wesley, M. A., Fleshing Out Wire Frames. IBM J. Res. Develop. 24(1980)5, p. 582-597.

9. Mäntylä, M., Computational Topology, Acta Polytechnical Scandinavica, Series Ma 37, Helsinki, 1983.

10. Mäntylä, M. and Sulonen, R., GWB - A Solid Modeler With Euler Operators. IEEE Computer Graphics and Applications 2(1982)7, p. 17-31.

11. Okino, N. et al., TIPS-1. Institute of Precision Engineering, Hokkaido University, Japan, 1978.

12. Requicha, A. A. G., Representations of Rigid Solids - Theory, Methods, and Systems. ACM Computing Surveys 12(1980)4, p. 437-464.

13. Requicha, A. A. G. and Voelcker, H. B., An Introduction to Geometric Modeling and Its Applications in Mechanical Design and Production. In J. Tou (ed.), Advances in Information Systems Sciences, Vol. 8, Plenum Publ. Co., 1981.

14. Roth, S.D., Ray Casting for Modeling Solids. Computer Graphics and Image Processing 18(1982)2, p. 109-144.

15. Sutherland, I.E., Computer Displays. Scientific American, June 1970.

16. Tilove, R.B., Exploiting Spatial and Structural Locality in Geometric Modeling. Tech. Memo. No TM-38, Production Automation Project, University of Rochester, 1981.

17. Tilove, R.B., Extending Solid Modeling Systems for Mechanical Design and Kinematic Simulation. IEEE Computer Graphics and Applications 3(1983)3, p. 9-19.

18. Wesley, M.A., Construction and Use of Geometric Models. In: J. Encarnacao (ed.), Computer Aided Design - Modeling, Systems Engineering, CAD-Systems. Springer Verlag, 1980.

Symbolic Computation

Managing Editors: **J. Encarnação, P. Hayes**

Computer Graphics

Editors: **K. Bø, J. D. Foley, R. Guedj, J. W. ten Hagen, F. R. A. Hopgood, M. Hosaka, M. Lucas, A. G. Requicha**

G. Enderle, K. Kansy, G. Pfaff

Computer Graphics Programming

GKS – The Graphics Standard

1984. 93 figures, some in color. XVI, 542 pages
ISBN 3-540-11525-0

Contents: Introduction to Computer Graphics Based on GKS. – The Process of Generating a Standard. – Graphics Kernel System Programming. – The GKS Environment. – Appendix 1: GKS Metafile Format. – Appendix 2: Vocabulary. – References. – Index.

The book covers computer graphics programming on the base of the Graphical Kernel System GKS. GKS is the first international standard for the functions of a computer graphics system. It offers capabilities for creation and representation of two-dimensional pictures, handling input from graphical work-stations, structuring and manipulating pictures, and for storing and retrieving them. It represents a methodological framework for the concepts of computer graphics and establishes a common understanding for computer graphics systems, methods and applications. This book gives an overview over the GKS concepts, the history of the GKS design and the various system interfaces. A significant part of the book is devoted to a detailed description of the application of GKS functions both in a Pascal and a FORTRAN-Language environment.

Springer-Verlag
Berlin
Heidelberg
New York
Tokyo

Symbolic Computation

Managing Editors:
J. Encarnação, P. Hayes

Computer Graphics

Editors: K. Bø,
J. D. Foley, R. Guedj,
J. W. ten Hagen,
F. R. A. Hopgood,
M. Hosaka, M. Lucas,
A. G. Requicha

J. Encarnação, E. G. Schlechtendahl

Computer Aided Design

Fundamentals and System Architectures
1983. 176 figures (12 of them in color).
IX, 348 pages. ISBN 3-540-11526-9

Contents: Introduction. – History and Basic Components of CAD. – The Process Aspect of CAD. – The Architecture of CAD Systems. – Implementation Methodology. – Engineering Methods of CAD. – CAD Application Examples. – Trends. – Subject Index. – Author Index. – Color Plates.

This outstanding work is a thorough introduction to the fundamentals of CAD. Both computer science and engineering sciences contribute to the particular flavor of CAD. Design is interpreted as an interactive process involving specification, synthesis, analysis, and evaluation, with CAD as a tool to provide computer assistance in all these phases.

The book is intended primarily for computer scientists and engineers seeking to become proficient in CAD. It will help them obtain the necessary expertise in designing, evaluating or implementing CAD systems and embedding them into existing design environments. Major topics of the book are: system architecture, components and interfaces, the data base aspects in CAD, man-machine communication, computer graphics for geometrical design, drafting and data representation, the interrelationship between CAD and numerical methods, simulation, and optimization. Economic, ergonomic, and social aspects are considered as well.

Springer-Verlag
Berlin
Heidelberg
New York
Tokyo